The
Wize Wize
Beasts
of the
Wizarding
Wizdoms

story & art by
NAGABE

contents

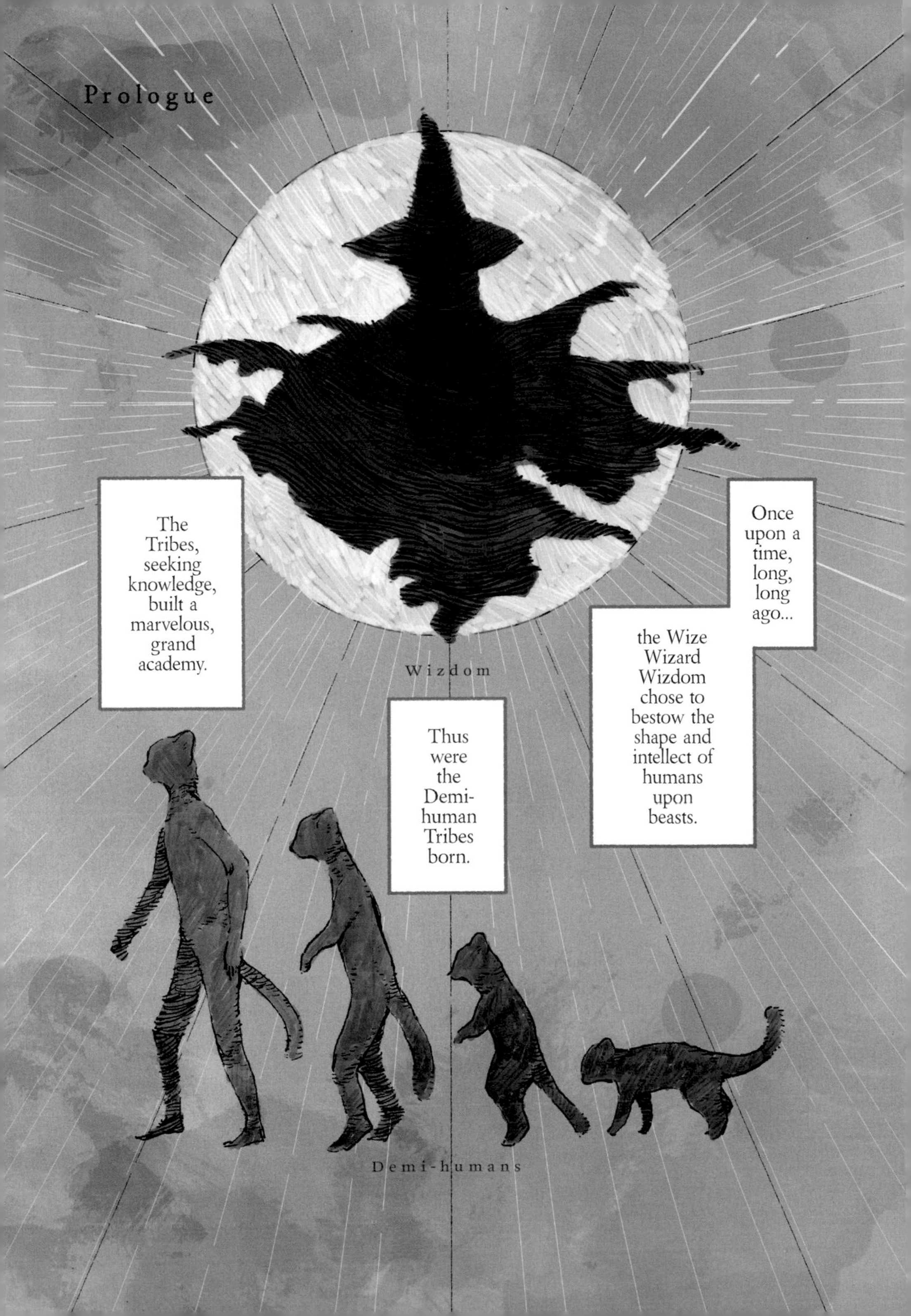
Prologue
Once upon a time, long, long ago...
the Wize Wizard Wizdom chose to bestow the shape and intellect of humans upon beasts.
Wizdom
Thus were the Demi-human Tribes born.
The Tribes, seeking knowledge, built a marvelous, grand academy.
Demi-humans

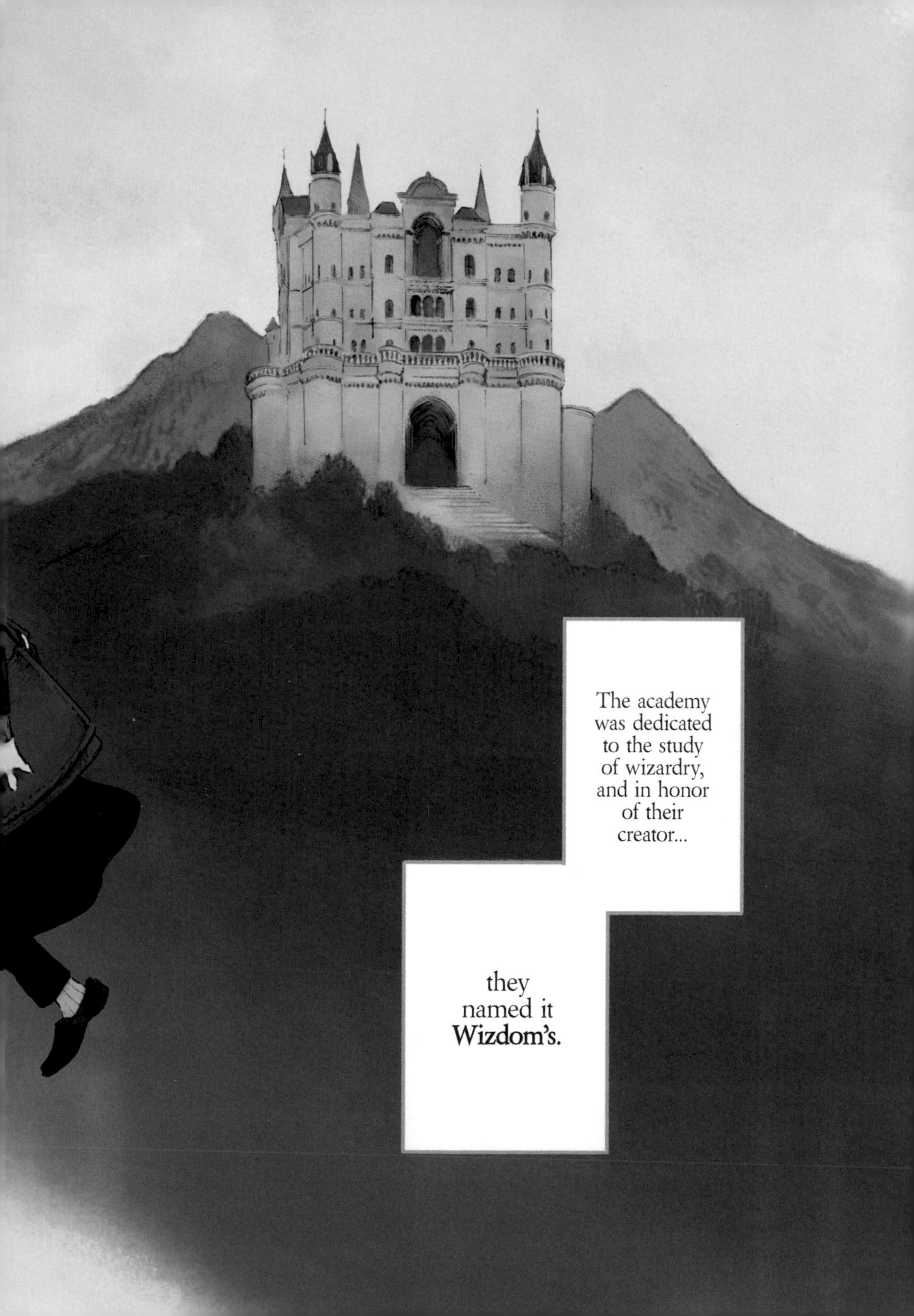
The academy was dedicated to the study of wizardry, and in honor of their creator...
they named it **Wizdom's.**

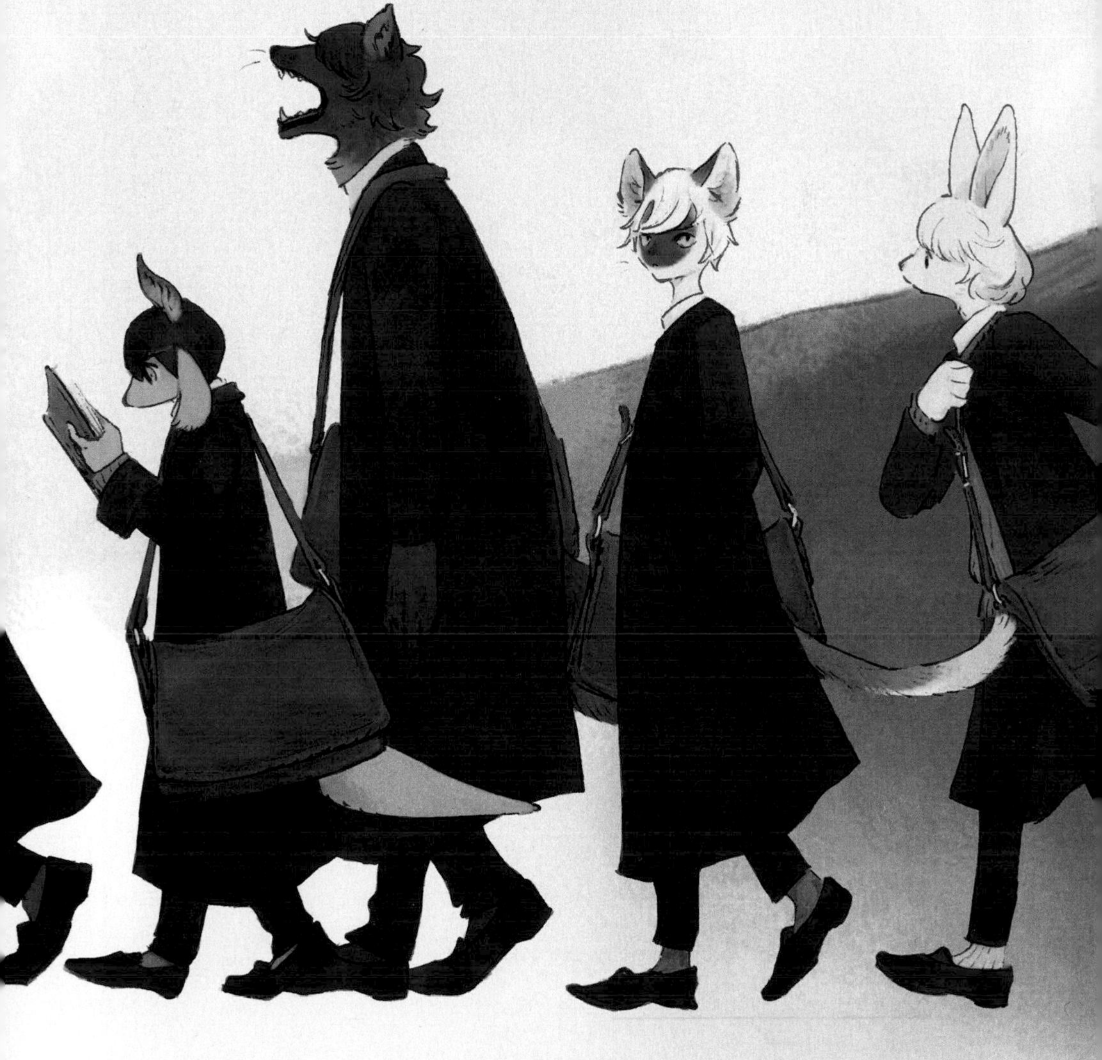

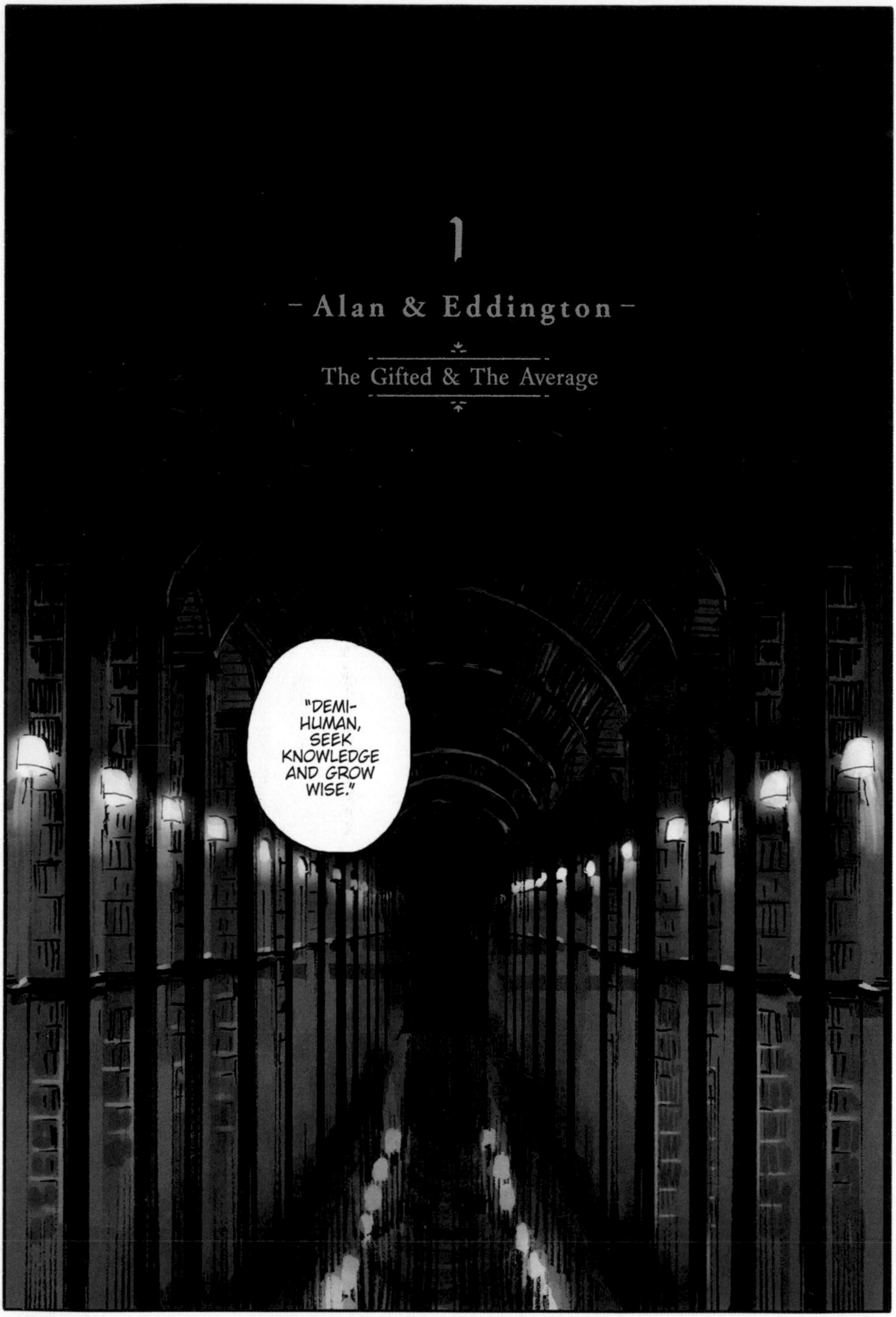
1
- Alan & Eddington -
The Gifted & The Average
"DEMI-HUMAN, SEEK KNOWLEDGE AND GROW WISE."

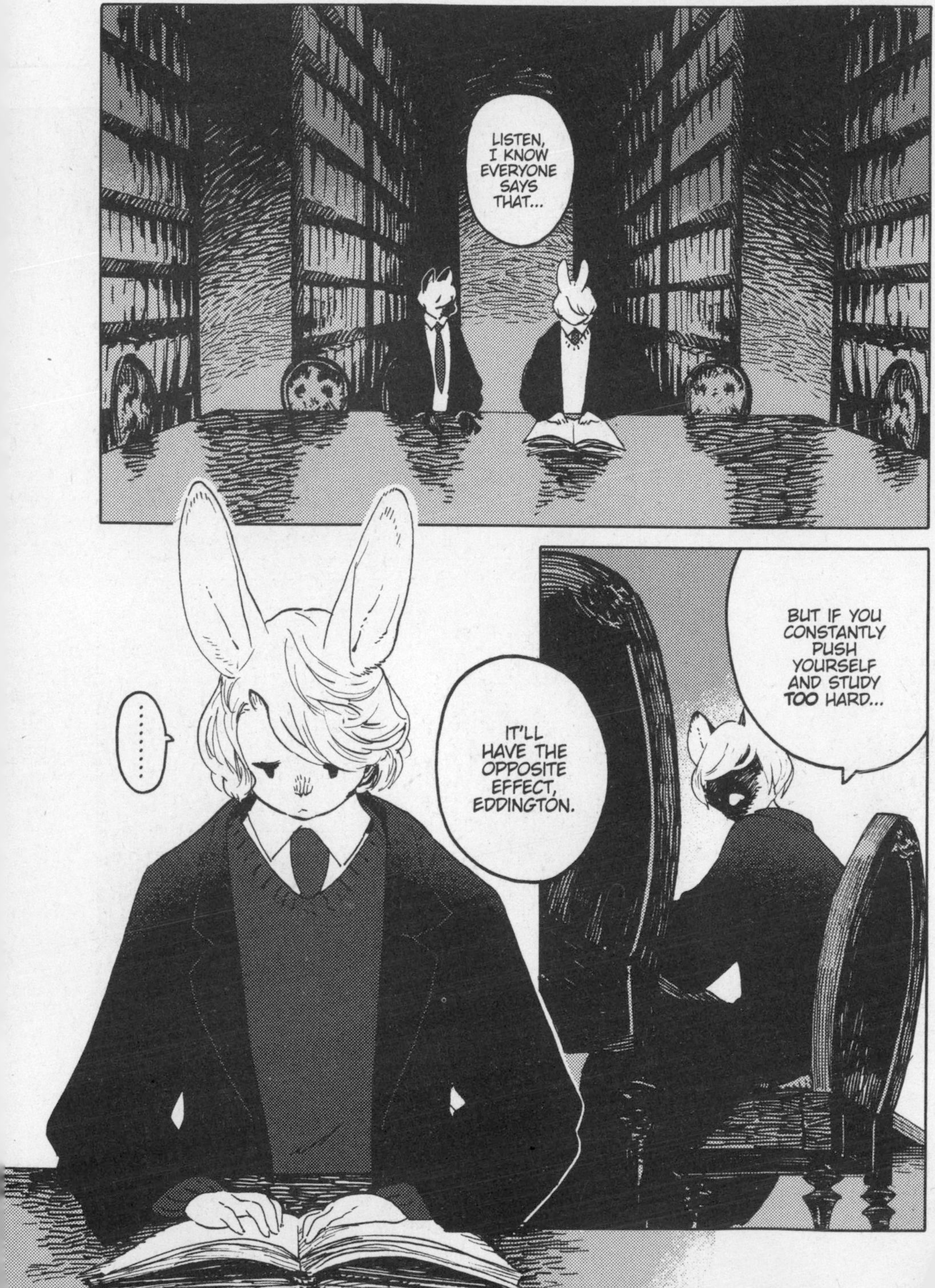
LISTEN, I KNOW EVERYONE SAYS THAT...
BUT IF YOU CONSTANTLY PUSH YOURSELF AND STUDY **TOO** HARD...
IT'LL HAVE THE OPPOSITE EFFECT, EDDINGTON.
....

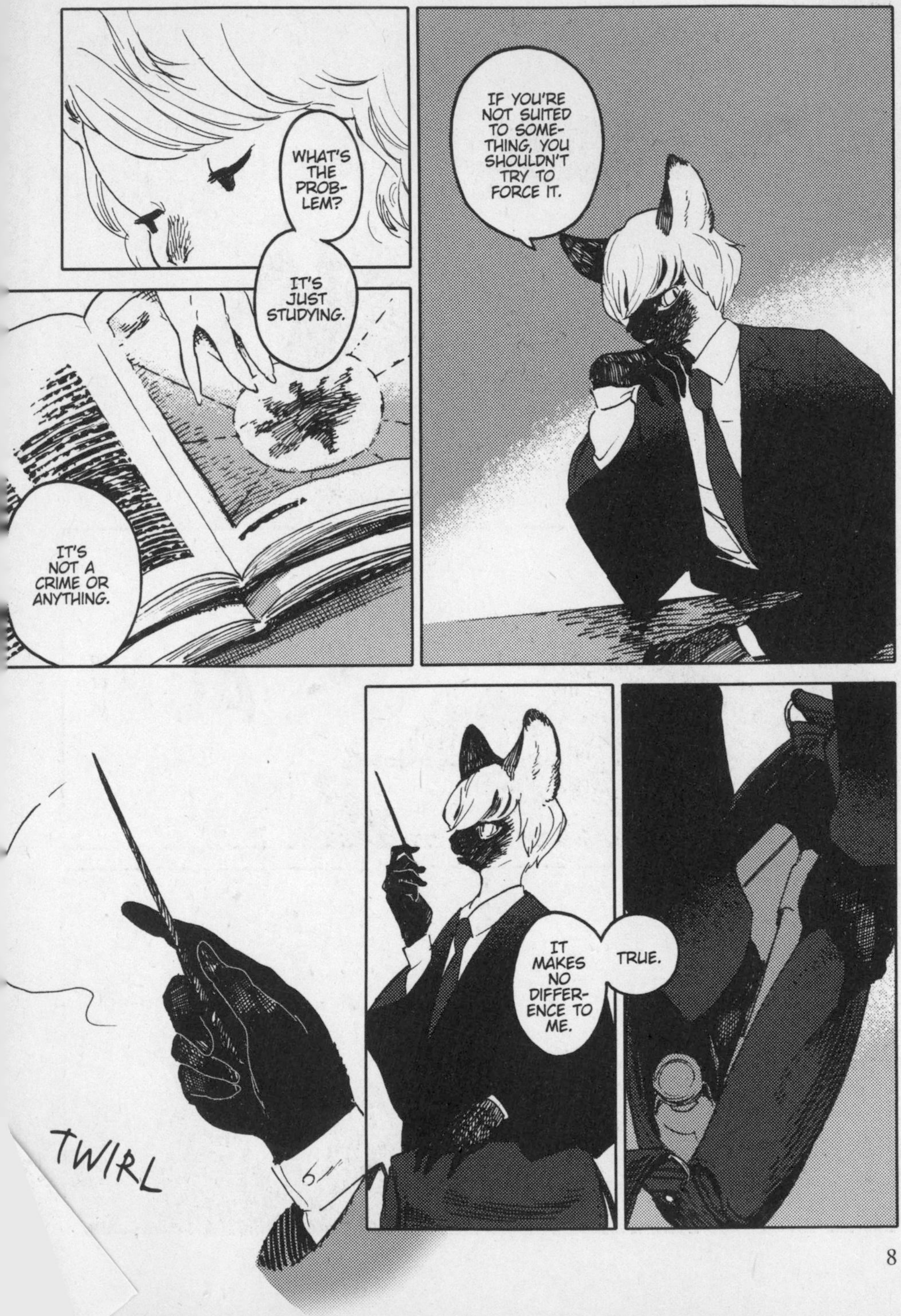
IF YOU'RE NOT SUITED TO SOME-THING, YOU SHOULDN'T TRY TO FORCE IT.
WHAT'S THE PROB-LEM?
IT'S JUST STUDYING.
IT'S NOT A CRIME OR ANYTHING.
TRUE.
IT MAKES NO DIFFER-ENCE TO ME.
TWIRL

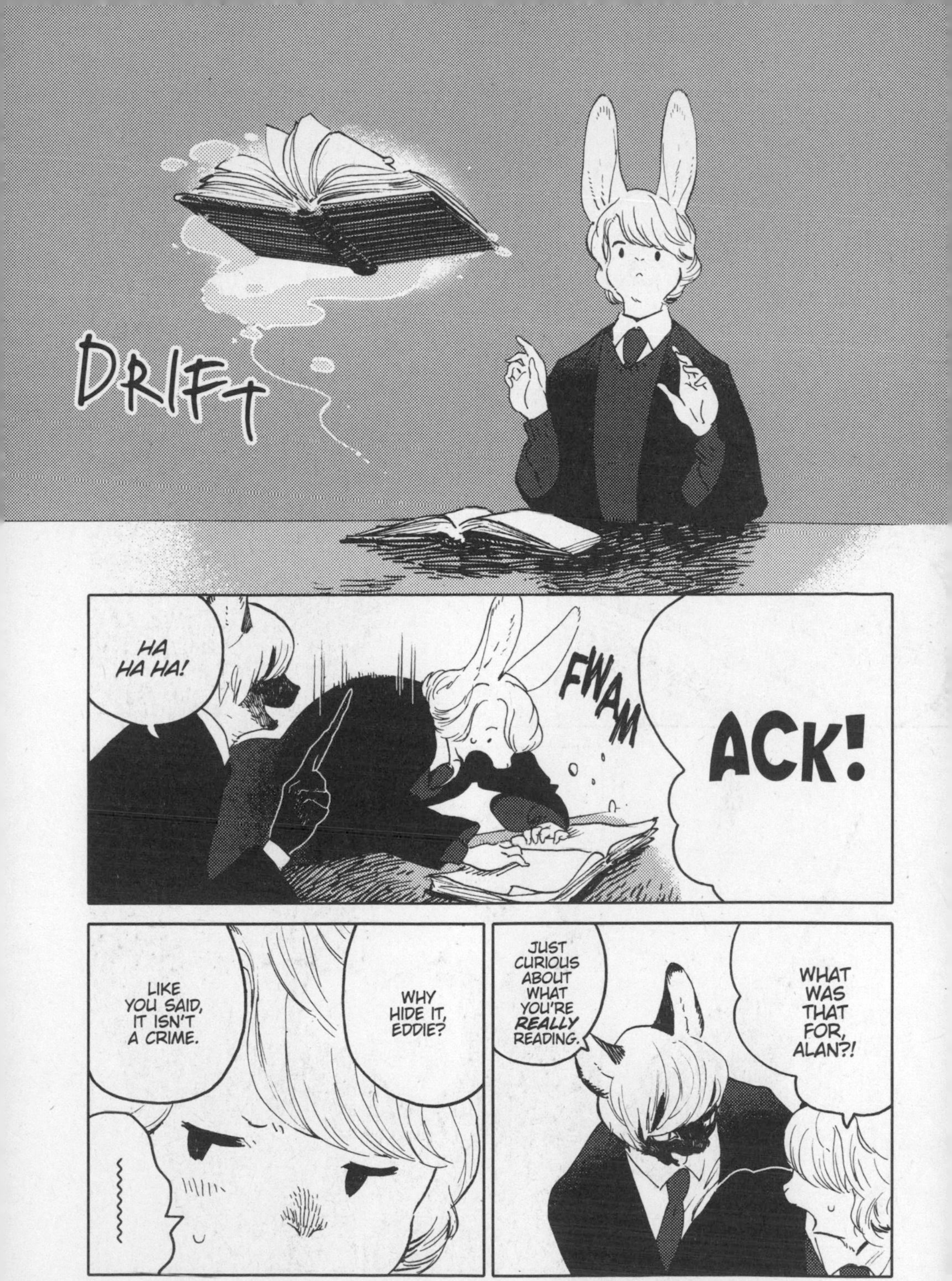
DRIFT
ACK!
FWAM
HA HA HA!
WHAT WAS THAT FOR, ALAN?!
JUST CURIOUS ABOUT WHAT YOU'RE *REALLY* READING.
WHY HIDE IT, EDDIE?
LIKE YOU SAID, IT ISN'T A CRIME.

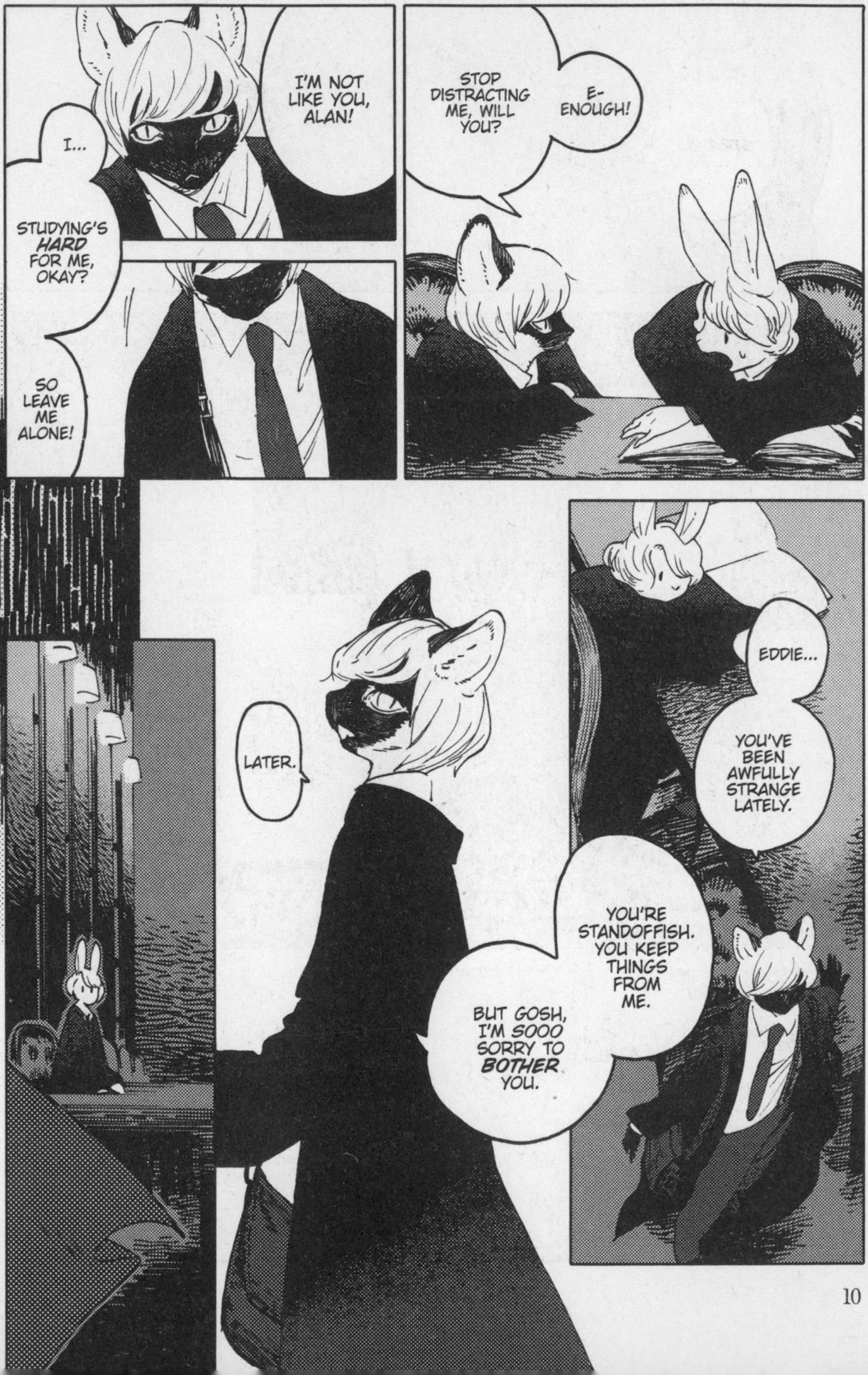
E-ENOUGH!
STOP DISTRACTING ME, WILL YOU?
I'M NOT LIKE YOU, ALAN!
I...
STUDYING'S *HARD* FOR ME, OKAY?
SO LEAVE ME ALONE!
EDDIE...
YOU'VE BEEN AWFULLY STRANGE LATELY.
YOU'RE STANDOFFISH. YOU KEEP THINGS FROM ME.
BUT GOSH, I'M *SOOO* SORRY TO ***BOTHER*** YOU.
LATER.

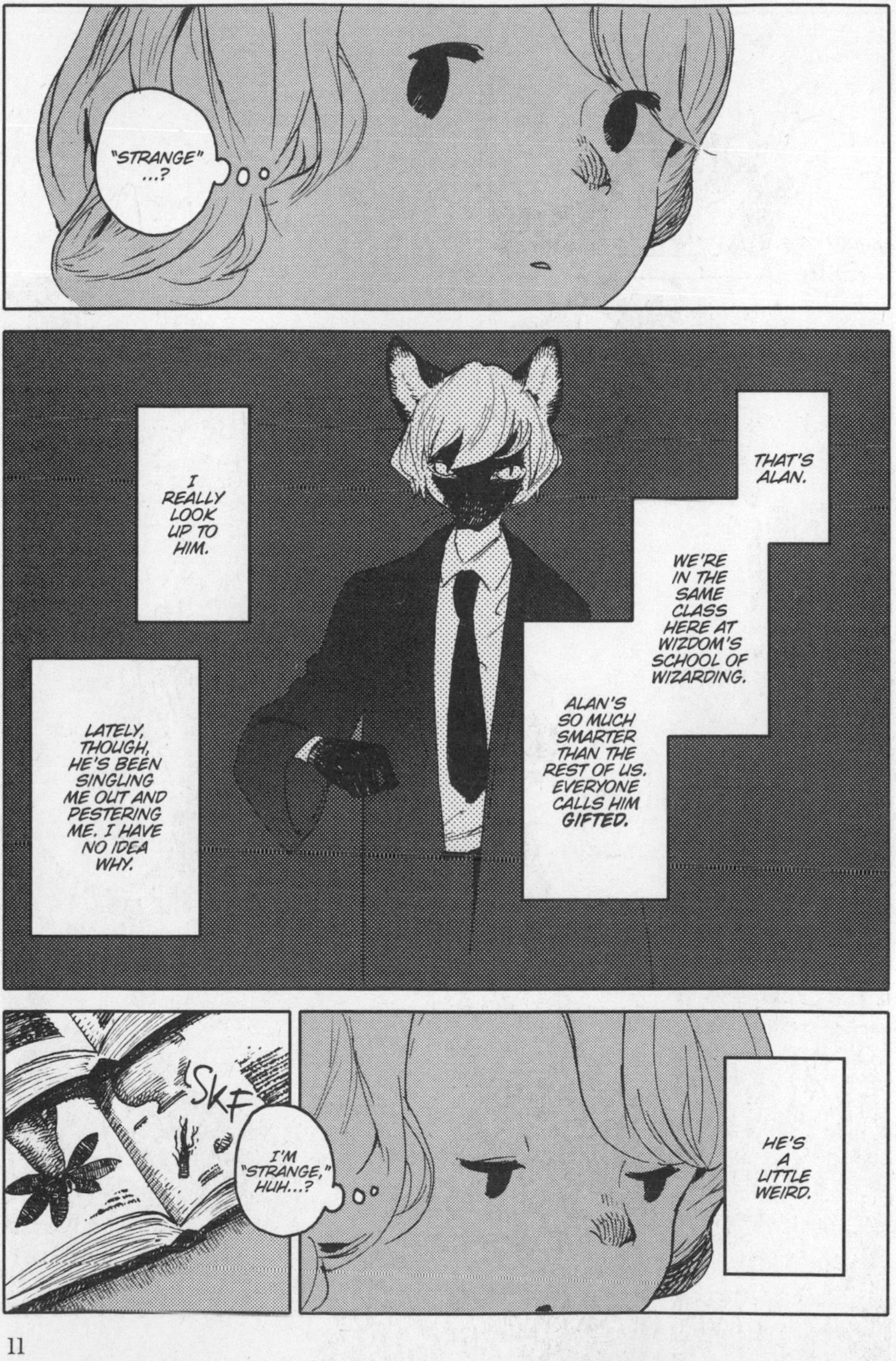
"STRANGE" ...?
THAT'S ALAN.
WE'RE IN THE SAME CLASS HERE AT WIZDOM'S SCHOOL OF WIZARDING.
ALAN'S SO MUCH SMARTER THAN THE REST OF US. EVERYONE CALLS HIM GIFTED.
I REALLY LOOK UP TO HIM.
LATELY, THOUGH, HE'S BEEN SINGLING ME OUT AND PESTERING ME. I HAVE NO IDEA WHY.
HE'S A LITTLE WEIRD.
I'M "STRANGE," HUH...?
SKF

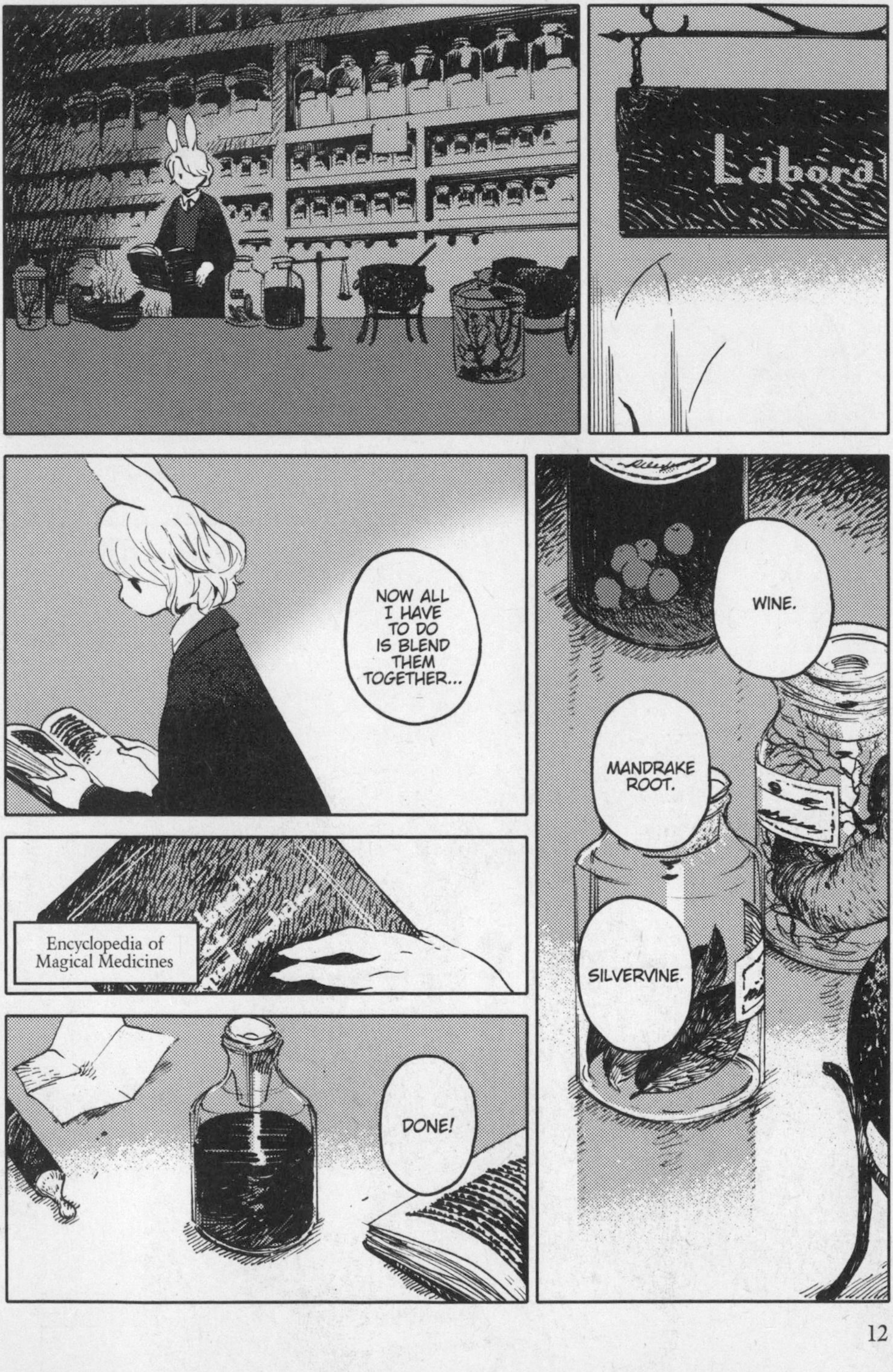
Labora
WINE.
MANDRAKE ROOT.
SILVERVINE.
NOW ALL I HAVE TO DO IS BLEND THEM TOGETHER...
Encyclopedia of Magical Medicines
DONE!

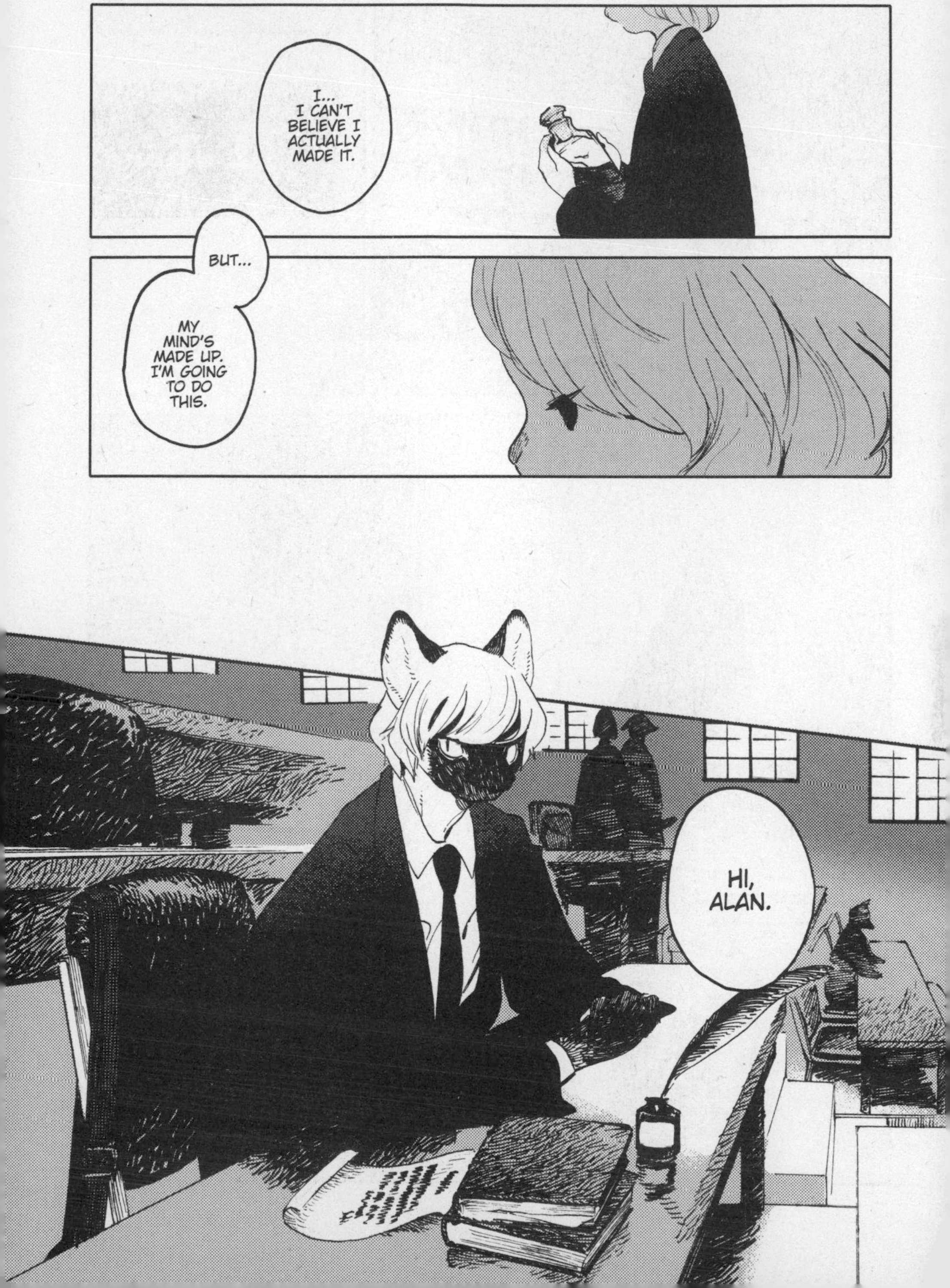
I... I CAN'T BELIEVE I ACTUALLY MADE IT.
BUT...
MY MIND'S MADE UP. I'M GOING TO DO THIS.
HI, ALAN.

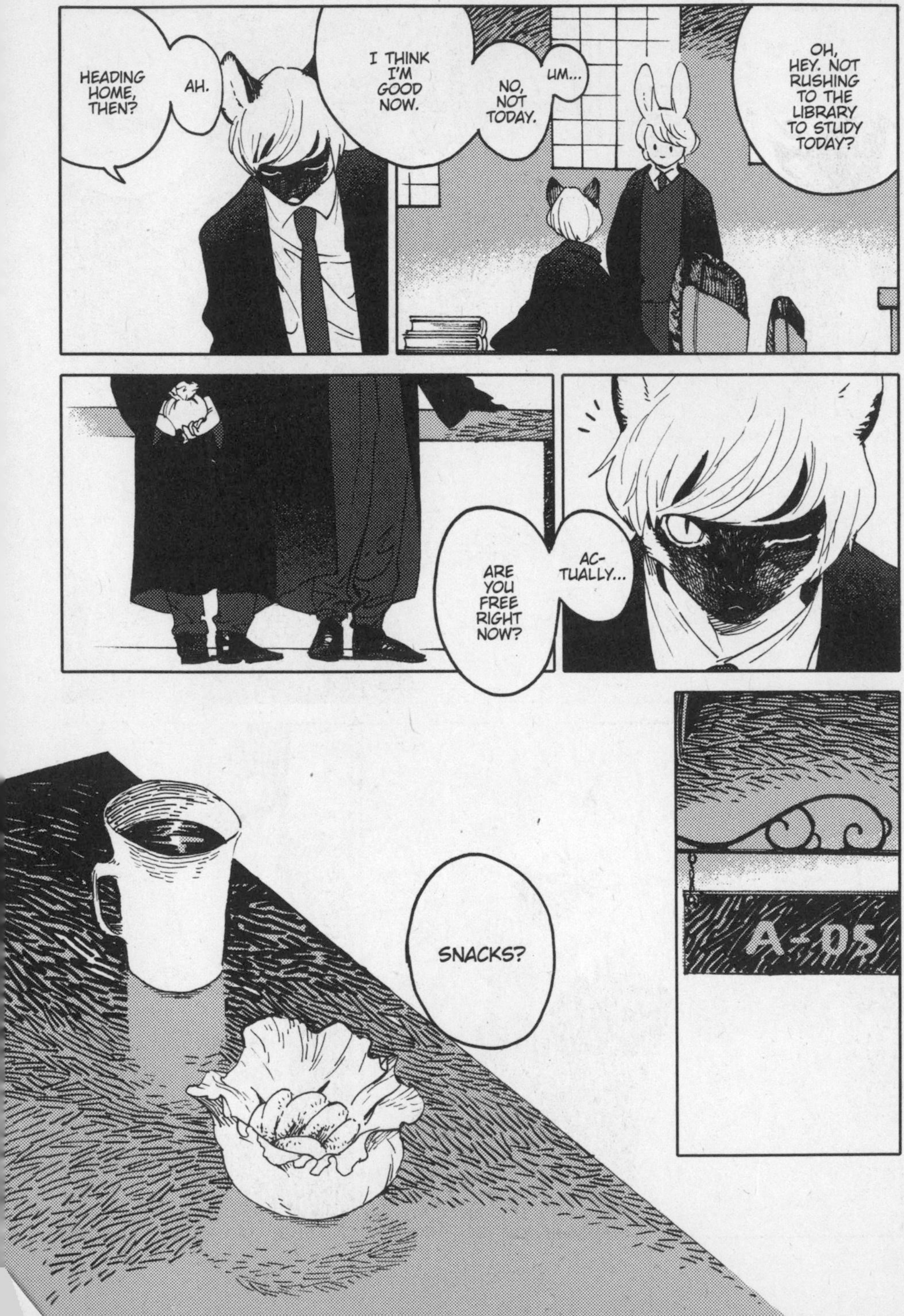
OH, HEY. NOT RUSHING TO THE LIBRARY TO STUDY TODAY?
UM...
NO, NOT TODAY.
I THINK I'M GOOD NOW.
AH.
HEADING HOME, THEN?
AC-TUALLY...
ARE YOU FREE RIGHT NOW?
A-05
SNACKS?

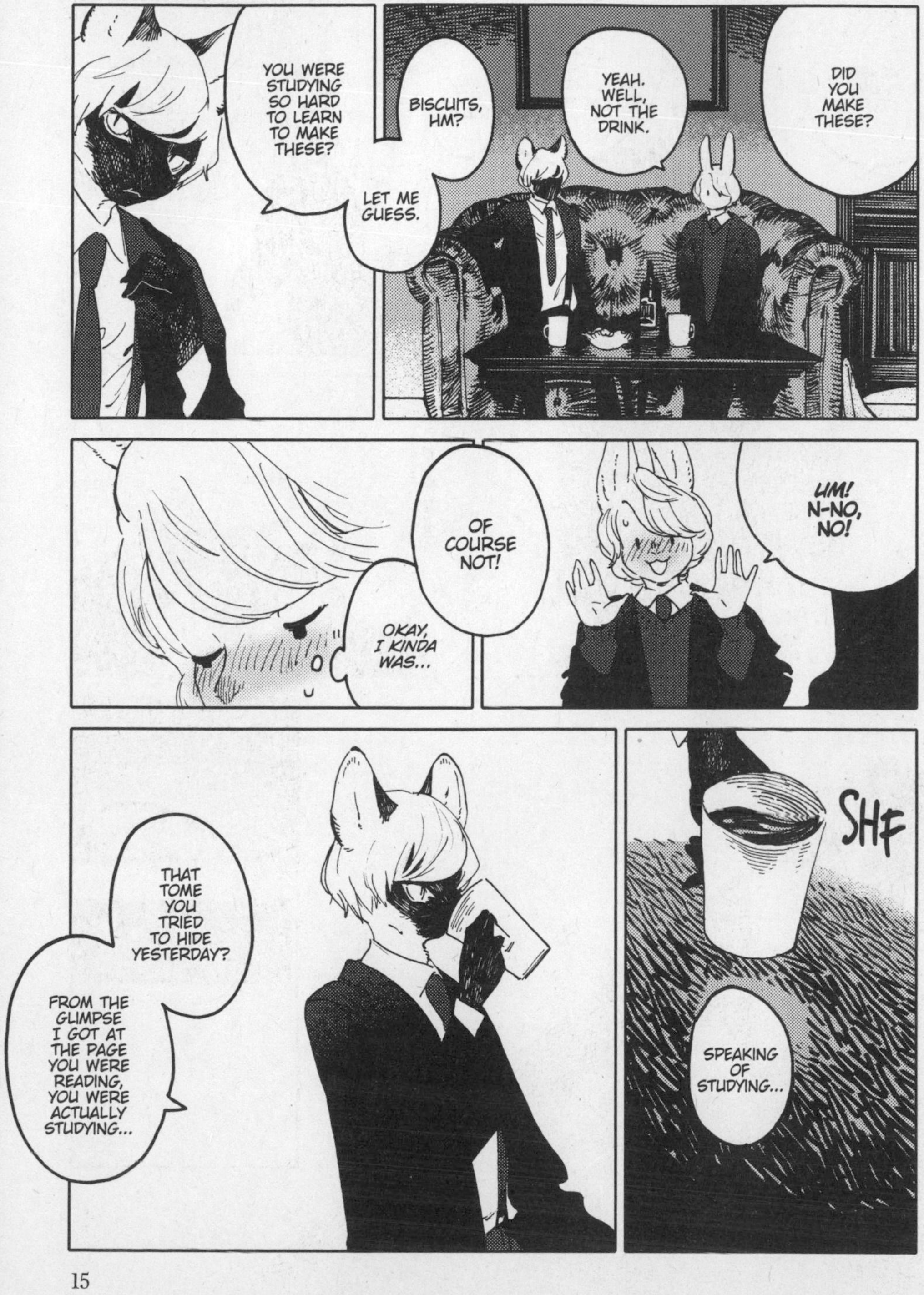
DID YOU MAKE THESE?
YEAH. WELL, NOT THE DRINK.
BISCUITS, HM?
LET ME GUESS.
YOU WERE STUDYING SO HARD TO LEARN TO MAKE THESE?
UM! N-NO, NO!
OF COURSE NOT!
OKAY, I KINDA WAS...
SHF
SPEAKING OF STUDYING...
THAT TOME YOU TRIED TO HIDE YESTERDAY?
FROM THE GLIMPSE I GOT AT THE PAGE YOU WERE READING, YOU WERE ACTUALLY STUDYING...

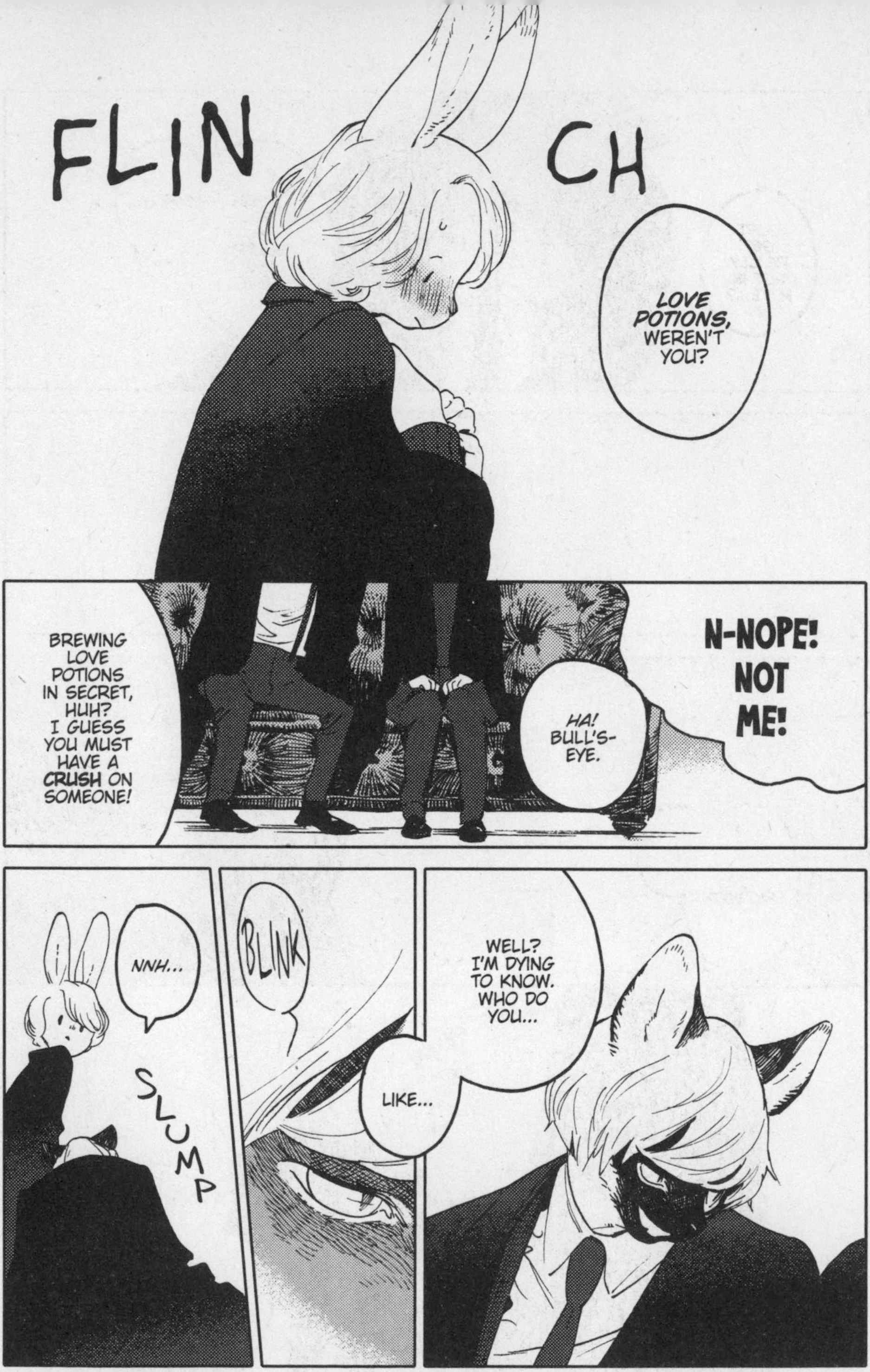
FLINCH
LOVE POTIONS, WEREN'T YOU?
N-NOPE! NOT ME!
HA! BULL'S-EYE.
BREWING LOVE POTIONS IN SECRET, HUH? I GUESS YOU MUST HAVE A CRUSH ON SOMEONE!
WELL? I'M DYING TO KNOW. WHO DO YOU...
LIKE...
BLINK
NNH...
SLUMP

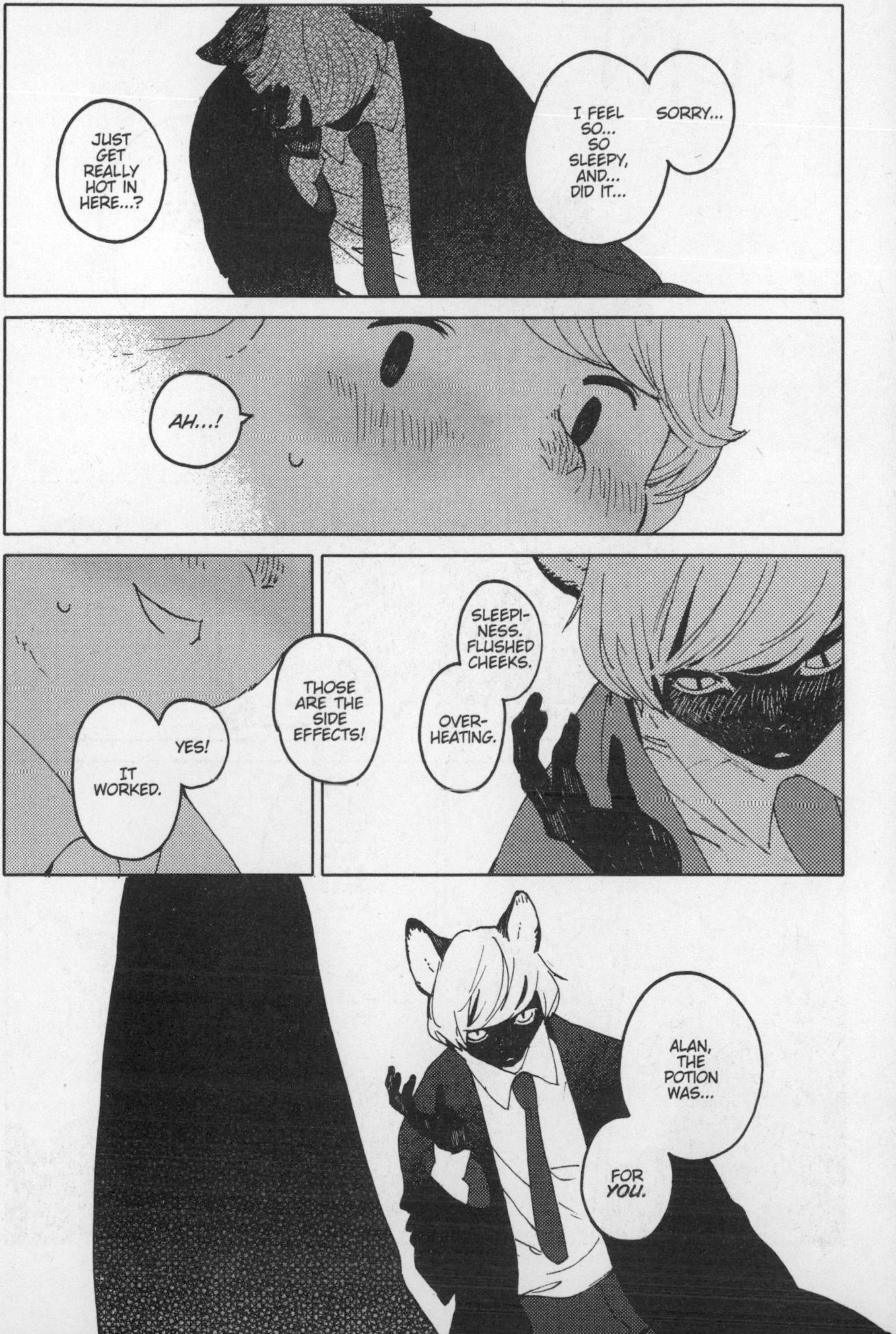
SORRY...
I FEEL SO... SO SLEEPY, AND... DID IT...
JUST GET REALLY HOT IN HERE...?
AH...!
SLEEPI-NESS. FLUSHED CHEEKS.
OVER-HEATING.
THOSE ARE THE SIDE EFFECTS!
YES!
IT WORKED.
ALAN, THE POTION WAS...
FOR *YOU*.

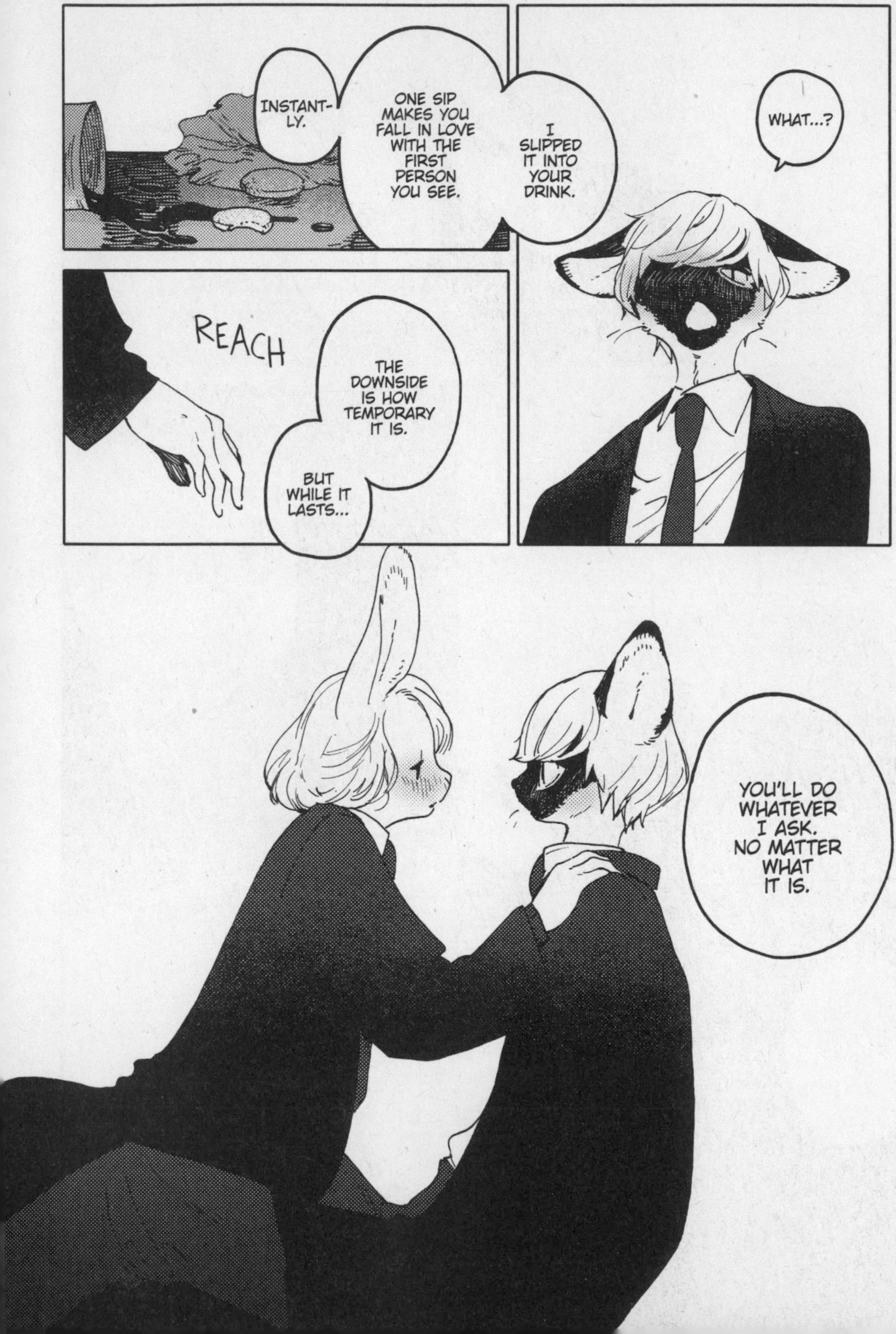
WHAT...?
I SLIPPED IT INTO YOUR DRINK.
ONE SIP MAKES YOU FALL IN LOVE WITH THE FIRST PERSON YOU SEE.
INSTANT-LY.
THE DOWNSIDE IS HOW TEMPORARY IT IS.
REACH
BUT WHILE IT LASTS...
YOU'LL DO WHATEVER I ASK. NO MATTER WHAT IT IS.

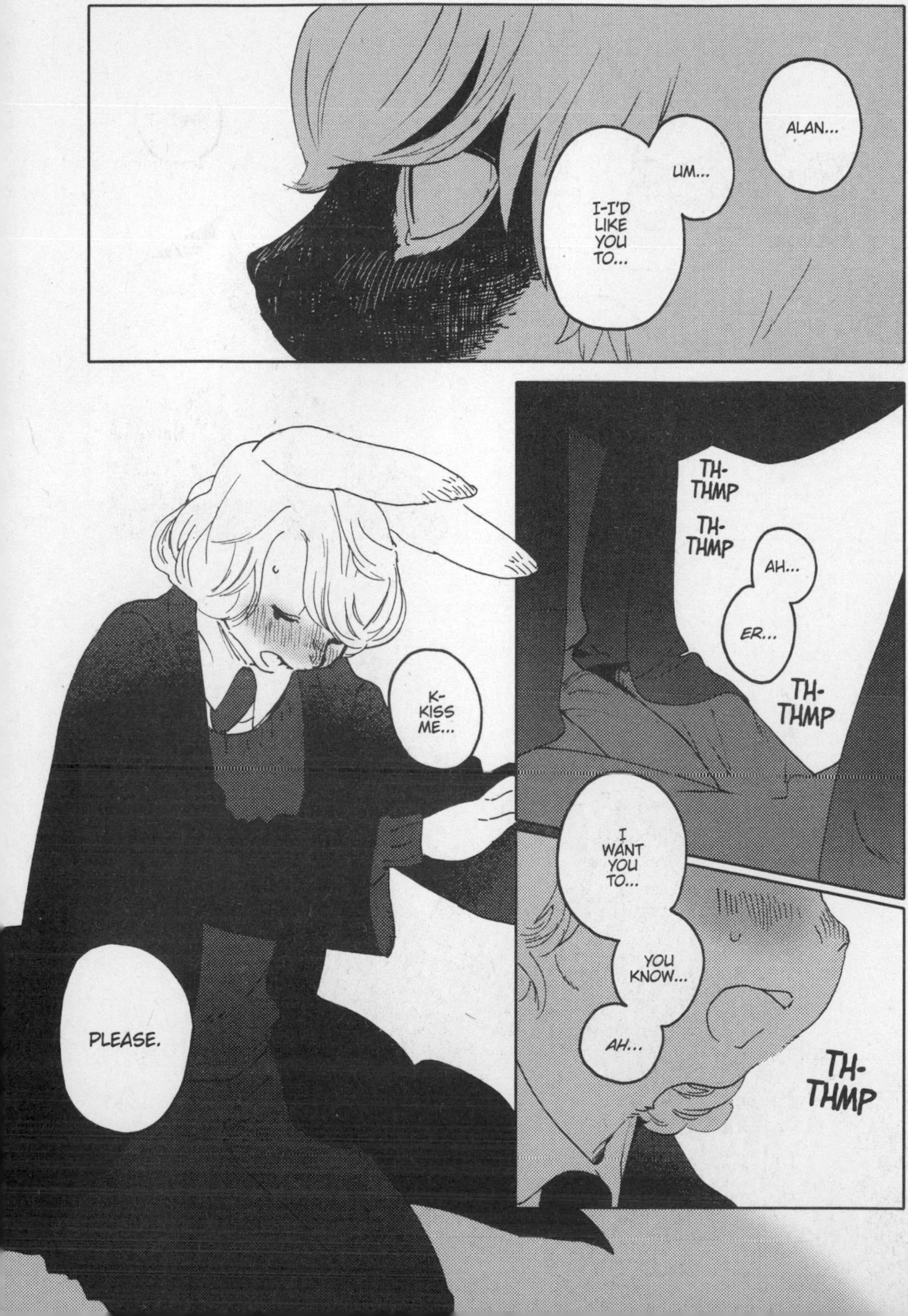
ALAN...
UM...
I-I'D LIKE YOU TO...
TH-THMP
TH-THMP
AH...
ER...
TH-THMP
I WANT YOU TO...
YOU KNOW...
AH...
TH-THMP
K-KISS ME...
PLEASE.

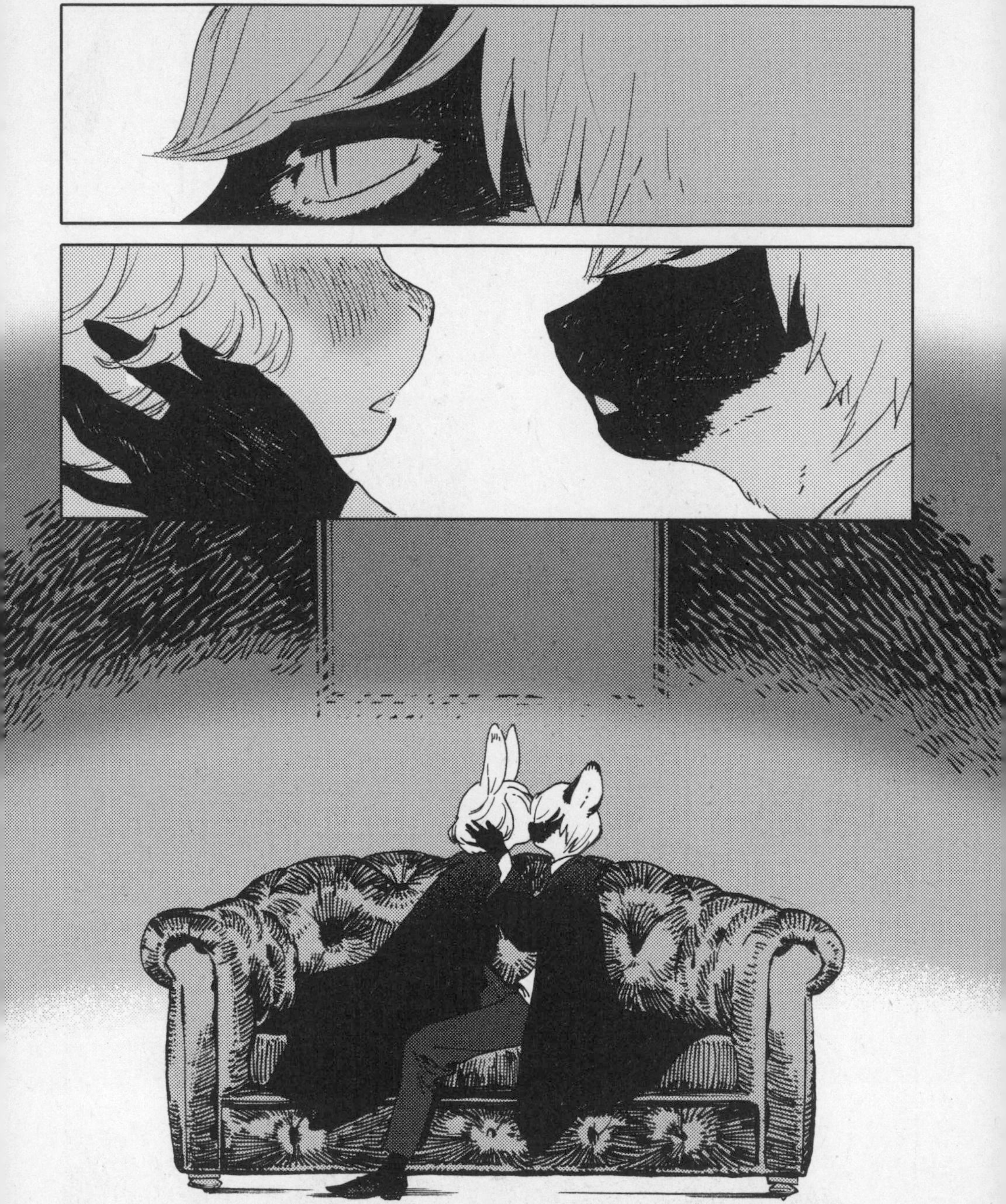

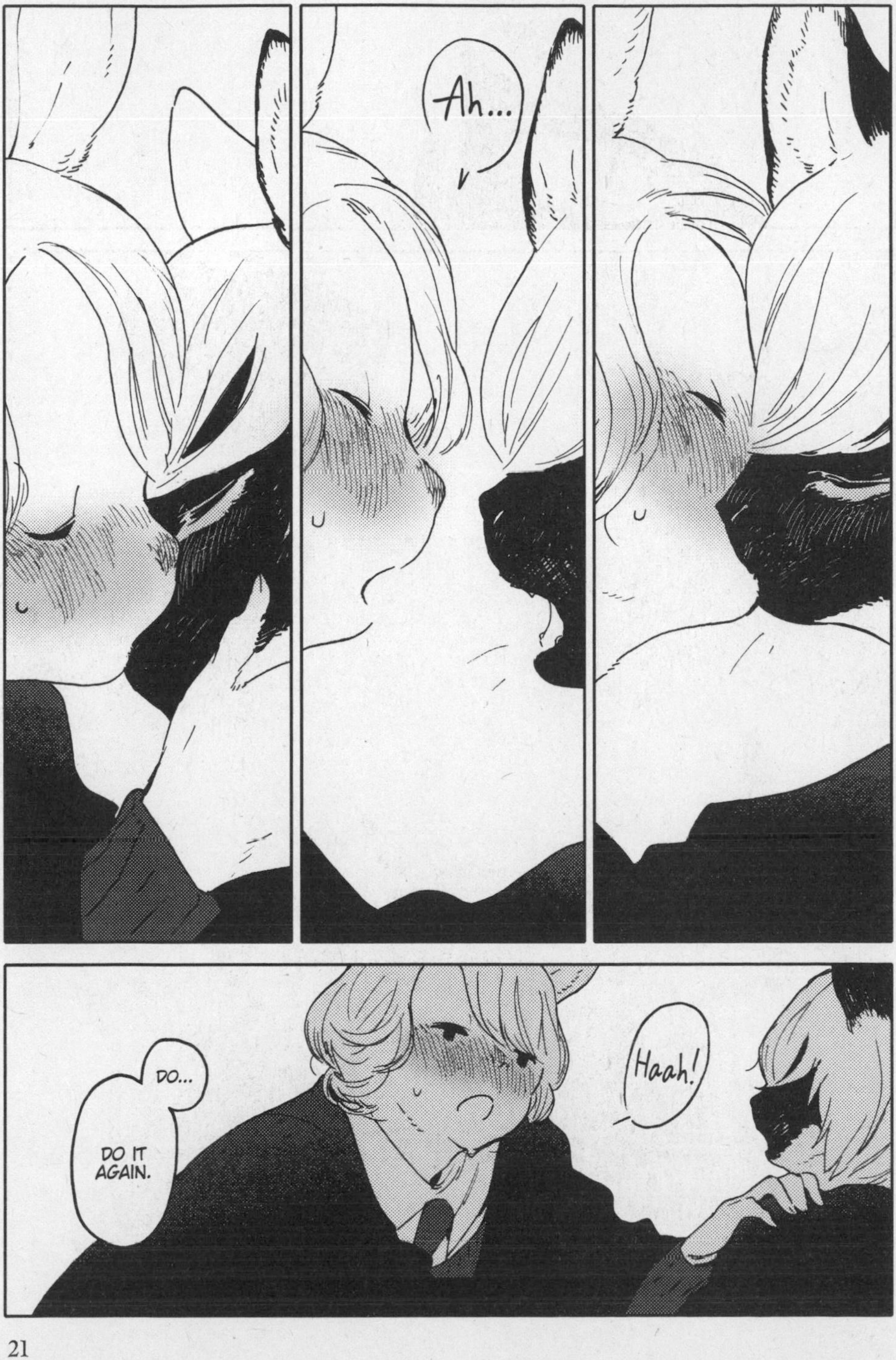
Ah...
Haah!
DO...
DO IT AGAIN.

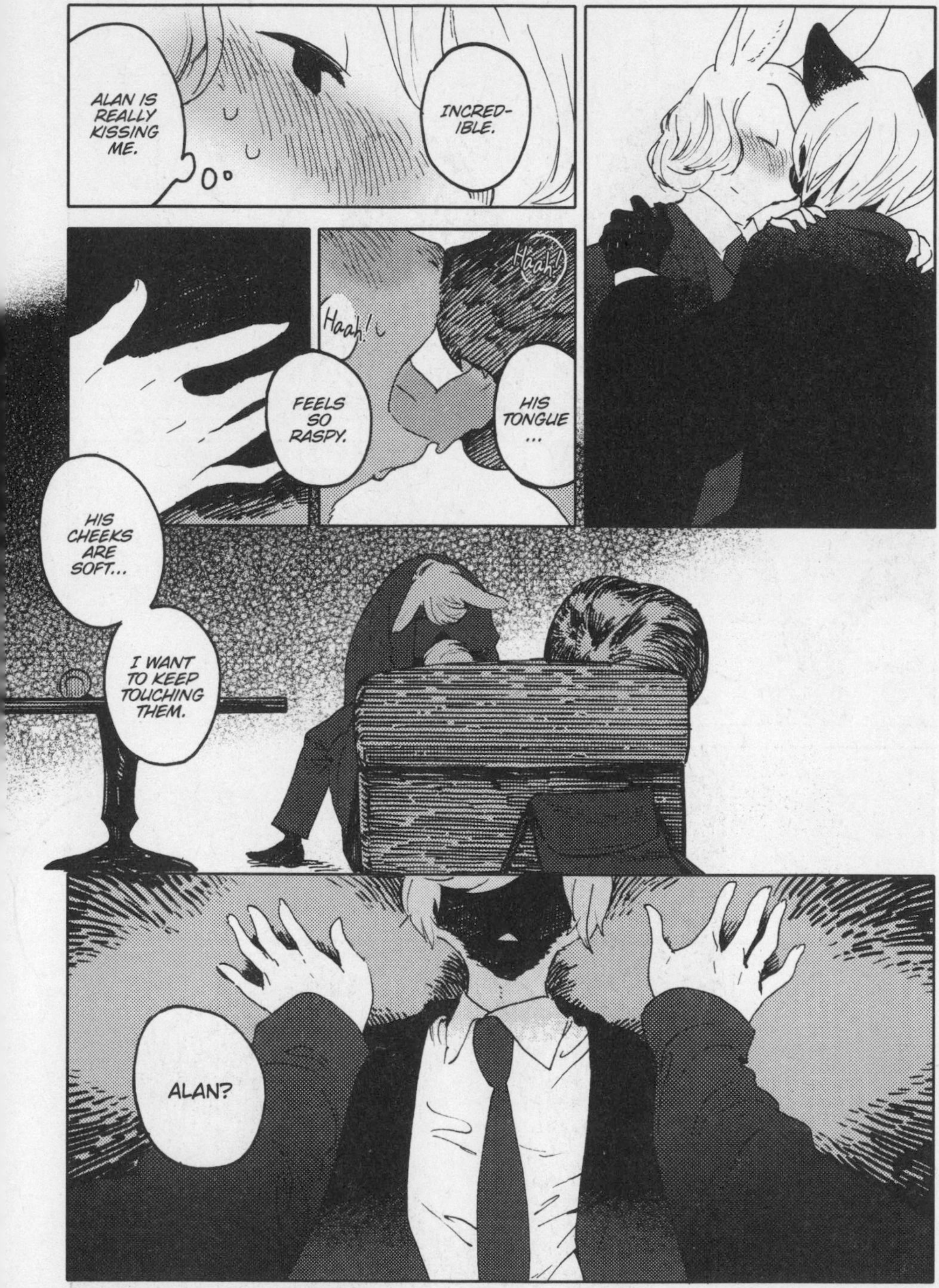
INCRED-IBLE.
ALAN IS REALLY KISSING ME.
Haaah!
Haah!
HIS TONGUE...
FEELS SO RASPY.
HIS CHEEKS ARE SOFT...
I WANT TO KEEP TOUCHING THEM.
ALAN?

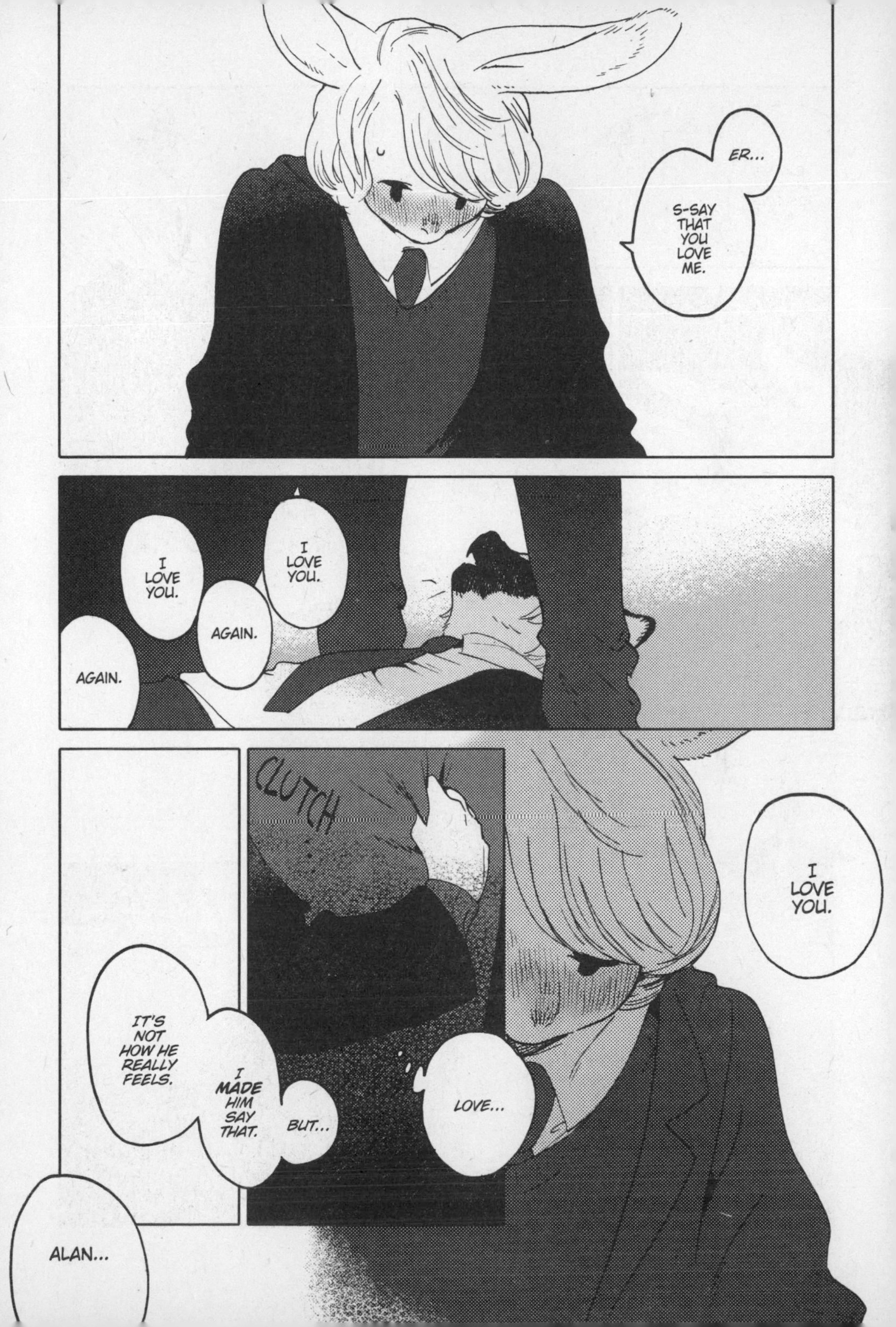
ER...
S-SAY THAT YOU LOVE ME.
I LOVE YOU.
I LOVE YOU.
AGAIN.
AGAIN.
I LOVE YOU.
CLUTCH
LOVE...
BUT...
I MADE HIM SAY THAT.
IT'S NOT HOW HE REALLY FEELS.
ALAN...

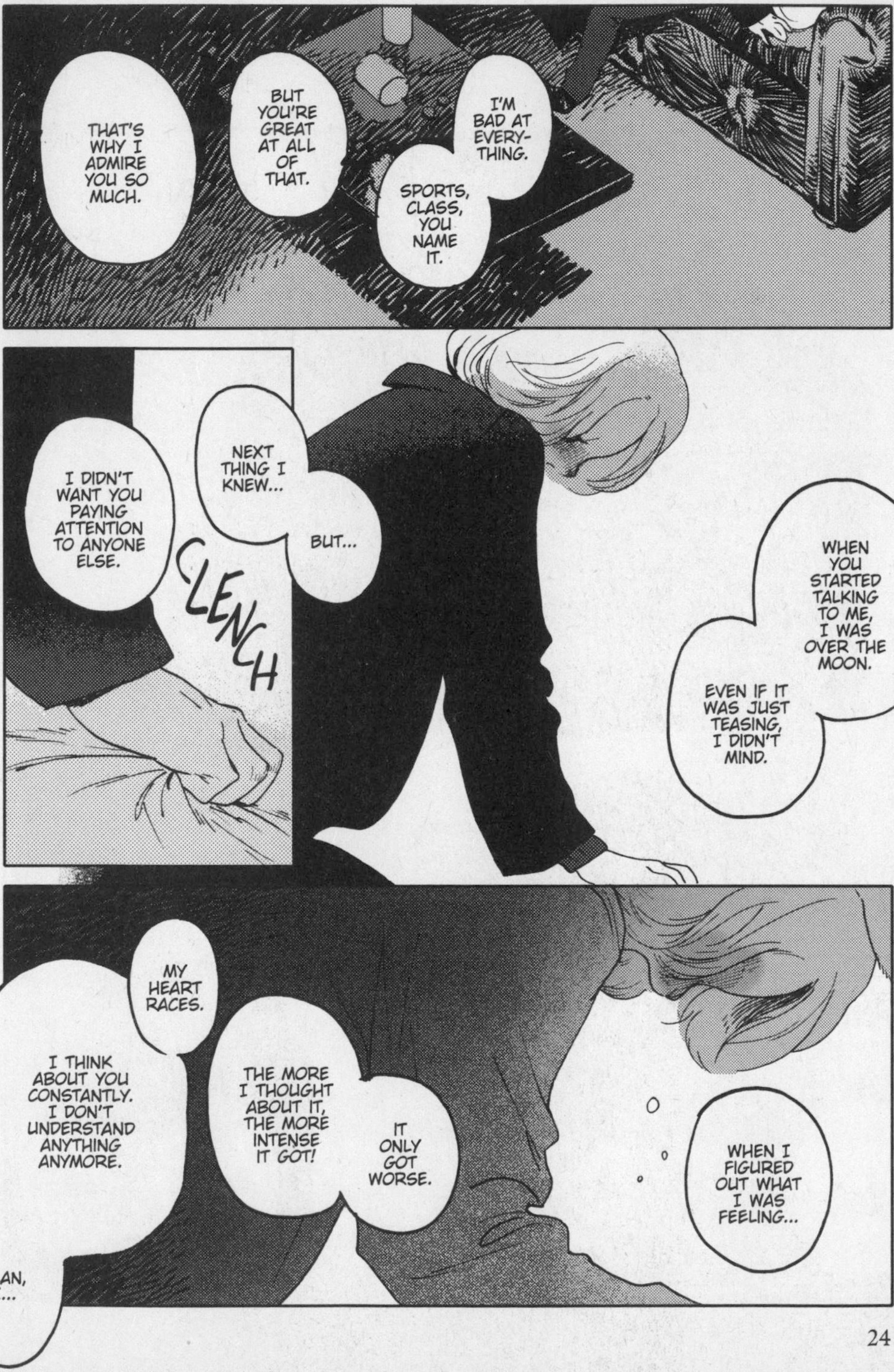
I'M BAD AT EVERYTHING.
SPORTS, CLASS, YOU NAME IT.
BUT YOU'RE GREAT AT ALL OF THAT.
THAT'S WHY I ADMIRE YOU SO MUCH.
WHEN YOU STARTED TALKING TO ME, I WAS OVER THE MOON.
EVEN IF IT WAS JUST TEASING, I DIDN'T MIND.
BUT...
NEXT THING I KNEW...
I DIDN'T WANT YOU PAYING ATTENTION TO ANYONE ELSE.
CLENCH
WHEN I FIGURED OUT WHAT I WAS FEELING...
IT ONLY GOT WORSE.
THE MORE I THOUGHT ABOUT IT, THE MORE INTENSE IT GOT!
MY HEART RACES.
I THINK ABOUT YOU CONSTANTLY. I DON'T UNDERSTAND ANYTHING ANYMORE.
ALAN, I...

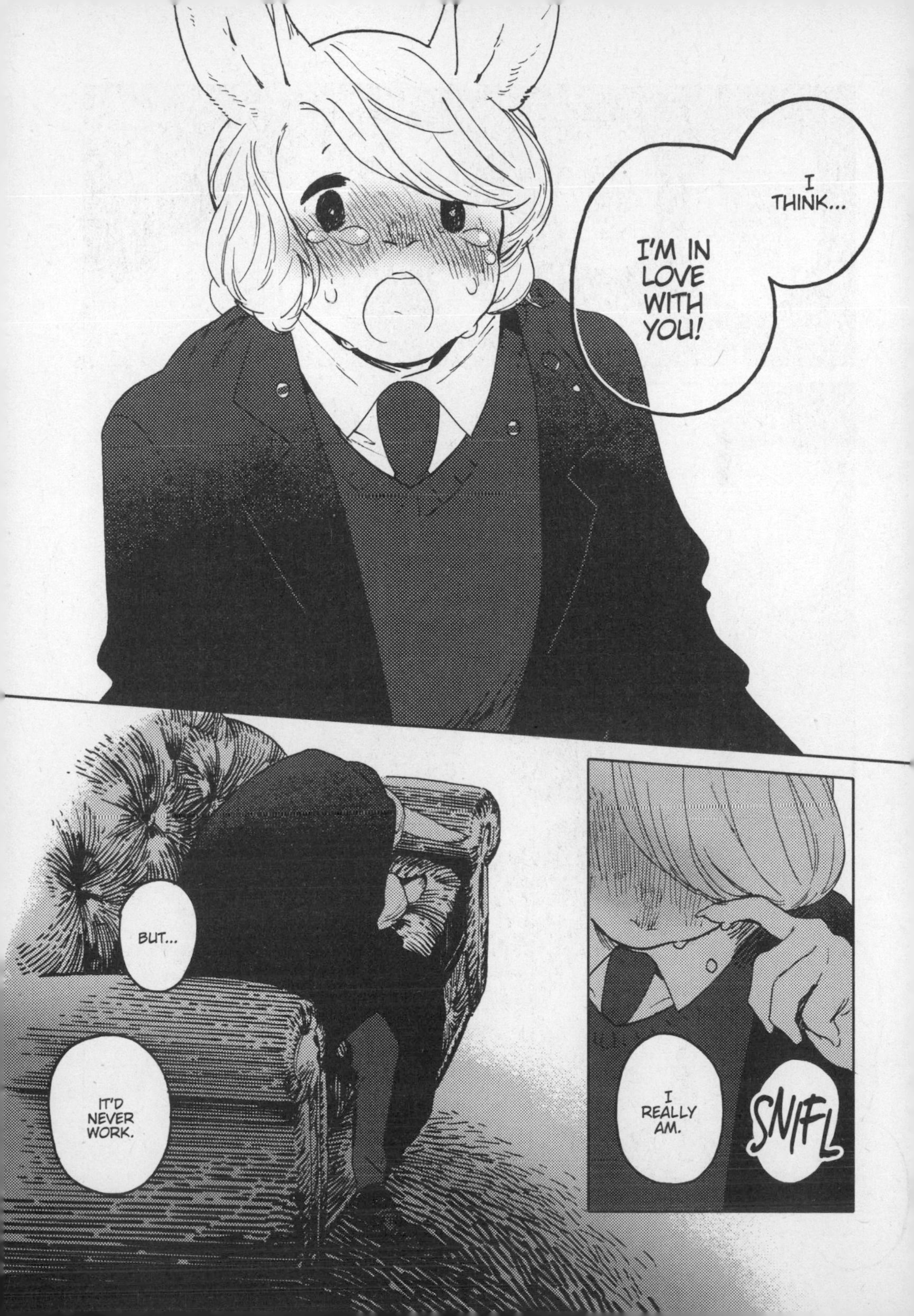
I THINK...
I'M IN LOVE WITH YOU!
I REALLY AM.
SNIFL
BUT...
IT'D NEVER WORK.

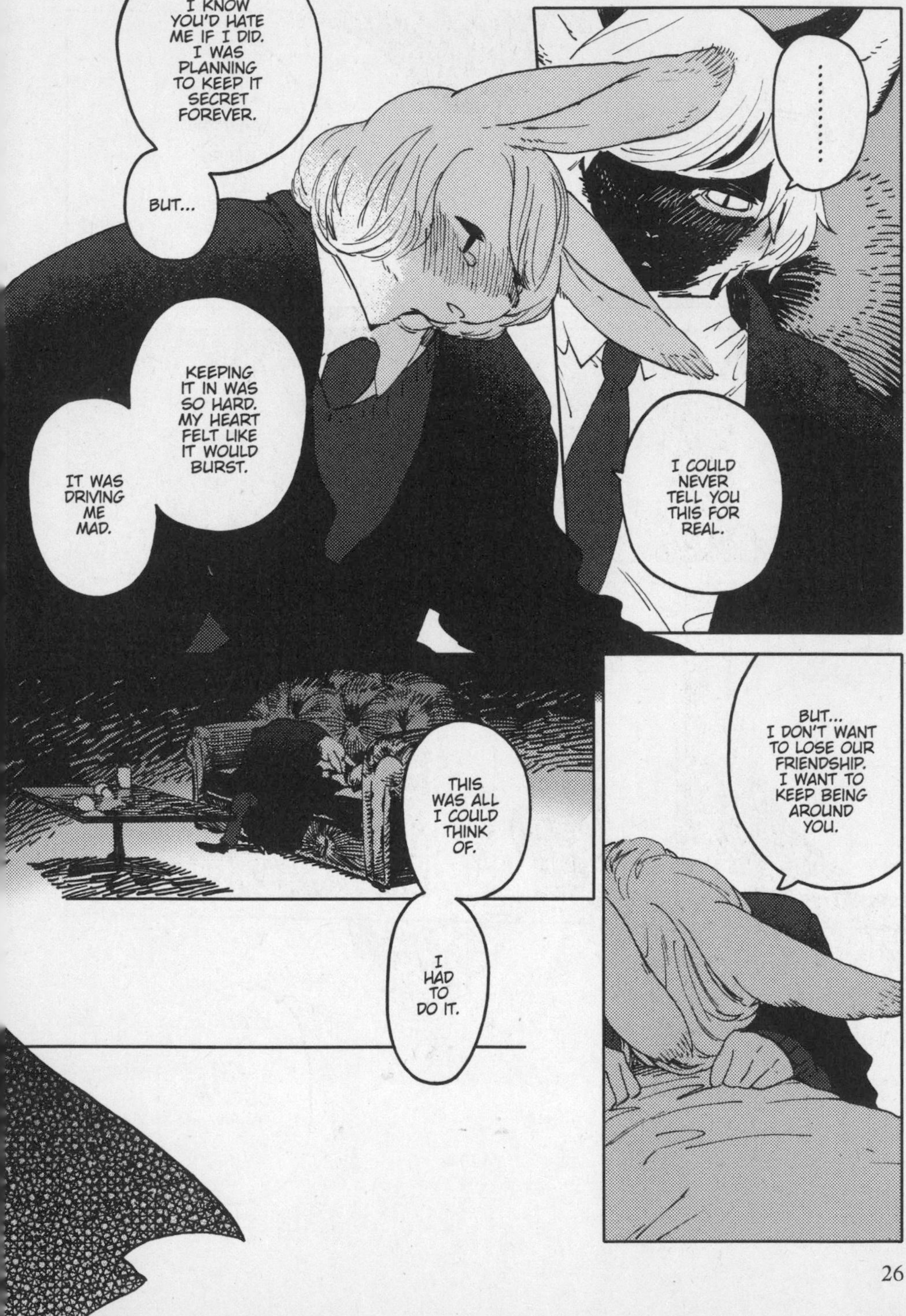
......
I KNOW YOU'D HATE ME IF I DID. I WAS PLANNING TO KEEP IT SECRET FOREVER.
BUT...
I COULD NEVER TELL YOU THIS FOR REAL.
KEEPING IT IN WAS SO HARD. MY HEART FELT LIKE IT WOULD BURST.
IT WAS DRIVING ME MAD.
BUT... I DON'T WANT TO LOSE OUR FRIENDSHIP. I WANT TO KEEP BEING AROUND YOU.
THIS WAS ALL I COULD THINK OF.
I HAD TO DO IT.

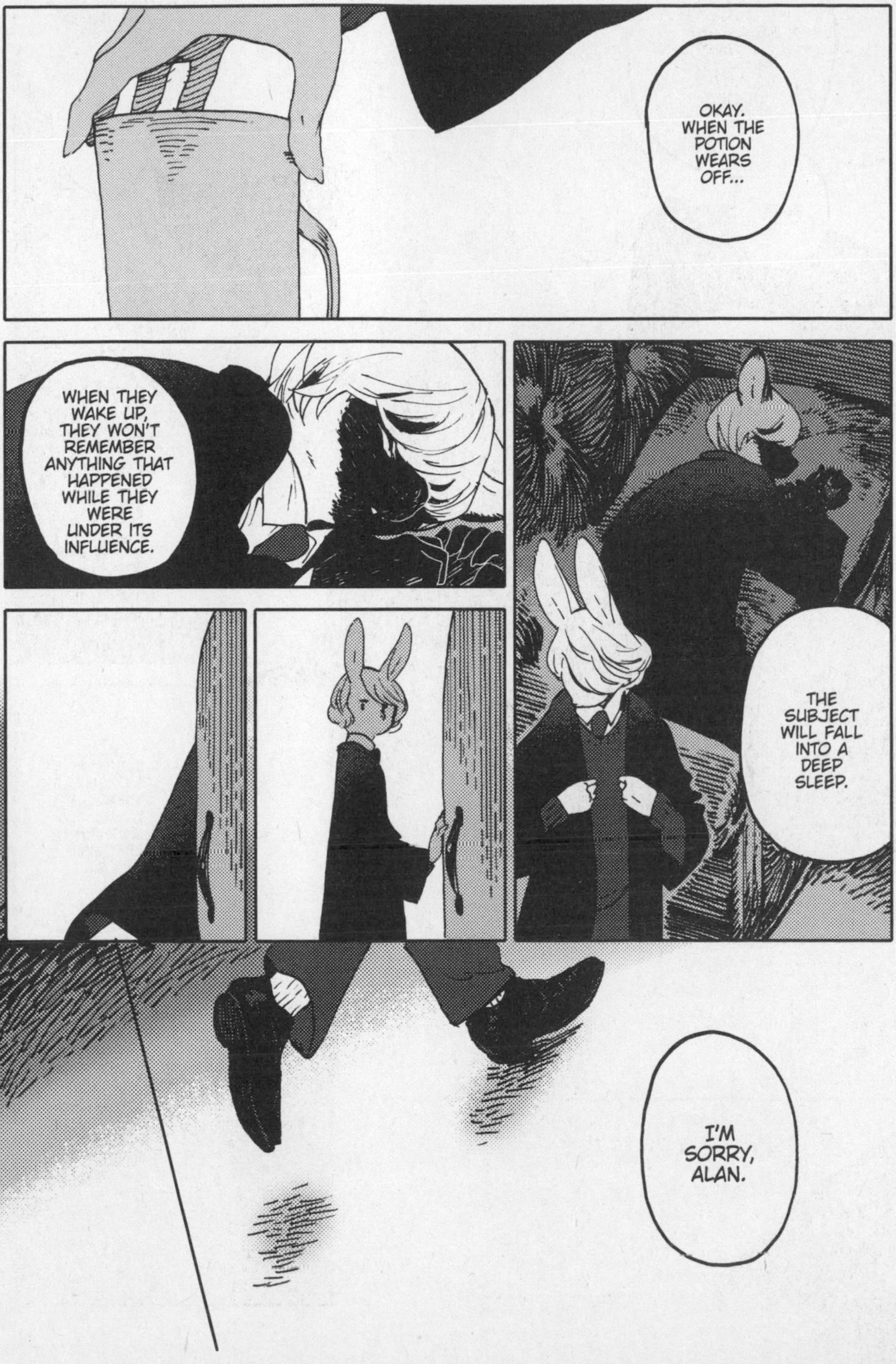
OKAY. WHEN THE POTION WEARS OFF...
THE SUBJECT WILL FALL INTO A DEEP SLEEP.
WHEN THEY WAKE UP, THEY WON'T REMEMBER ANYTHING THAT HAPPENED WHILE THEY WERE UNDER ITS INFLUENCE.
I'M SORRY, ALAN.

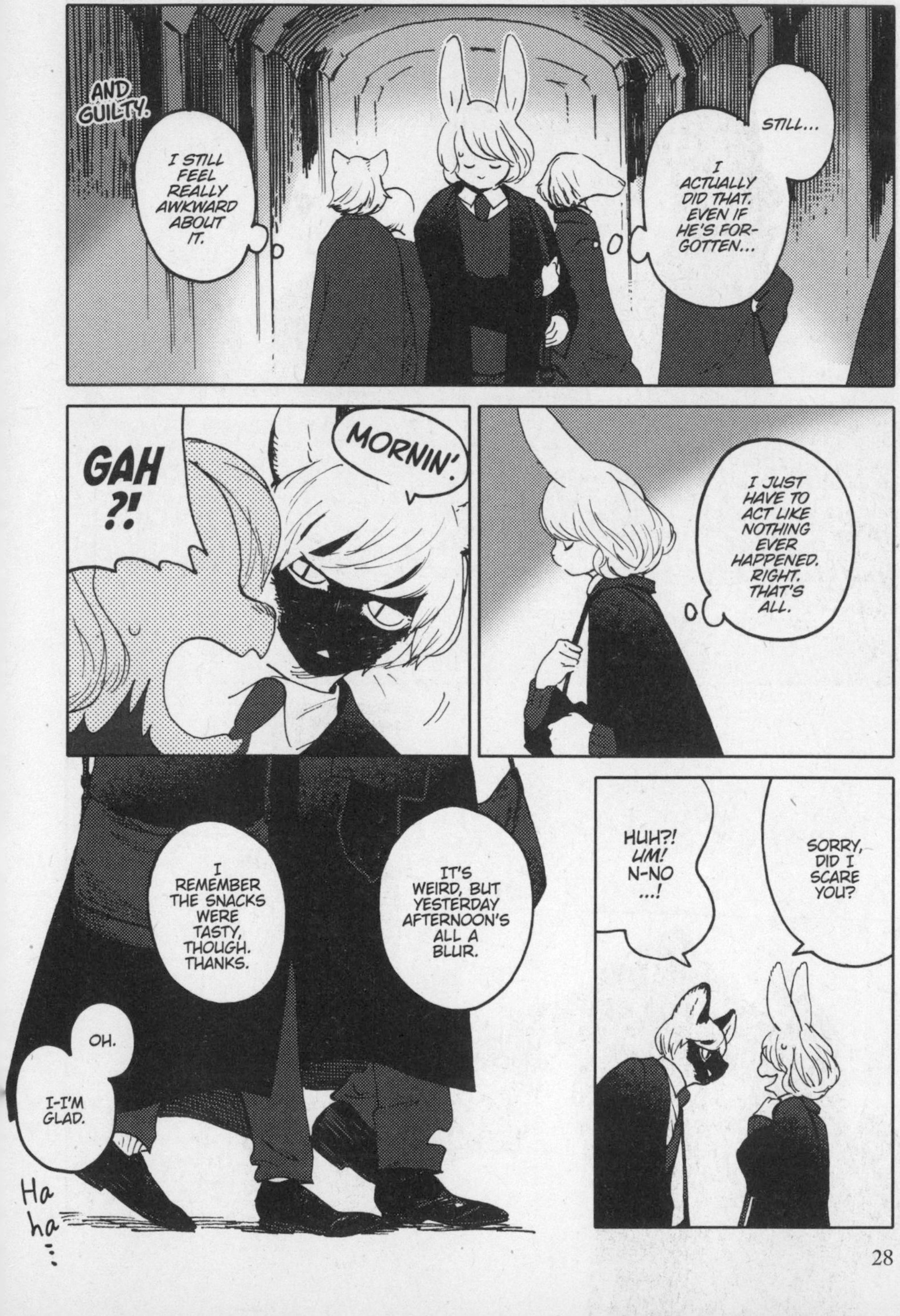
STILL... I ACTUALLY DID THAT. EVEN IF HE'S FORGOTTEN...
I STILL FEEL REALLY AWKWARD ABOUT IT.
AND GUILTY.
I JUST HAVE TO ACT LIKE NOTHING EVER HAPPENED. RIGHT. THAT'S ALL.
MORNIN'.
GAH ?!
SORRY, DID I SCARE YOU?
HUH?! UM! N-NO ...!
IT'S WEIRD, BUT YESTERDAY AFTERNOON'S ALL A BLUR.
I REMEMBER THE SNACKS WERE TASTY, THOUGH. THANKS.
OH.
I-I'M GLAD.
Ha ha...

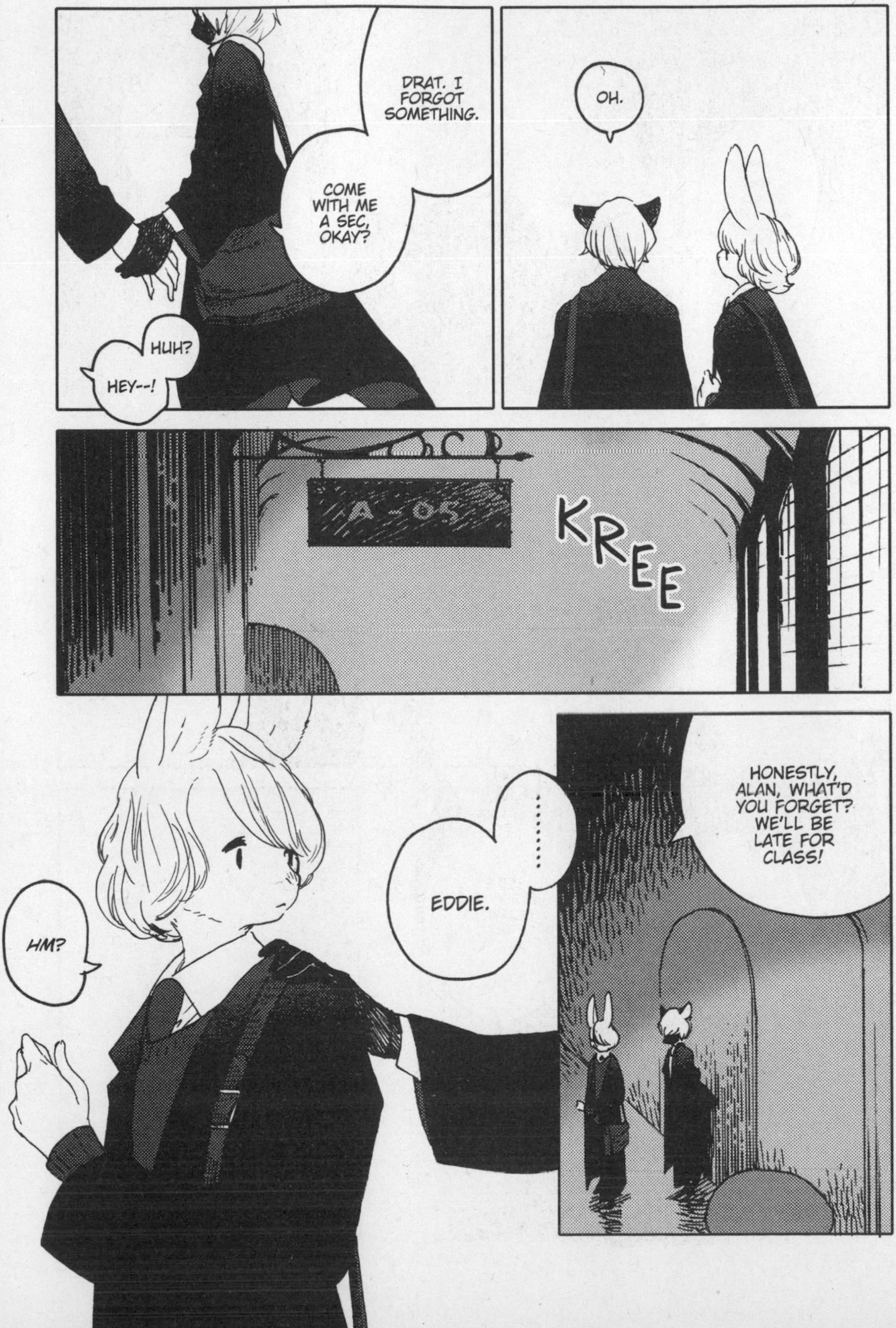
OH.
DRAT. I FORGOT SOMETHING.
COME WITH ME A SEC, OKAY?
HUH?
HEY--!
A-05
KREE
HONESTLY, ALAN, WHAT'D YOU FORGET? WE'LL BE LATE FOR CLASS!
......
EDDIE.
HM?

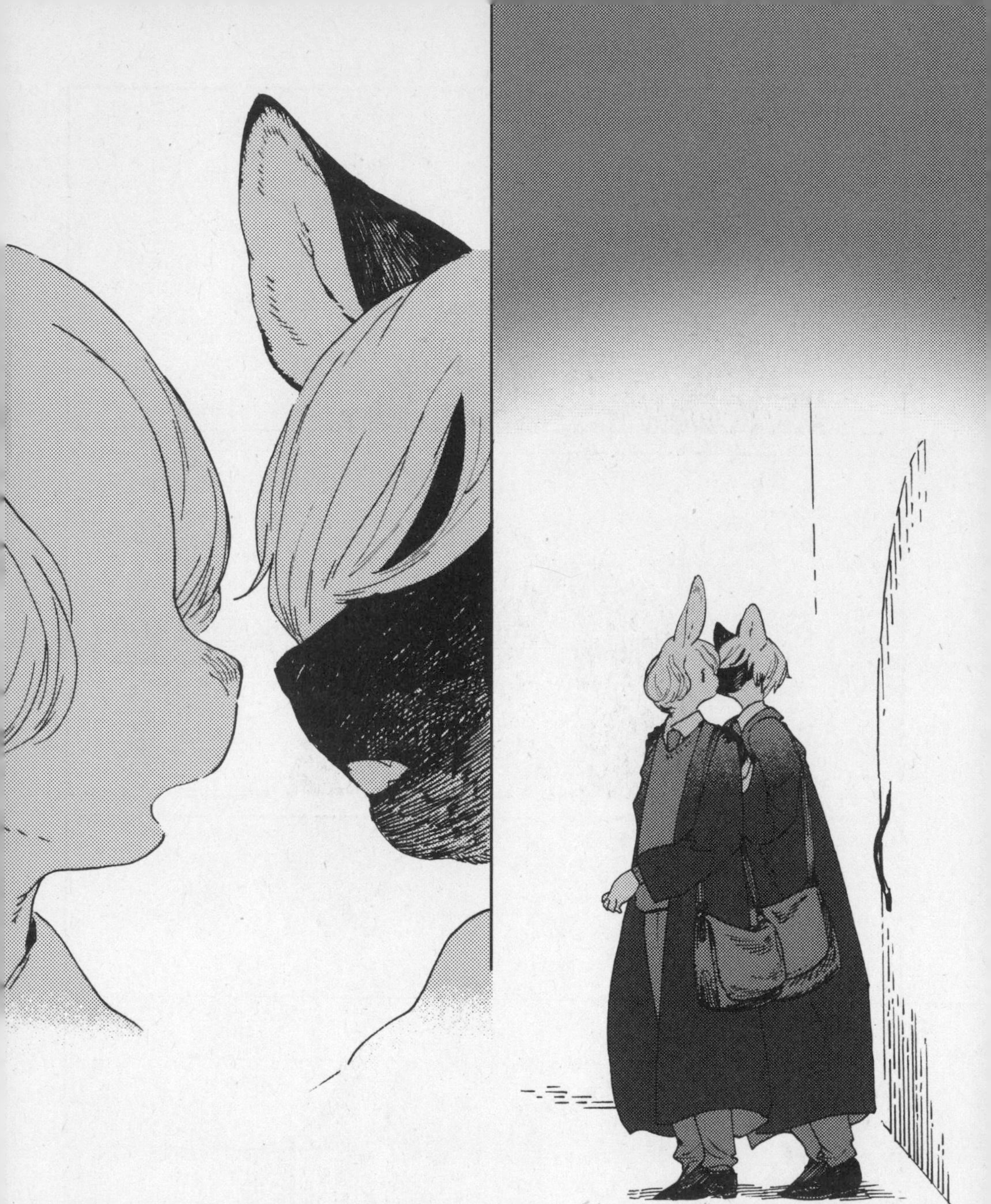

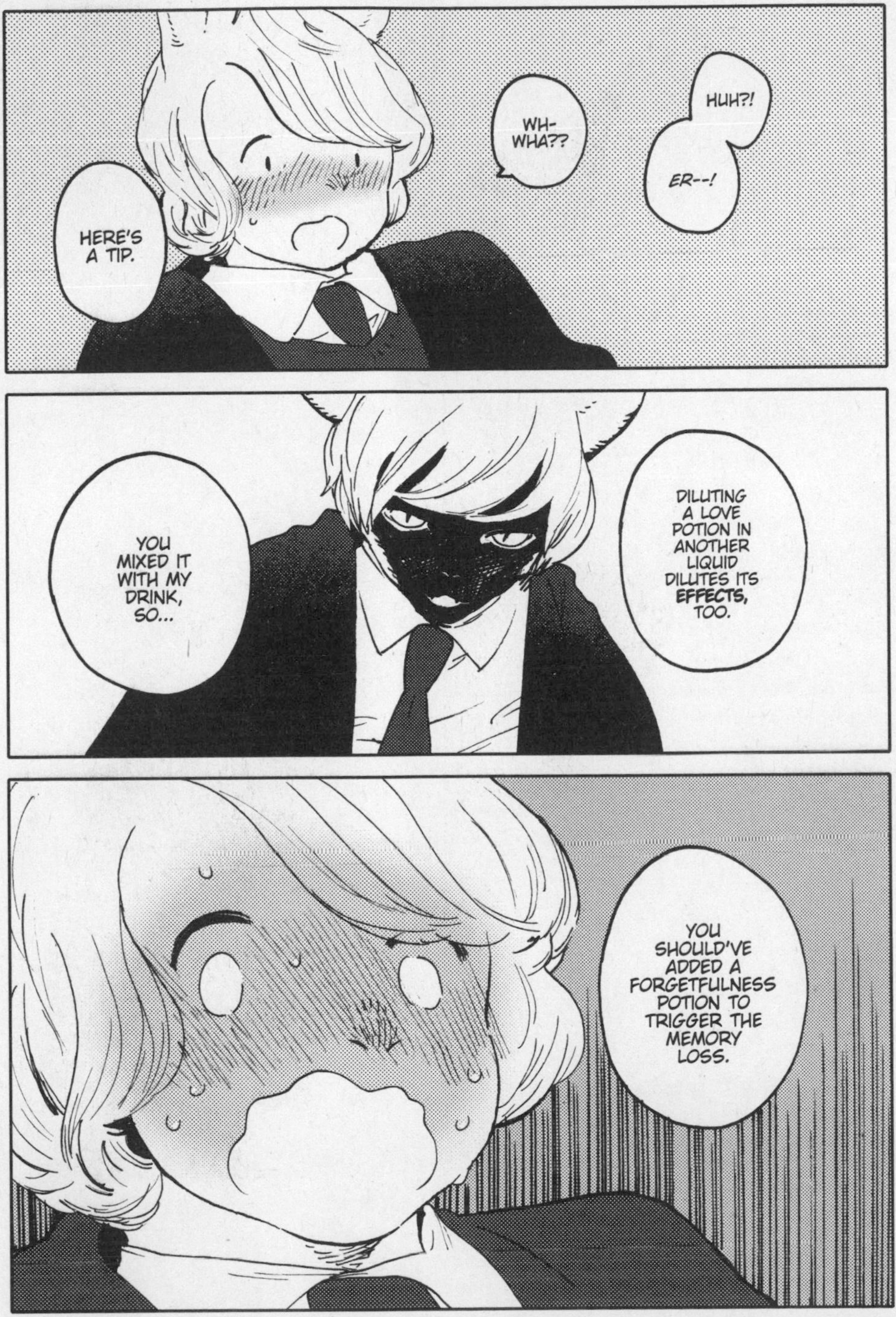
HUH?!
ER--!
WH-WHA??
HERE'S A TIP.
DILUTING A LOVE POTION IN ANOTHER LIQUID DILUTES ITS EFFECTS, TOO.
YOU MIXED IT WITH MY DRINK, SO...
YOU SHOULD'VE ADDED A FORGETFULNESS POTION TO TRIGGER THE MEMORY LOSS.

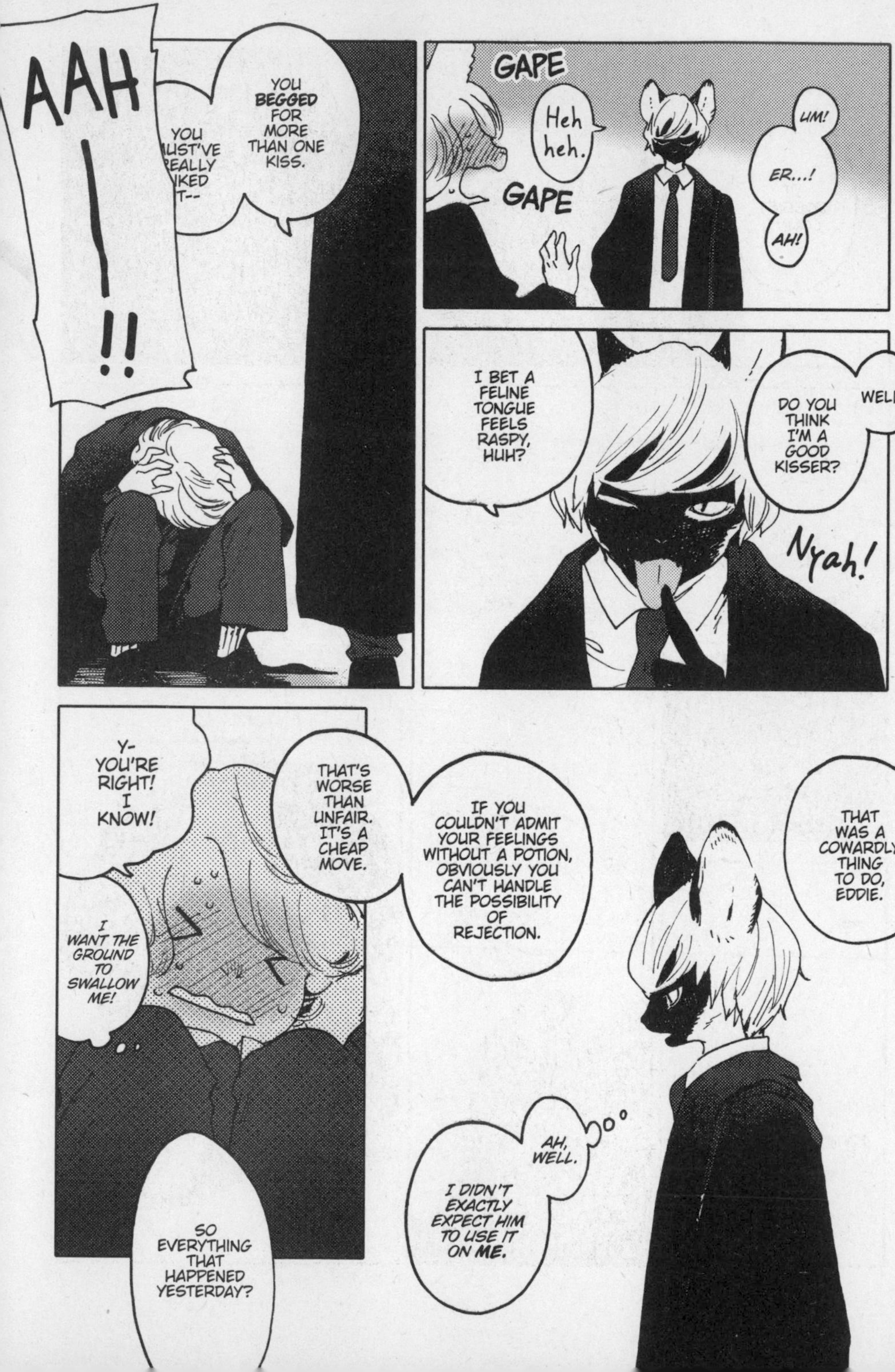
UM!
ER...!
AH!
Heh heh.
GAPE
GAPE
WELL?
DO YOU THINK I'M A GOOD KISSER?
Nyah!
I BET A FELINE TONGUE FEELS RASPY, HUH?
YOU BEGGED FOR MORE THAN ONE KISS.
YOU MUST'VE REALLY LIKED IT--
AAH!!
THAT WAS A COWARDLY THING TO DO, EDDIE.
IF YOU COULDN'T ADMIT YOUR FEELINGS WITHOUT A POTION, OBVIOUSLY YOU CAN'T HANDLE THE POSSIBILITY OF REJECTION.
THAT'S WORSE THAN UNFAIR. IT'S A CHEAP MOVE.
AH, WELL.
I DIDN'T EXACTLY EXPECT HIM TO USE IT ON ME.
Y-YOU'RE RIGHT! I KNOW!
I WANT THE GROUND TO SWALLOW ME!
SO EVERYTHING THAT HAPPENED YESTERDAY?

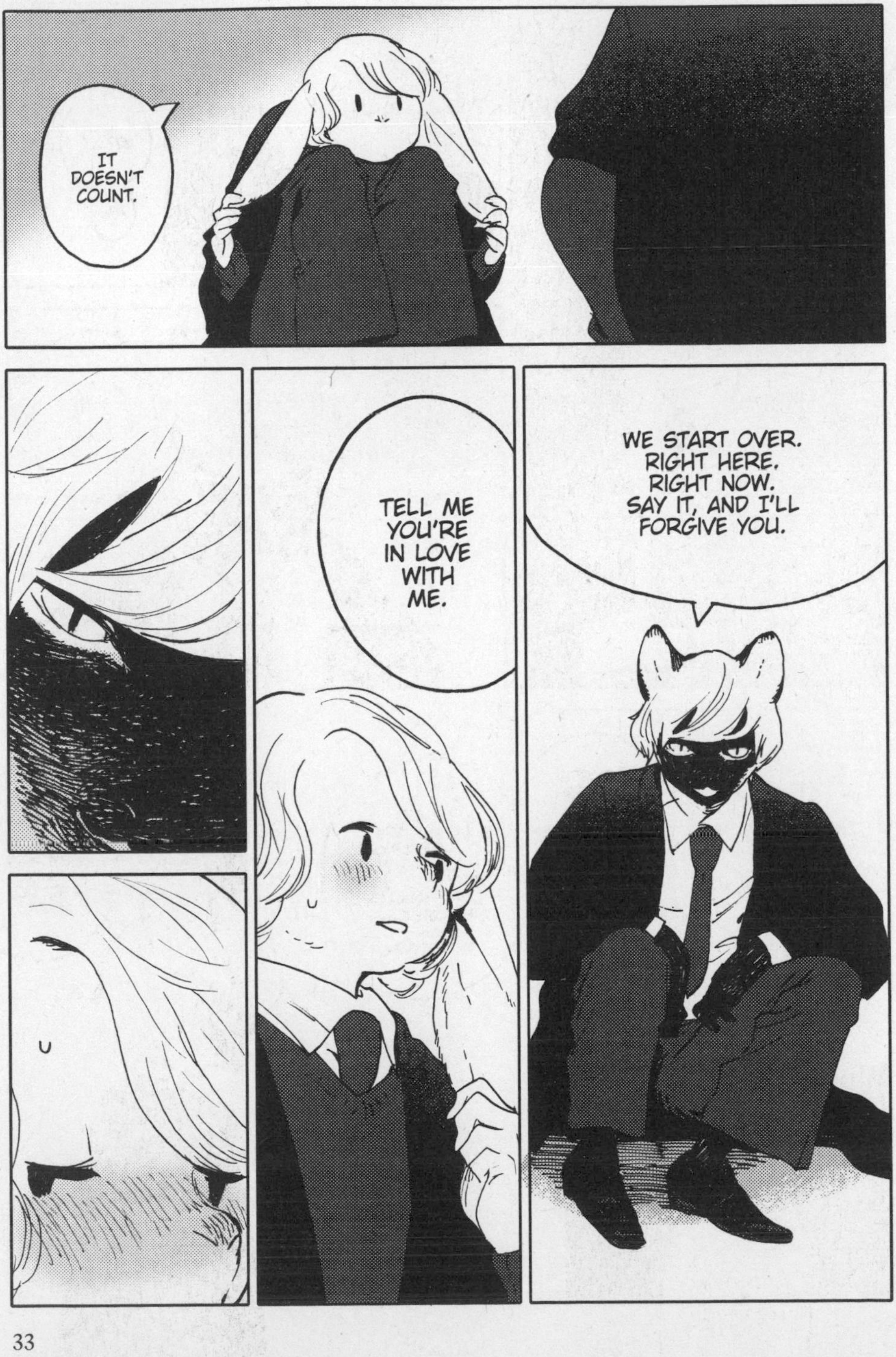
IT DOESN'T COUNT.
WE START OVER. RIGHT HERE. RIGHT NOW. SAY IT, AND I'LL FORGIVE YOU.
TELL ME YOU'RE IN LOVE WITH ME.

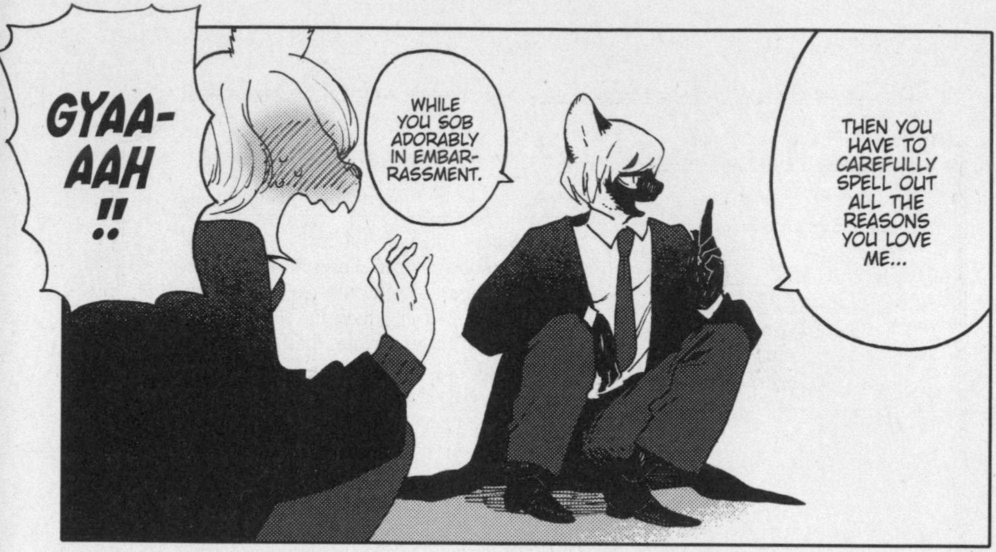
THEN YOU HAVE TO CAREFULLY SPELL OUT ALL THE REASONS YOU LOVE ME...
WHILE YOU SOB ADORABLY IN EMBAR-RASSMENT.
GYAA-AAH!!

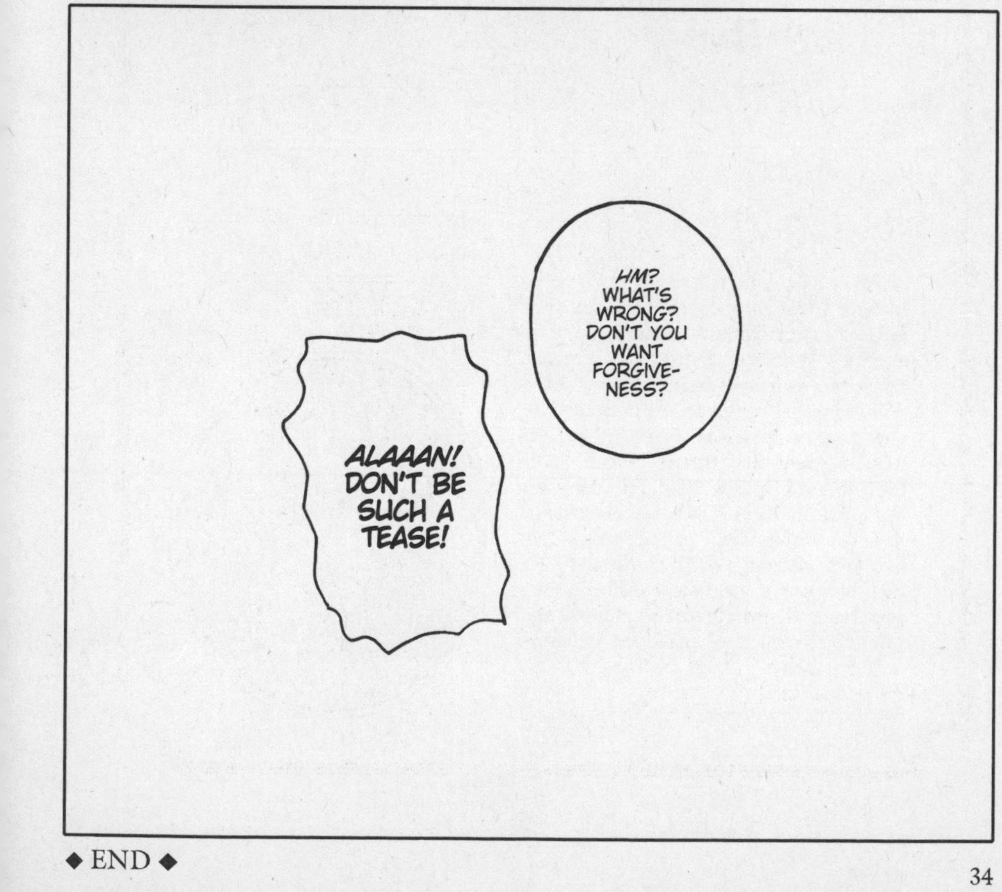
HM? WHAT'S WRONG? DON'T YOU WANT FORGIVE-NESS?
ALAAAN! DON'T BE SUCH A TEASE!

◆ END ◆

CAT

Felis

Carnivora | Felidae *Felis*

Felines are lithe animals with well-muscled bodies, keen senses, quick reflexes, and tremendously effective teeth and claws. Adapted for stealth, their fur patterns provide camouflage, while their eyes--with pupils that open wide--and their sensitive whiskers help them maneuver in the dark.

Their tongues have spines called papillae that function as a stiff brush for grooming themselves and scraping meat from prey bones. Siamese cats, a distinctive Asian breed, are known for having strong personalities and for being social, affectionate, intelligent, and occasionally arrogant. They can be incredibly loyal to any human they accept as "theirs."

Lagomorpha | Leporidae *Lepus*

HARE

Lepus

Hares have not one but two sets of front incisors. They are the only mammal with kinetic—that is, jointed—skulls. They have extremely large ears, and their eyes are set on the sides of their head, allowing for a 360-degree field of vision. As prey animals, they have evolved extra-large and powerfully muscled hindquarters, which allow them to reach speeds up to 56 kilometers and evade predators. The fur on the base of their paws gives them firm traction when they run. Hares are herbivorous and have high birthrates to help them maintain their population despite predation. Stimulation from copulation is what induces a female hare to ovulate. Unlike rabbits, hares are solitary animals.

The Wize Wize Beasts
of the Wizarding Wizdoms
by Nagabe

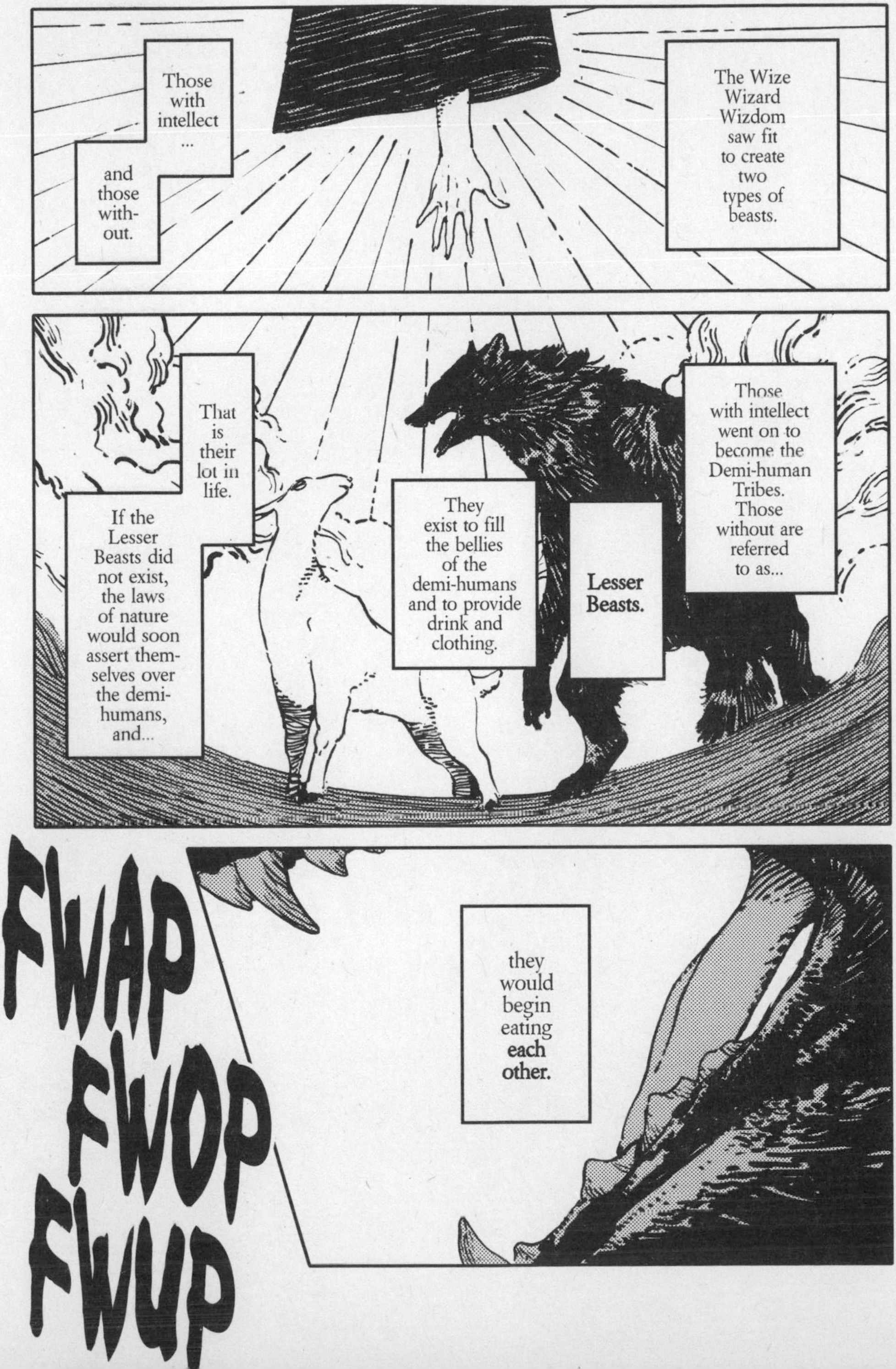
The Wize Wizard Wizdom saw fit to create two types of beasts.
Those with intellect ...
and those with-out.
Those with intellect went on to become the Demi-human Tribes. Those without are referred to as...
Lesser Beasts.
They exist to fill the bellies of the demi-humans and to provide drink and clothing.
That is their lot in life.
If the Lesser Beasts did not exist, the laws of nature would soon assert them-selves over the demi-humans, and...
they would begin eating **each other.**
FWAP FWOP FWUP

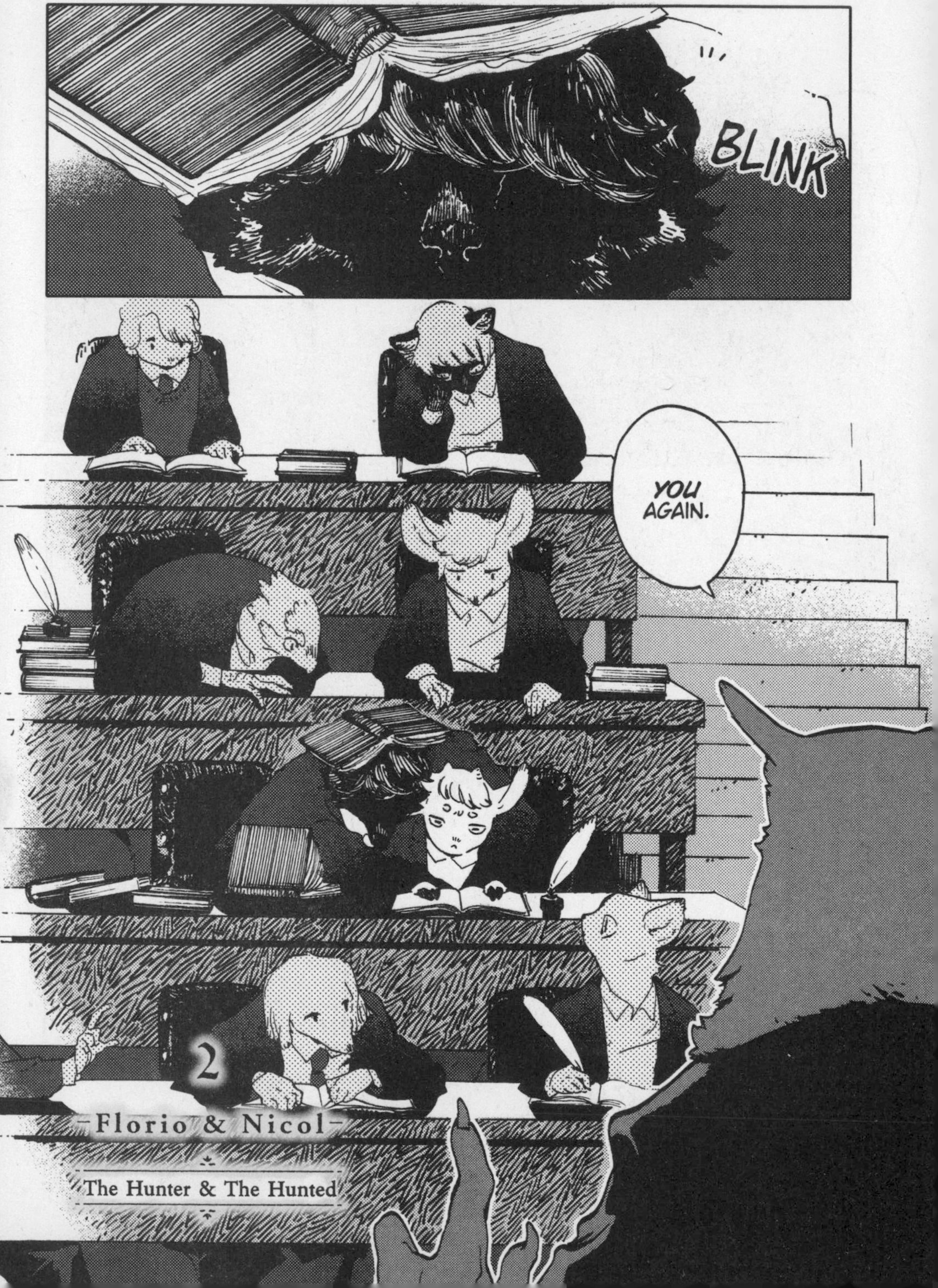
BLINK
YOU AGAIN.
2
-Florio & Nicol-
The Hunter & The Hunted

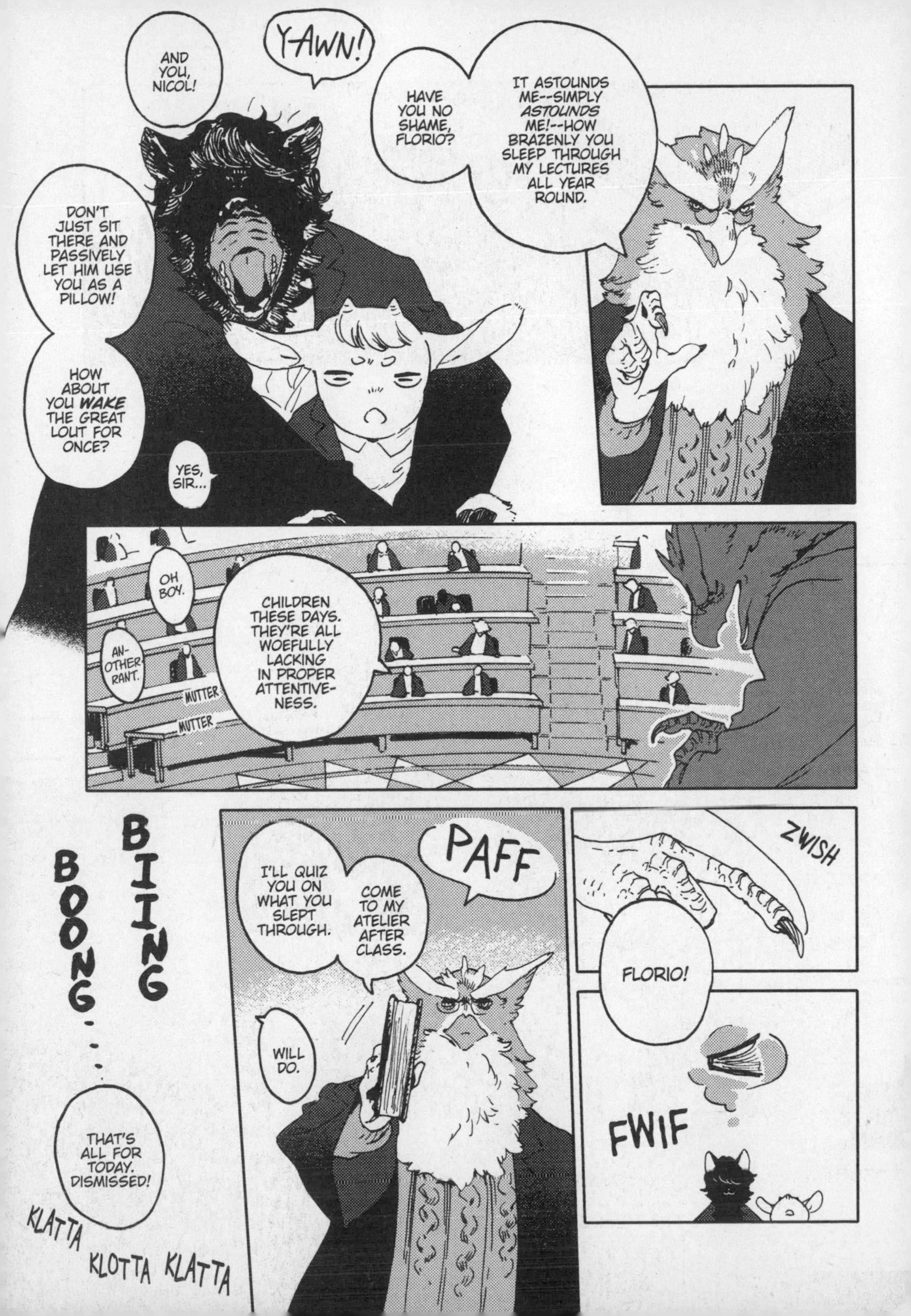
IT ASTOUNDS ME--SIMPLY *ASTOUNDS* ME!--HOW BRAZENLY YOU SLEEP THROUGH MY LECTURES ALL YEAR ROUND.
HAVE YOU NO SHAME, FLORIO?
Y-AWN!
AND YOU, NICOL!
DON'T JUST SIT THERE AND PASSIVELY LET HIM USE YOU AS A PILLOW!
HOW ABOUT YOU ***WAKE*** THE GREAT LOUT FOR ONCE?
YES, SIR...
CHILDREN THESE DAYS. THEY'RE ALL WOEFULLY LACKING IN PROPER ATTENTIVENESS.
OH BOY.
ANOTHER RANT.
MUTTER
MUTTER
ZWISH
FLORIO!
FWIF
PAFF
COME TO MY ATELIER AFTER CLASS.
I'LL QUIZ YOU ON WHAT YOU SLEPT THROUGH.
WILL DO.
BIIING
BOONG...
THAT'S ALL FOR TODAY. DISMISSED!
KLATTA KLOTTA KLATTA

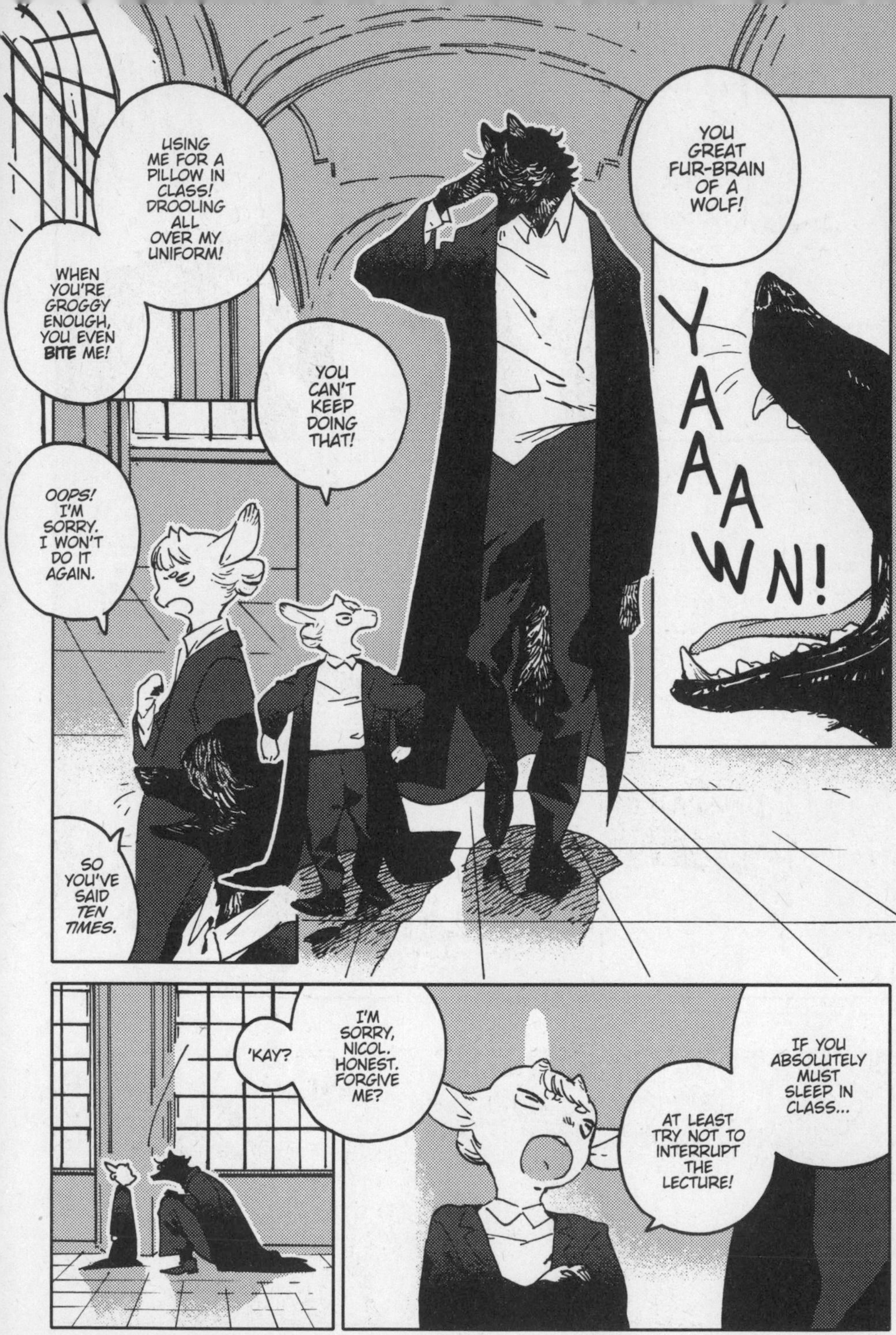

YOU GREAT FUR-BRAIN OF A WOLF!
YAAAWN!
USING ME FOR A PILLOW IN CLASS! DROOLING ALL OVER MY UNIFORM!
WHEN YOU'RE GROGGY ENOUGH, YOU EVEN **BITE** ME!
YOU CAN'T KEEP DOING THAT!
OOPS! I'M SORRY. I WON'T DO IT AGAIN.
SO YOU'VE SAID *TEN TIMES.*
IF YOU ABSOLUTELY MUST SLEEP IN CLASS...
AT LEAST TRY NOT TO INTERRUPT THE LECTURE!
I'M SORRY, NICOL. HONEST. FORGIVE ME?
'KAY?

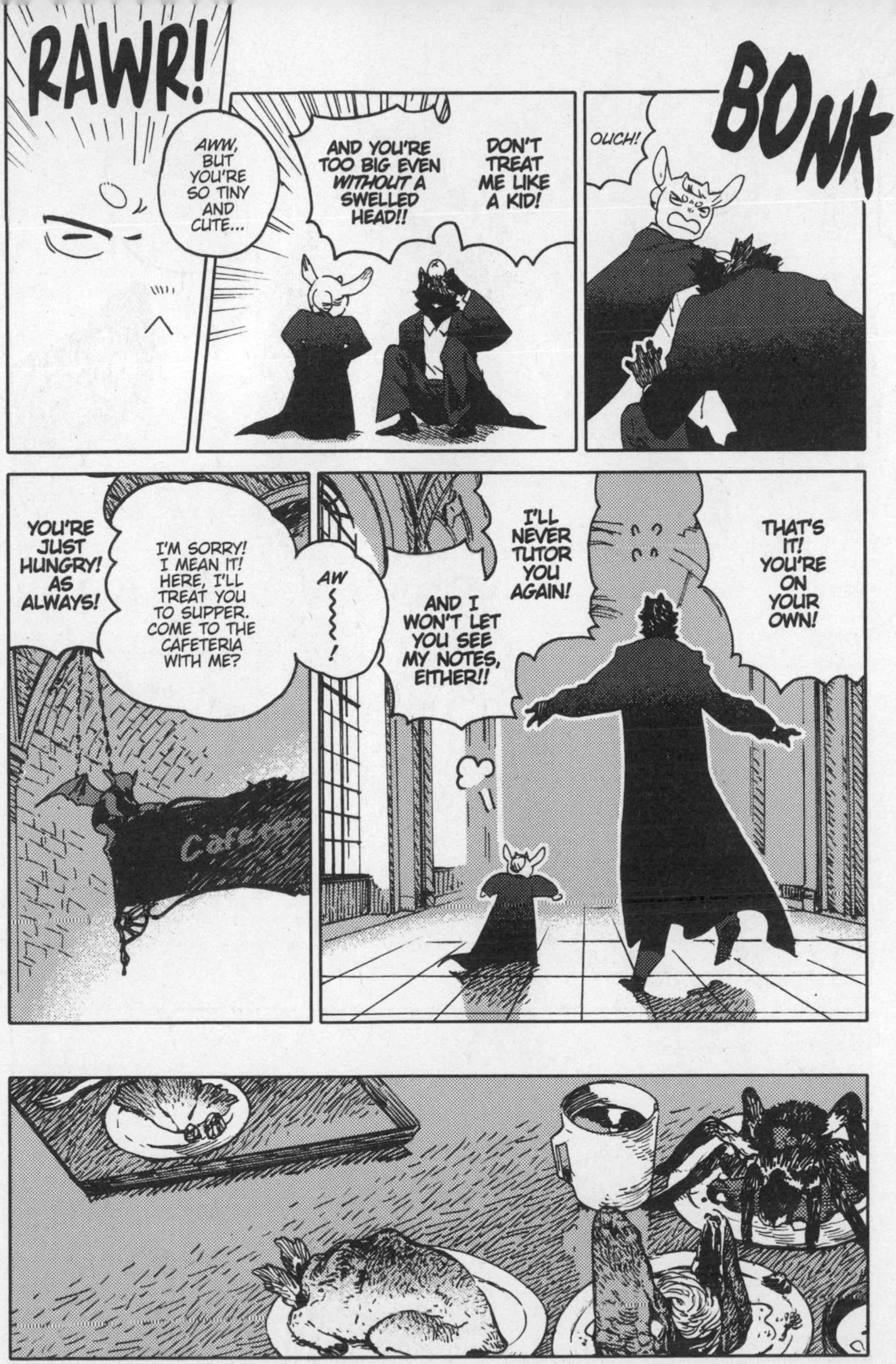
BONK
OUCH!
DON'T TREAT ME LIKE A KID!
AND YOU'RE TOO BIG EVEN *WITHOUT* A SWELLED HEAD!!
AWW, BUT YOU'RE SO TINY AND CUTE...
RAWR!
THAT'S IT! YOU'RE ON YOUR OWN!
I'LL NEVER TUTOR YOU AGAIN!
AND I WON'T LET YOU SEE MY NOTES, EITHER!!
AW~~~!
I'M SORRY! I MEAN IT! HERE, I'LL TREAT YOU TO SUPPER. COME TO THE CAFETERIA WITH ME?
YOU'RE JUST HUNGRY! AS ALWAYS!

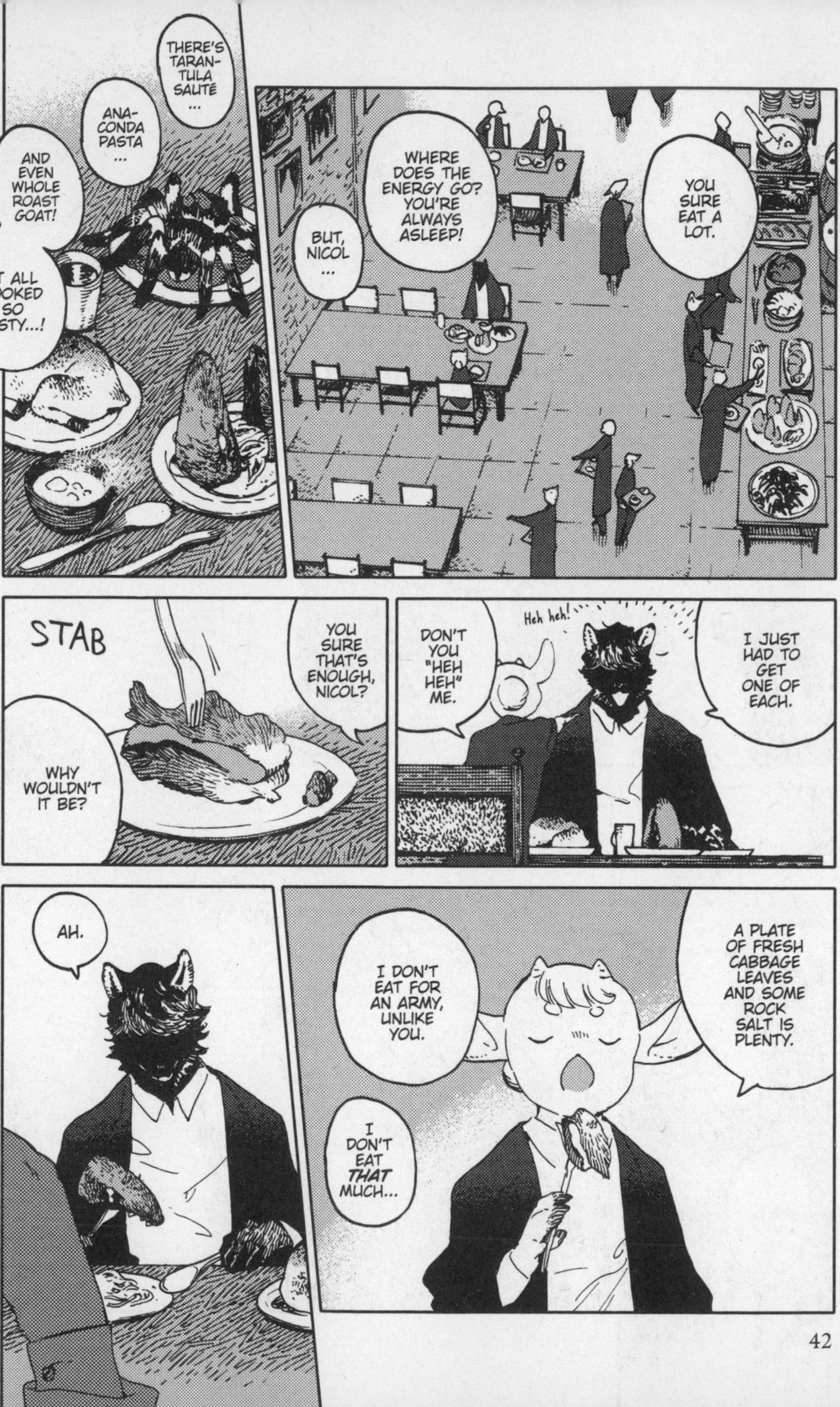
YOU SURE EAT A LOT.
WHERE DOES THE ENERGY GO? YOU'RE ALWAYS ASLEEP!
BUT, NICOL...
THERE'S TARANTULA SAUTÉ...
ANACONDA PASTA...
AND EVEN WHOLE ROAST GOAT!
IT ALL LOOKED SO TASTY...!
Heh heh!
I JUST HAD TO GET ONE OF EACH.
DON'T YOU "HEH HEH" ME.
YOU SURE THAT'S ENOUGH, NICOL?
STAB
WHY WOULDN'T IT BE?
A PLATE OF FRESH CABBAGE LEAVES AND SOME ROCK SALT IS PLENTY.
I DON'T EAT FOR AN ARMY, UNLIKE YOU.
I DON'T EAT *THAT* MUCH...
AH.

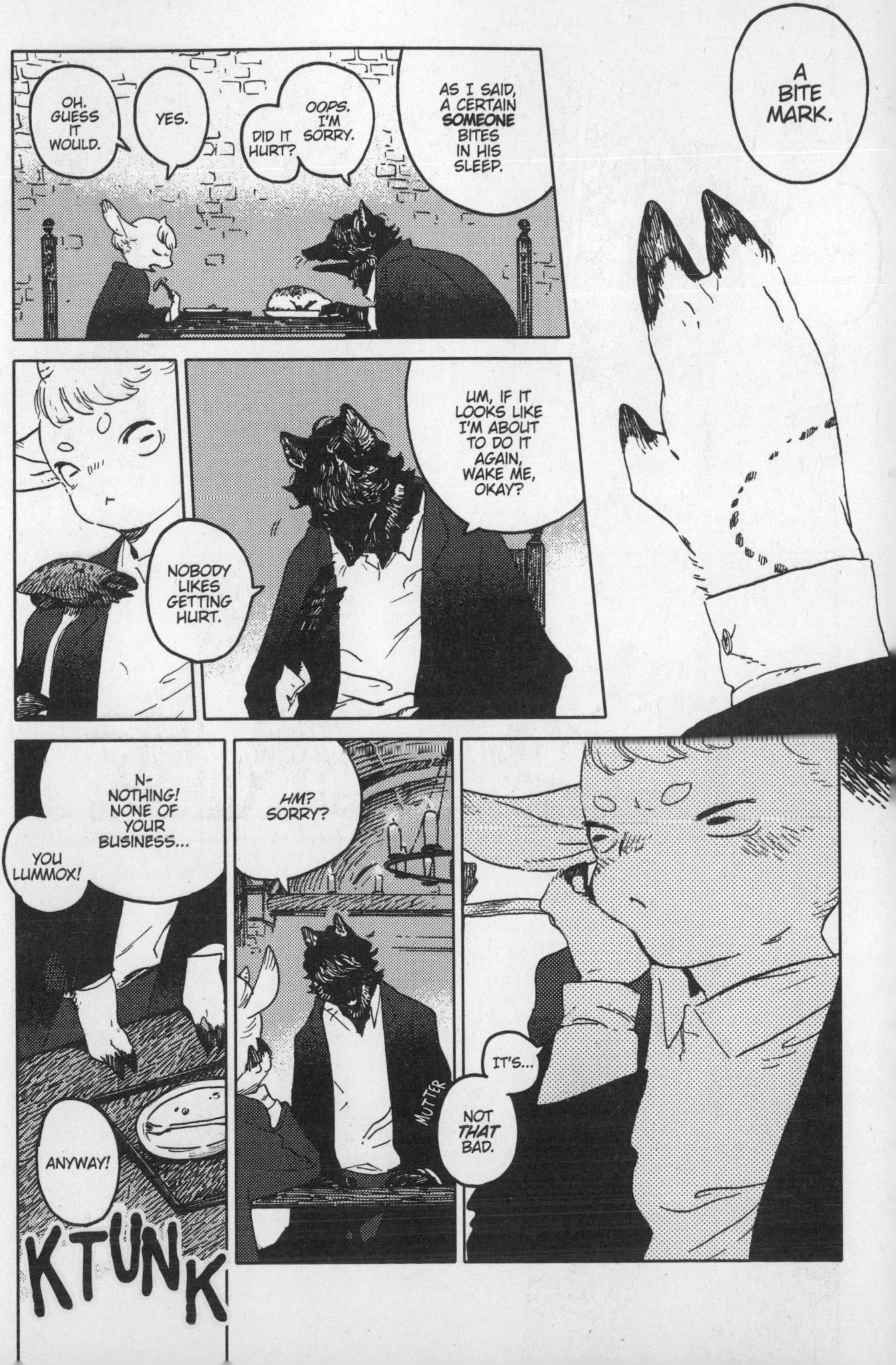
A BITE MARK.
AS I SAID, A CERTAIN **SOMEONE** BITES IN HIS SLEEP.
OOPS. I'M SORRY.
DID IT HURT?
YES.
OH. GUESS IT WOULD.
UM, IF IT LOOKS LIKE I'M ABOUT TO DO IT AGAIN, WAKE ME, OKAY?
NOBODY LIKES GETTING HURT.
IT'S...
NOT *THAT* BAD.
MUTTER
HM? SORRY?
N- NOTHING! NONE OF YOUR BUSINESS...
YOU LUMMOX!
ANYWAY!
KTUNK

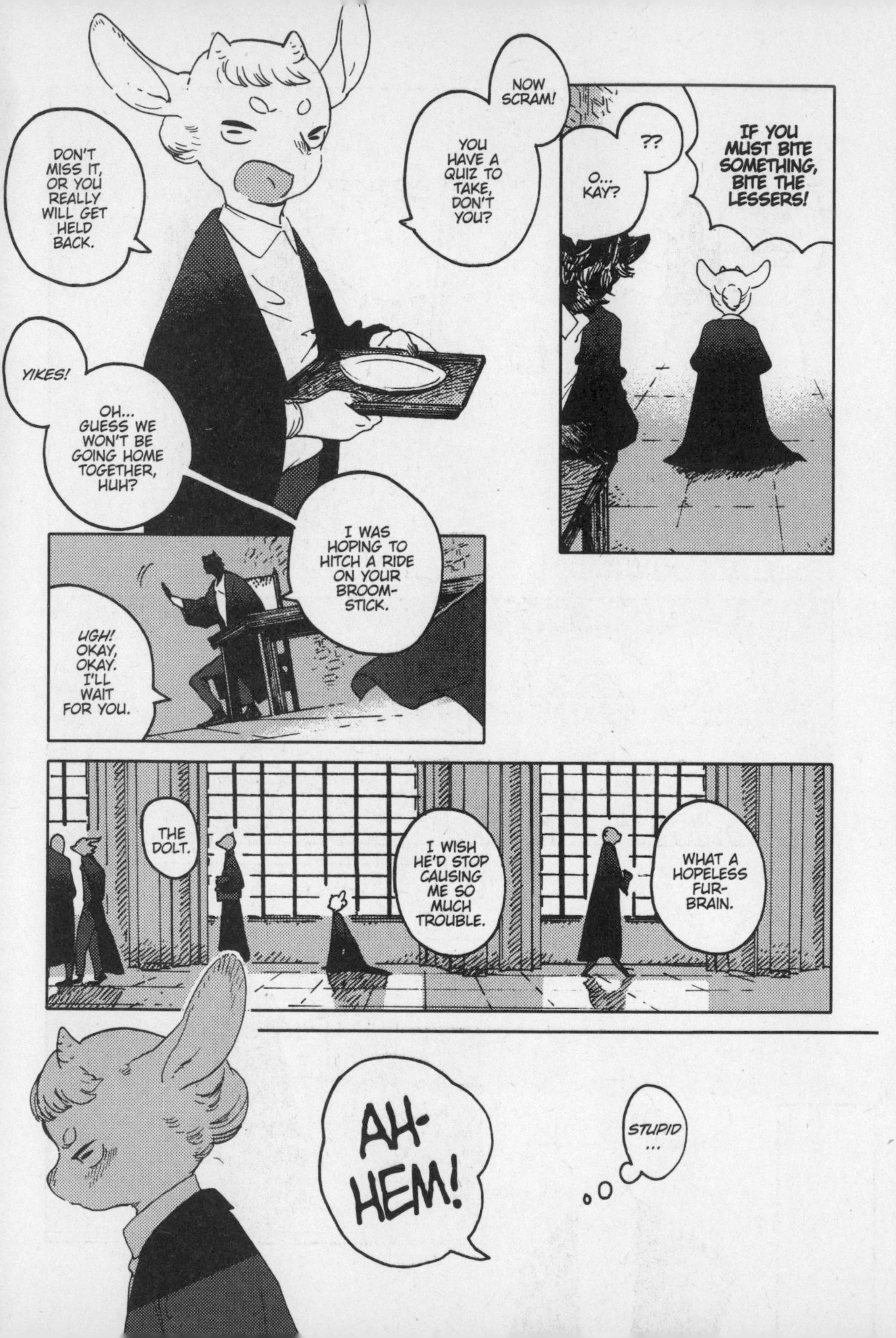

IF YOU MUST BITE SOMETHING, BITE THE LESSERS!
??
O... KAY?
NOW SCRAM!
YOU HAVE A QUIZ TO TAKE, DON'T YOU?
DON'T MISS IT, OR YOU REALLY WILL GET HELD BACK.
YIKES!
OH... GUESS WE WON'T BE GOING HOME TOGETHER, HUH?
I WAS HOPING TO HITCH A RIDE ON YOUR BROOM-STICK.
UGH! OKAY, OKAY. I'LL WAIT FOR YOU.
WHAT A HOPELESS FUR-BRAIN.
I WISH HE'D STOP CAUSING ME SO MUCH TROUBLE.
THE DOLT.
STUPID ...
AH-HEM!

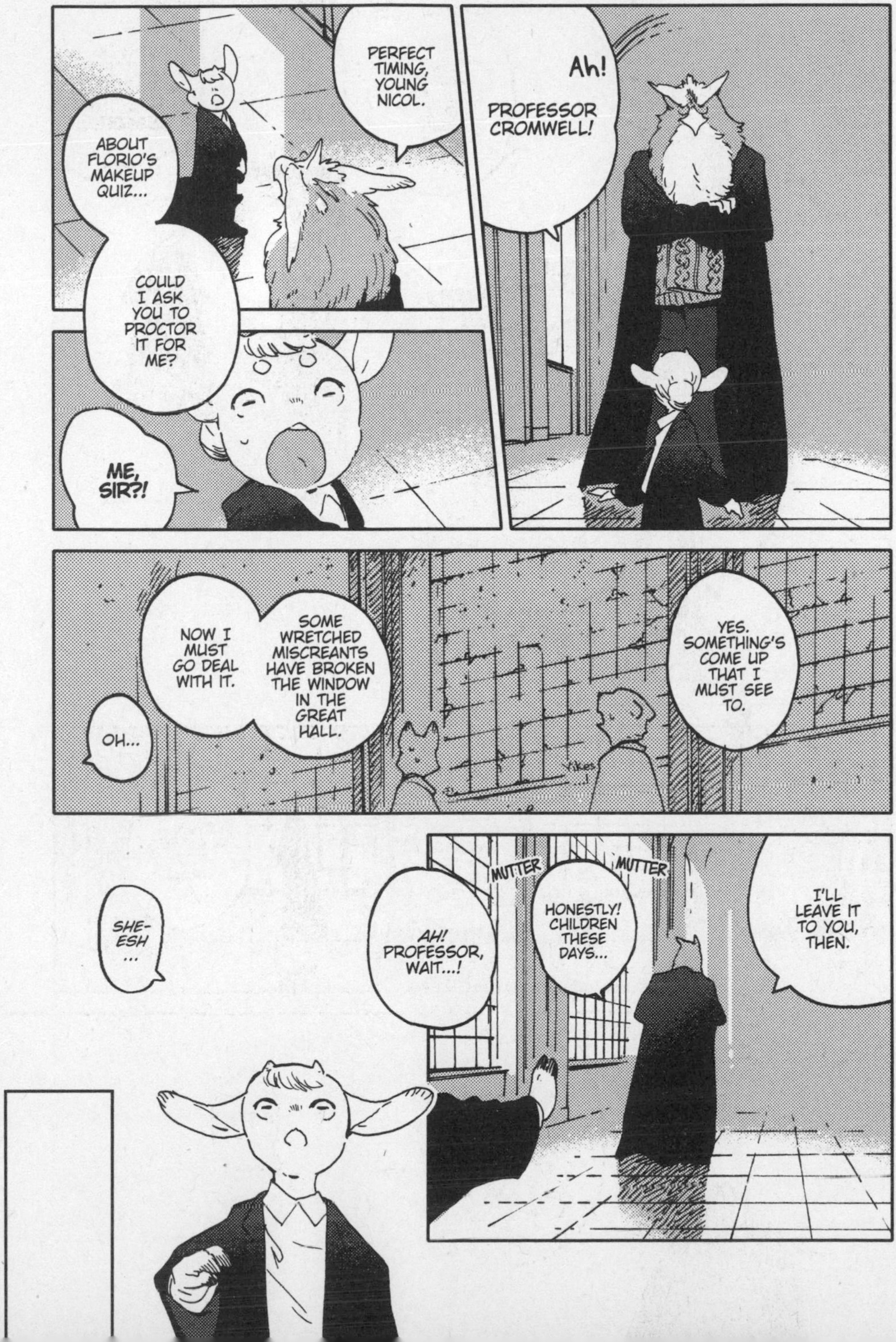
Ah!
PROFESSOR CROMWELL!
PERFECT TIMING, YOUNG NICOL.
ABOUT FLORIO'S MAKEUP QUIZ...
COULD I ASK YOU TO PROCTOR IT FOR ME?
ME, SIR?!
YES. SOMETHING'S COME UP THAT I MUST SEE TO.
Yikes
SOME WRETCHED MISCREANTS HAVE BROKEN THE WINDOW IN THE GREAT HALL.
NOW I MUST GO DEAL WITH IT.
OH...
I'LL LEAVE IT TO YOU, THEN.
MUTTER
MUTTER
HONESTLY! CHILDREN THESE DAYS...
AH! PROFESSOR, WAIT...!
SHE-ESH...

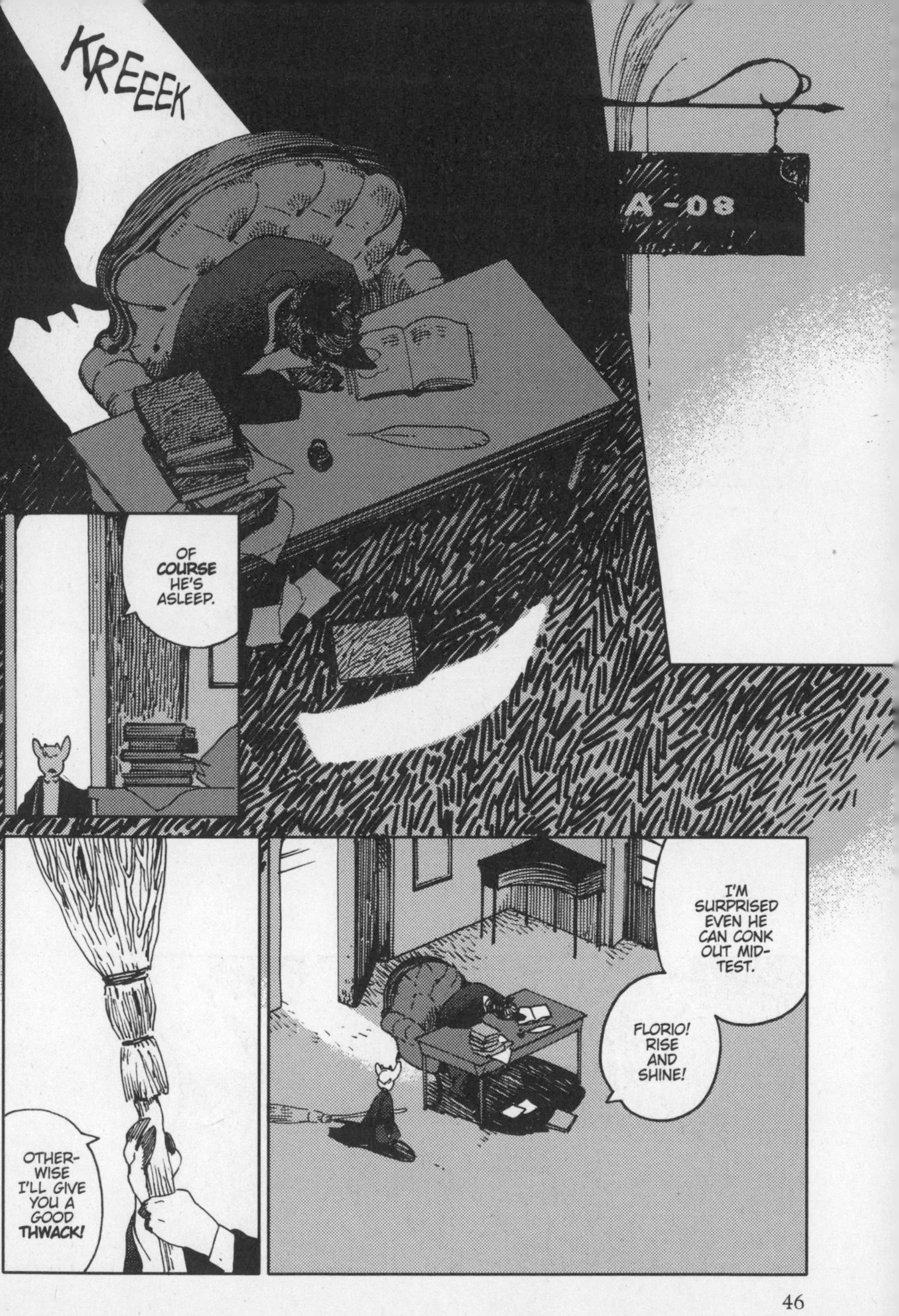
KREEEK
A-08
OF COURSE HE'S ASLEEP.
I'M SURPRISED EVEN HE CAN CONK OUT MID-TEST.
FLORIO! RISE AND SHINE!
OTHER-WISE I'LL GIVE YOU A GOOD THWACK!

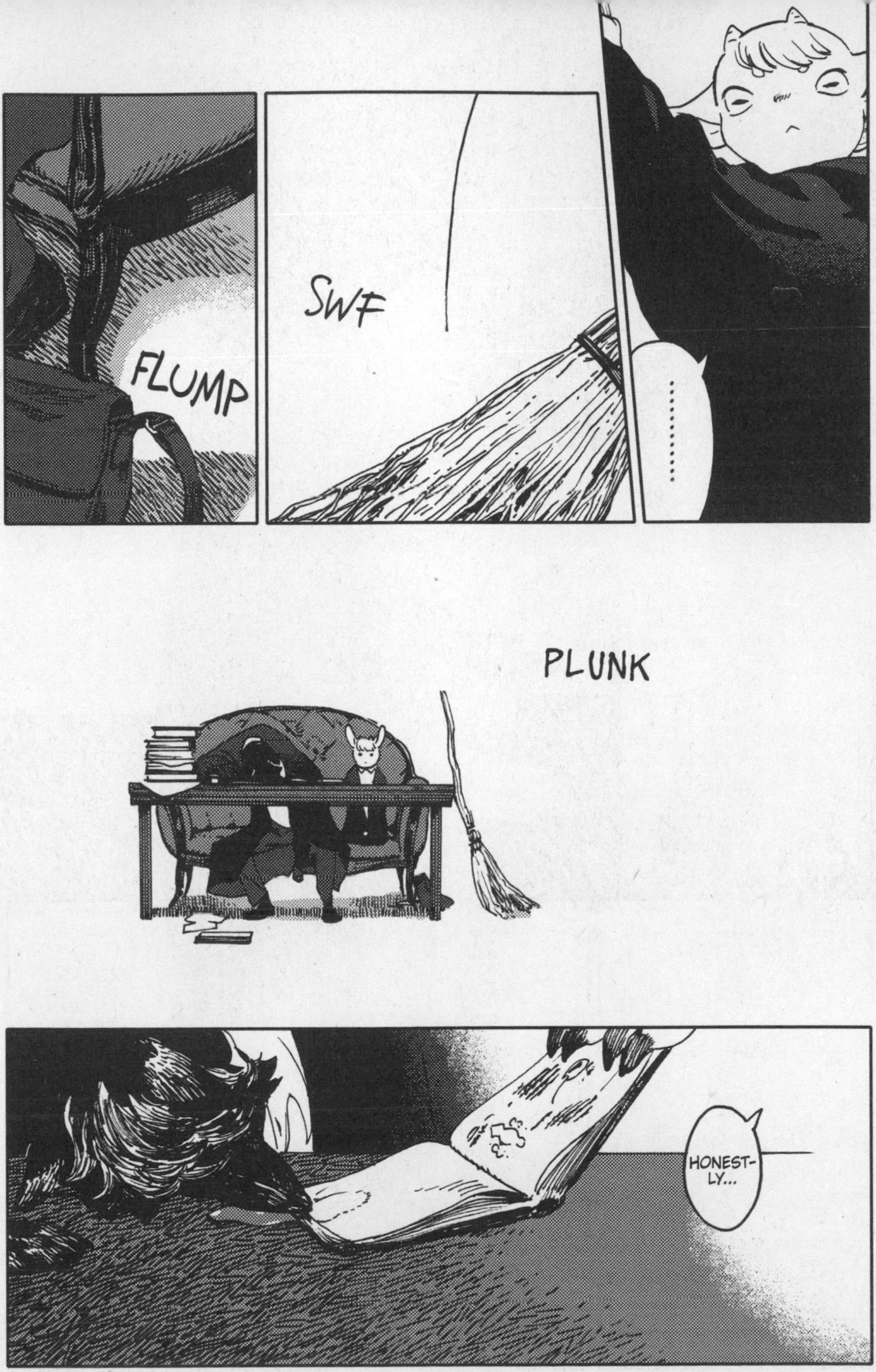
SWF
FLUMP
PLUNK
HONEST-LY...

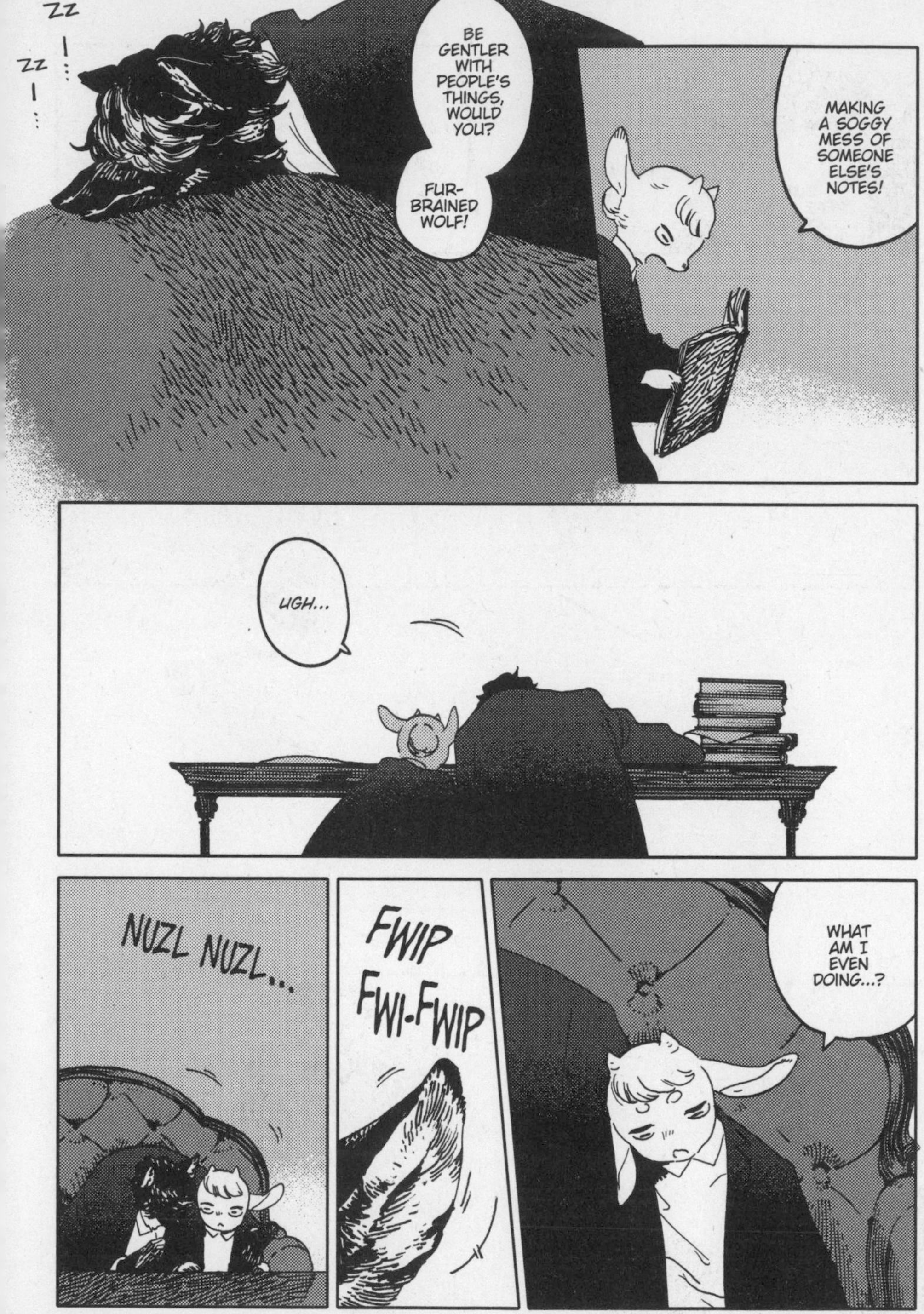
MAKING A SOGGY MESS OF SOMEONE ELSE'S NOTES!
BE GENTLER WITH PEOPLE'S THINGS, WOULD YOU?
FUR-BRAINED WOLF!
ZZ
ZZ
UGH...
WHAT AM I EVEN DOING...?
FWIP FWI-FWIP
NUZL NUZL...

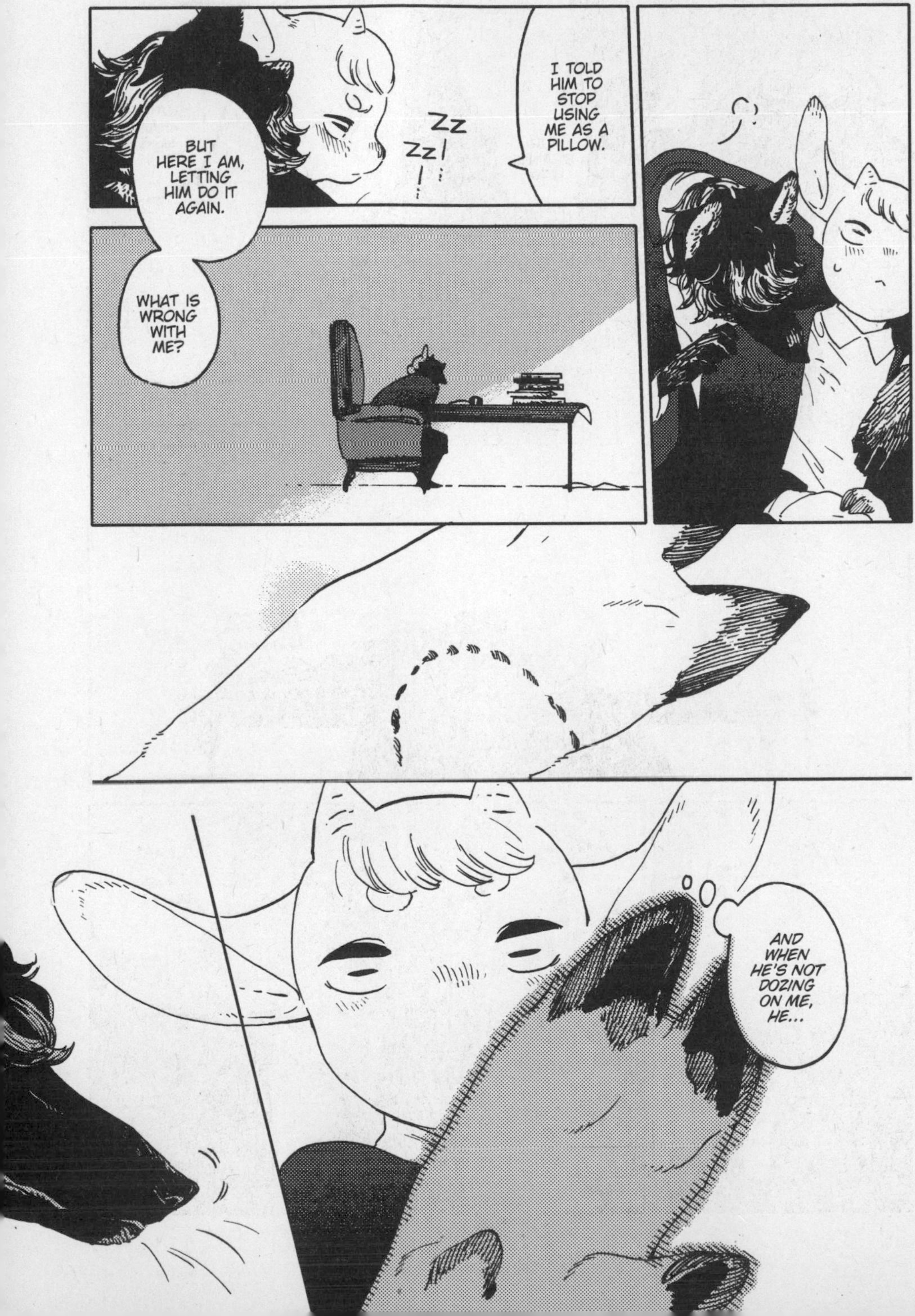
I TOLD HIM TO STOP USING ME AS A PILLOW.
Zz
Zz
BUT HERE I AM, LETTING HIM DO IT AGAIN.
WHAT IS WRONG WITH ME?
AND WHEN HE'S NOT DOZING ON ME, HE...

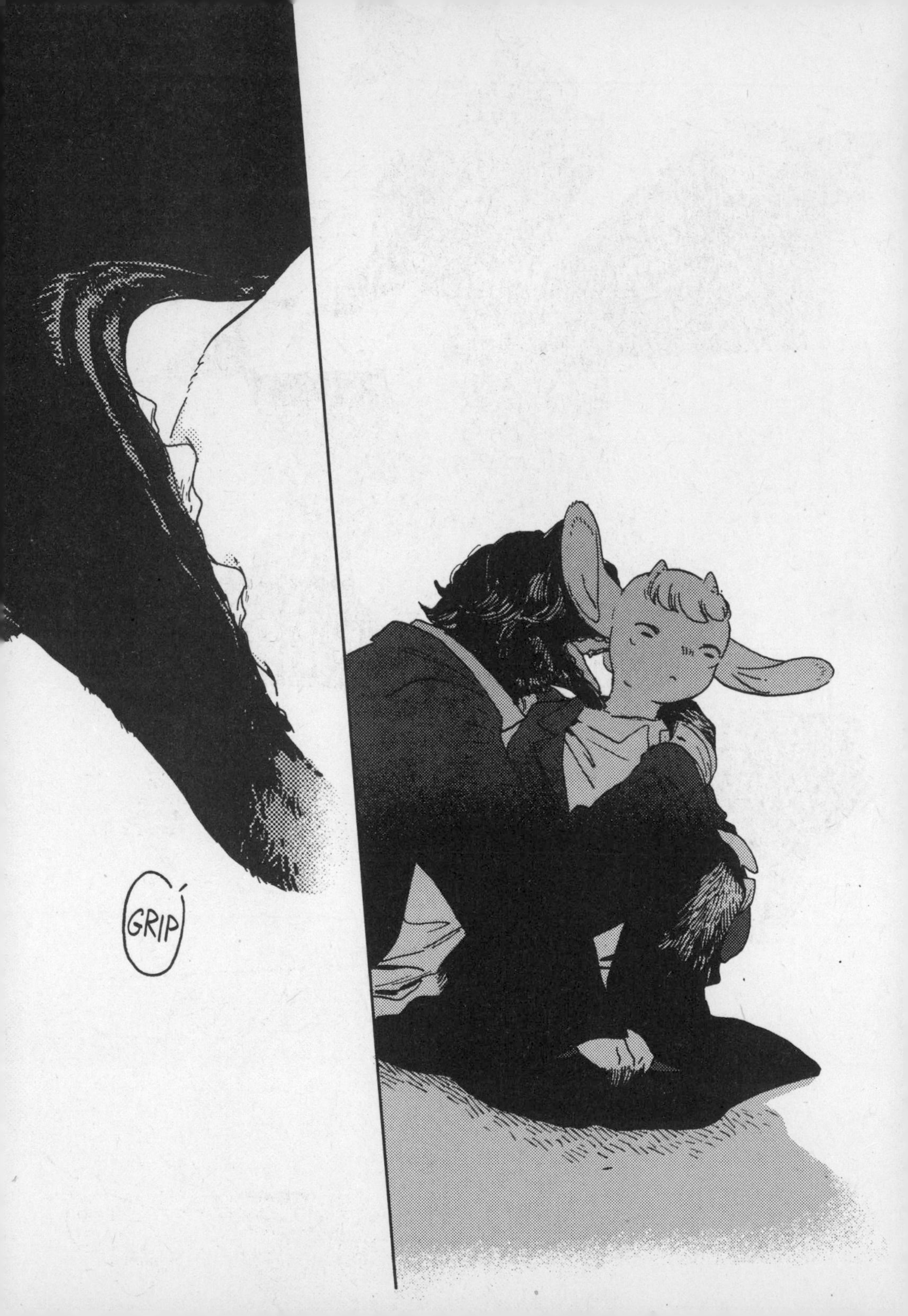
GRIP

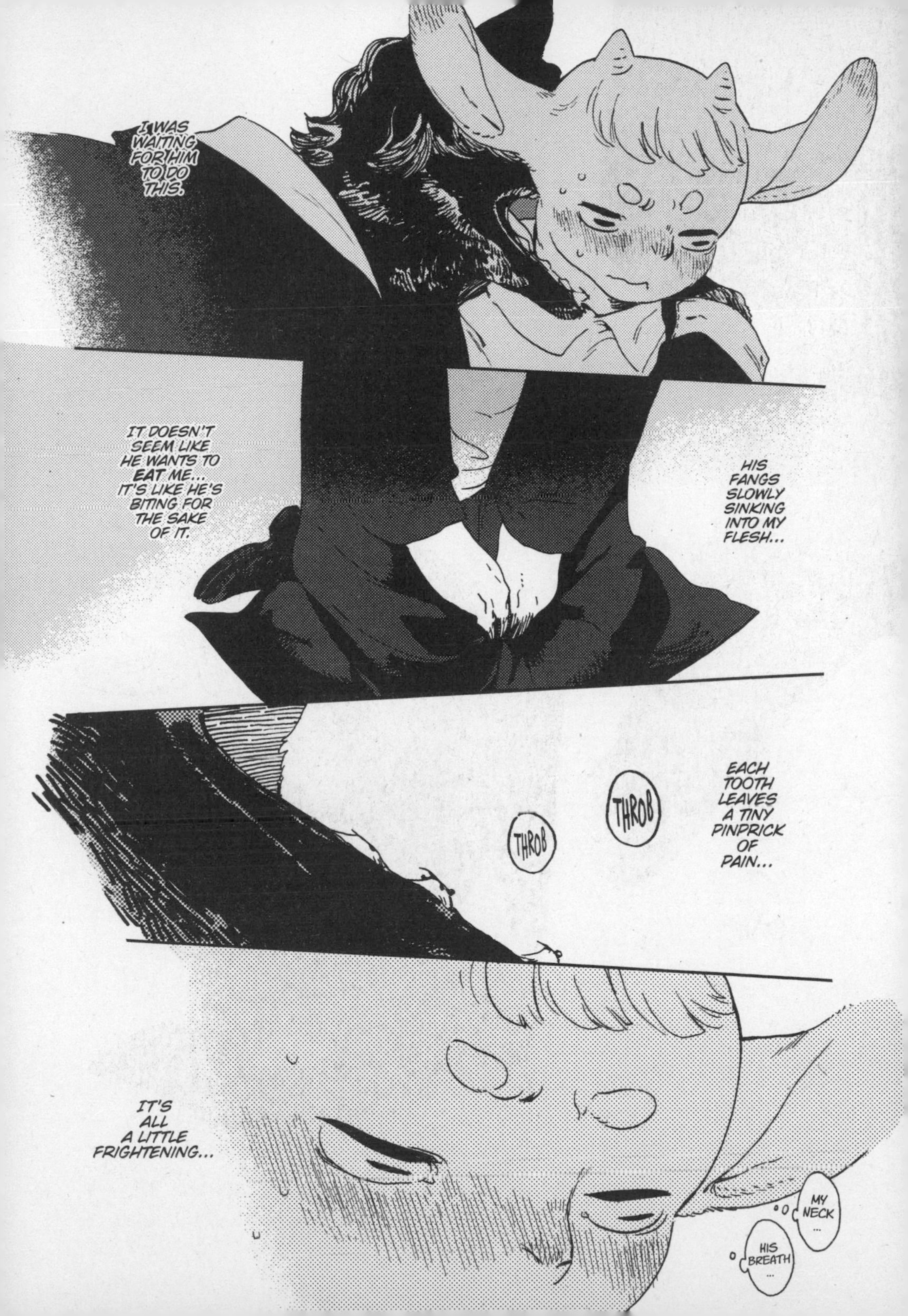

I WAS WAITING FOR HIM TO DO THIS.
HIS FANGS SLOWLY SINKING INTO MY FLESH...
IT DOESN'T SEEM LIKE HE WANTS TO EAT ME... IT'S LIKE HE'S BITING FOR THE SAKE OF IT.
EACH TOOTH LEAVES A TINY PINPRICK OF PAIN...
THROB
THROB
MY NECK...
HIS BREATH...
IT'S ALL A LITTLE FRIGHTENING...

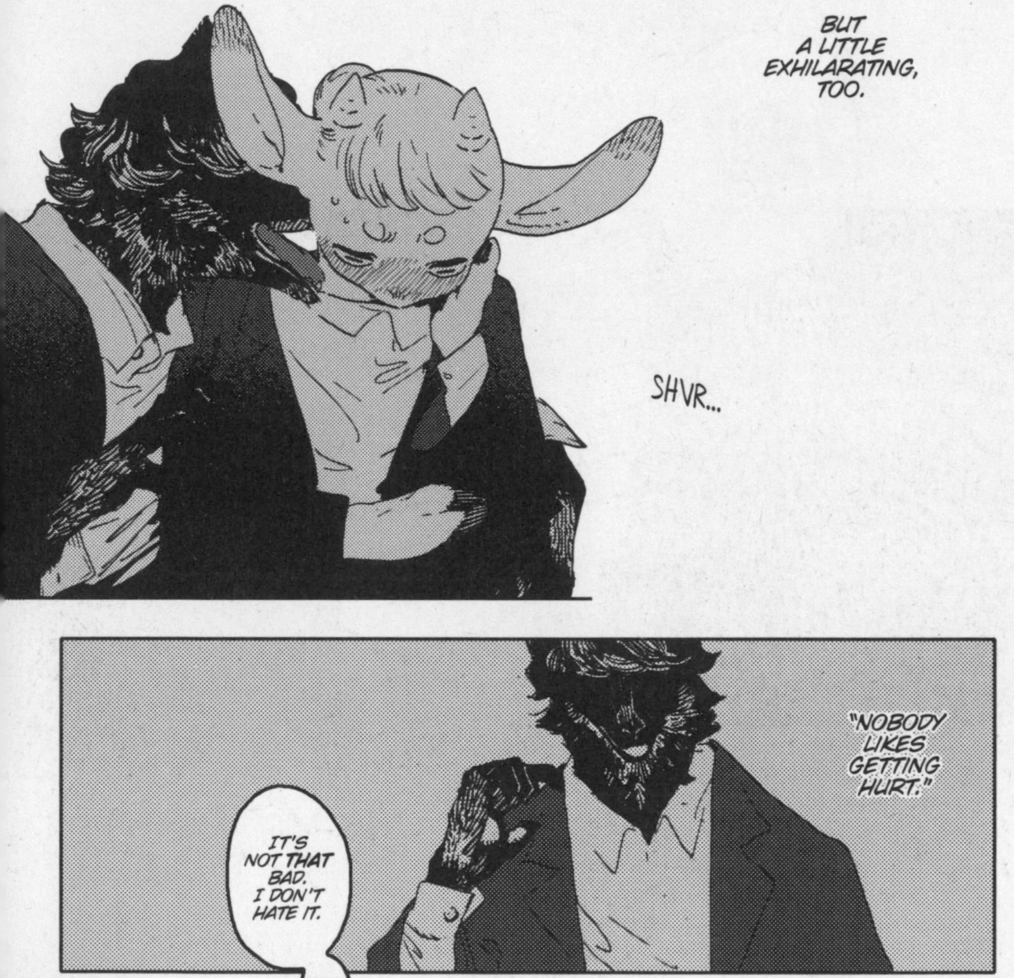
BUT A LITTLE EXHILARATING, TOO.
SHVR...
"NOBODY LIKES GETTING HURT."
IT'S NOT THAT BAD. I DON'T HATE IT.
IN FACT...
(Haah...)

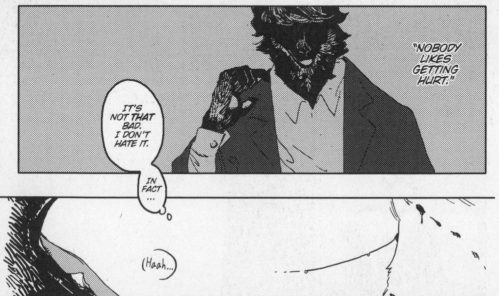

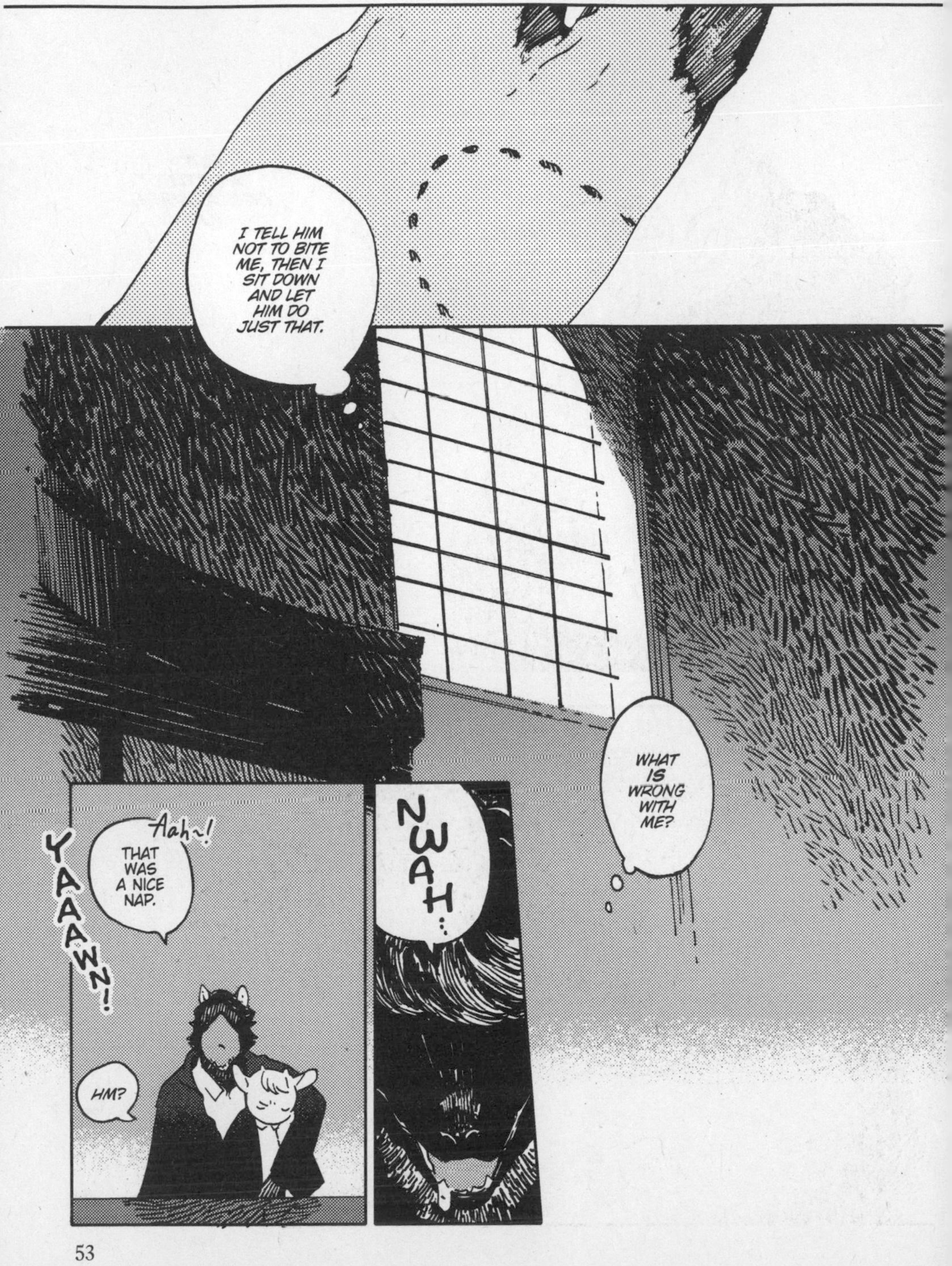
I TELL HIM NOT TO BITE ME, THEN I SIT DOWN AND LET HIM DO JUST THAT.
WHAT IS WRONG WITH ME?
NWAH...
Aah~!
THAT WAS A NICE NAP.
YAAAWN!
HM?

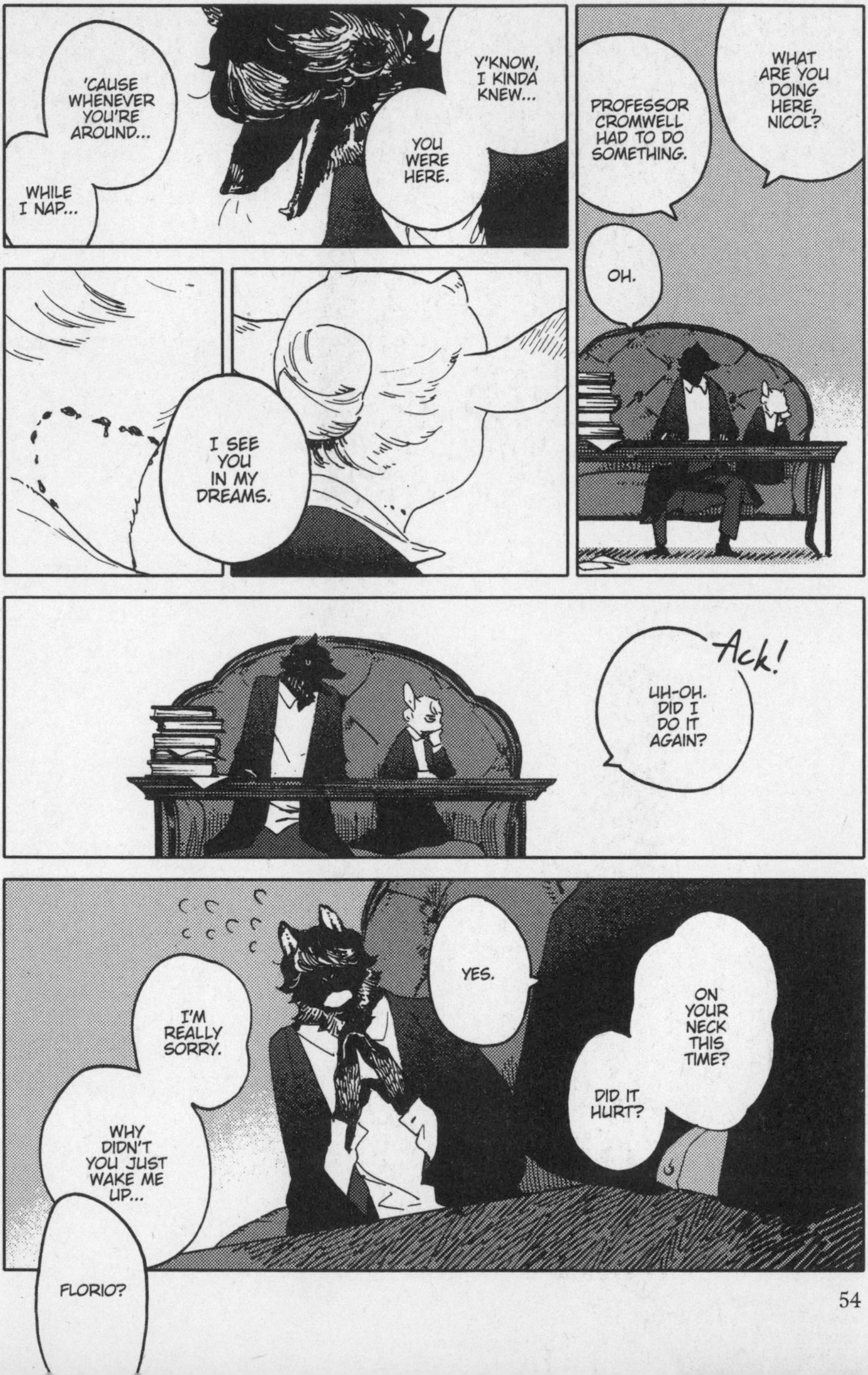
WHAT ARE YOU DOING HERE, NICOL?
PROFESSOR CROMWELL HAD TO DO SOMETHING.
OH.
Y'KNOW, I KINDA KNEW...
YOU WERE HERE.
'CAUSE WHENEVER YOU'RE AROUND...
WHILE I NAP...
I SEE YOU IN MY DREAMS.
Ack!
UH-OH. DID I DO IT AGAIN?
ON YOUR NECK THIS TIME?
DID IT HURT?
YES.
I'M REALLY SORRY.
WHY DIDN'T YOU JUST WAKE ME UP...
FLORIO?

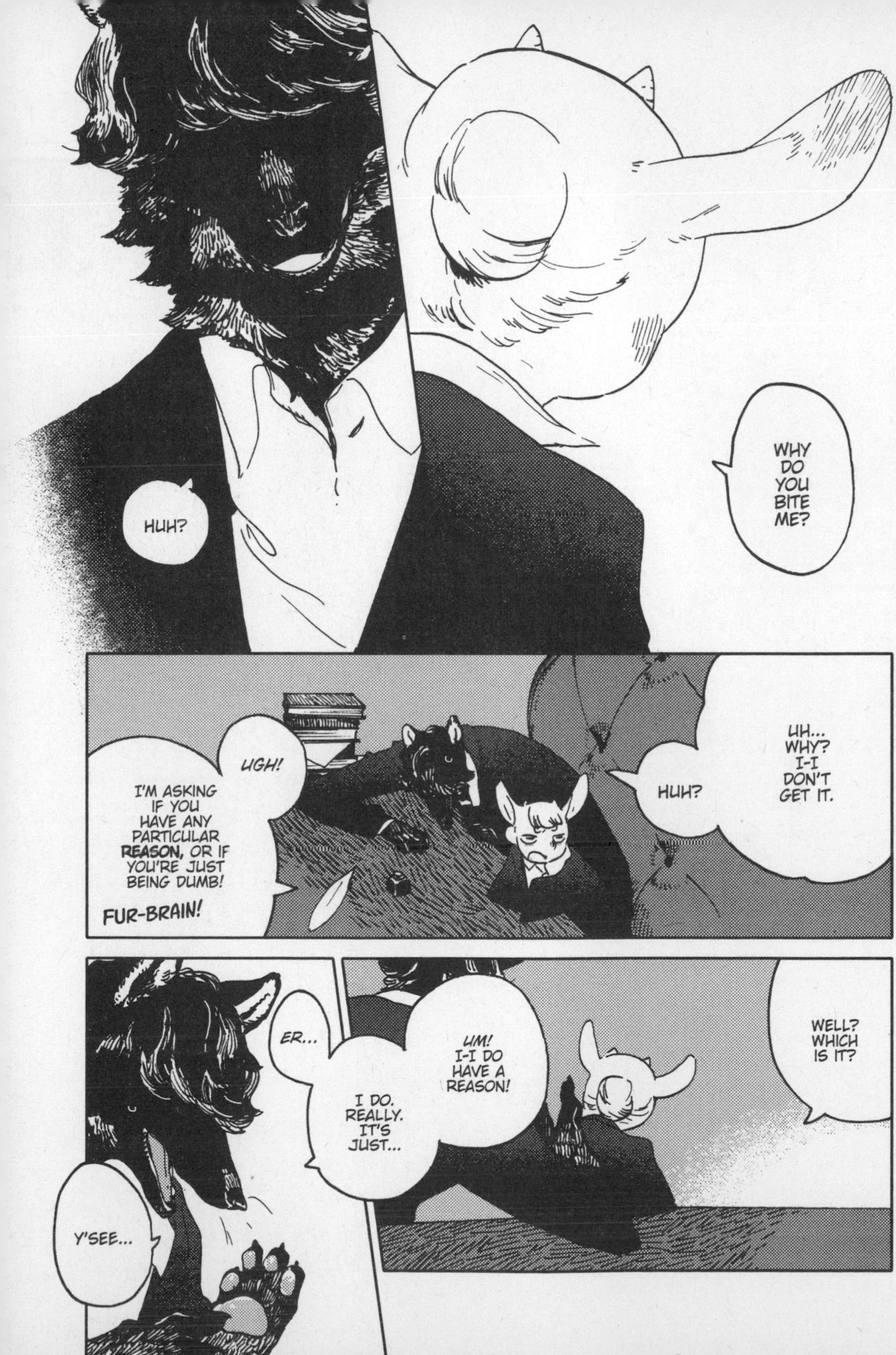
WHY DO YOU BITE ME?
HUH?
UH... WHY? I-I DON'T GET IT.
HUH?
UGH!
I'M ASKING IF YOU HAVE ANY PARTICULAR **REASON**, OR IF YOU'RE JUST BEING DUMB!
FUR-BRAIN!
WELL? WHICH IS IT?
UM! I-I DO HAVE A REASON!
I DO. REALLY. IT'S JUST...
ER...
Y'SEE...

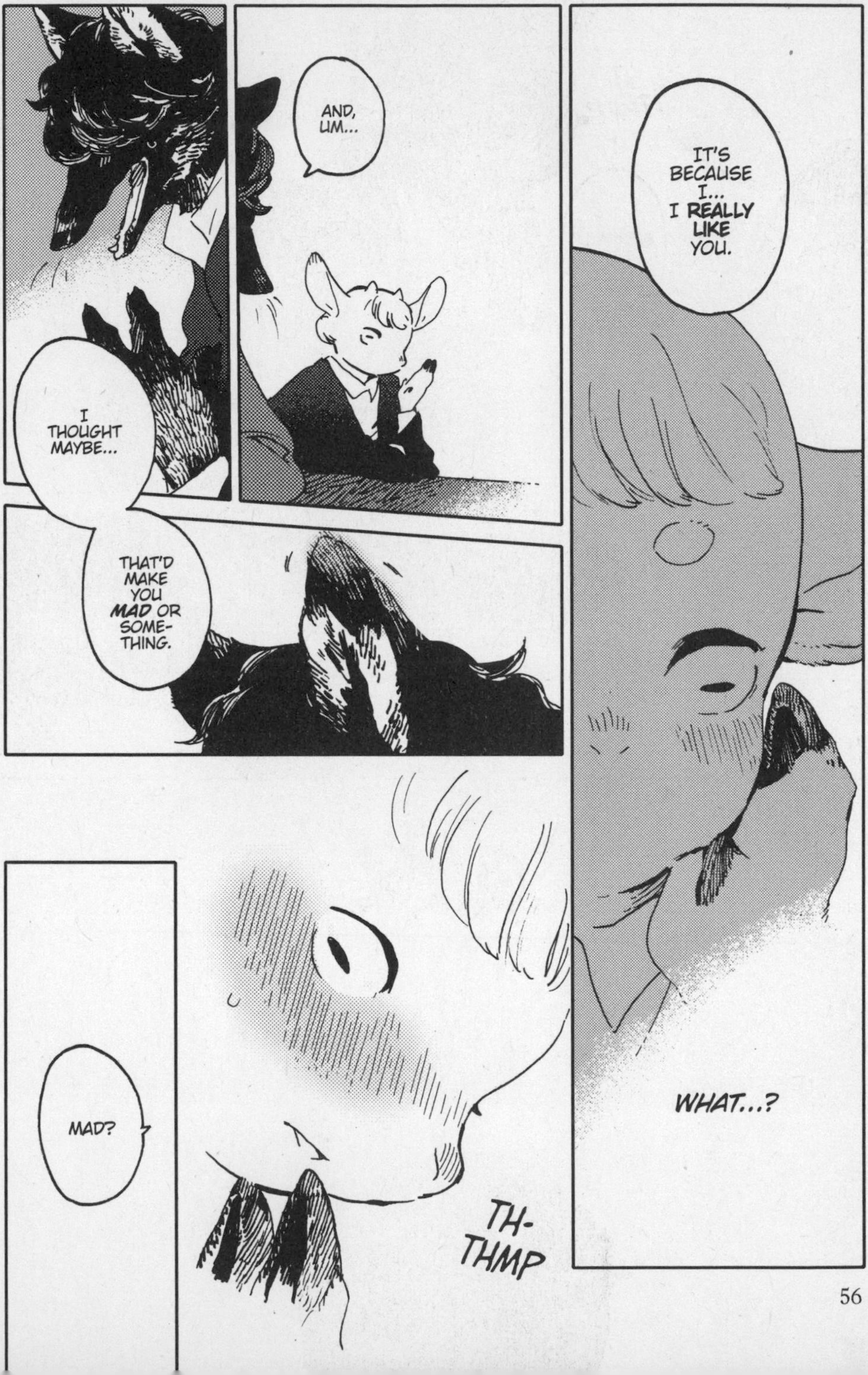
IT'S BECAUSE I... I REALLY LIKE YOU.
WHAT...?
AND, UM...
I THOUGHT MAYBE...
THAT'D MAKE YOU MAD OR SOMETHING.
TH-THMP
MAD?

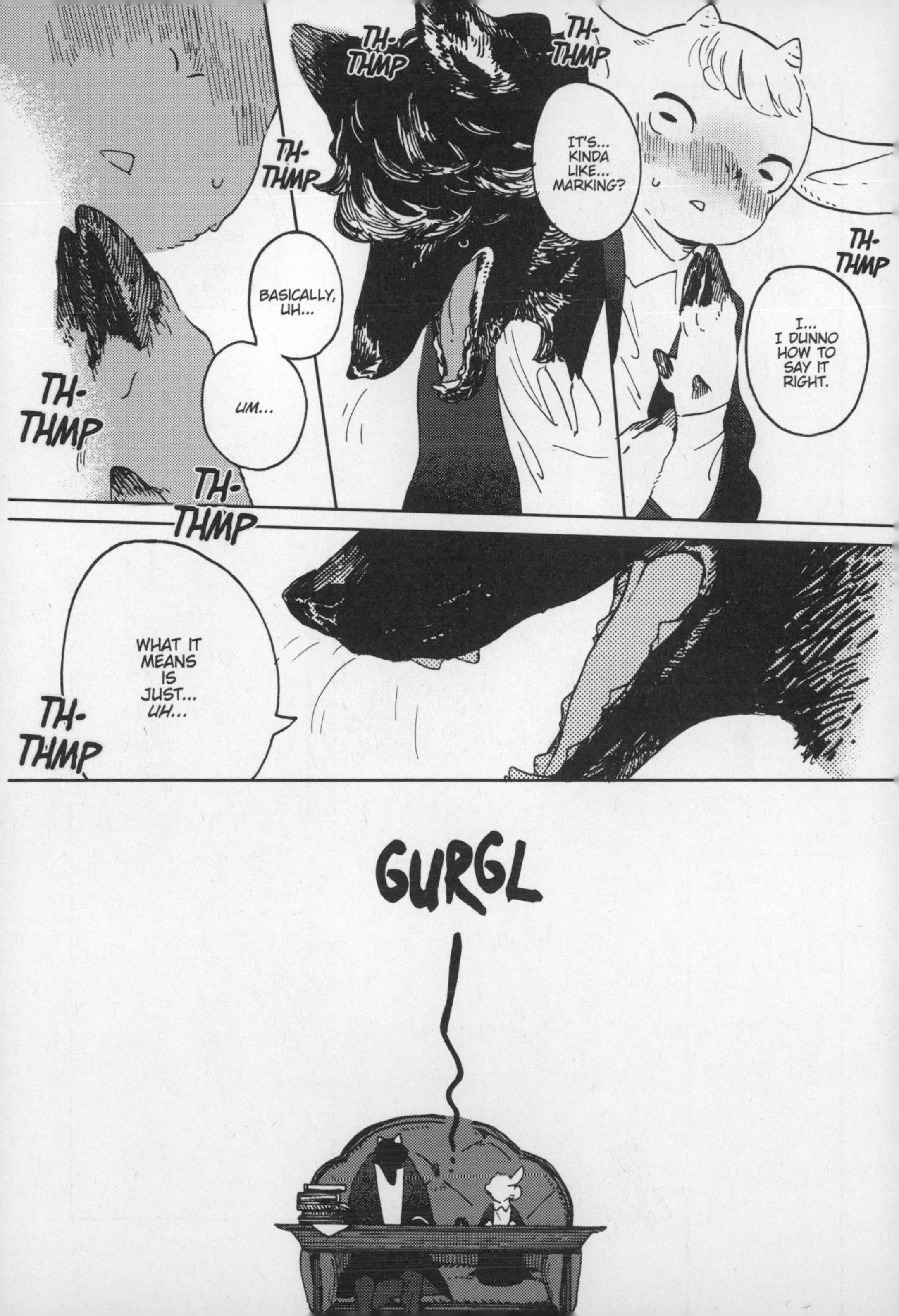
TH-THMP
TH-THMP
IT'S... KINDA LIKE... MARKING?
TH-THMP
I... I DUNNO HOW TO SAY IT RIGHT.
TH-THMP
BASICALLY, UH...
UM...
TH-THMP
TH-THMP
WHAT IT MEANS IS JUST... UH...
TH-THMP
GURGL

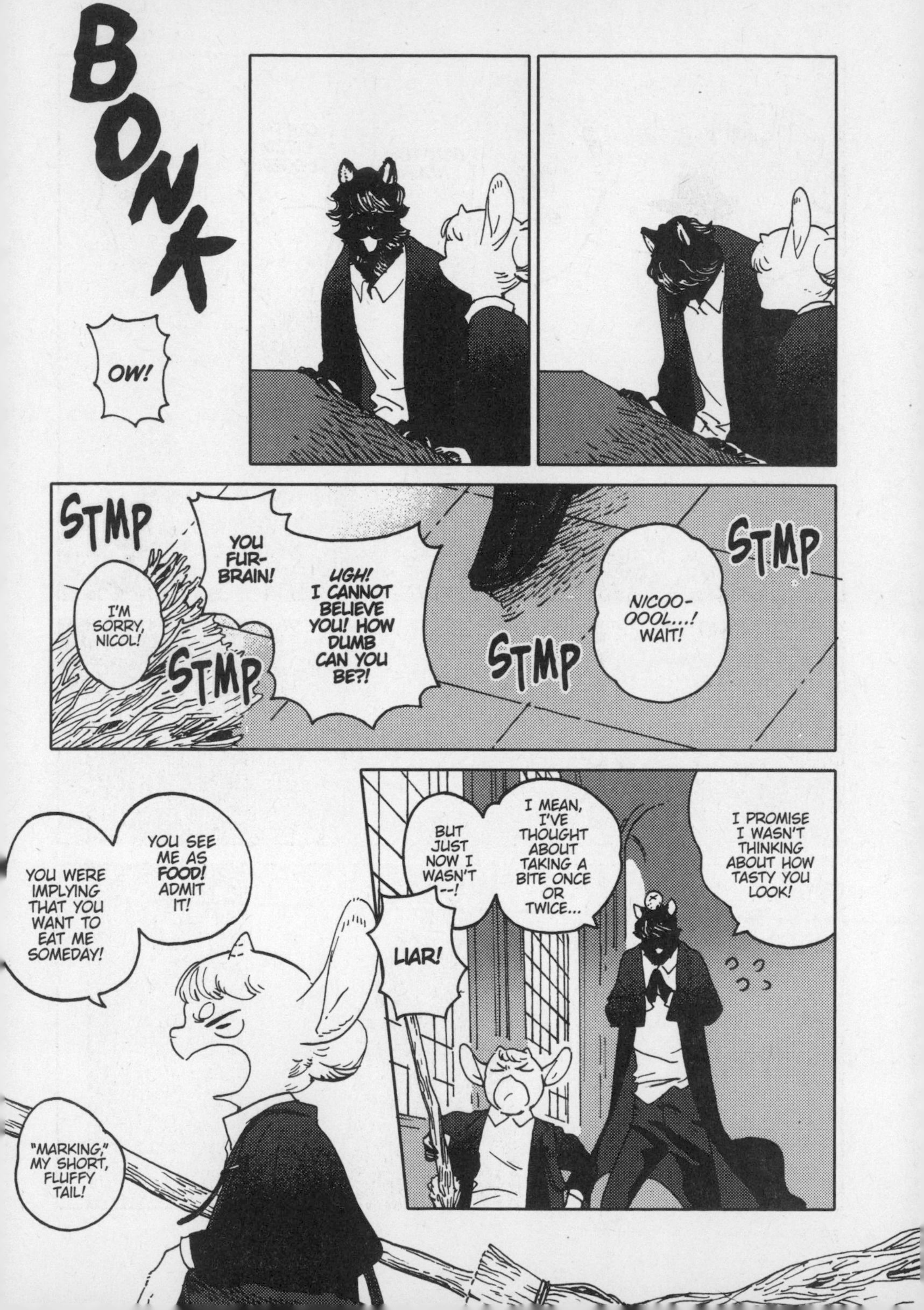
BONK
OW!
STMP
NICOO-OOOL...! WAIT!
STMP
YOU FUR-BRAIN!
UGH! I CANNOT BELIEVE YOU! HOW DUMB CAN YOU BE?!
STMP
I'M SORRY, NICOL!
STMP
I PROMISE I WASN'T THINKING ABOUT HOW TASTY YOU LOOK!
I MEAN, I'VE THOUGHT ABOUT TAKING A BITE ONCE OR TWICE...
BUT JUST NOW I WASN'T --!
LIAR!
YOU SEE ME AS FOOD! ADMIT IT!
YOU WERE IMPLYING THAT YOU WANT TO EAT ME SOMEDAY!
"MARKING," MY SHORT, FLUFFY TAIL!

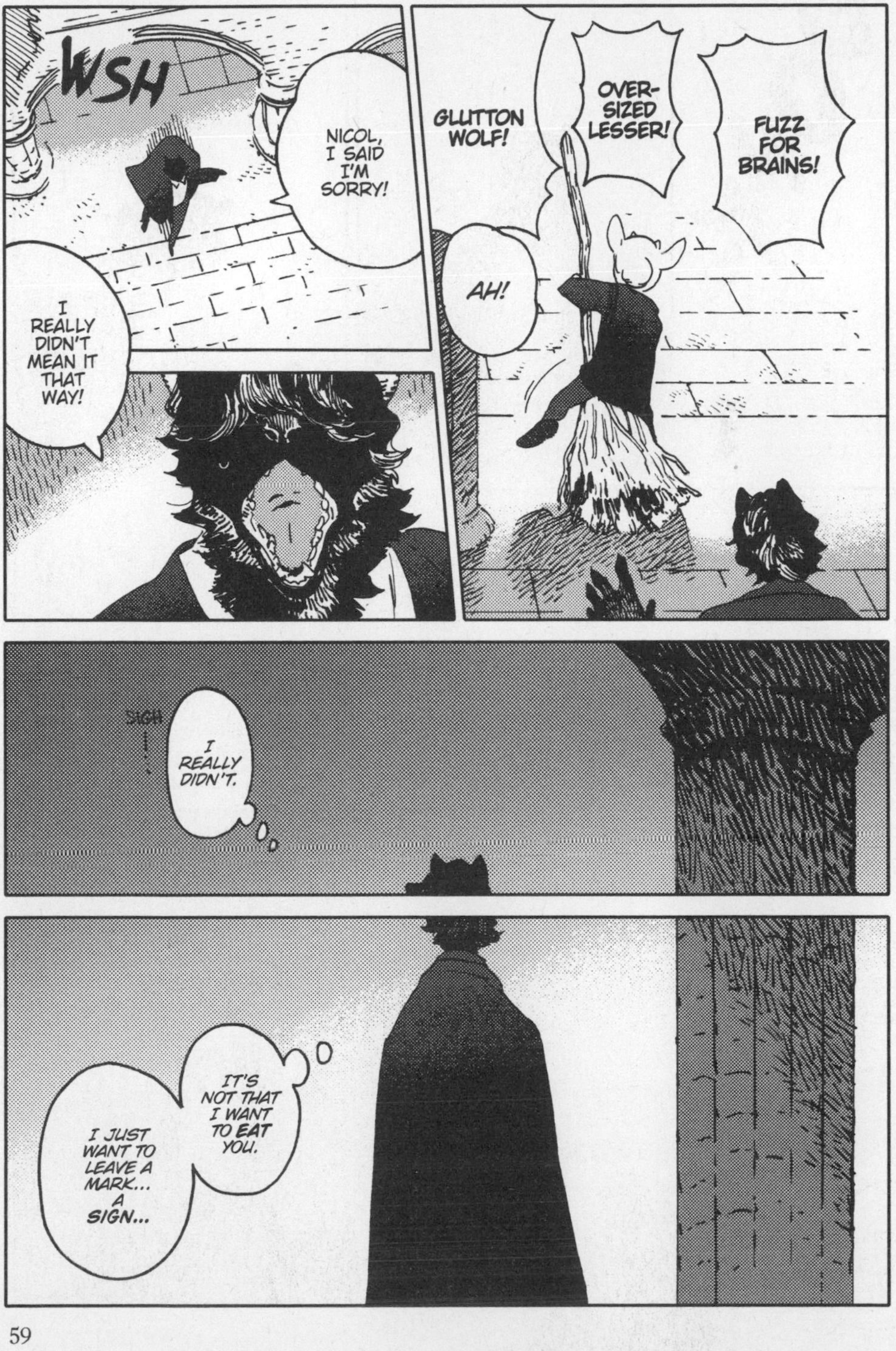
FUZZ FOR BRAINS!
OVER-SIZED LESSER!
GLUTTON WOLF!
AH!
WSH
NICOL, I SAID I'M SORRY!
I REALLY DIDN'T MEAN IT THAT WAY!
SIGH...
I REALLY DIDN'T.
IT'S NOT THAT I WANT TO EAT YOU.
I JUST WANT TO LEAVE A MARK... A SIGN...

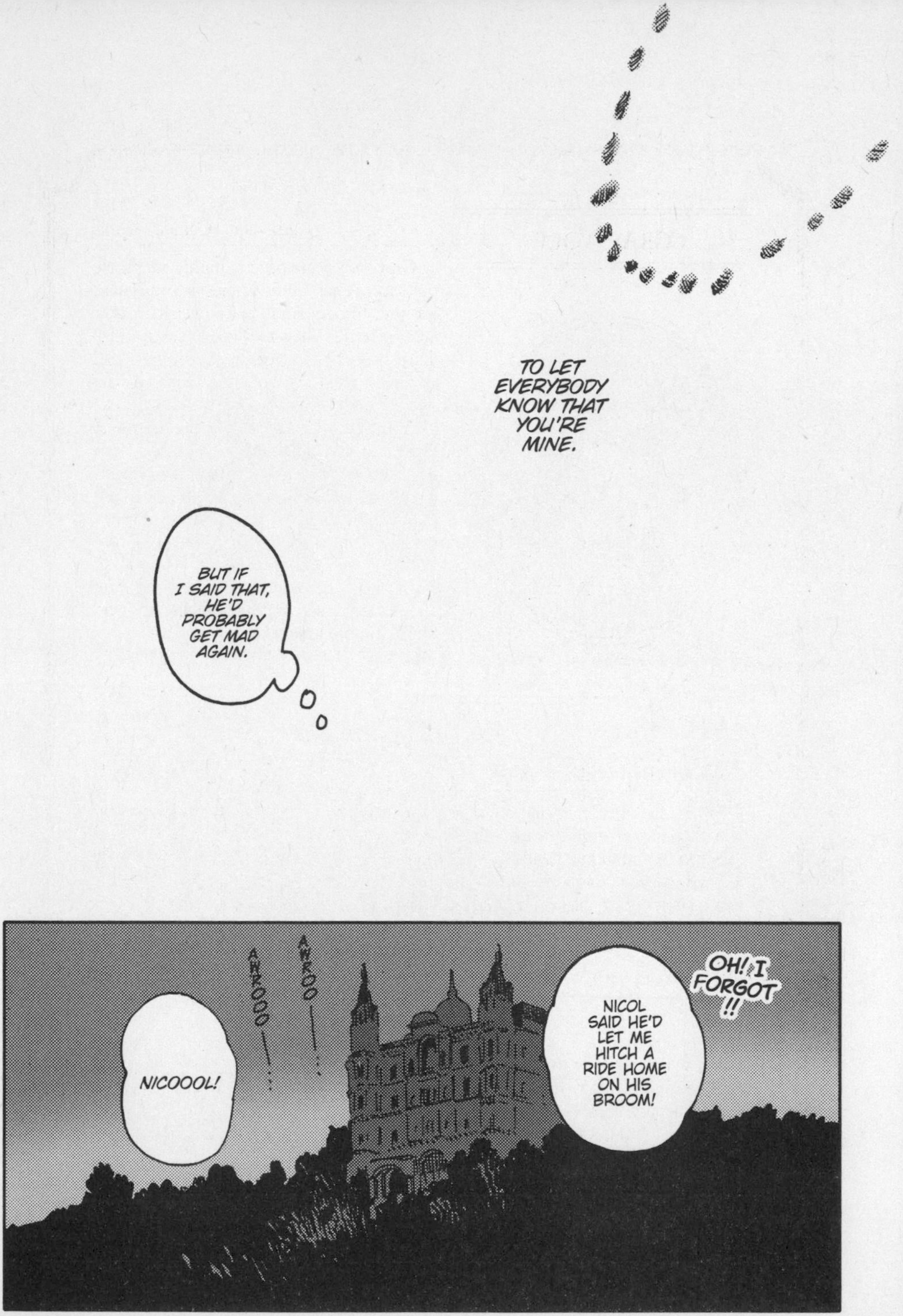
TO LET EVERYBODY KNOW THAT YOU'RE MINE.
BUT IF I SAID THAT, HE'D PROBABLY GET MAD AGAIN.
OH! I FORGOT !!
NICOL SAID HE'D LET ME HITCH A RIDE HOME ON HIS BROOM!
AWROO
AWROOO
NICOOOL!

◆ END ◆

GRAY WOLF

Canis lupus

Carnivora | Canidae *Canis*

Gray wolves are patient, highly adaptable predators. Their entire bodies are muscular, but their hindquarters are especially tough and powerful. They have long, narrow jaws that sport highly developed canines and carnassial teeth. At the end of their narrow muzzle sits a sensitive nose, which they use to hunt and track prey. It is so keen that they can smell individual prey animals from up to 1.5 kilometers away. Gray wolves are a gregarious species, living in groups called packs and protecting a communal territory that they mark with their urine. They are an extremely emotive species, using their scents, body language such as tail-wagging and licking, and vocalizations like yips and howls to communicate.

Artiodactyla | Bovidae *Capra*

GOAT

Capra

Goats are closely related to sheep and cows. Living in large groups called herds, they can be found in a variety of geographical areas, from high mountain pastures and cliffs to grassy plains and forests. They are prey animals and herbivores, eating primarily grass, leaves, and twigs, which they digest in a four-chambered stomach. Males and females alike grow two short, curving horns, and their wide-set eyes and horizontally split pupils give them panoramic vision while reducing the sun's glare. Their eyes can rotate up to fifty degrees in their sockets, letting them keep watch in multiple directions while they eat. Aside from keen vision, they also have large, sharp ears and a remarkable sense of smell.

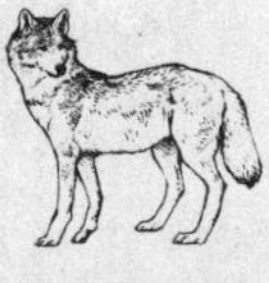

The Wize Wize Beasts
of the Wizarding Wizdoms
by Nagabe

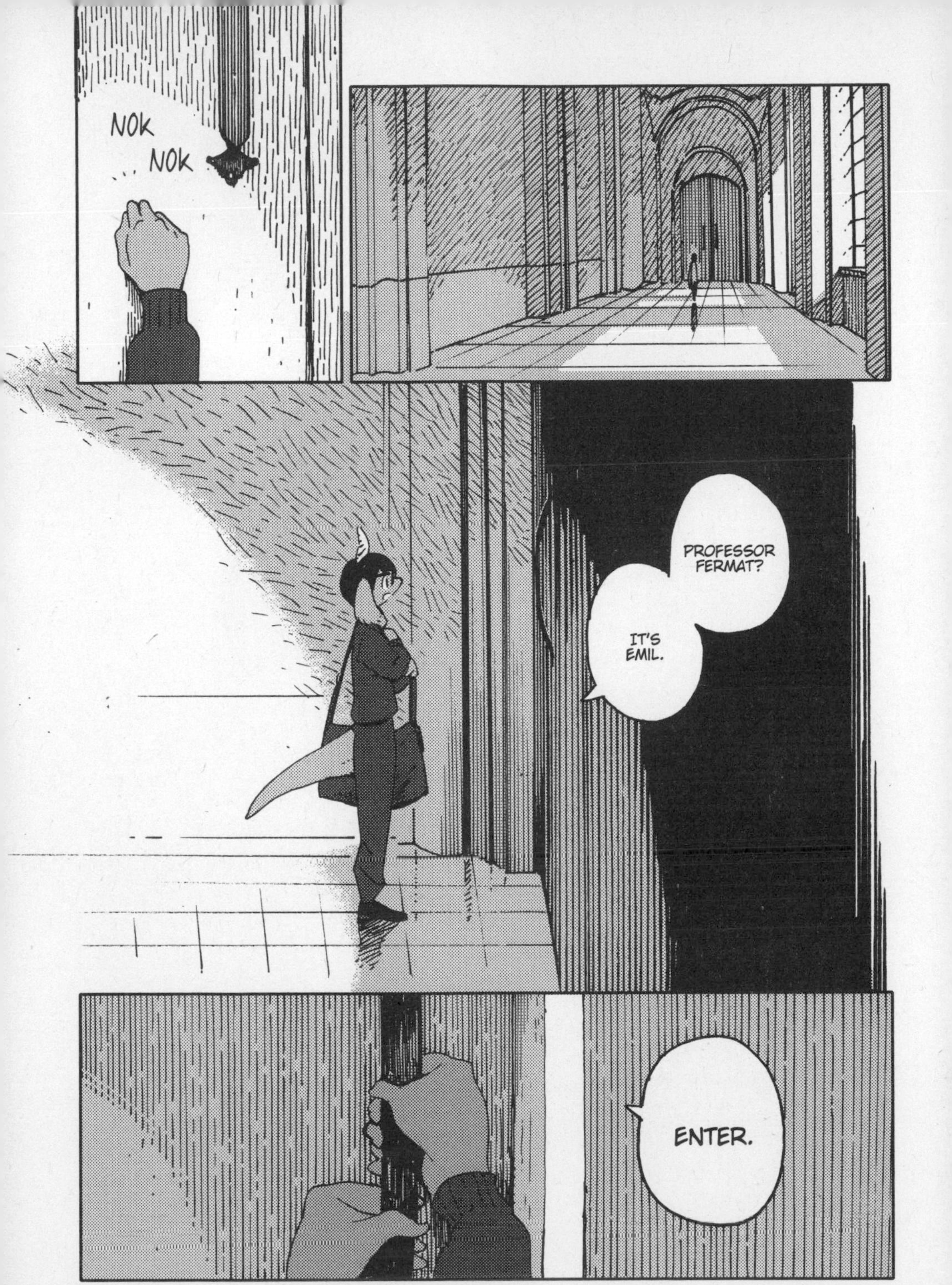
NOK NOK
PROFESSOR FERMAT?
IT'S EMIL.
ENTER.

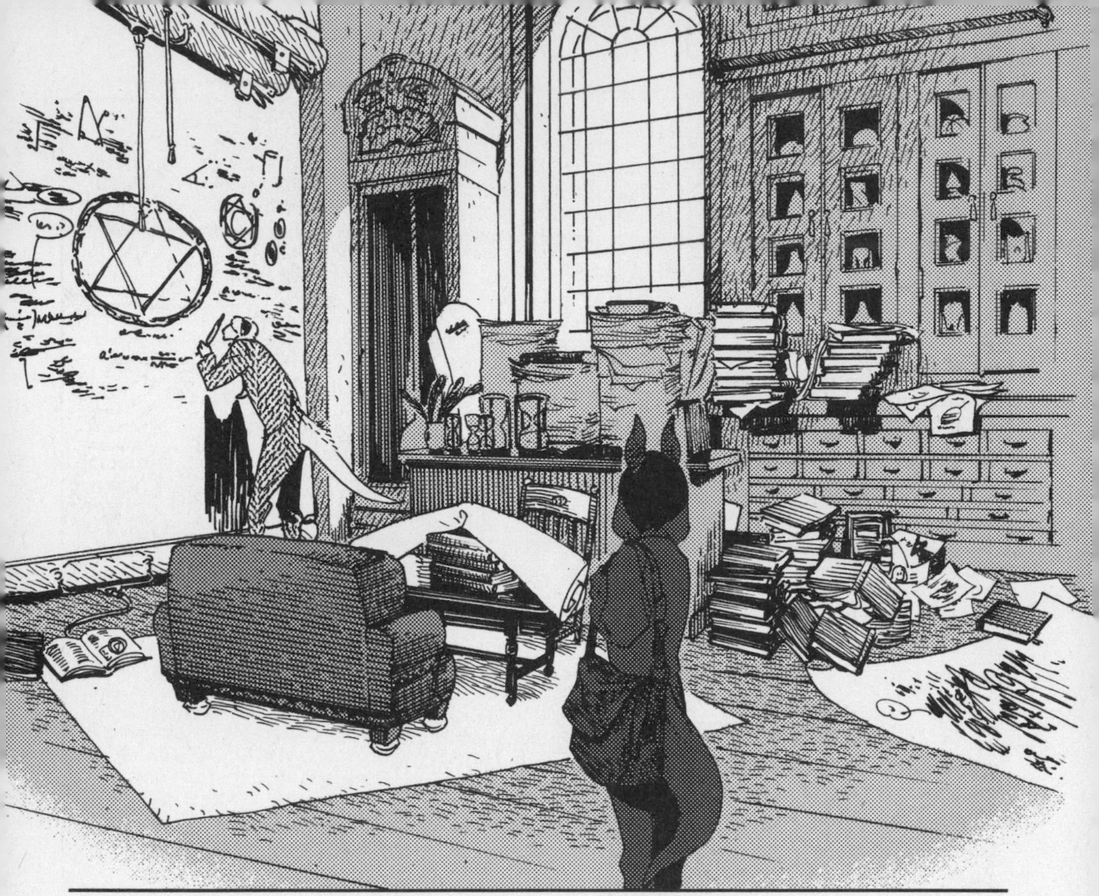

3

-Fermat & Emil-

The Teacher & The Pupil

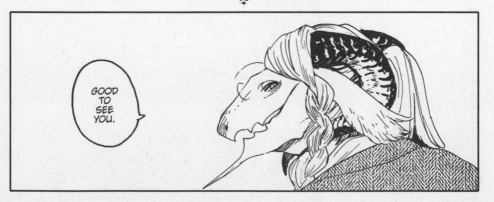

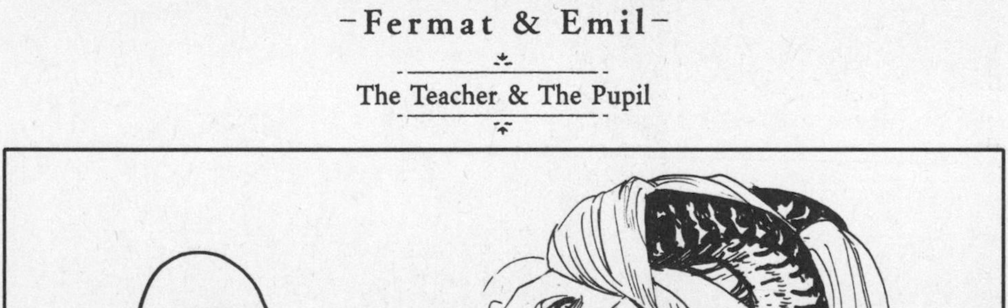
GOOD TO SEE YOU.

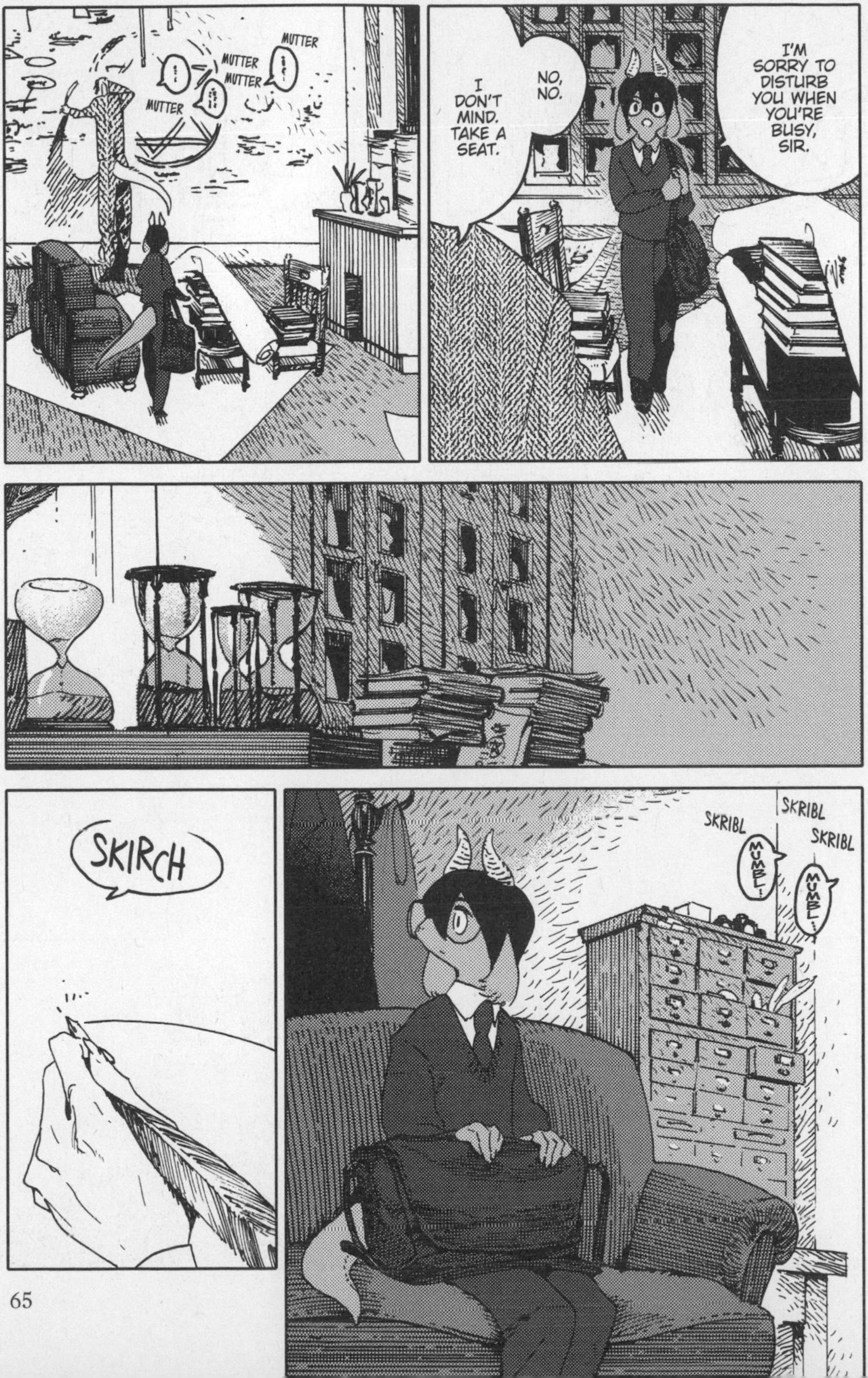
I'M SORRY TO DISTURB YOU WHEN YOU'RE BUSY, SIR.
NO, NO.
I DON'T MIND. TAKE A SEAT.
MUTTER
MUTTER
MUTTER
MUTTER
SKRIBL
SKRIBL
SKRIBL
MUMBL...
MUMBL...
SKIRCH

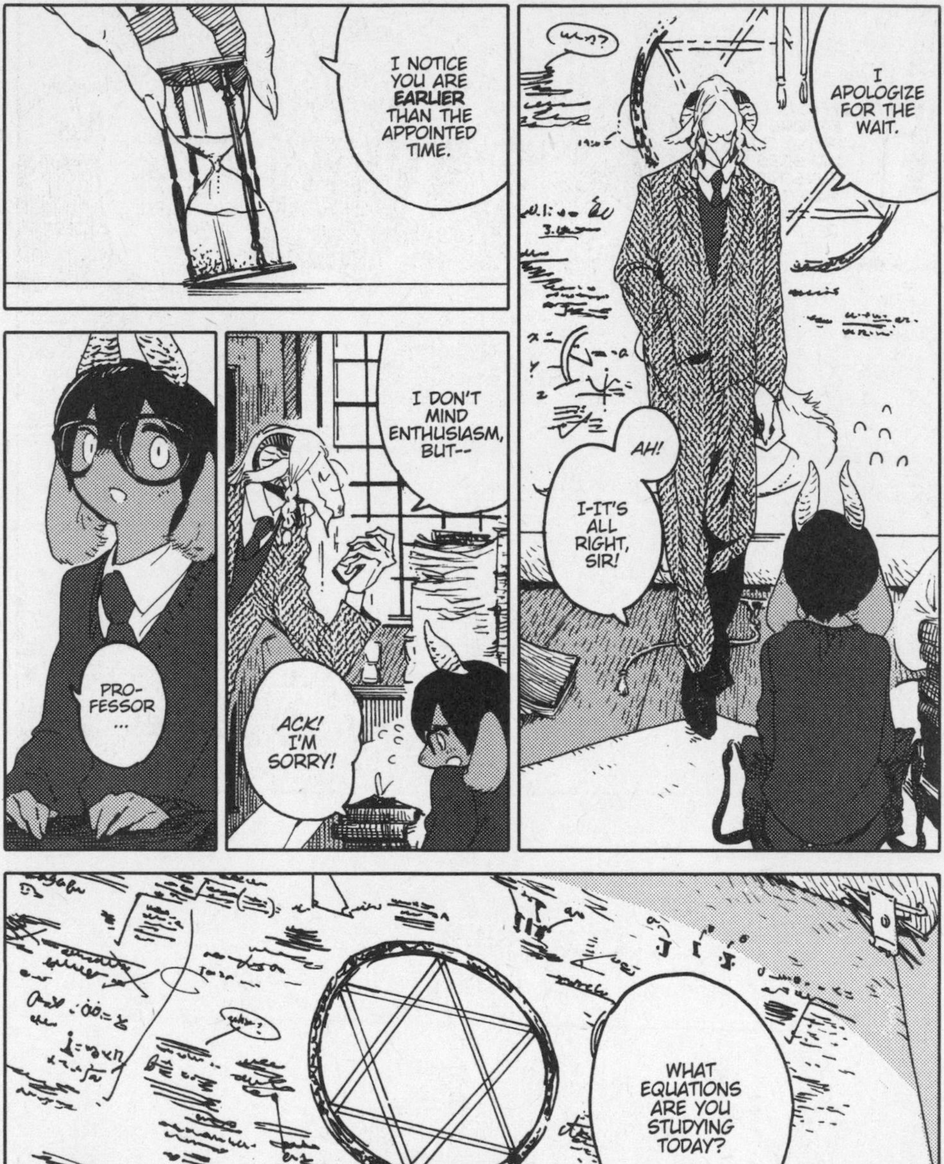
I APOLOGIZE FOR THE WAIT.
AH!
I-IT'S ALL RIGHT, SIR!
I NOTICE YOU ARE **EARLIER** THAN THE APPOINTED TIME.
I DON'T MIND ENTHUSIASM, BUT--
ACK! I'M SORRY!
PRO-FESSOR ...
WHAT EQUATIONS ARE YOU STUDYING TODAY?

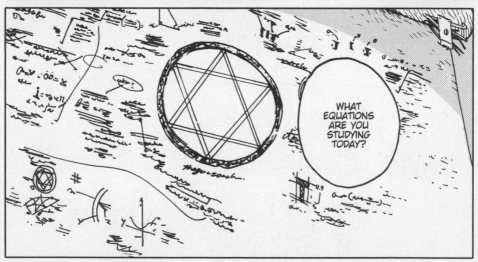

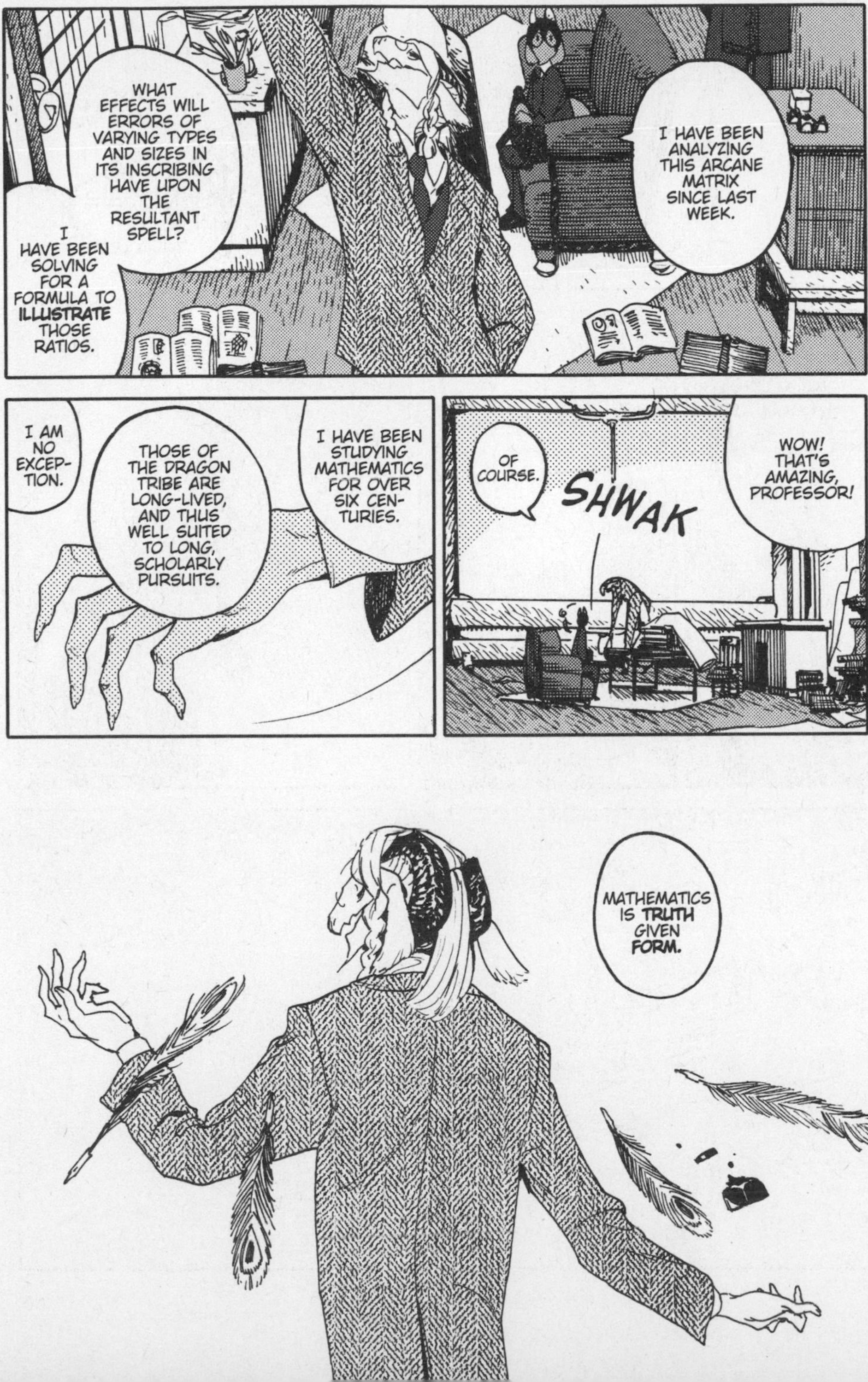
I HAVE BEEN ANALYZING THIS ARCANE MATRIX SINCE LAST WEEK.
WHAT EFFECTS WILL ERRORS OF VARYING TYPES AND SIZES IN ITS INSCRIBING HAVE UPON THE RESULTANT SPELL?
I HAVE BEEN SOLVING FOR A FORMULA TO **ILLUSTRATE** THOSE RATIOS.
WOW! THAT'S AMAZING, PROFESSOR!
SHWAK
OF COURSE.
I HAVE BEEN STUDYING MATHEMATICS FOR OVER SIX CEN-TURIES.
THOSE OF THE DRAGON TRIBE ARE LONG-LIVED, AND THUS WELL SUITED TO LONG, SCHOLARLY PURSUITS.
I AM NO EXCEP-TION.
MATHEMATICS IS **TRUTH** GIVEN **FORM.**

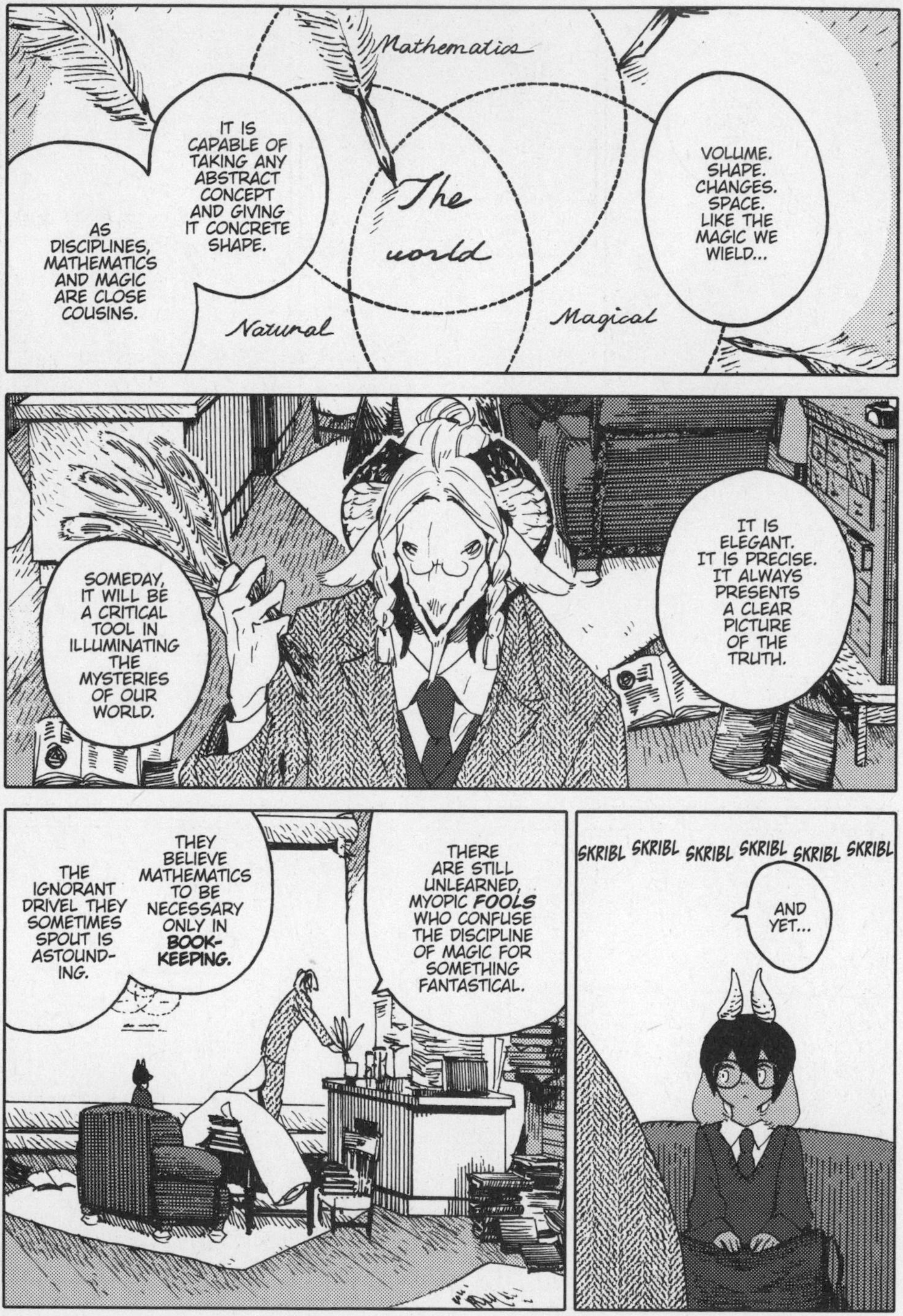
Mathematics
VOLUME. SHAPE. CHANGES. SPACE. LIKE THE MAGIC WE WIELD...
IT IS CAPABLE OF TAKING ANY ABSTRACT CONCEPT AND GIVING IT CONCRETE SHAPE.
The world
AS DISCIPLINES, MATHEMATICS AND MAGIC ARE CLOSE COUSINS.
Magical
Natural
IT IS ELEGANT. IT IS PRECISE. IT ALWAYS PRESENTS A CLEAR PICTURE OF THE TRUTH.
SOMEDAY, IT WILL BE A CRITICAL TOOL IN ILLUMINATING THE MYSTERIES OF OUR WORLD.
SKRIBL SKRIBL SKRIBL SKRIBL SKRIBL SKRIBL
AND YET...
THERE ARE STILL UNLEARNED, MYOPIC **FOOLS** WHO CONFUSE THE DISCIPLINE OF MAGIC FOR SOMETHING FANTASTICAL.
THEY BELIEVE MATHEMATICS TO BE NECESSARY ONLY IN **BOOK-KEEPING.**
THE IGNORANT DRIVEL THEY SOMETIMES SPOUT IS ASTOUND-ING.

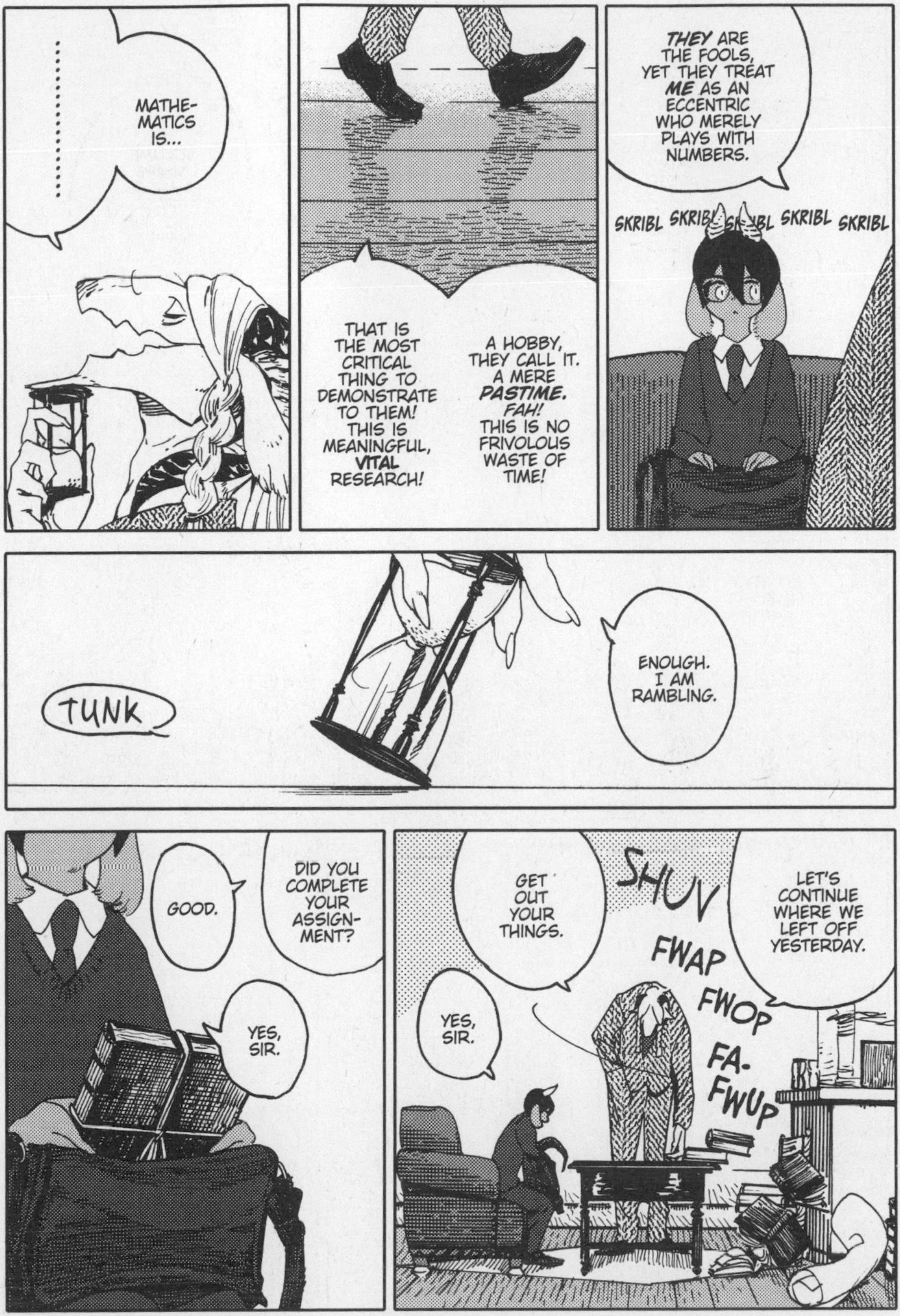
THEY ARE THE FOOLS, YET THEY TREAT ME AS AN ECCENTRIC WHO MERELY PLAYS WITH NUMBERS.
SKRIBL SKRIBL SKRIBL SKRIBL SKRIBL SKRIBL
A HOBBY, THEY CALL IT. A MERE PASTIME. FAH! THIS IS NO FRIVOLOUS WASTE OF TIME!
THAT IS THE MOST CRITICAL THING TO DEMONSTRATE TO THEM! THIS IS MEANINGFUL, VITAL RESEARCH!
MATHE-MATICS IS...
ENOUGH. I AM RAMBLING.
TUNK
LET'S CONTINUE WHERE WE LEFT OFF YESTERDAY.
SHUV
GET OUT YOUR THINGS.
FWAP
FWOP
FA-FWUP
YES, SIR.
DID YOU COMPLETE YOUR ASSIGN-MENT?
GOOD.
YES, SIR.

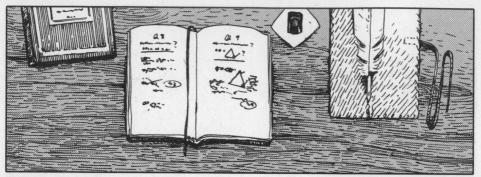

LET ME SEE.

IN-CORRECT.

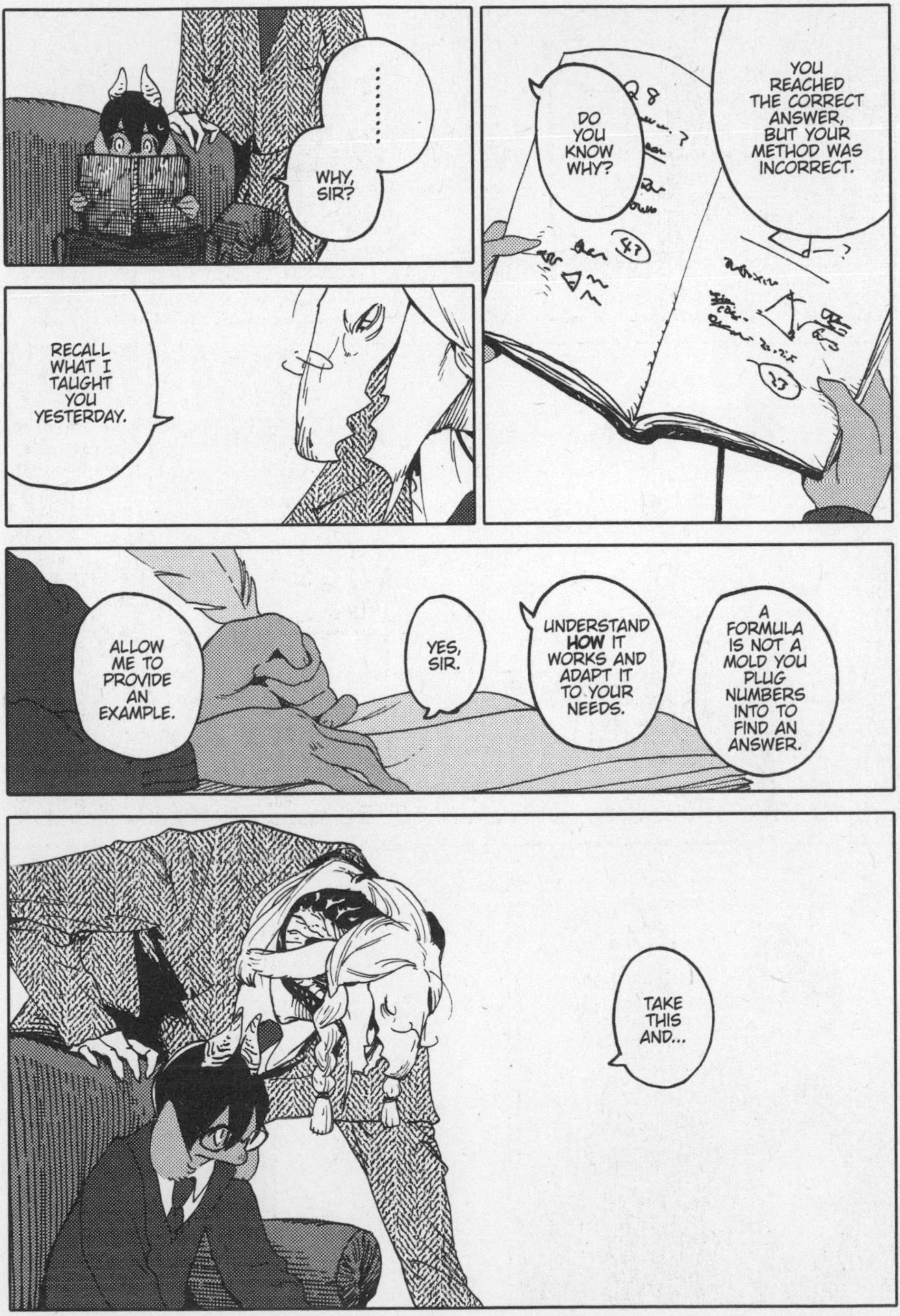
YOU REACHED THE CORRECT ANSWER, BUT YOUR METHOD WAS INCORRECT.
DO YOU KNOW WHY?
......
WHY, SIR?
RECALL WHAT I TAUGHT YOU YESTERDAY.
A FORMULA IS NOT A MOLD YOU PLUG NUMBERS INTO TO FIND AN ANSWER.
UNDERSTAND **HOW** IT WORKS AND ADAPT IT TO YOUR NEEDS.
YES, SIR.
ALLOW ME TO PROVIDE AN EXAMPLE.
TAKE THIS AND...

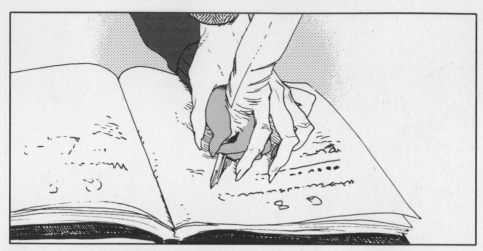

CHOOSE A SYMBOL TO REPRESENT THE MISSING NUMBER.

TAKE THIS AND...

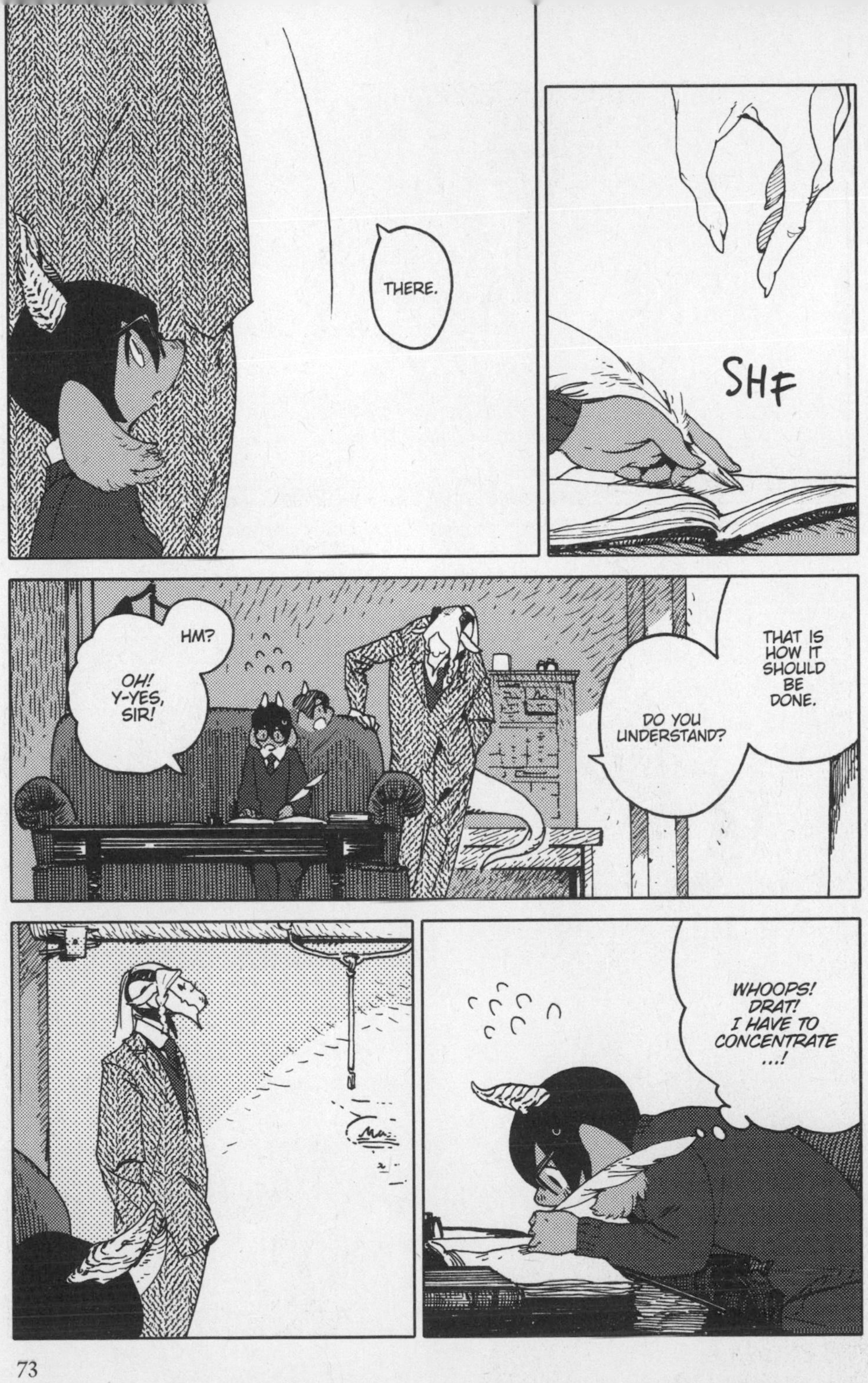
SHF
THERE.
THAT IS HOW IT SHOULD BE DONE.
DO YOU UNDERSTAND?
HM?
OH! Y-YES, SIR!
WHOOPS! DRAT! I HAVE TO CONCENTRATE ...!

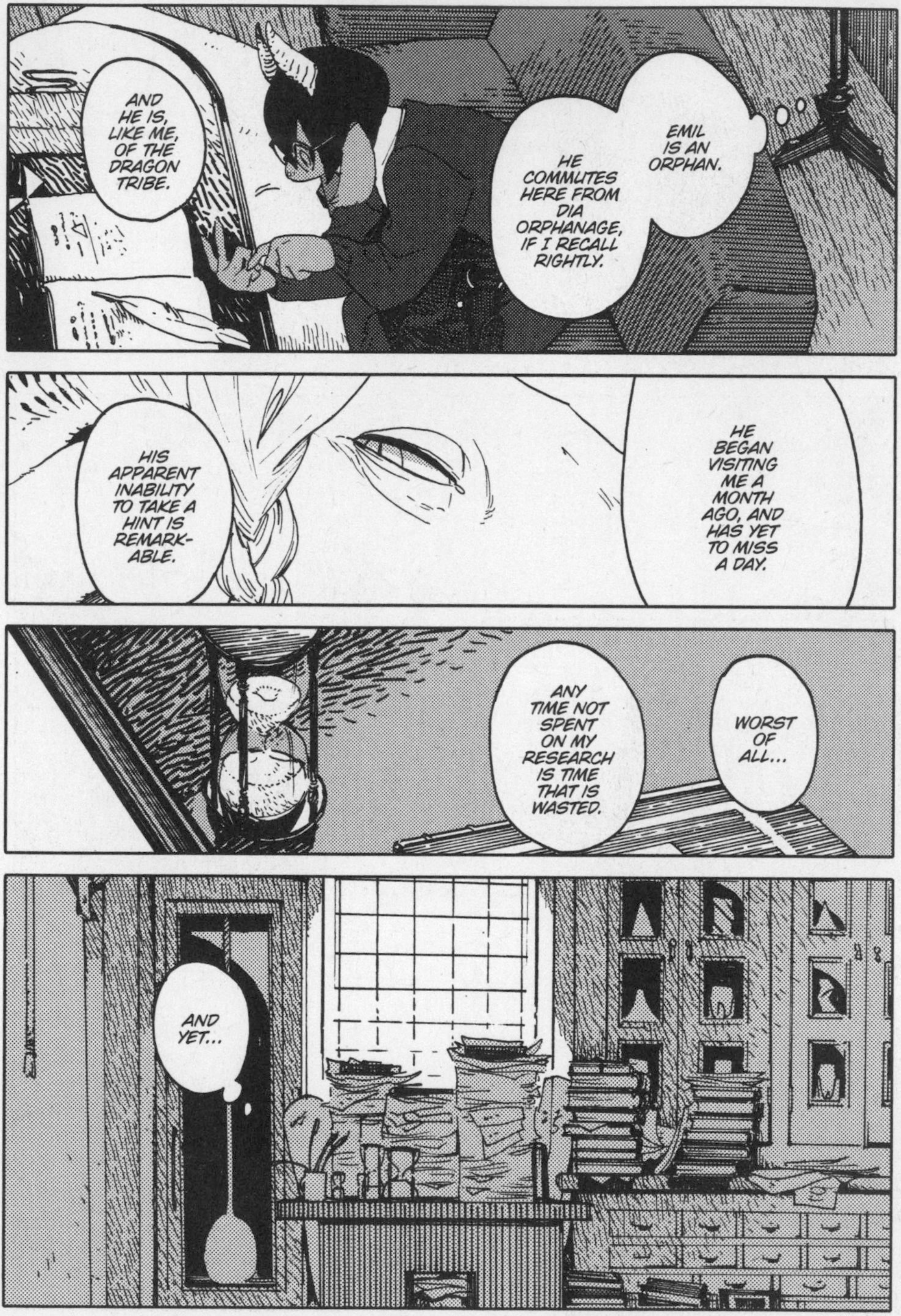
EMIL IS AN ORPHAN.
HE COMMUTES HERE FROM DIA ORPHANAGE, IF I RECALL RIGHTLY.
AND HE IS, LIKE ME, OF THE DRAGON TRIBE.
HE BEGAN VISITING ME A MONTH AGO, AND HAS YET TO MISS A DAY.
HIS APPARENT INABILITY TO TAKE A HINT IS REMARK-ABLE.
WORST OF ALL...
ANY TIME NOT SPENT ON MY RESEARCH IS TIME THAT IS WASTED.
AND YET...

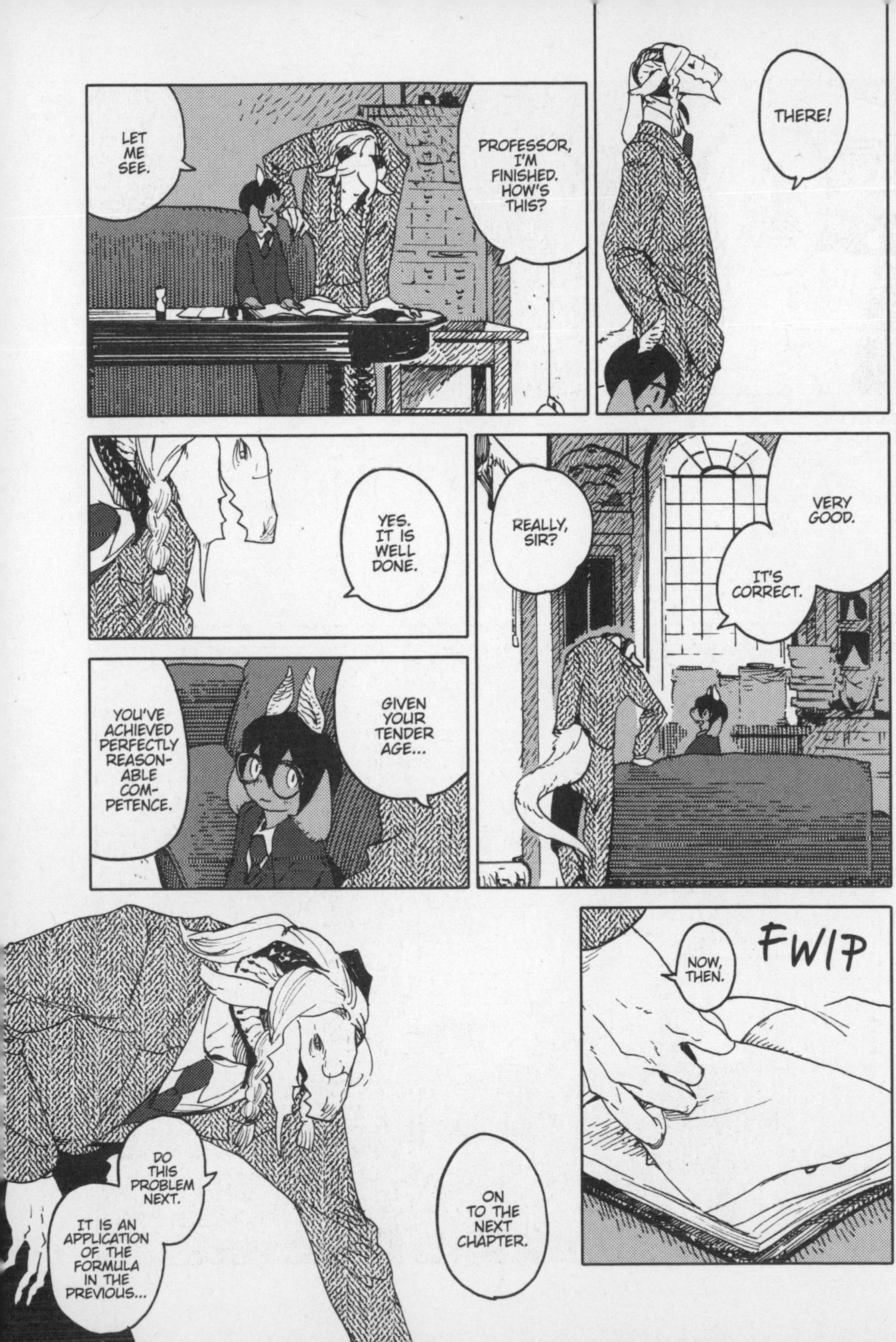
THERE!
PROFESSOR, I'M FINISHED. HOW'S THIS?
LET ME SEE.
VERY GOOD.
IT'S CORRECT.
REALLY, SIR?
YES. IT IS WELL DONE.
GIVEN YOUR TENDER AGE...
YOU'VE ACHIEVED PERFECTLY REASONABLE COMPETENCE.
FWIP
NOW, THEN.
ON TO THE NEXT CHAPTER.
DO THIS PROBLEM NEXT.
IT IS AN APPLICATION OF THE FORMULA IN THE PREVIOUS...

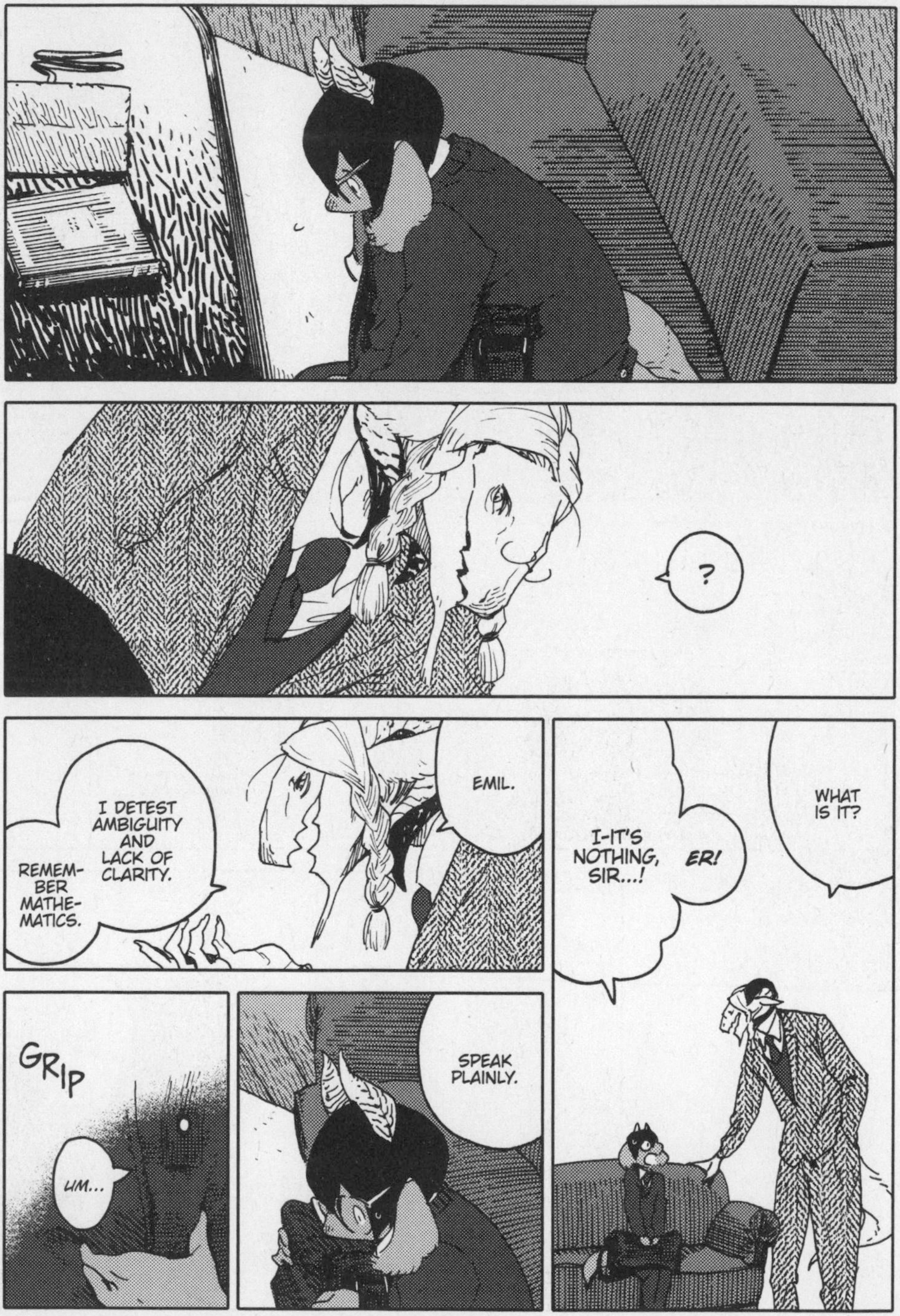
?
WHAT IS IT?
ER!
I-IT'S NOTHING, SIR...!
EMIL.
I DETEST AMBIGUITY AND LACK OF CLARITY.
REMEMBER MATHEMATICS.
SPEAK PLAINLY.
GRIP
UM...

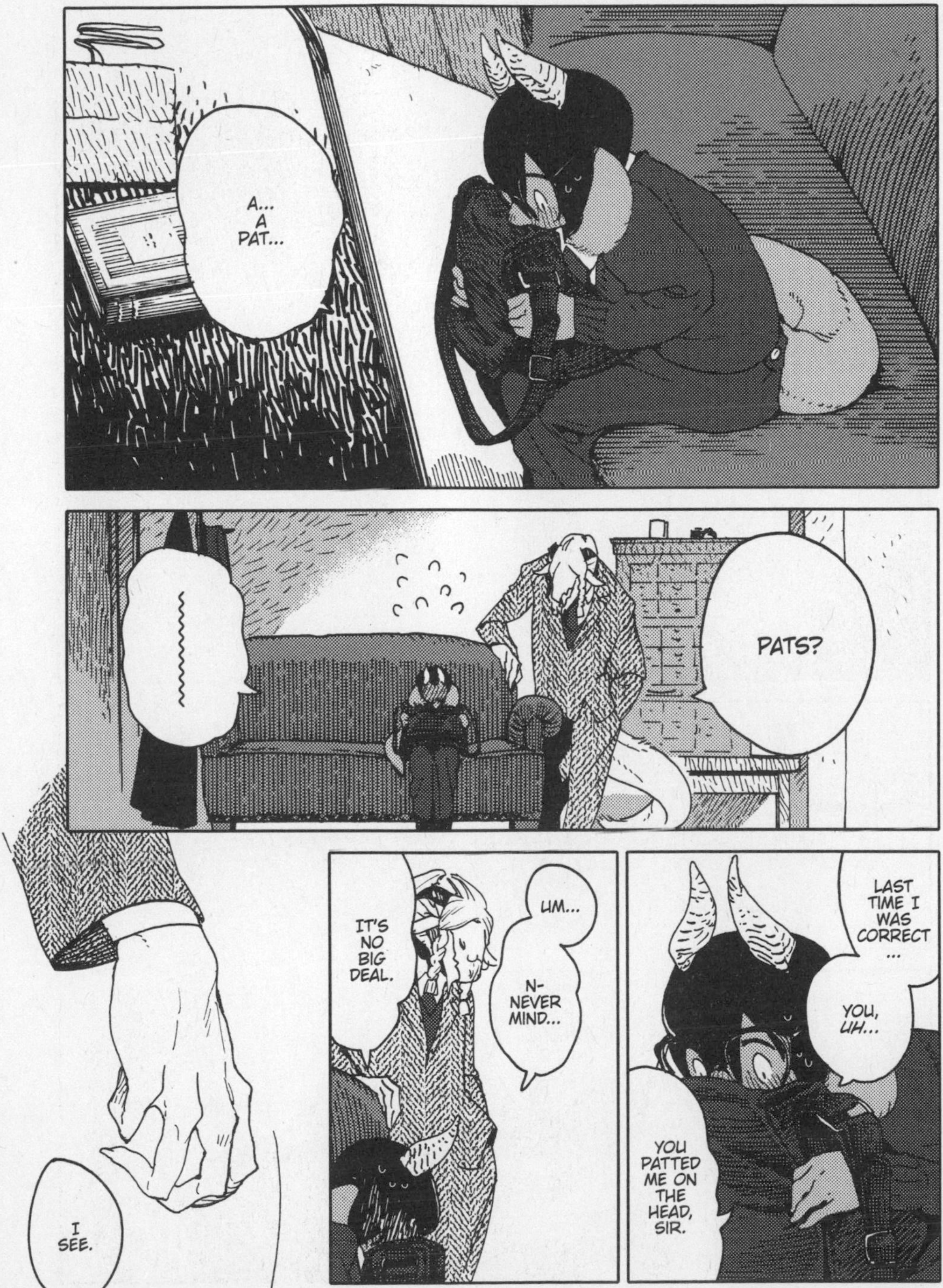
A... A PAT...
PATS?
LAST TIME I WAS CORRECT ...
YOU, UH...
YOU PATTED ME ON THE HEAD, SIR.
UM...
N-NEVER MIND...
IT'S NO BIG DEAL.
I SEE.

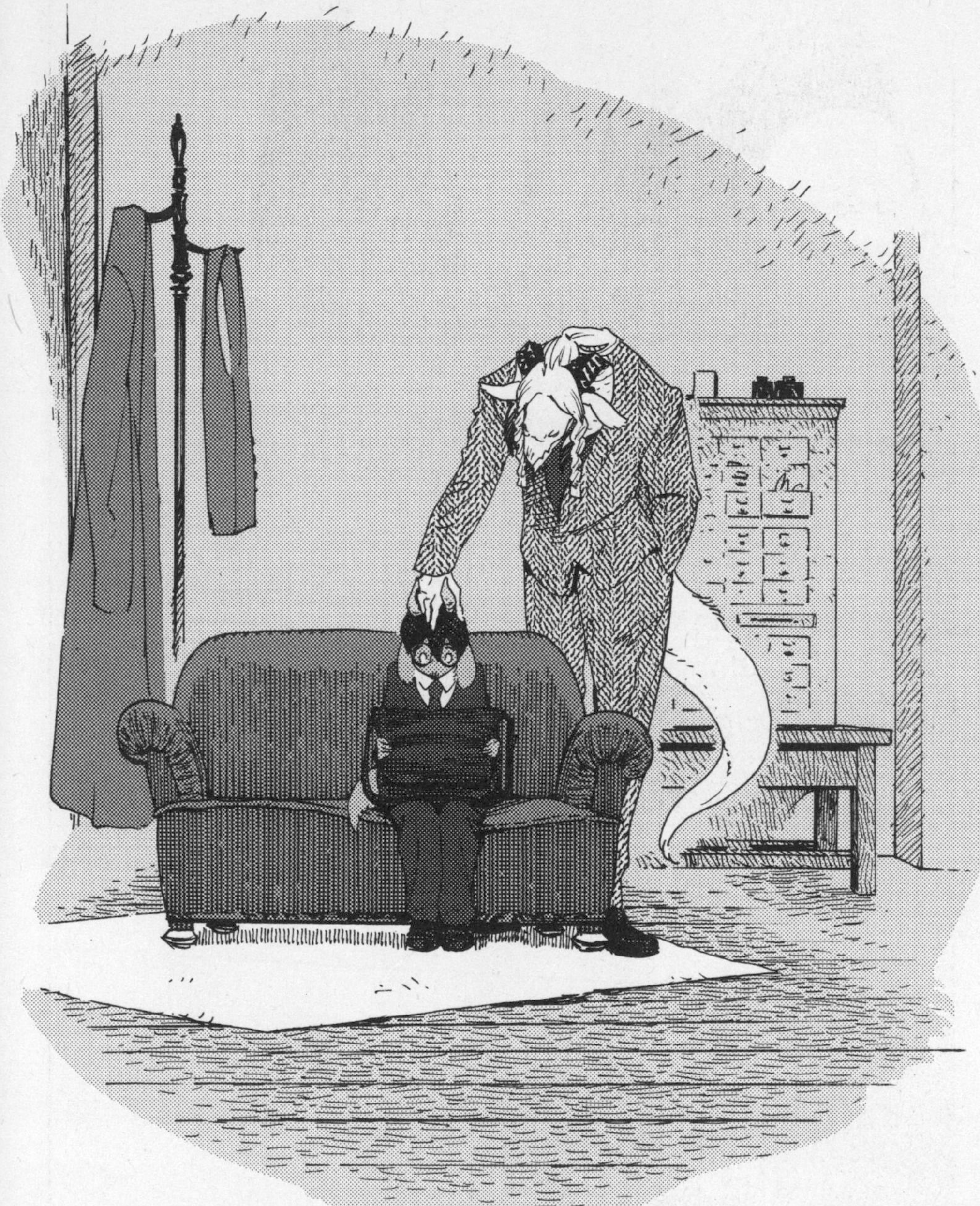

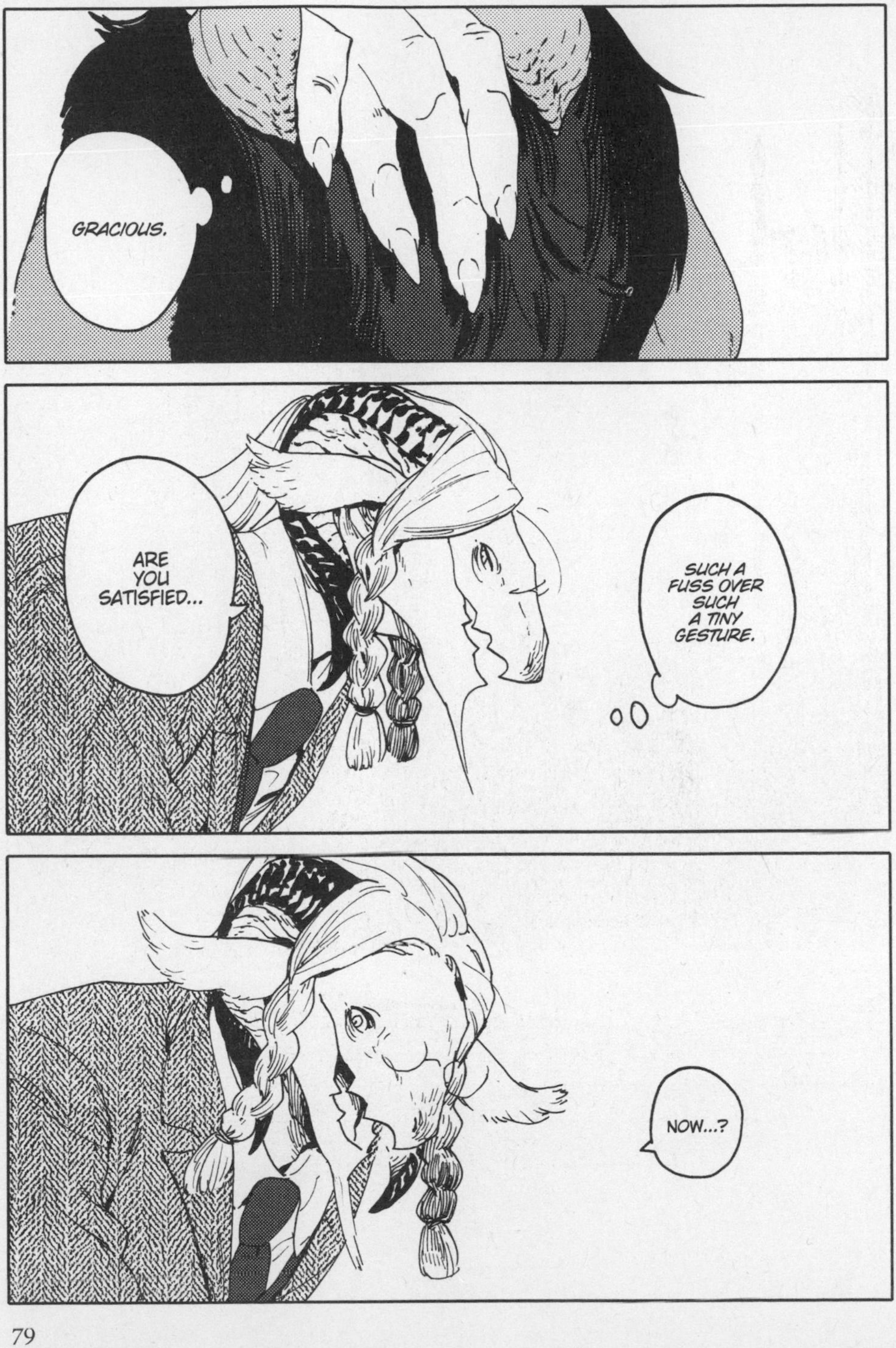
GRACIOUS.
SUCH A FUSS OVER SUCH A TINY GESTURE.
ARE YOU SATISFIED...
NOW...?

OH, GOSH.

I-I'M SORRY, SIR.

RUB RUB

I HAVE NO IDEA WHY THAT HAPPENED.

THAT'S SO STRANGE.

ACK!

HUH?

AH! DID THAT HURT?

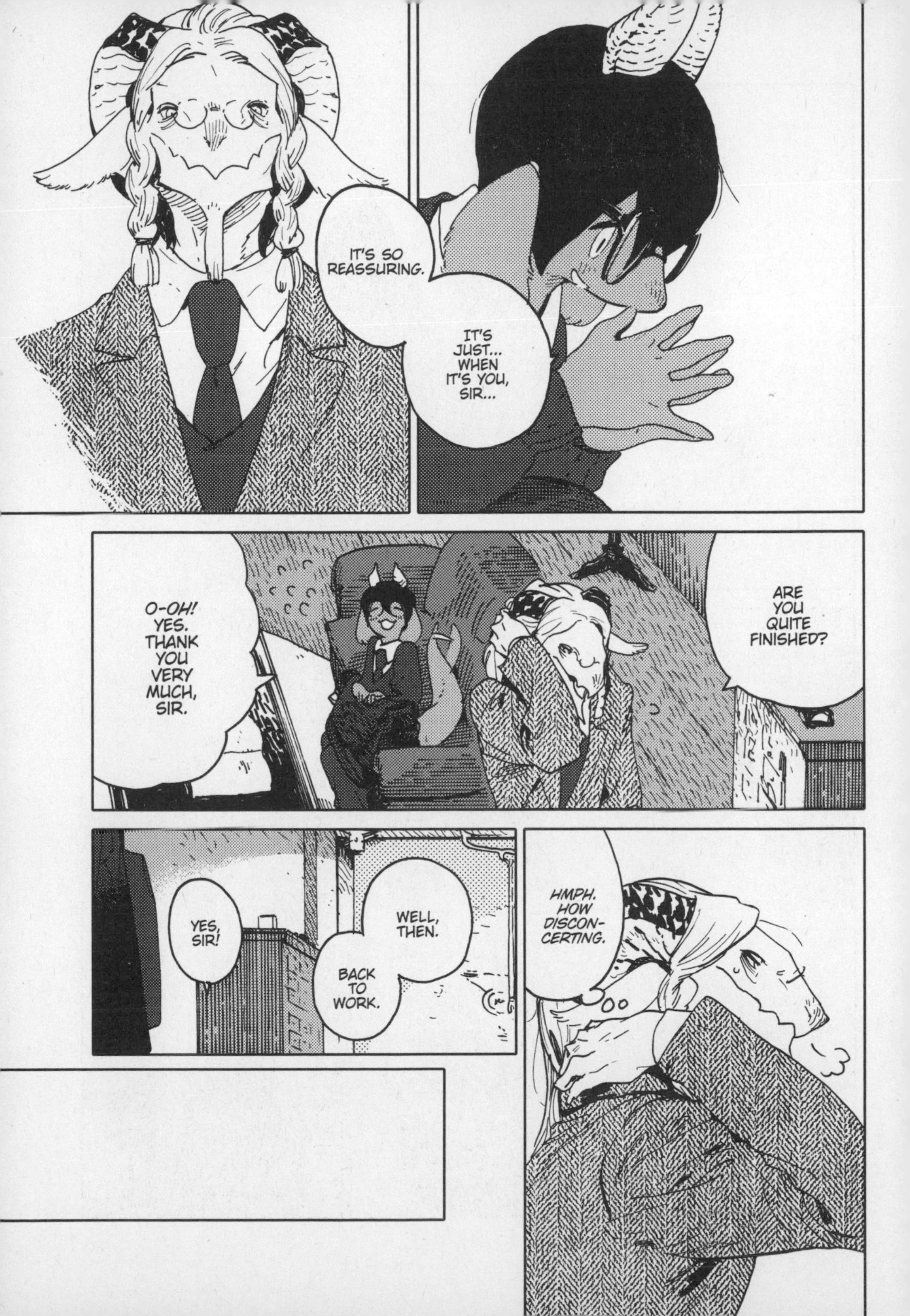
IT'S JUST... WHEN IT'S YOU, SIR...
IT'S SO REASSURING.
ARE YOU QUITE FINISHED?
O-OH! YES. THANK YOU VERY MUCH, SIR.
HMPH. HOW DISCON-CERTING.
WELL, THEN.
BACK TO WORK.
YES, SIR!

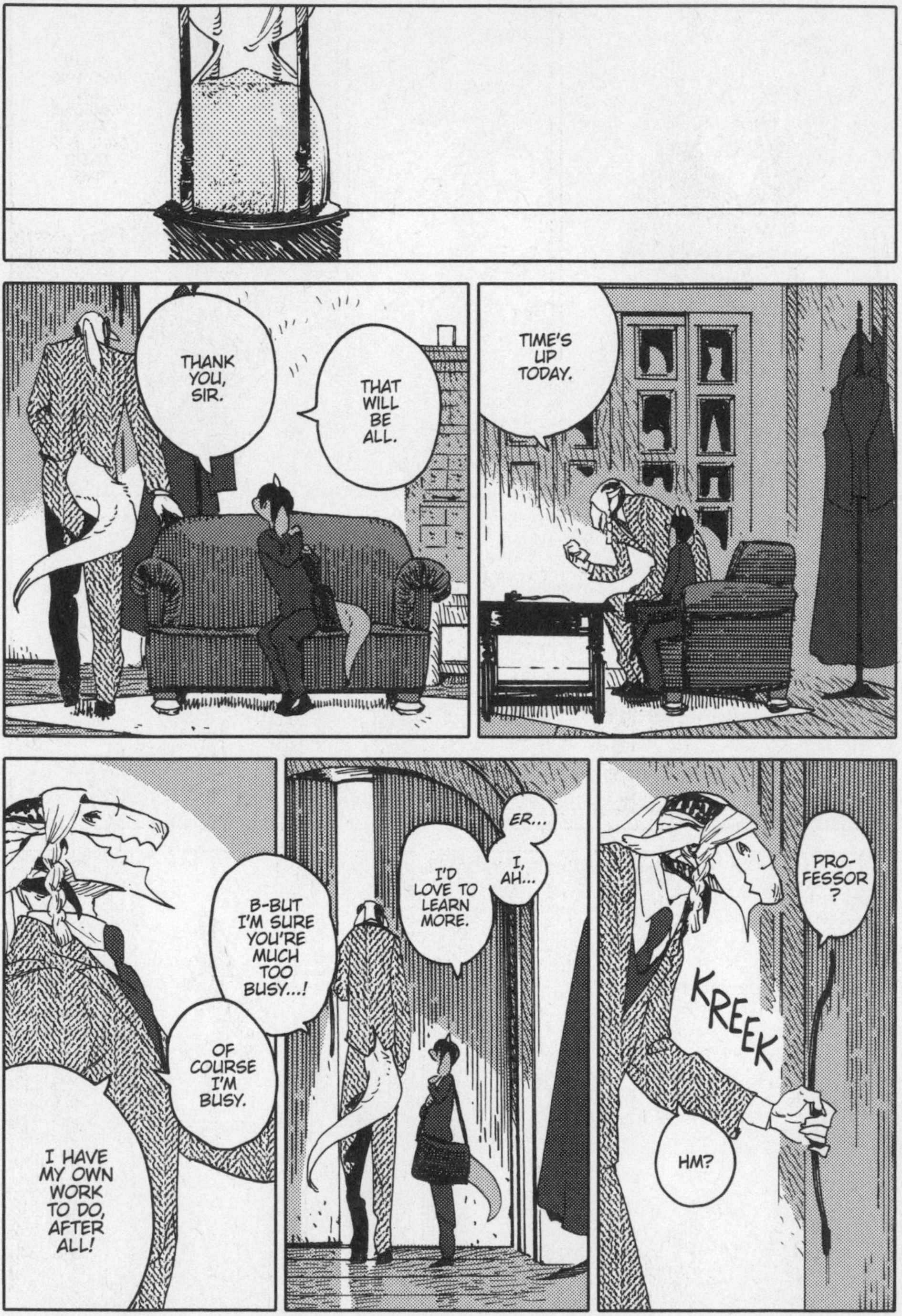
TIME'S UP TODAY.
THAT WILL BE ALL.
THANK YOU, SIR.
PRO-FESSOR?
KREEK
HM?
ER...
I, AH...
I'D LOVE TO LEARN MORE.
B-BUT I'M SURE YOU'RE MUCH TOO BUSY...!
OF COURSE I'M BUSY.
I HAVE MY OWN WORK TO DO, AFTER ALL!

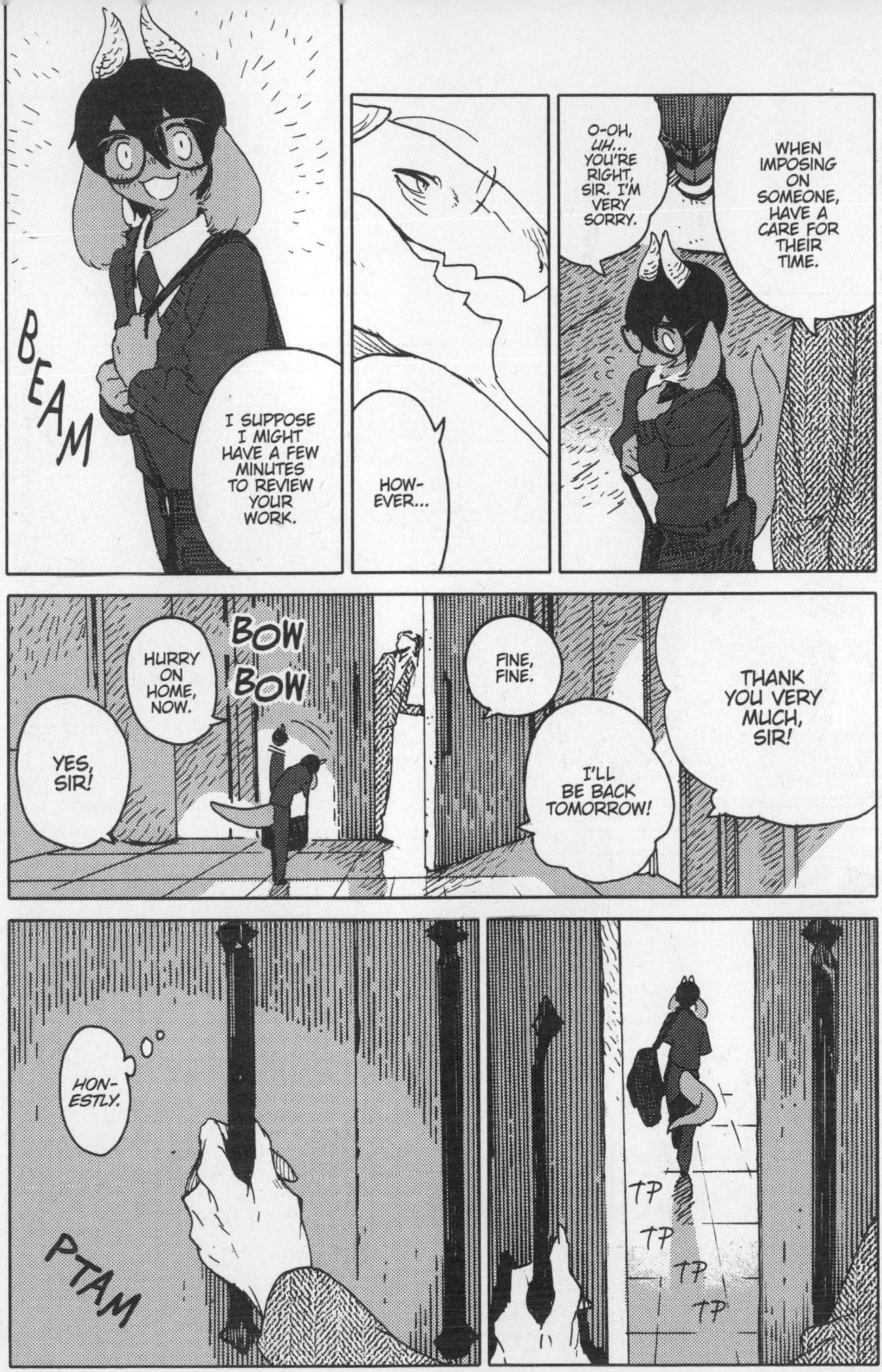
WHEN IMPOSING ON SOMEONE, HAVE A CARE FOR THEIR TIME.
O-OH, UH... YOU'RE RIGHT, SIR. I'M VERY SORRY.
HOW-EVER...
I SUPPOSE I MIGHT HAVE A FEW MINUTES TO REVIEW YOUR WORK.
BEAM
THANK YOU VERY MUCH, SIR!
I'LL BE BACK TOMORROW!
FINE, FINE.
BOW BOW
HURRY ON HOME, NOW.
YES, SIR!
TP
TP
TP
TP
HON-ESTLY.
PTAM

EVERYTHING HAS BEEN QUITE DISCOMBOBULATED SINCE HE STARTED COMING.
ME, TUTORING A PUPIL OUTSIDE OF LECTURE HOURS.
AND THERE'S THIS PECULIAR FEELING.
WHAT IS HAPPENING TO ME? I HAVE NO IDEA.
IT IS A PROBLEM.
I WILL SOLVE IT AS I WOULD ANY OTHER.
MY CURRENT CONDITION: "A."
MUTTER
MY PREVIOUS CONDITION: "L."
MUTTER
HE IS "E."
MUTTER
MMBL MMBL...
MUMBL...

◆ END ◆

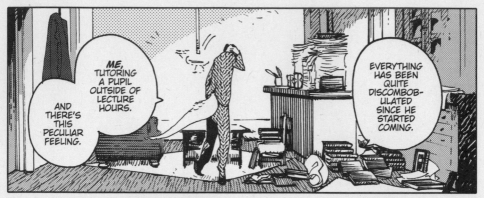

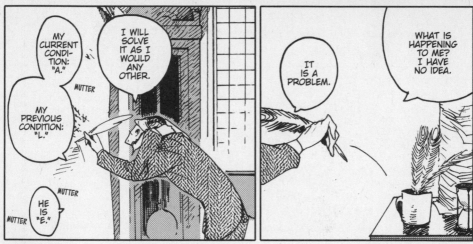

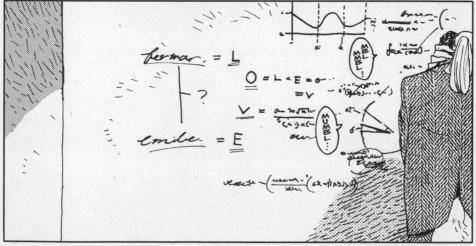

DRAGON

Dragon

Most dragons are scaled creatures with sharp fangs and talons. As they walk on land, have scales like a fish, and have wings like a bird, some consider them the Four Classical Elements given flesh. Some species can use their wings to fly. Other species are said to breathe fire. Still others are known to live in caves. Most are thought to live far longer than humans.

Some cultures regard dragons as evil, while others consider them wise sages. While theories about dragons abound, there has yet to be a single comprehensive description of them.

The Wize Wize Beasts
of the Wizarding Wizdoms
by Ragabe

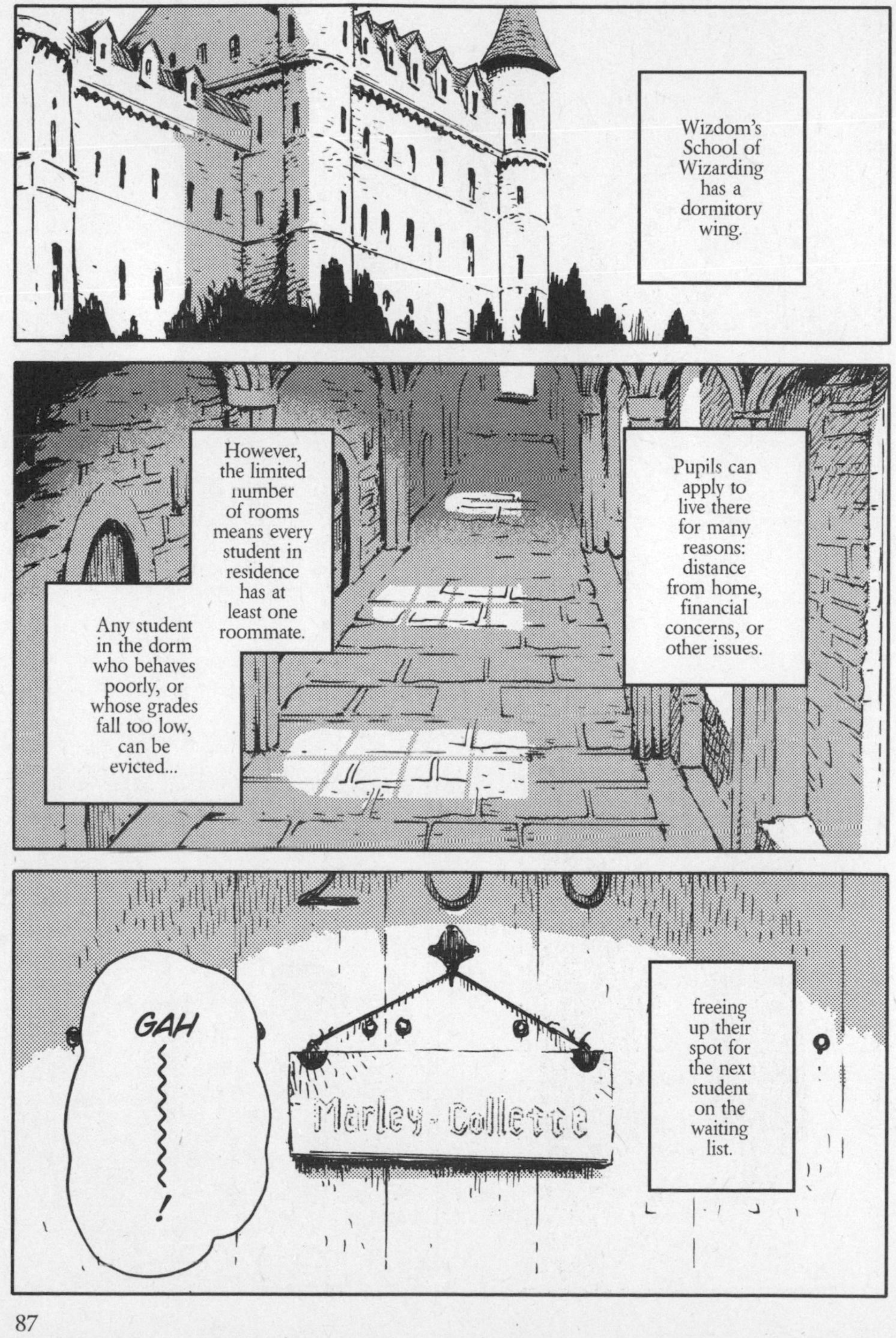
Wizdom's School of Wizarding has a dormitory wing.
Pupils can apply to live there for many reasons: distance from home, financial concerns, or other issues.
However, the limited number of rooms means every student in residence has at least one roommate.
Any student in the dorm who behaves poorly, or whose grades fall too low, can be evicted...
freeing up their spot for the next student on the waiting list.
Marley - Collette
GAH~~~!

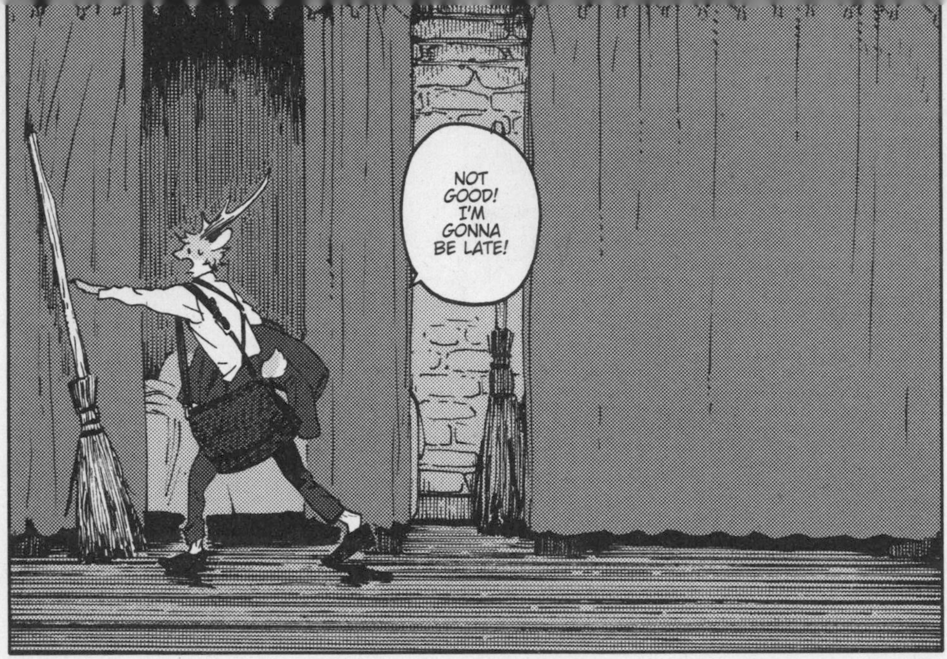
NOT GOOD! I'M GONNA BE LATE!

4

–Marley & Collette–

The Cold-Blooded & The Warm-Blooded

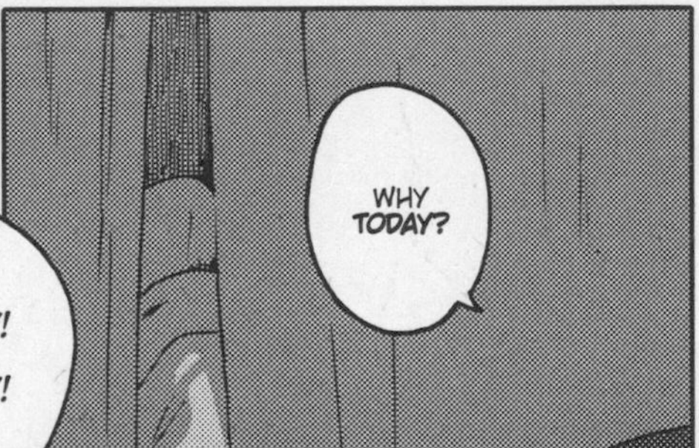
WHY TODAY?

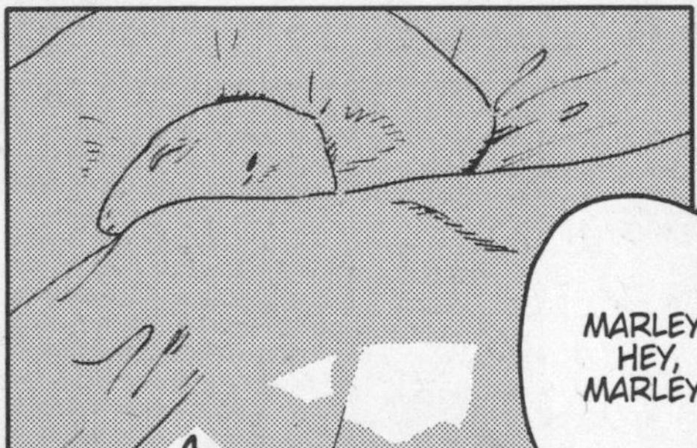
MARLEY! HEY, MARLEY!
C'MON, GET UP!
MNN...

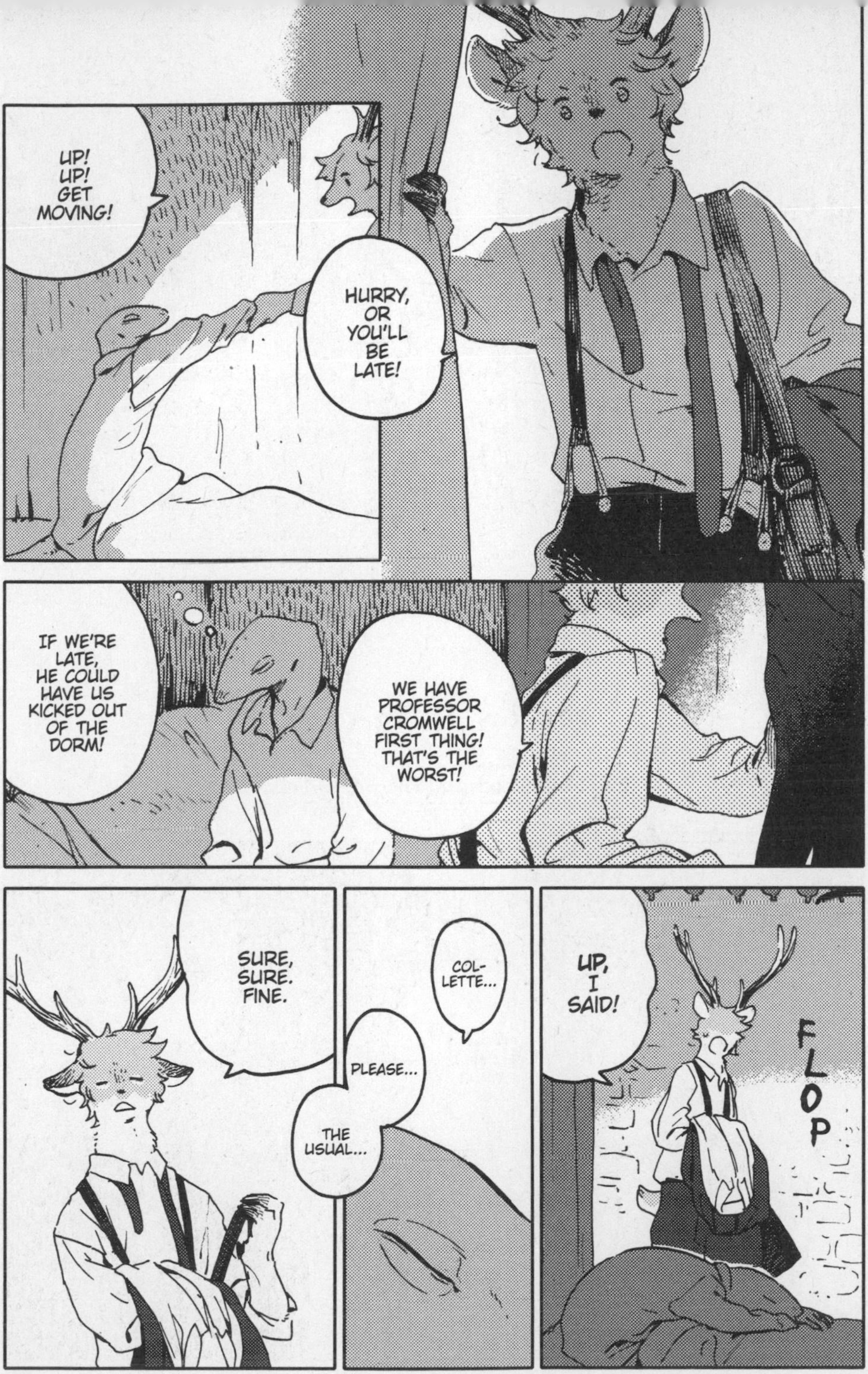
HURRY, OR YOU'LL BE LATE!
UP! UP! GET MOVING!
WE HAVE PROFESSOR CROMWELL FIRST THING! THAT'S THE WORST!
IF WE'RE LATE, HE COULD HAVE US KICKED OUT OF THE DORM!
UP, I SAID!
FLOP
COL-LETTE...
PLEASE...
THE USUAL...
SURE, SURE. FINE.

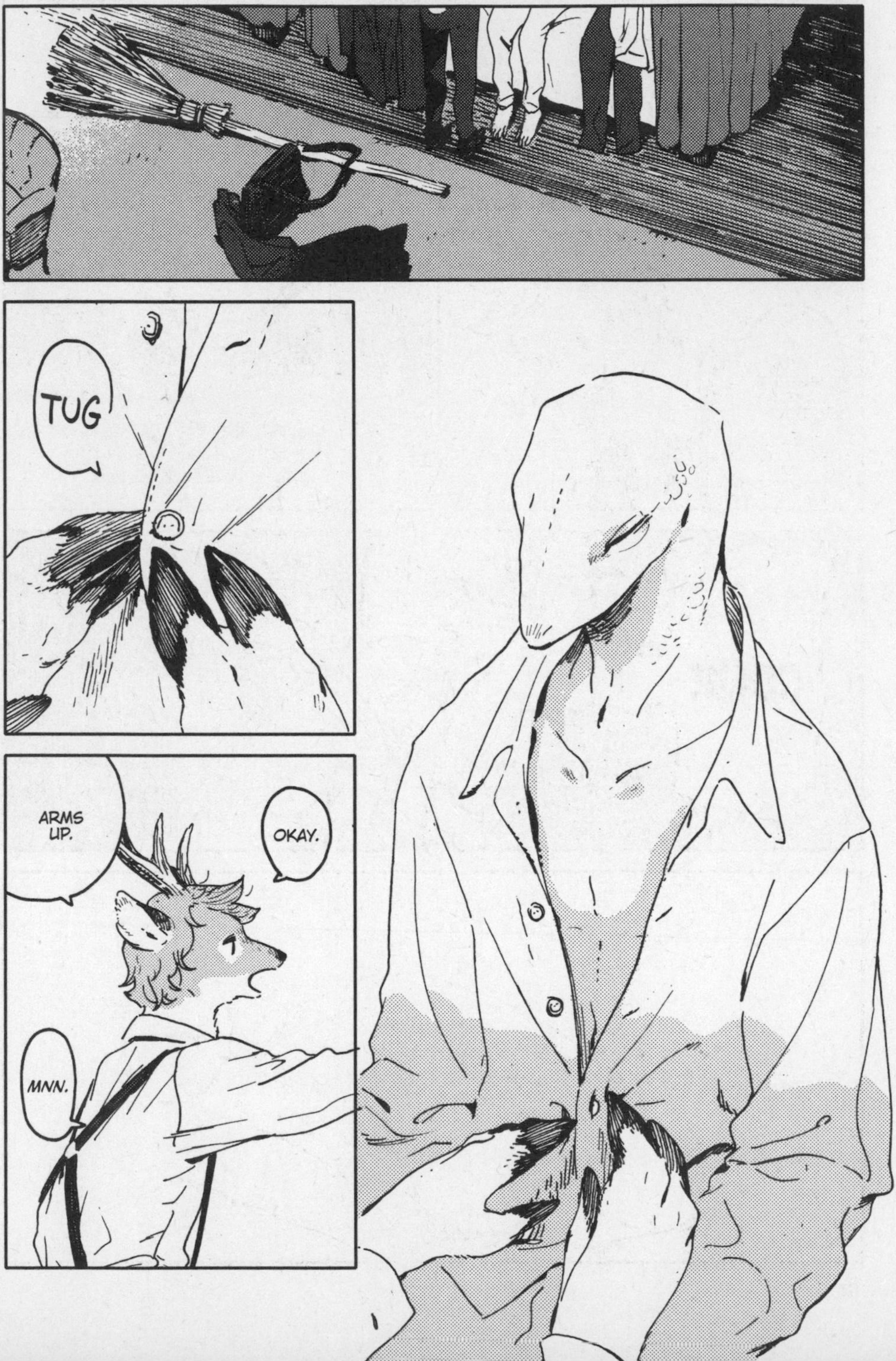
TUG
ARMS UP.
OKAY.
MNN.

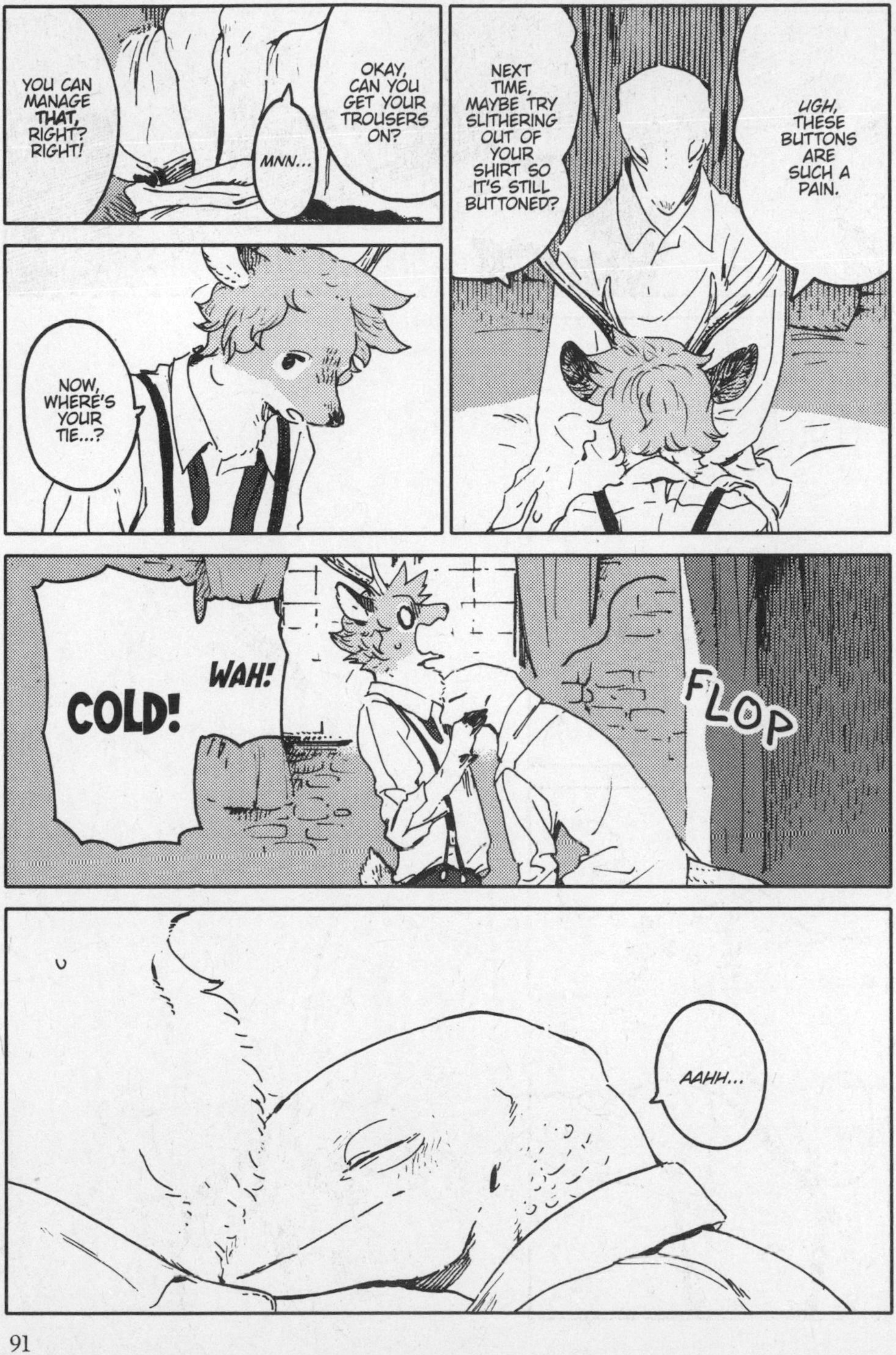
UGH, THESE BUTTONS ARE SUCH A PAIN.
NEXT TIME, MAYBE TRY SLITHERING OUT OF YOUR SHIRT SO IT'S STILL BUTTONED?
OKAY, CAN YOU GET YOUR TROUSERS ON?
MNN...
YOU CAN MANAGE **THAT**, RIGHT? RIGHT!
NOW, WHERE'S YOUR TIE...?
FLOP
WAH!
COLD!
AAHH...

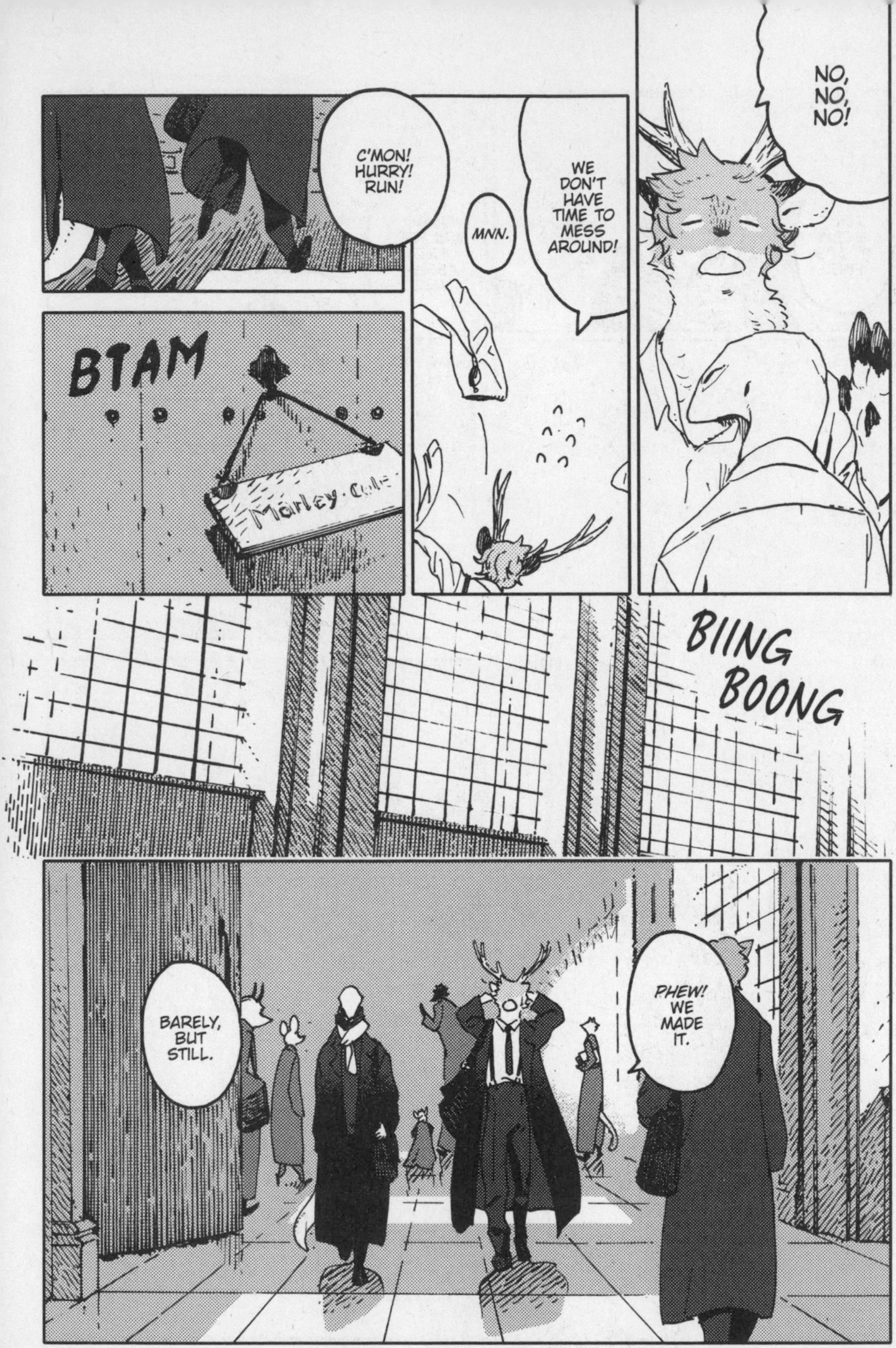
NO, NO, NO!
WE DON'T HAVE TIME TO MESS AROUND!
MNN.
C'MON! HURRY! RUN!
BTAM
BIING BOONG
PHEW! WE MADE IT.
BARELY, BUT STILL.

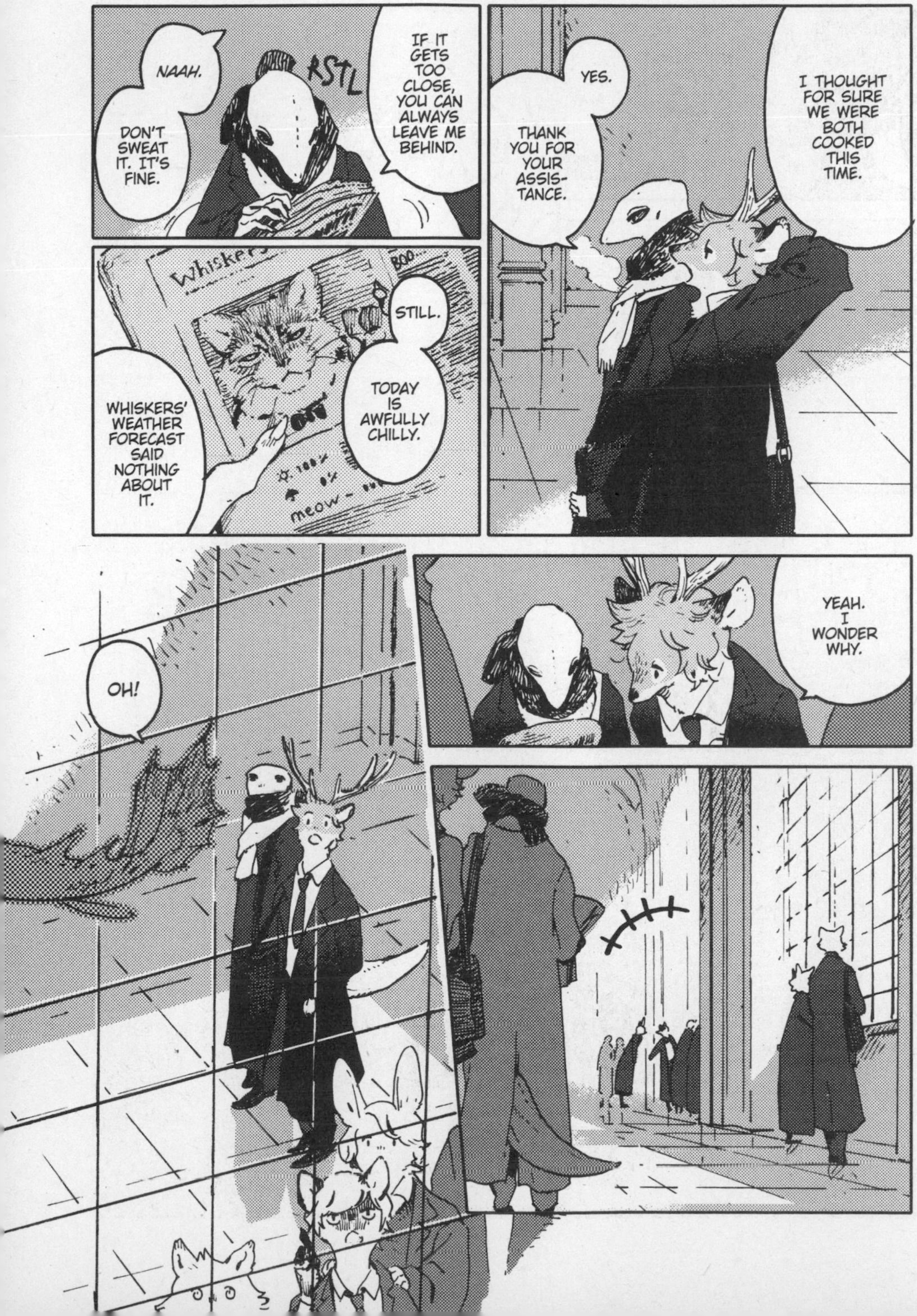
I THOUGHT FOR SURE WE WERE BOTH COOKED THIS TIME.
YES.
THANK YOU FOR YOUR ASSISTANCE.
IF IT GETS TOO CLOSE, YOU CAN ALWAYS LEAVE ME BEHIND.
RSTL
NAAH.
DON'T SWEAT IT. IT'S FINE.
STILL.
TODAY IS AWFULLY CHILLY.
WHISKERS' WEATHER FORECAST SAID NOTHING ABOUT IT.
meow
YEAH. I WONDER WHY.
OH!

LOOK! A WILD DRAGON!
IT'S SNOWING, TOO!
AH. IT MUST BE A SNOW DRAGON'S DOING, THEN.
OH, *WOW--!* THAT IS SO COOL! I'VE GOTTA GO SEE!
COME OUTSIDE AND LOOK WITH ME!
I'M KIDDING.
THANK YOU, BUT I'LL REFRAIN TODAY.
I'M RETURNING TO OUR ROOM TO STUDY.
'KAY.

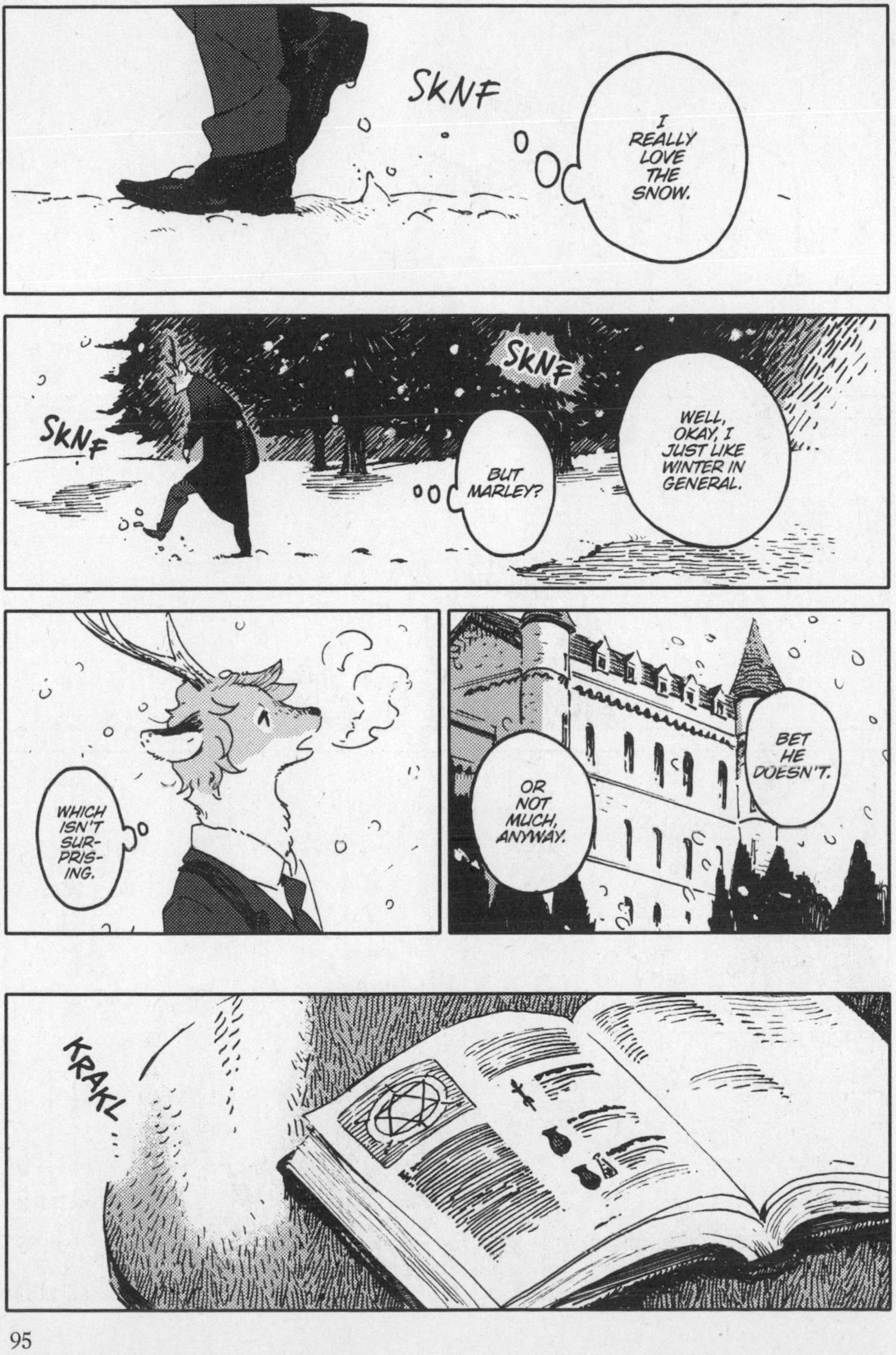

I REALLY LOVE THE SNOW.
SKNF
SKNF
WELL, OKAY, I JUST LIKE WINTER IN GENERAL.
BUT MARLEY?
SKNF
BET HE DOESN'T.
OR NOT MUCH, ANYWAY.
WHICH ISN'T SURPRISING.
KRAKL

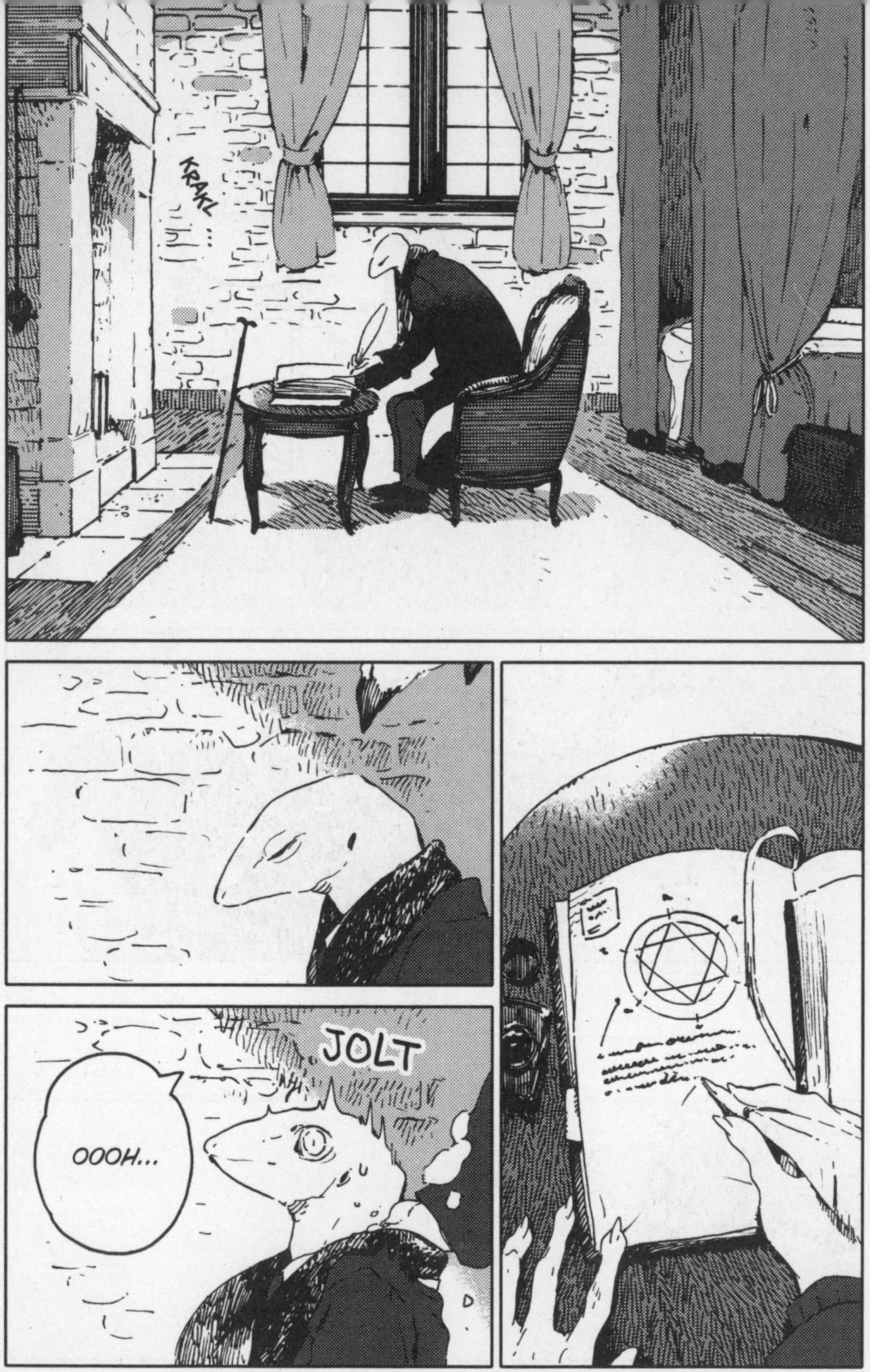
KRAKL...
JOLT
OOOH...

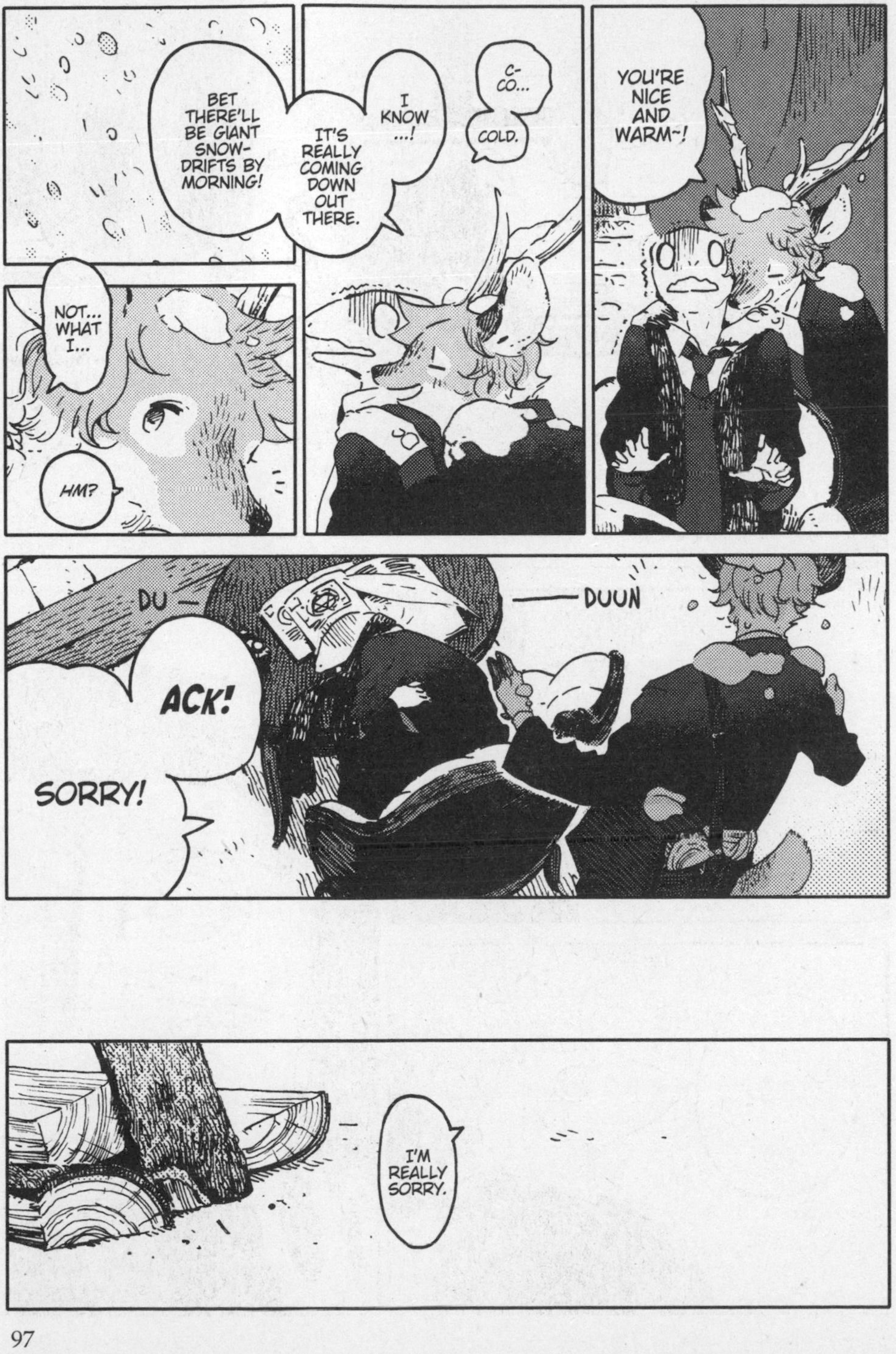
YOU'RE NICE AND WARM~!
C- CO...
COLD.
I KNOW ...!
IT'S REALLY COMING DOWN OUT THERE.
BET THERE'LL BE GIANT SNOW-DRIFTS BY MORNING!
NOT... WHAT I...
HM?
DU—
—DUUN
ACK!
SORRY!
I'M REALLY SORRY.

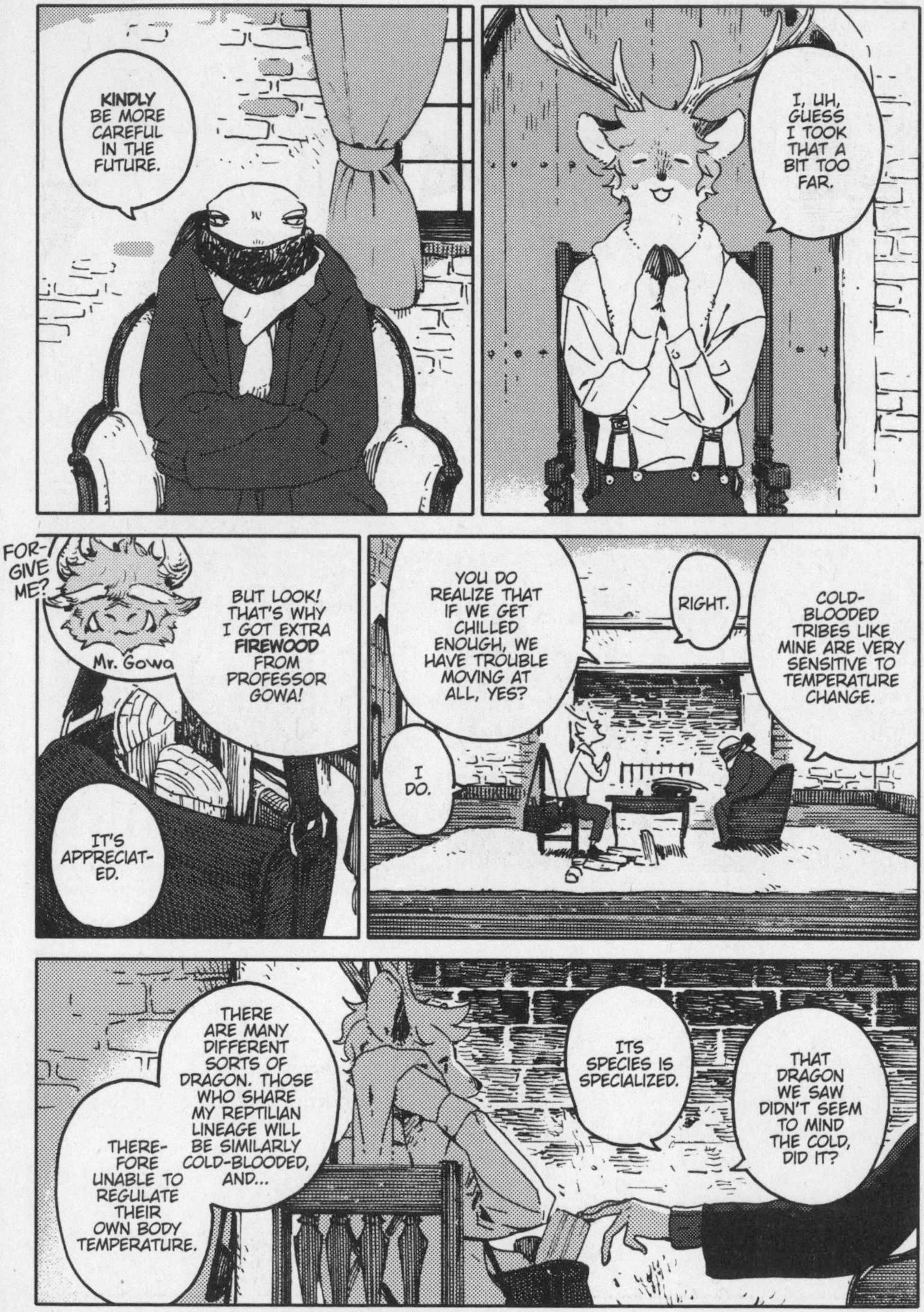
I, UH, GUESS I TOOK THAT A BIT TOO FAR.
KINDLY BE MORE CAREFUL IN THE FUTURE.
COLD-BLOODED TRIBES LIKE MINE ARE VERY SENSITIVE TO TEMPERATURE CHANGE.
RIGHT.
YOU DO REALIZE THAT IF WE GET CHILLED ENOUGH, WE HAVE TROUBLE MOVING AT ALL, YES?
I DO.
BUT LOOK! THAT'S WHY I GOT EXTRA **FIREWOOD** FROM PROFESSOR GOWA!
Mr. Gowa
FOR-GIVE ME?
IT'S APPRECIAT-ED.
THAT DRAGON WE SAW DIDN'T SEEM TO MIND THE COLD, DID IT?
ITS SPECIES IS SPECIALIZED.
THERE ARE MANY DIFFERENT SORTS OF DRAGON. THOSE WHO SHARE MY REPTILIAN LINEAGE WILL BE SIMILARLY COLD-BLOODED, AND...
THERE-FORE UNABLE TO REGULATE THEIR OWN BODY TEMPERATURE.

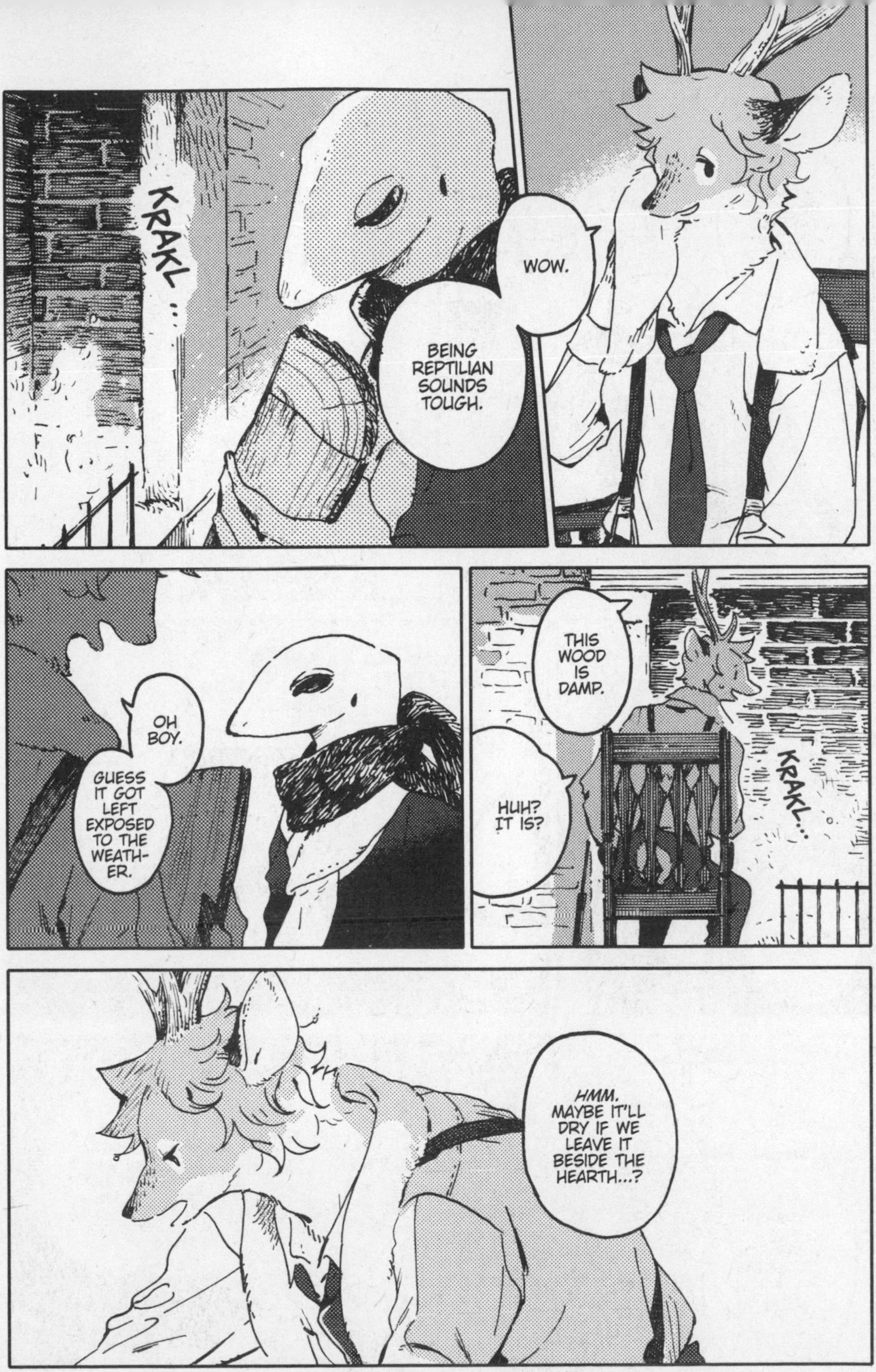
WOW.
BEING REPTILIAN SOUNDS TOUGH.
KRAKL...
THIS WOOD IS DAMP.
HUH? IT IS?
KRAKL...
OH BOY.
GUESS IT GOT LEFT EXPOSED TO THE WEATHER.
HMM. MAYBE IT'LL DRY IF WE LEAVE IT BESIDE THE HEARTH...?

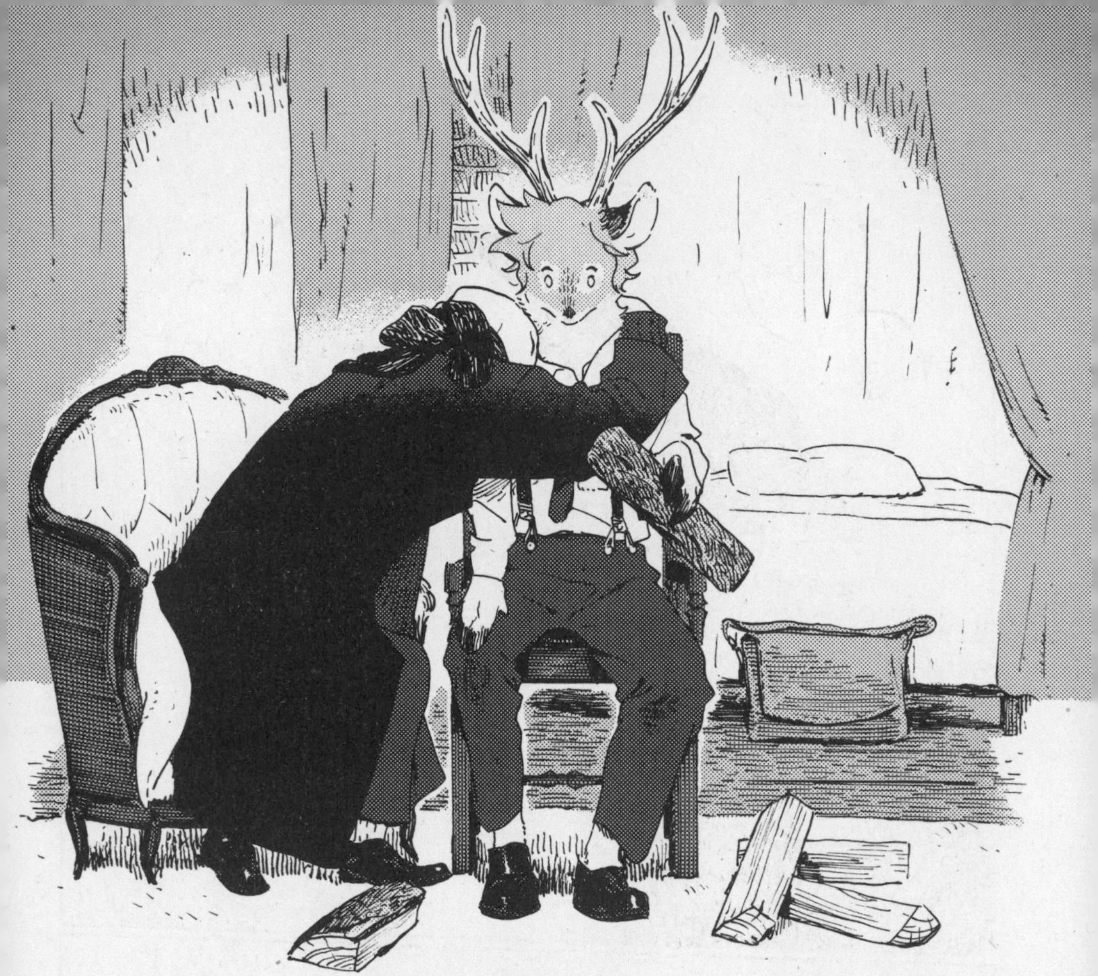

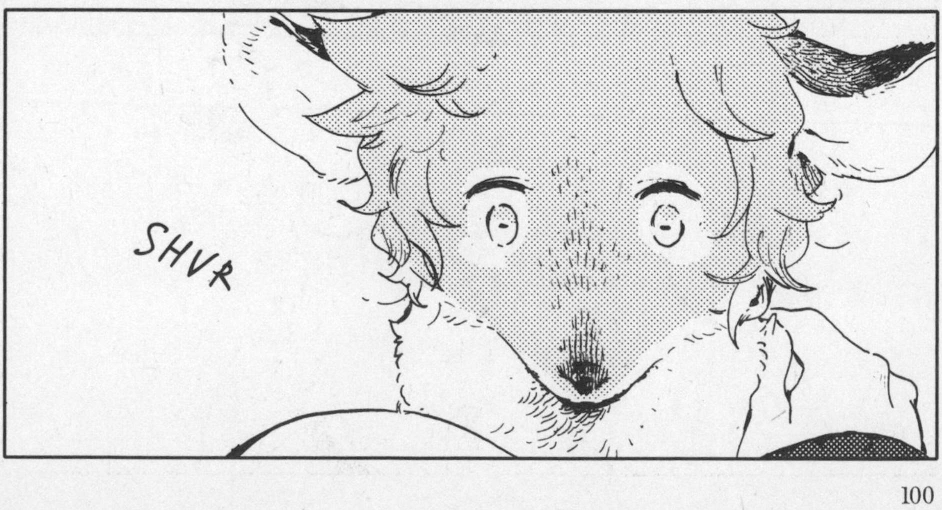
SHVR

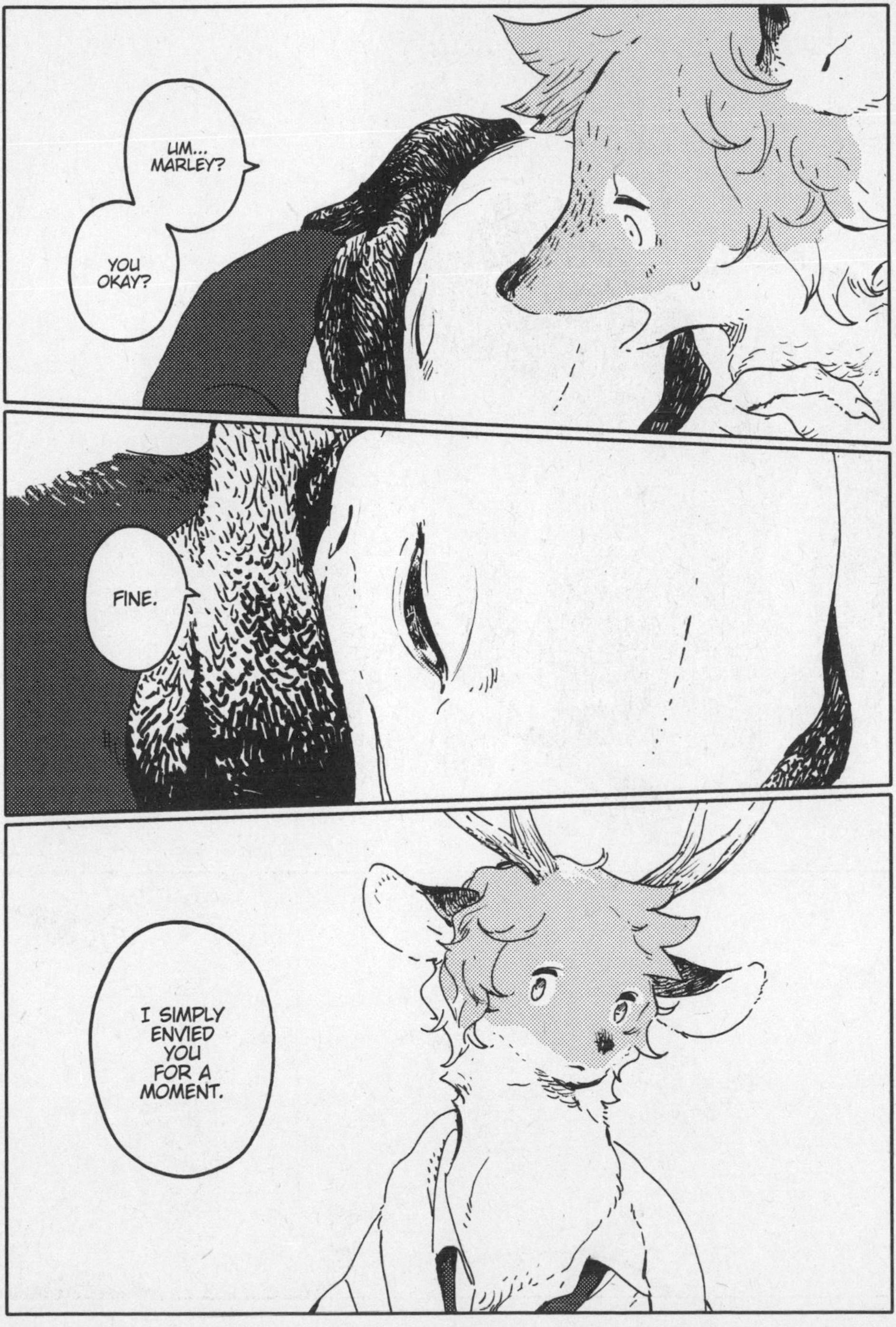
UM... MARLEY?
YOU OKAY?
FINE.
I SIMPLY ENVIED YOU FOR A MOMENT.

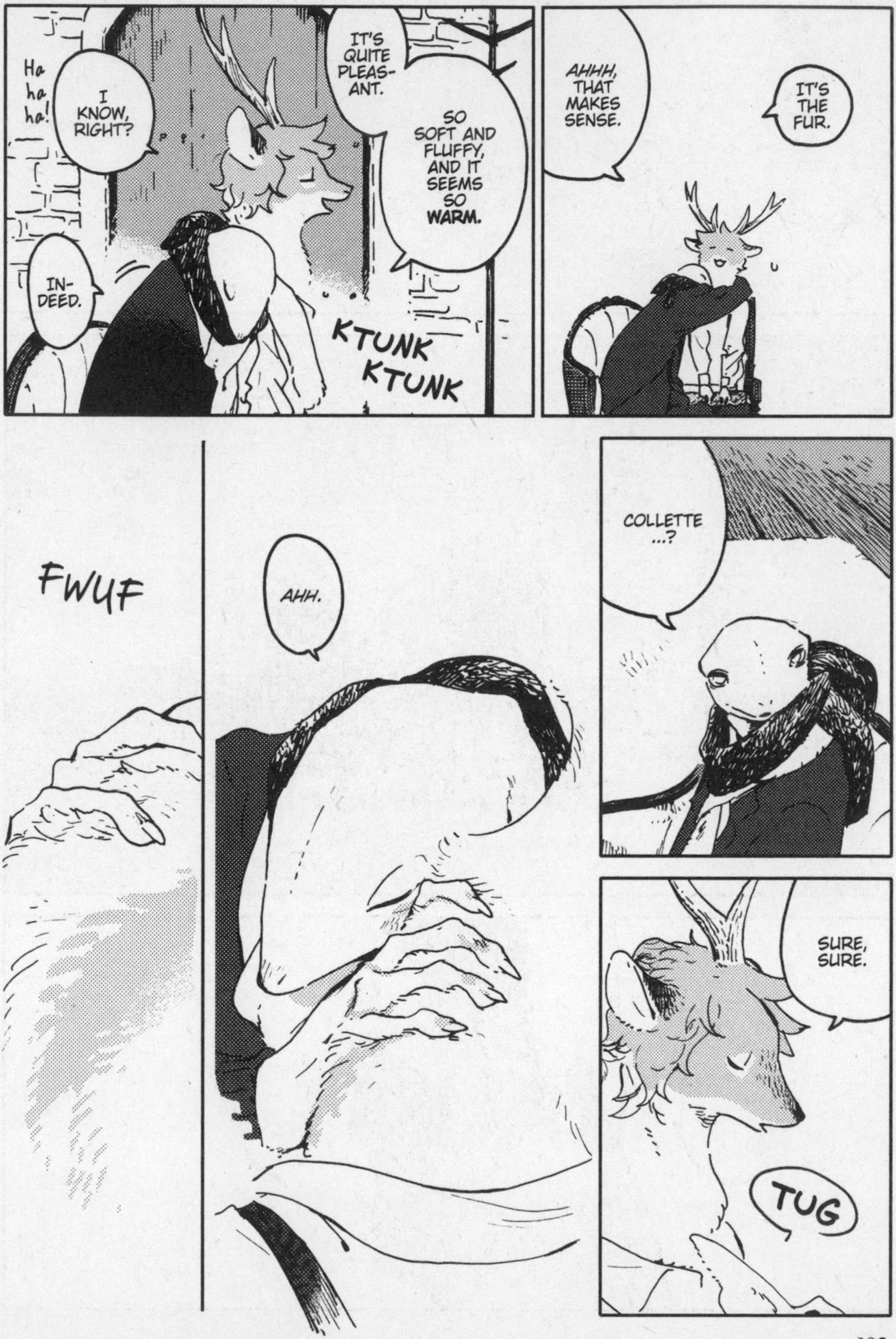
IT'S THE FUR.
AHHH, THAT MAKES SENSE.
IT'S QUITE PLEASANT.
SO SOFT AND FLUFFY, AND IT SEEMS SO WARM.
I KNOW, RIGHT?
Ha ha ha!
INDEED.
KTUNK KTUNK
COLLETTE ...?
SURE, SURE.
TUG
AHH.
FWUF

KRAKL...

KRAKL...

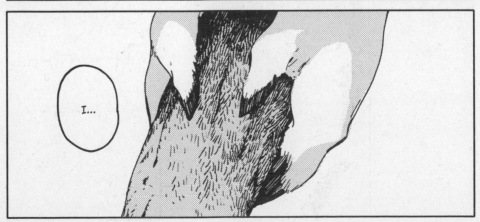

I...

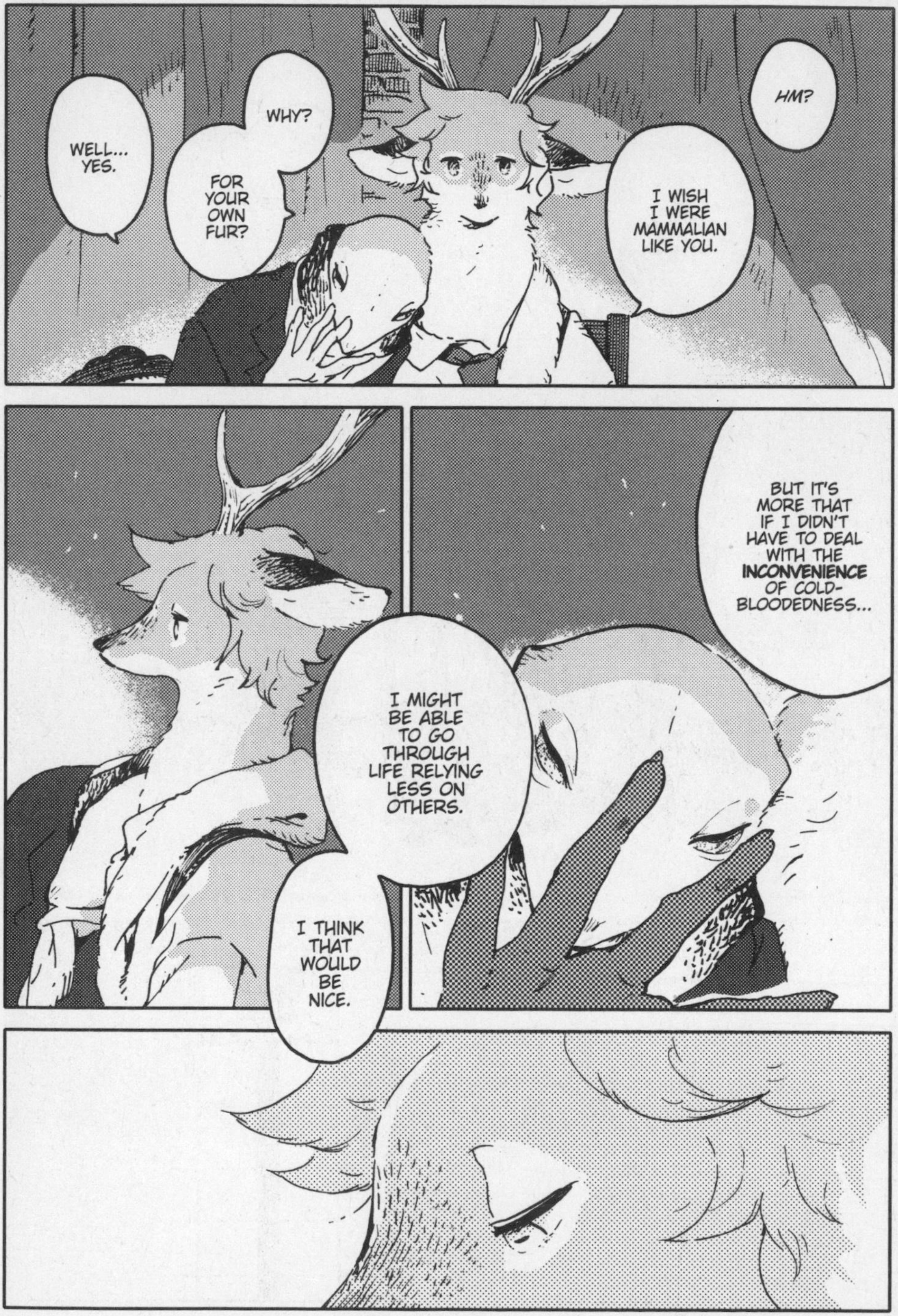
HM?
I WISH I WERE MAMMALIAN LIKE YOU.
WHY?
FOR YOUR OWN FUR?
WELL... YES.
BUT IT'S MORE THAT IF I DIDN'T HAVE TO DEAL WITH THE **INCONVENIENCE** OF COLD-BLOODEDNESS...
I MIGHT BE ABLE TO GO THROUGH LIFE RELYING LESS ON OTHERS.
I THINK THAT WOULD BE NICE.

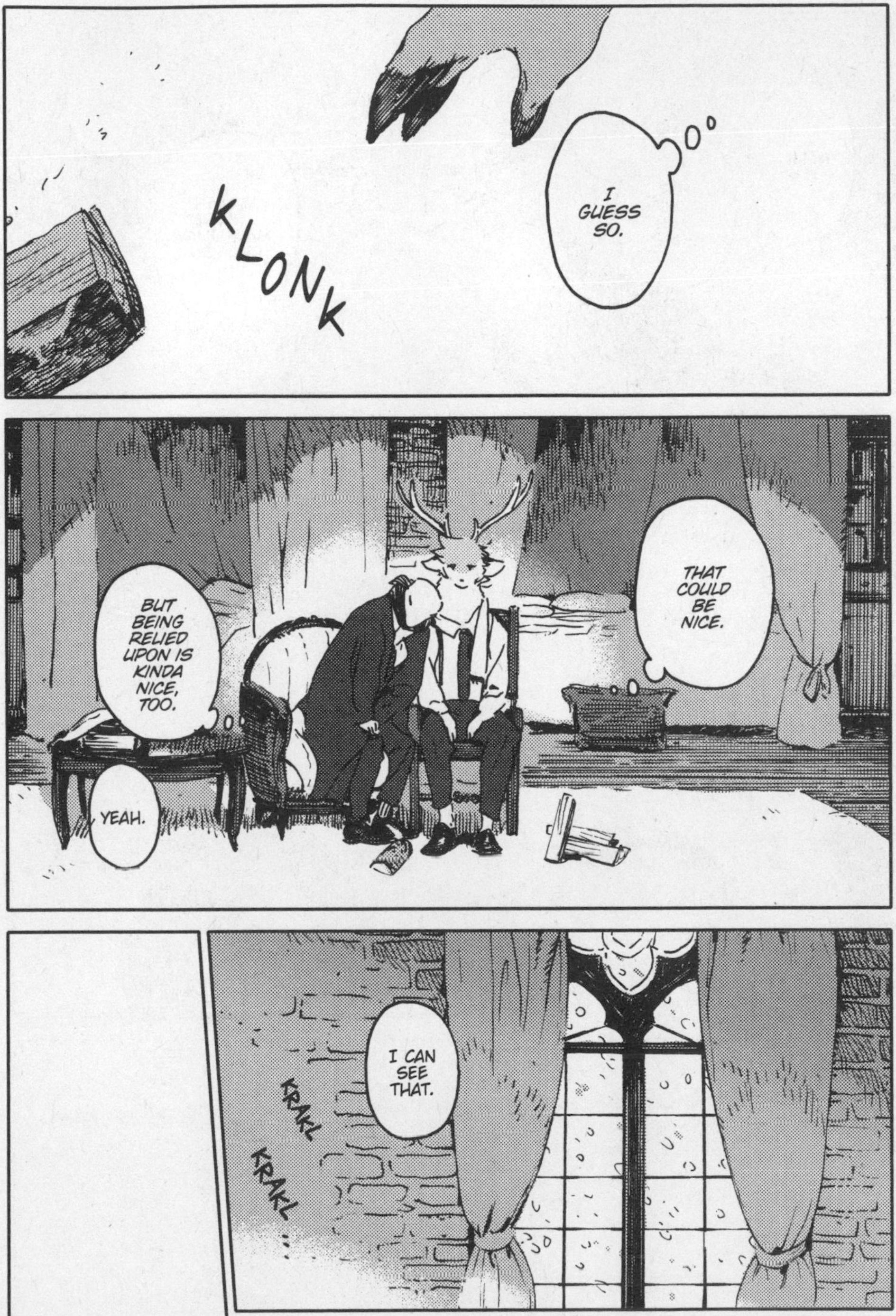
KLONK
I GUESS SO.
THAT COULD BE NICE.
BUT BEING RELIED UPON IS KINDA NICE, TOO.
YEAH.
I CAN SEE THAT.
KRAKL
KRAKL...

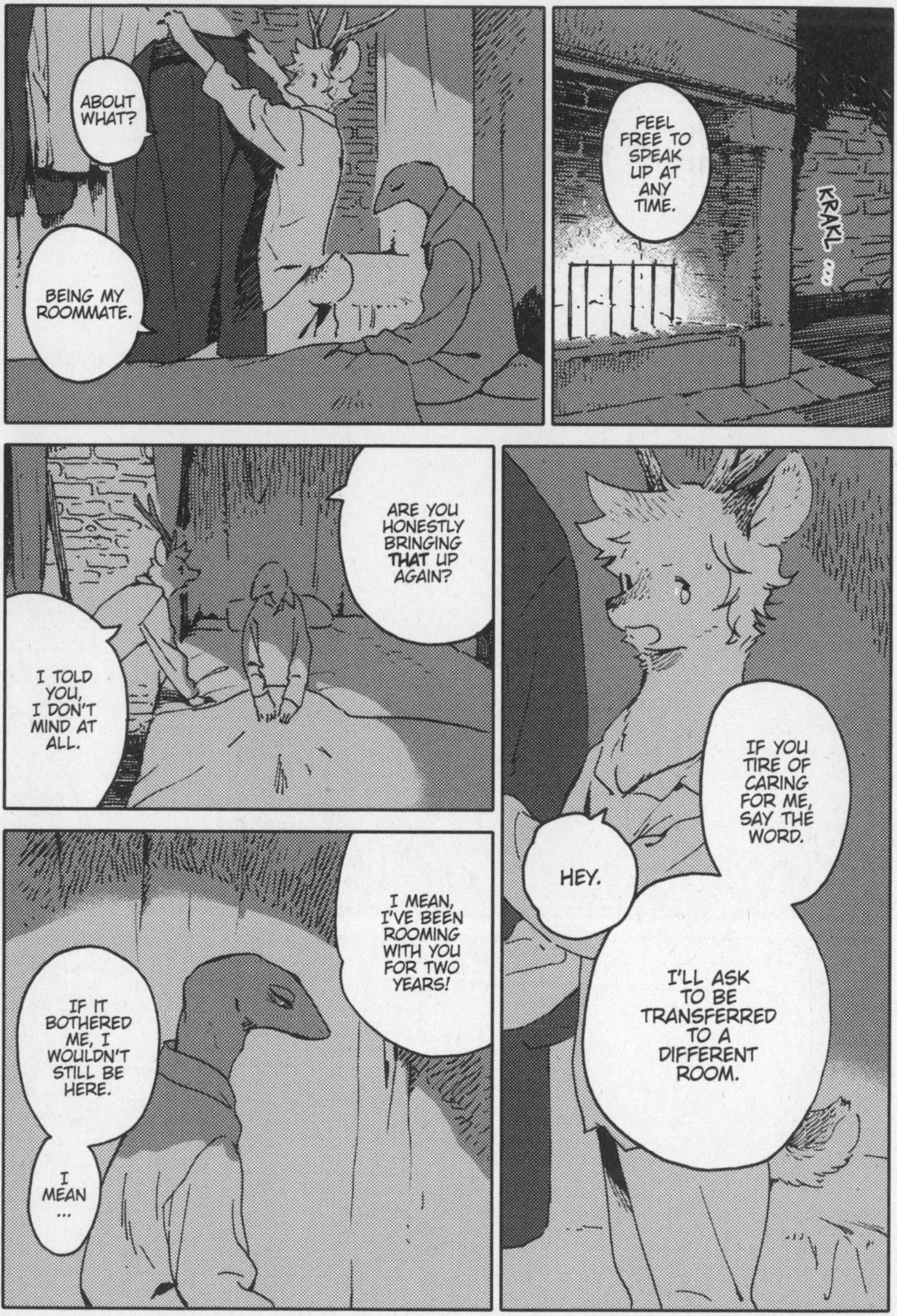
FEEL FREE TO SPEAK UP AT ANY TIME.
KRAKL...
ABOUT WHAT?
BEING MY ROOMMATE.
IF YOU TIRE OF CARING FOR ME, SAY THE WORD.
I'LL ASK TO BE TRANSFERRED TO A DIFFERENT ROOM.
HEY.
ARE YOU HONESTLY BRINGING **THAT** UP AGAIN?
I TOLD YOU, I DON'T MIND AT ALL.
I MEAN, I'VE BEEN ROOMING WITH YOU FOR TWO YEARS!
IF IT BOTHERED ME, I WOULDN'T STILL BE HERE.
I MEAN...

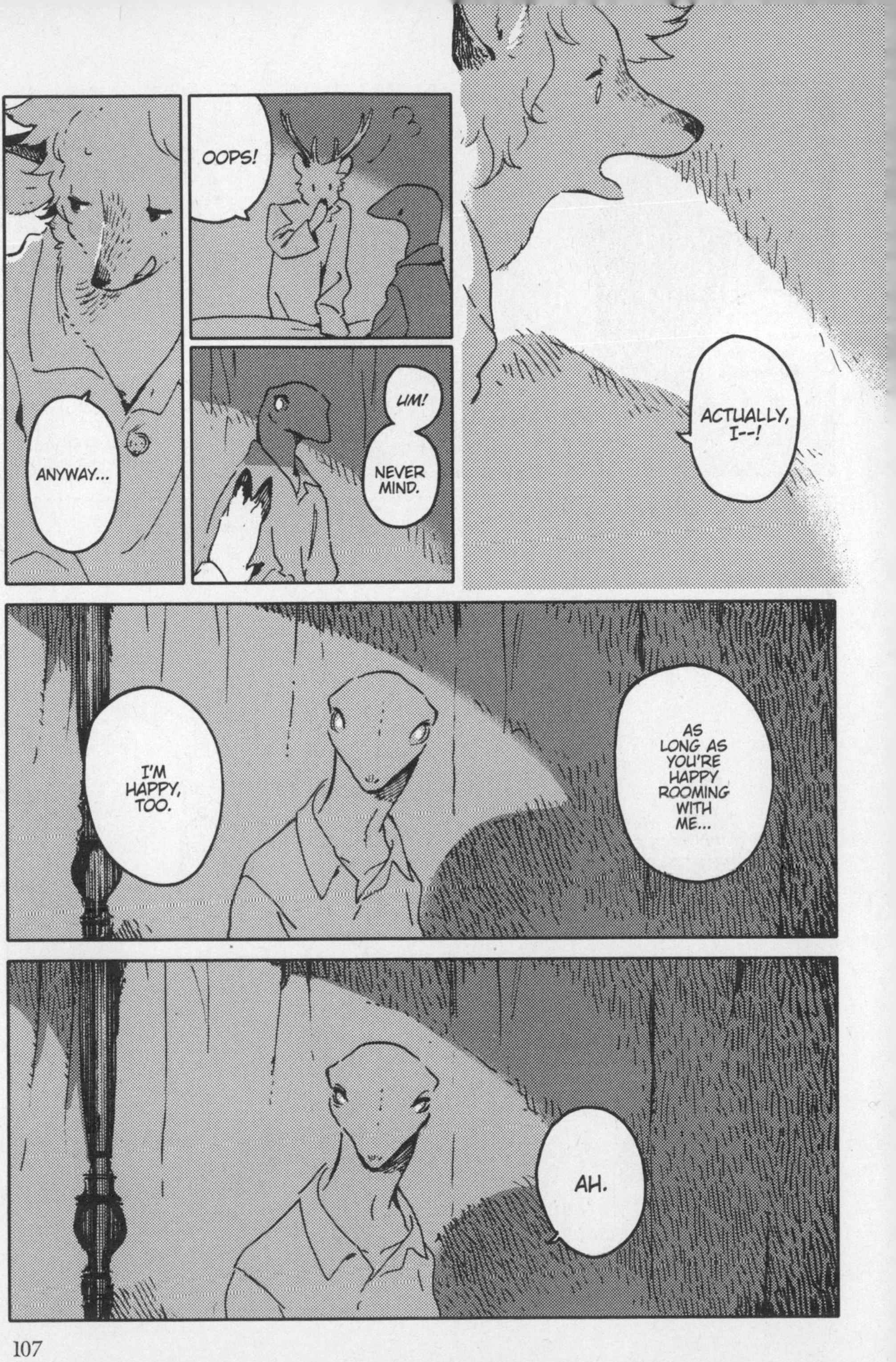
ACTUALLY, I--!
OOPS!
UM!
NEVER MIND.
ANYWAY...
AS LONG AS YOU'RE HAPPY ROOMING WITH ME...
I'M HAPPY, TOO.
AH.

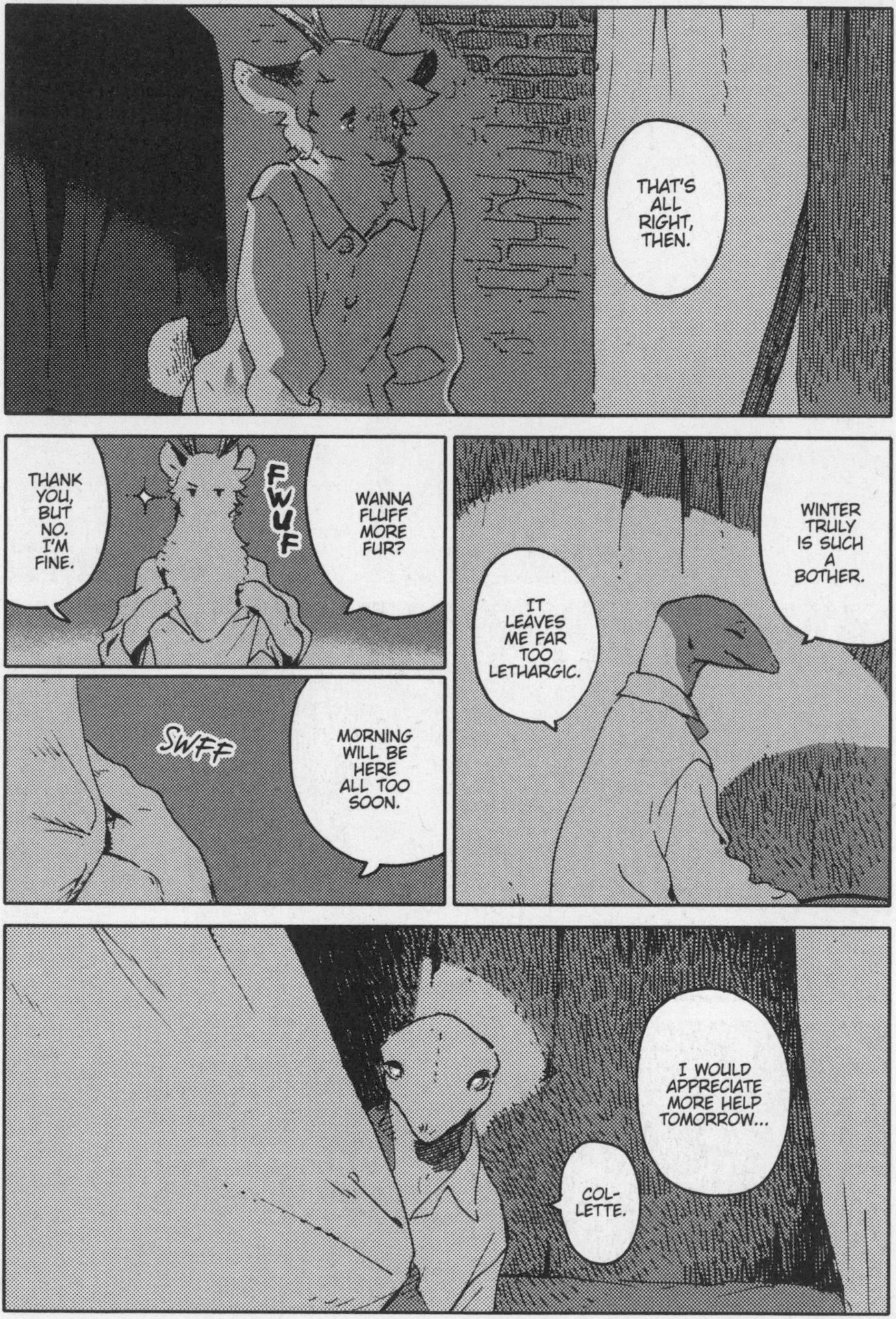
THAT'S ALL RIGHT, THEN.
WINTER TRULY IS SUCH A BOTHER.
IT LEAVES ME FAR TOO LETHARGIC.
WANNA FLUFF MORE FUR?
FWUF
THANK YOU, BUT NO. I'M FINE.
MORNING WILL BE HERE ALL TOO SOON.
SWFF
I WOULD APPRECIATE MORE HELP TOMORROW...
COL-LETTE.

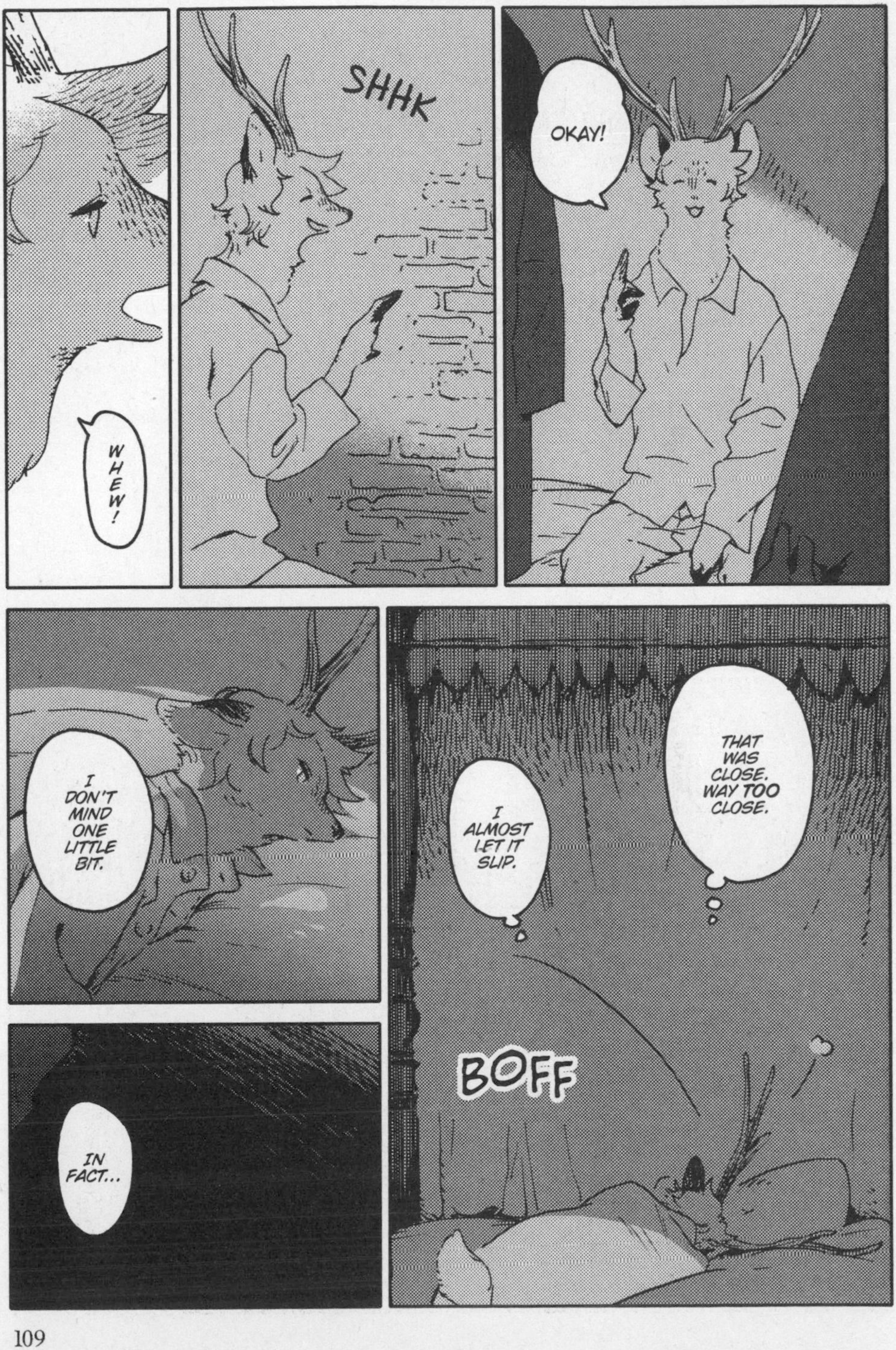
OKAY!
SHHK
WHEW!
THAT WAS CLOSE. WAY TOO CLOSE.
I ALMOST LET IT SLIP.
BOFF
I DON'T MIND ONE LITTLE BIT.
IN FACT...

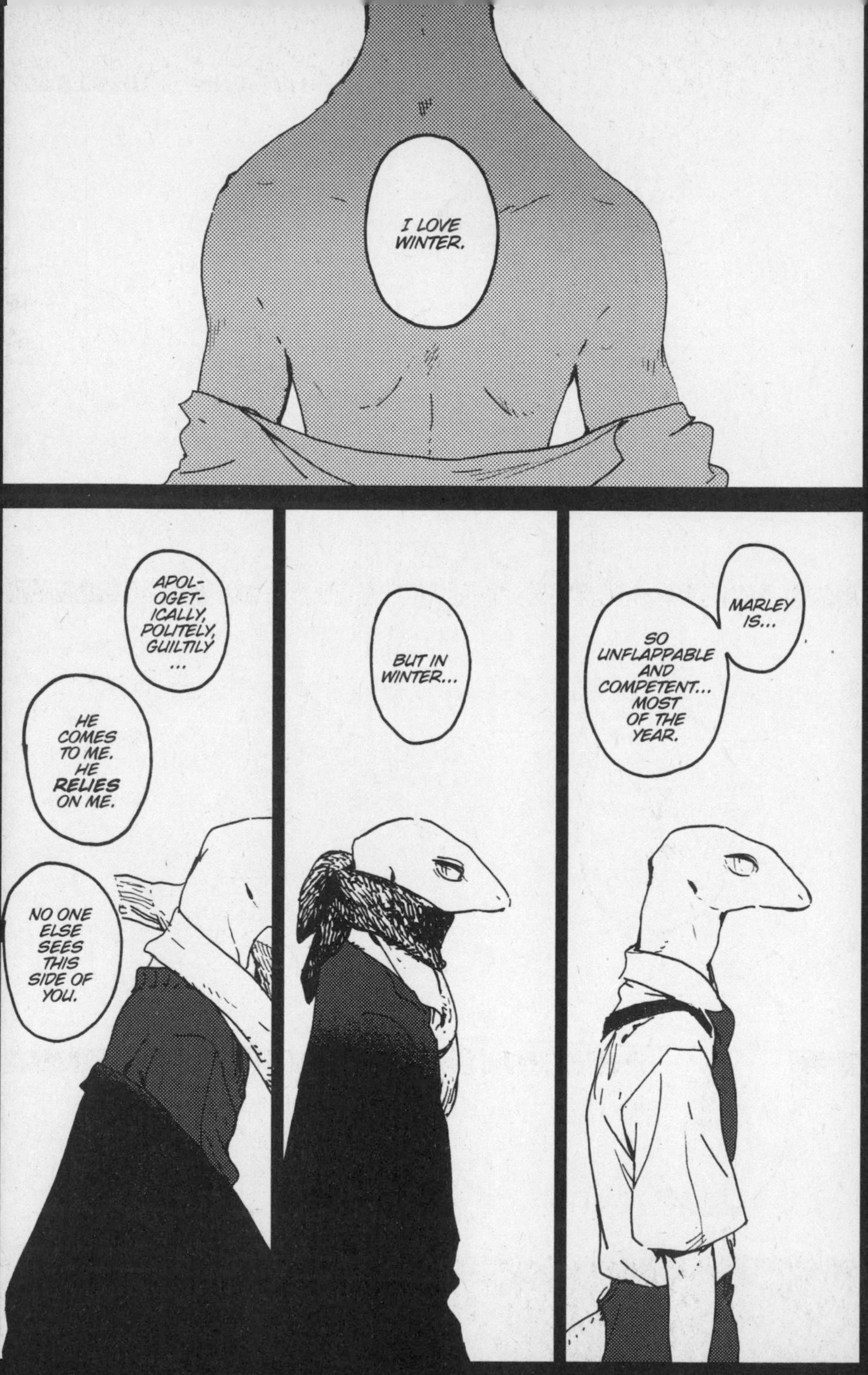
I LOVE WINTER.
MARLEY IS...
SO UNFLAPPABLE AND COMPETENT... MOST OF THE YEAR.
BUT IN WINTER...
APOLOGETICALLY, POLITELY, GUILTILY ...
HE COMES TO ME. HE **RELIES** ON ME.
NO ONE ELSE SEES THIS SIDE OF YOU.

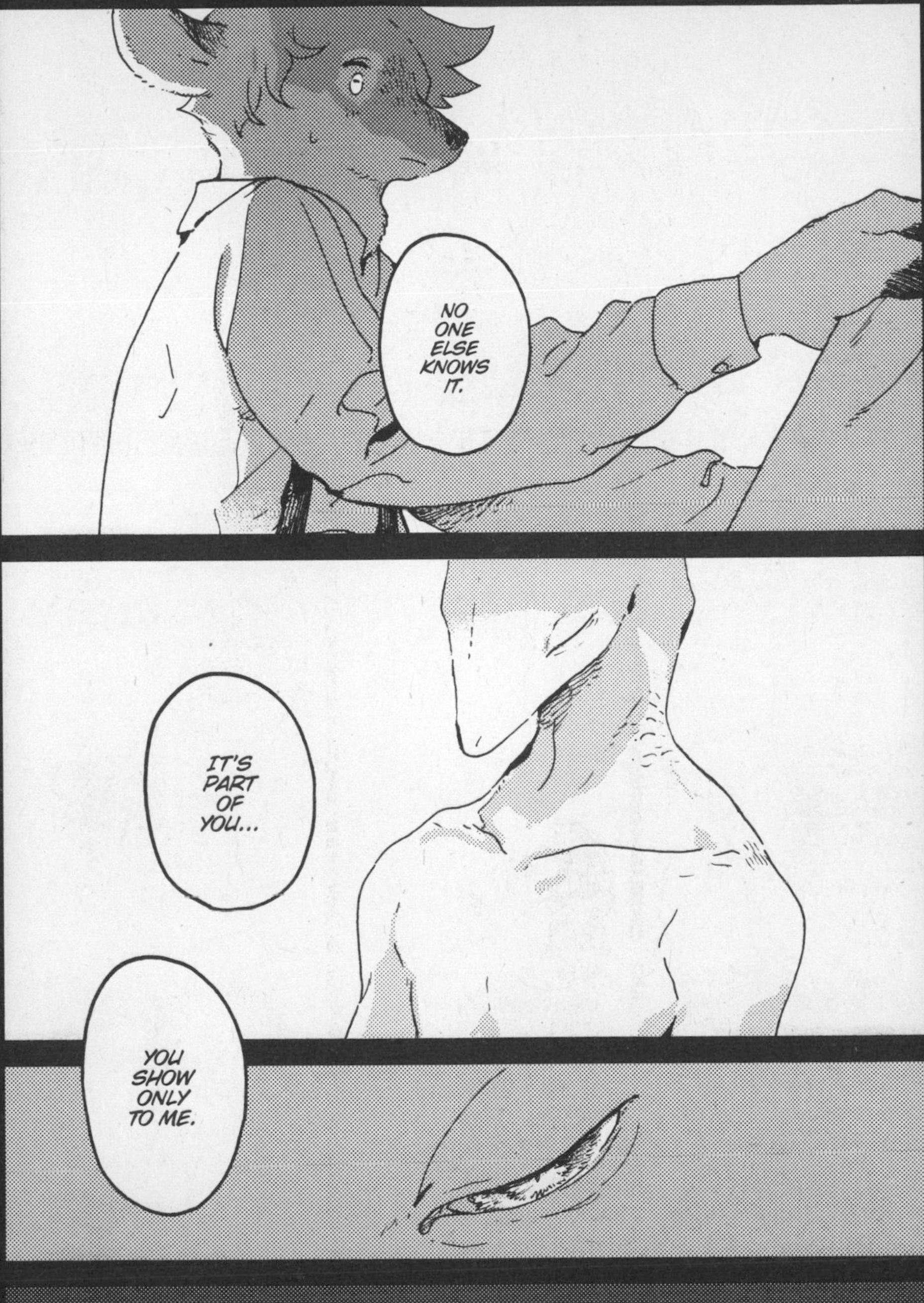
NO ONE ELSE KNOWS IT.
IT'S PART OF YOU...
YOU SHOW ONLY TO ME.

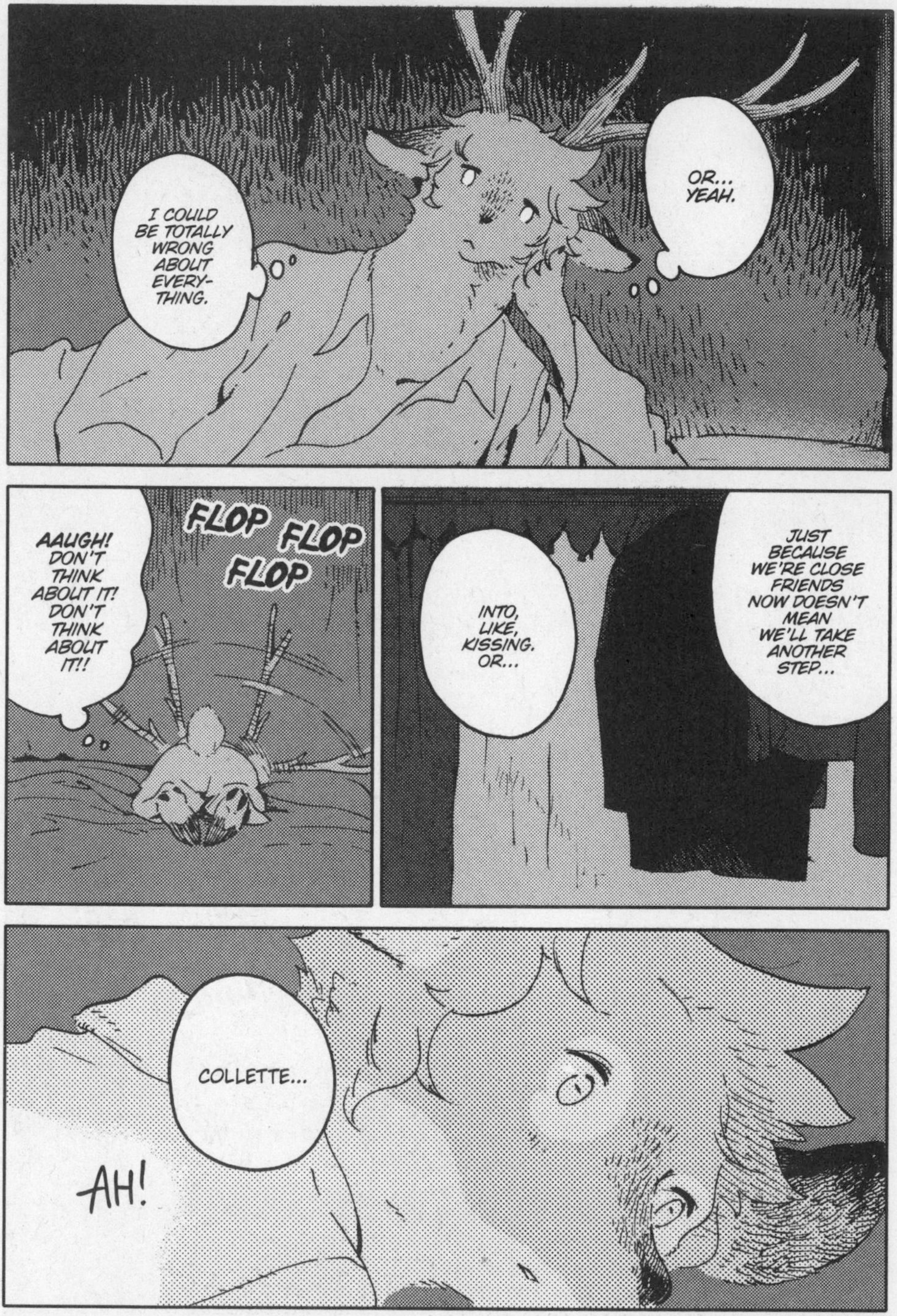
OR... YEAH.
I COULD BE TOTALLY WRONG ABOUT EVERY-THING.
JUST BECAUSE WE'RE CLOSE FRIENDS NOW DOESN'T MEAN WE'LL TAKE ANOTHER STEP...
INTO, LIKE, KISSING. OR...
FLOP FLOP FLOP
AAUGH! DON'T THINK ABOUT IT! DON'T THINK ABOUT IT!!
COLLETTE...
AH!

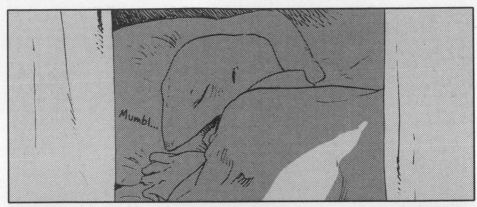

Mumbl...
TALKING IN HIS SLEEP...
AA-AAH! AAAA-AAH!!
FLAIL
FLAIL
FLAIL
I'VE GOTTA STOP...! I'VE GOT TO!
I CAN'T GET ALL BEWITCHED BY THAT SPECIAL WHATEVER-IT-IS REPTILES HAVE!
UGH... THIS IS ALL SO CONFUSING.

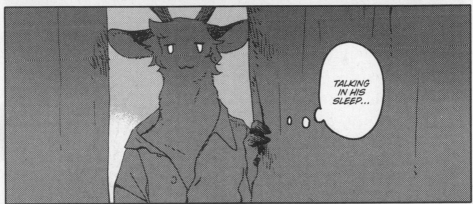

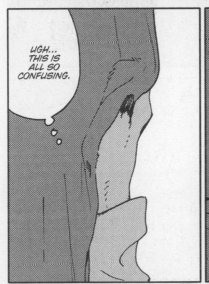

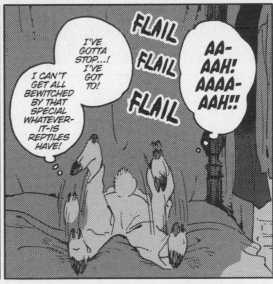

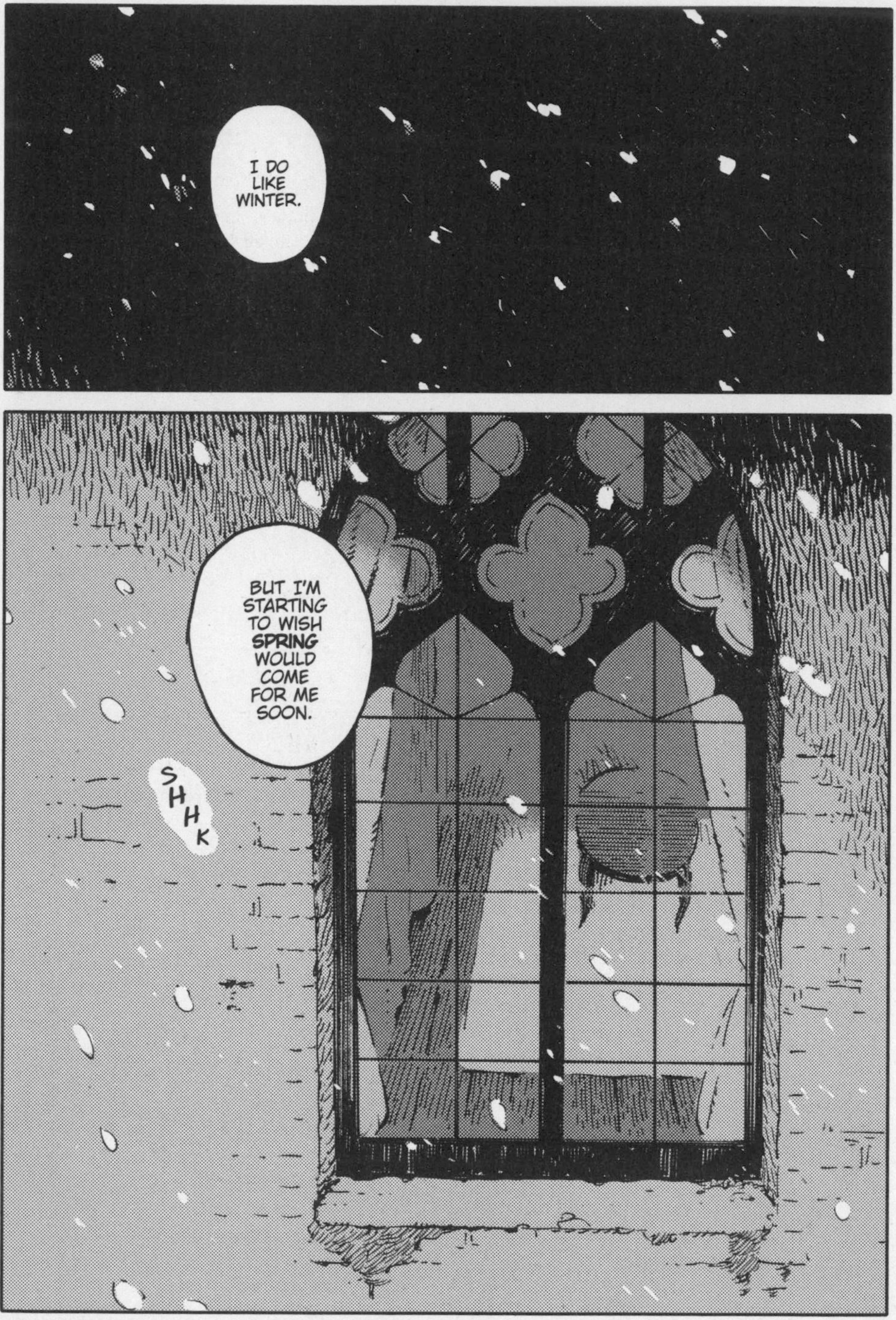
I DO LIKE WINTER.
BUT I'M STARTING TO WISH **SPRING** WOULD COME FOR ME SOON.
SHHK

◆ END ◆

LIZARD

Plestiodon

Squamata | Scincidae *Plestiodon*

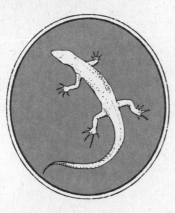

Flat elongated bodies, long tails, and wedge-shaped heads are all standard physical traits for lizards. Most have simple ear holes instead of fully developed external ears. Burrowing species have special transparent eyelids that allow them to see while digging underground. Other species have the ability to shed their tails, which are often brightly colored and will keep wiggling to draw predators' attention away from the lizard itself.

As they're cold-blooded, lizards are incapable of regulating their body heat. They often spend the daylight hours sunbathing to stay warm.

RED DEER

Cervus elaphus

Artiodactyla | Cervidae *C. elaphus*

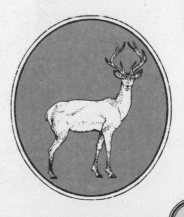

Red deer are a species group. They have large antlers, which they shed and regrow every year. They walk on what are effectively their third and fourth toes, which have evolved into cloven hooves. At least once a year, they shed and regrow their fur coats. While adults' coats are a solid color, the young have spotted coats for camouflage. Only the males, called stags, grow antlers. (However, male and female reindeer are both capable of growing antlers.) Come rutting season, stags fight each other for dominance, with the winner collecting a harem of females with which he will breed. Outside of that season, they are generally solitary.

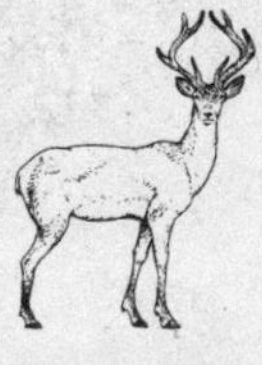

The Wize Wize Beasts
of the Wizarding Wizdoms
by Nagabe

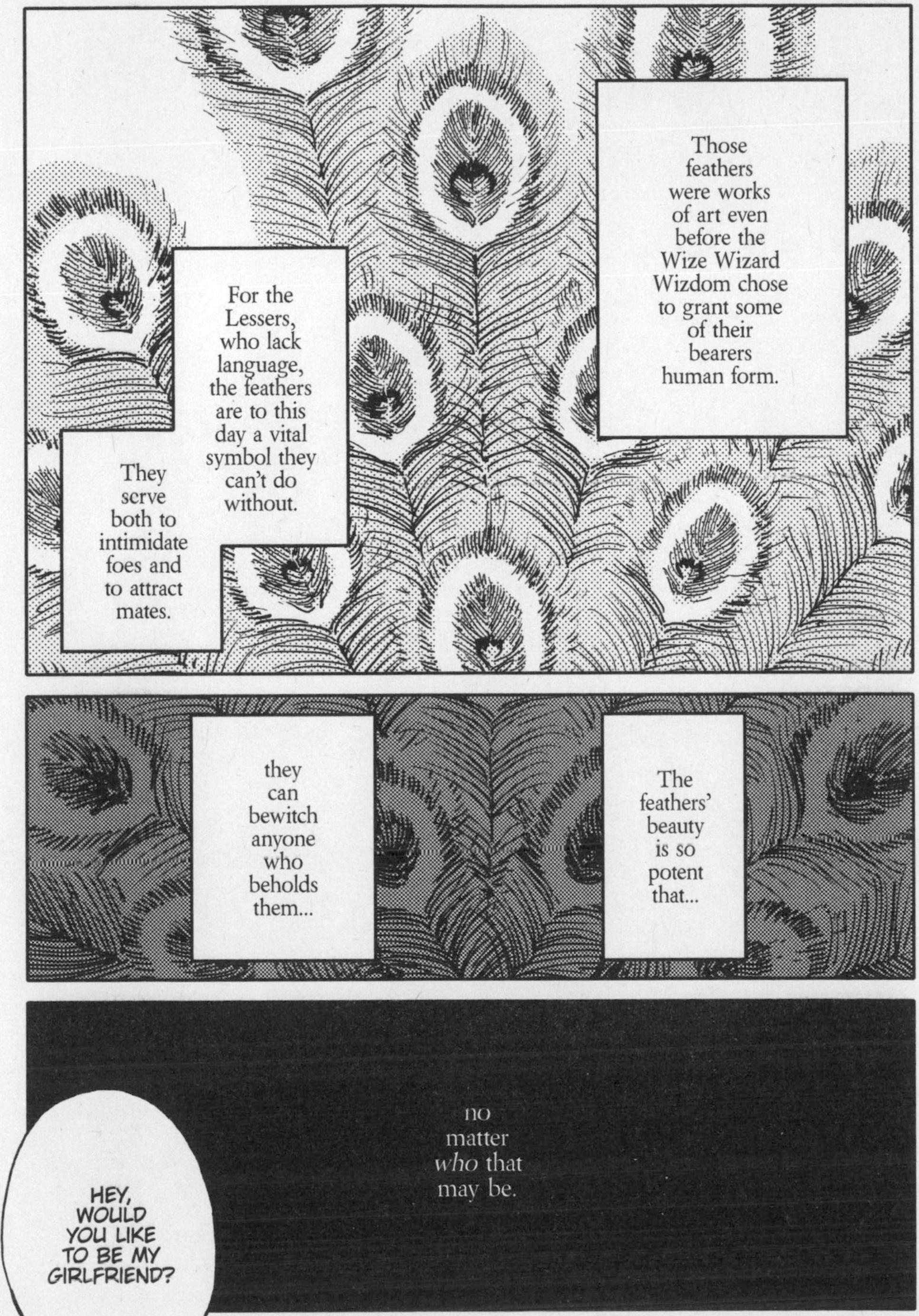
Those feathers were works of art even before the Wize Wizard Wizdom chose to grant some of their bearers human form.
For the Lessers, who lack language, the feathers are to this day a vital symbol they can't do without.
They serve both to intimidate foes and to attract mates.
The feathers' beauty is so potent that...
they can bewitch anyone who beholds them...
no matter *who* that may be.
HEY, WOULD YOU LIKE TO BE MY GIRLFRIEND?

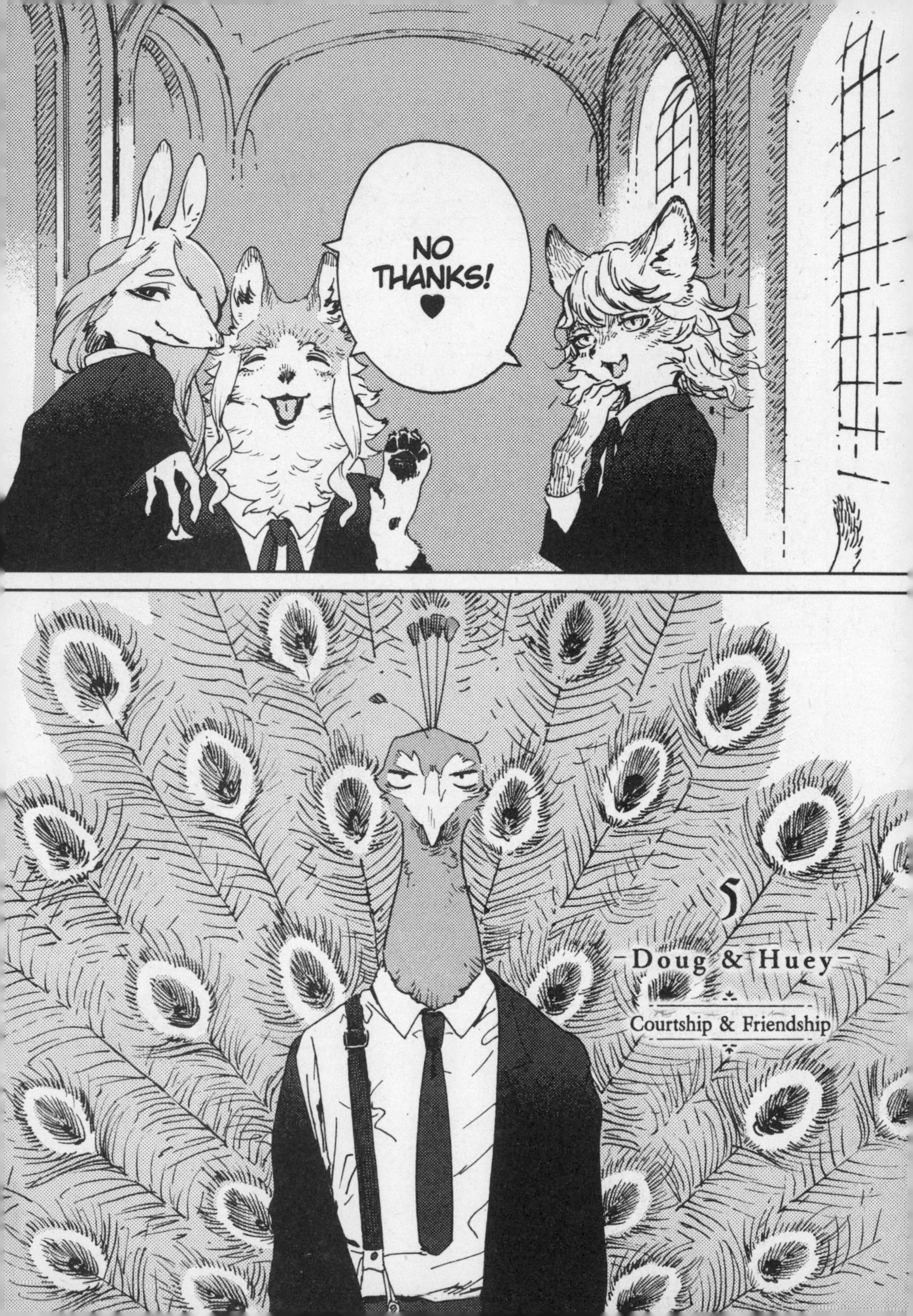
NO THANKS! ♥
5
Doug & Huey
Courtship & Friendship

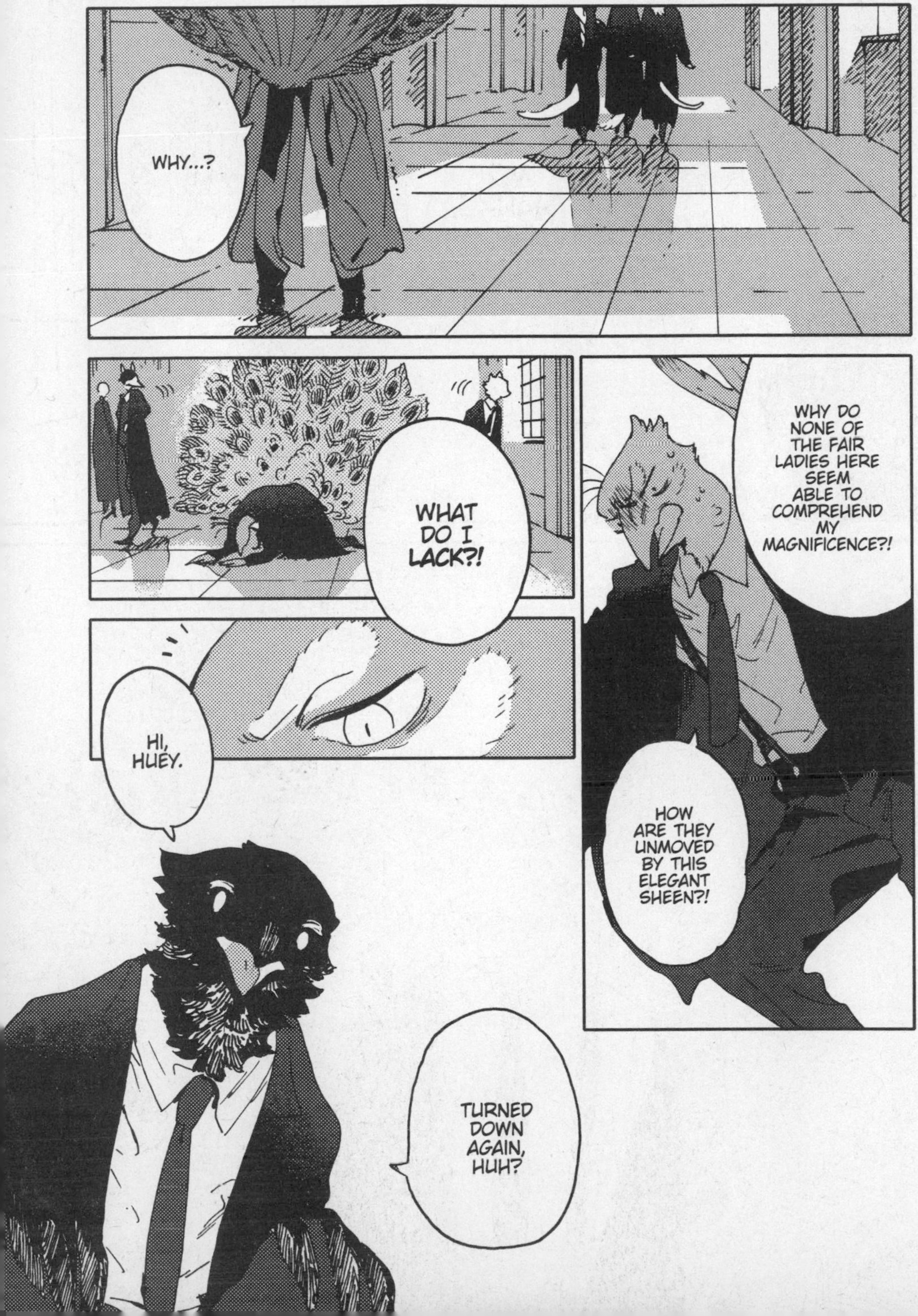
WHY...?
WHY DO NONE OF THE FAIR LADIES HERE SEEM ABLE TO COMPREHEND MY MAGNIFICENCE?!
HOW ARE THEY UNMOVED BY THIS ELEGANT SHEEN?!
WHAT DO I LACK?!
HI, HUEY.
TURNED DOWN AGAIN, HUH?

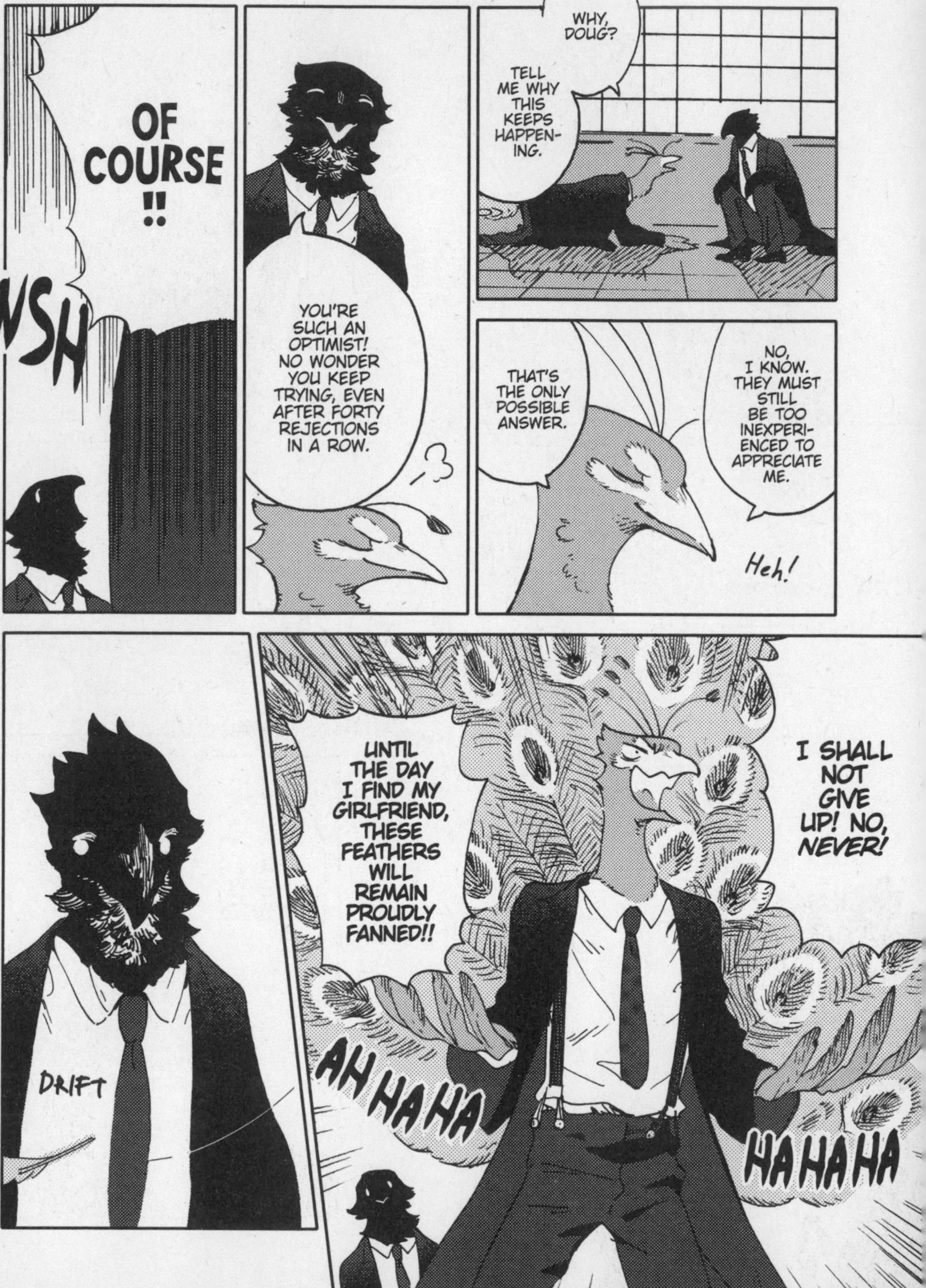
WHY, DOUG?
TELL ME WHY THIS KEEPS HAPPENING.
NO, I KNOW. THEY MUST STILL BE TOO INEXPERIENCED TO APPRECIATE ME.
THAT'S THE ONLY POSSIBLE ANSWER.
Heh!
YOU'RE SUCH AN OPTIMIST! NO WONDER YOU KEEP TRYING, EVEN AFTER FORTY REJECTIONS IN A ROW.
OF COURSE!!
WSH
I SHALL NOT GIVE UP! NO, NEVER!
UNTIL THE DAY I FIND MY GIRLFRIEND, THESE FEATHERS WILL REMAIN PROUDLY FANNED!!
HA HA HA
AH HA HA
DRIFT

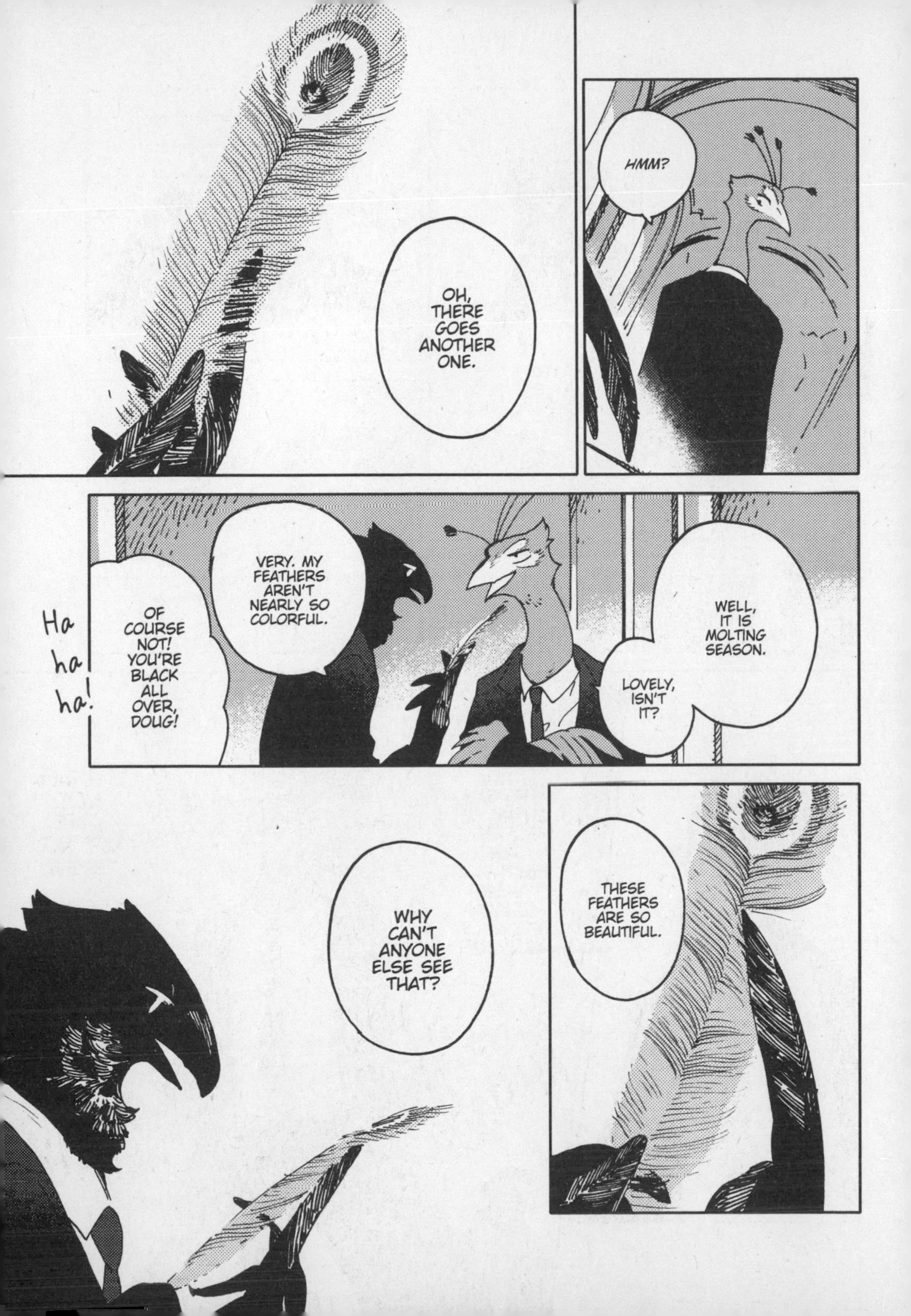
HMM?
OH, THERE GOES ANOTHER ONE.
WELL, IT IS MOLTING SEASON.
LOVELY, ISN'T IT?
VERY. MY FEATHERS AREN'T NEARLY SO COLORFUL.
OF COURSE NOT! YOU'RE BLACK ALL OVER, DOUG!
Ha ha ha!
THESE FEATHERS ARE SO BEAUTIFUL.
WHY CAN'T ANYONE ELSE SEE THAT?

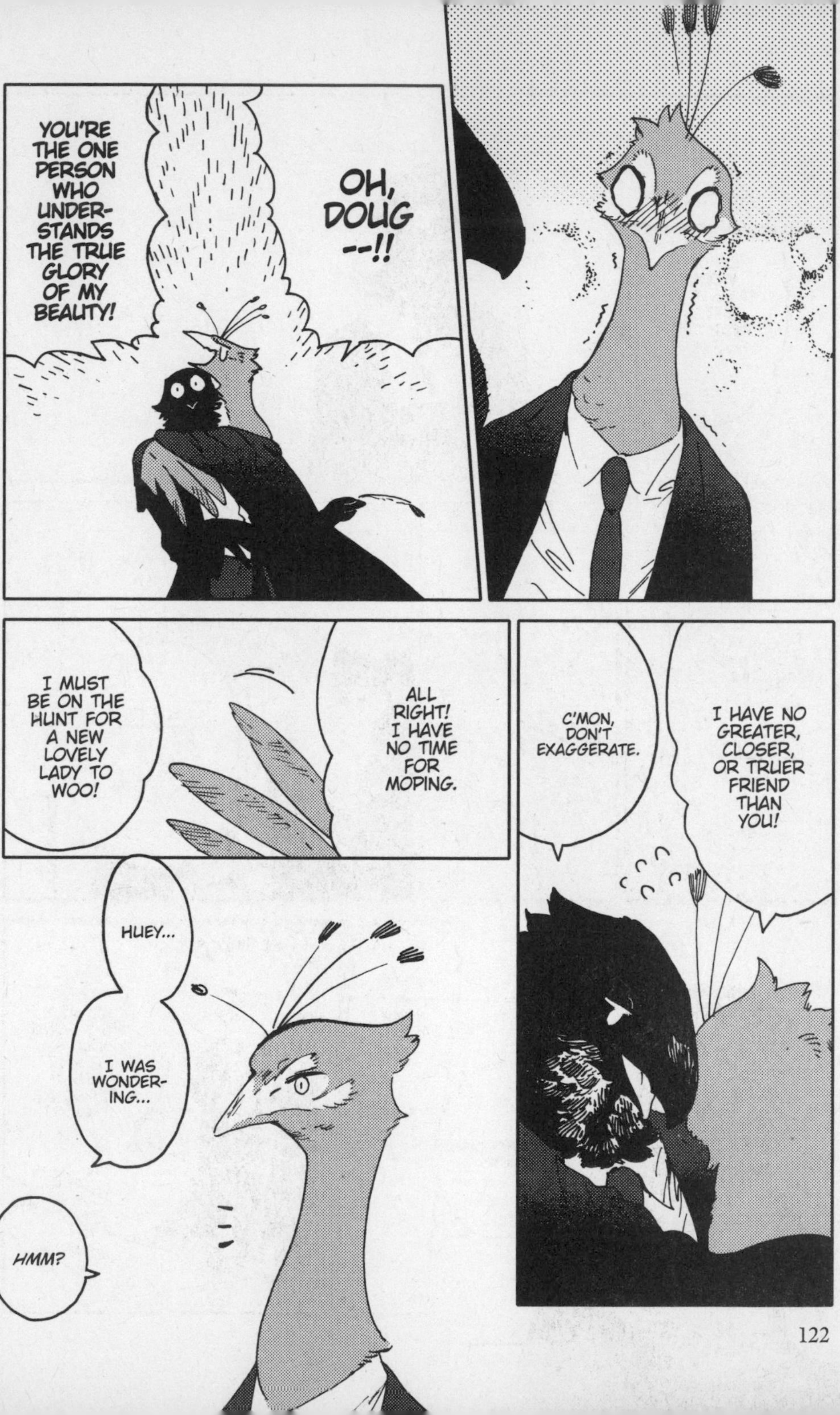

OH, DOUG--!!
YOU'RE THE ONE PERSON WHO UNDER-STANDS THE TRUE GLORY OF MY BEAUTY!
I HAVE NO GREATER, CLOSER, OR TRUER FRIEND THAN YOU!
C'MON, DON'T EXAGGERATE.
ALL RIGHT! I HAVE NO TIME FOR MOPING.
I MUST BE ON THE HUNT FOR A NEW LOVELY LADY TO WOO!
HUEY...
I WAS WONDER-ING...
HMM?

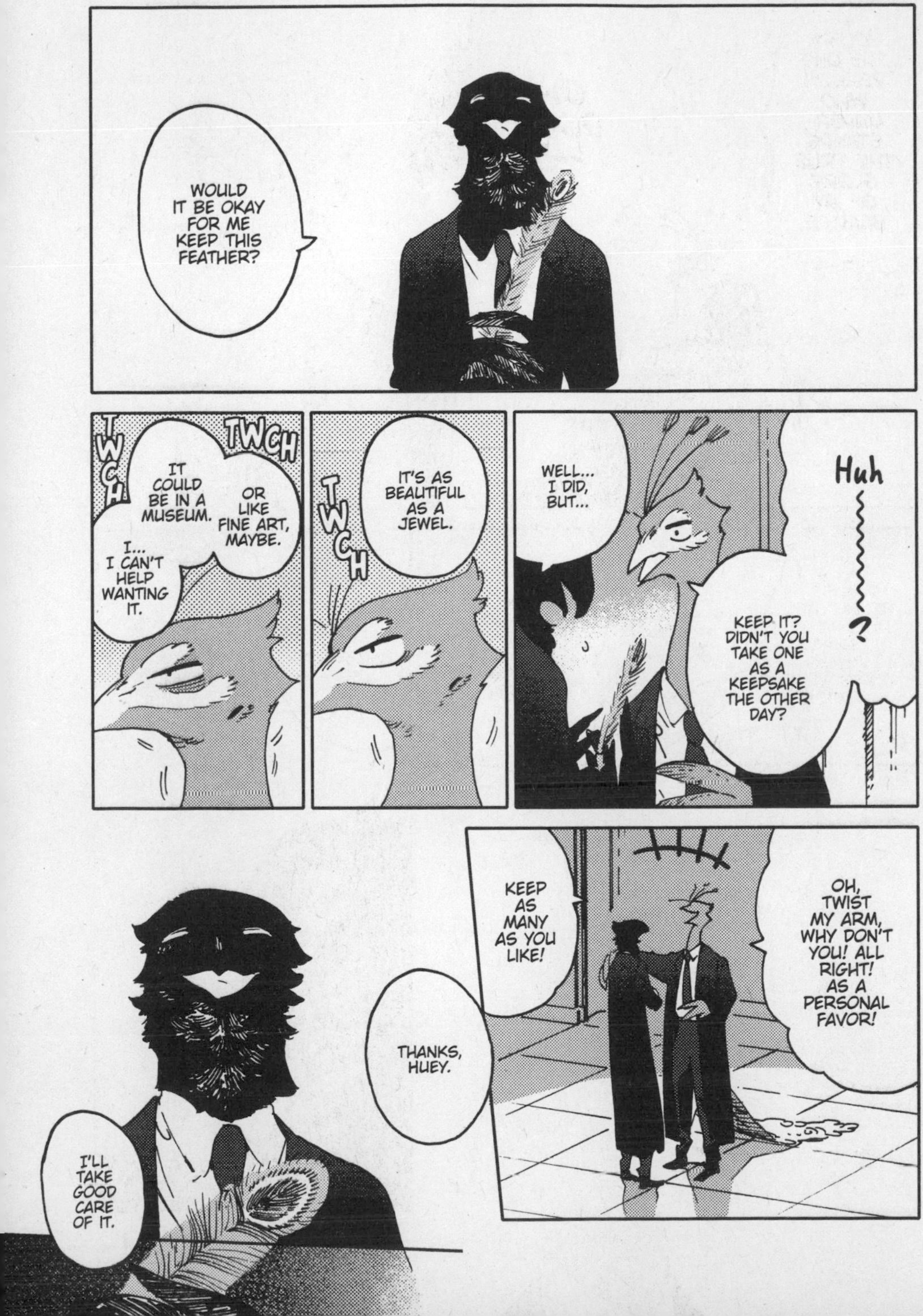
WOULD IT BE OKAY FOR ME KEEP THIS FEATHER?
Huh ~ ?
KEEP IT? DIDN'T YOU TAKE ONE AS A KEEPSAKE THE OTHER DAY?
WELL... I DID, BUT...
TWCH
IT'S AS BEAUTIFUL AS A JEWEL.
TWCH
TWCH
IT COULD BE IN A MUSEUM.
OR LIKE FINE ART, MAYBE.
I... I CAN'T HELP WANTING IT.
OH, TWIST MY ARM, WHY DON'T YOU! ALL RIGHT! AS A PERSONAL FAVOR!
KEEP AS MANY AS YOU LIKE!
THANKS, HUEY.
I'LL TAKE GOOD CARE OF IT.

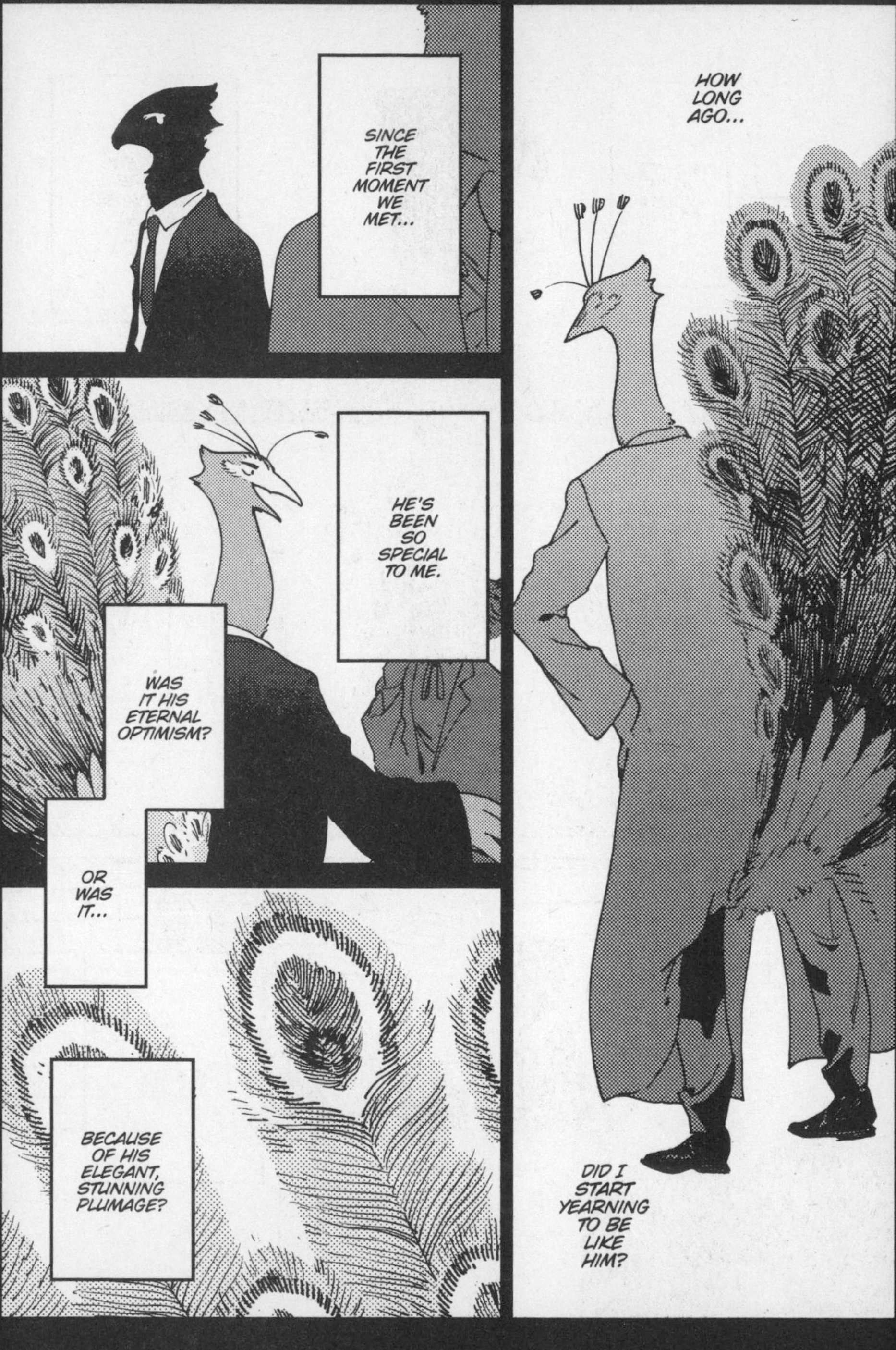
HOW LONG AGO...
DID I START YEARNING TO BE LIKE HIM?
SINCE THE FIRST MOMENT WE MET...
HE'S BEEN SO SPECIAL TO ME.
WAS IT HIS ETERNAL OPTIMISM?
OR WAS IT...
BECAUSE OF HIS ELEGANT, STUNNING PLUMAGE?

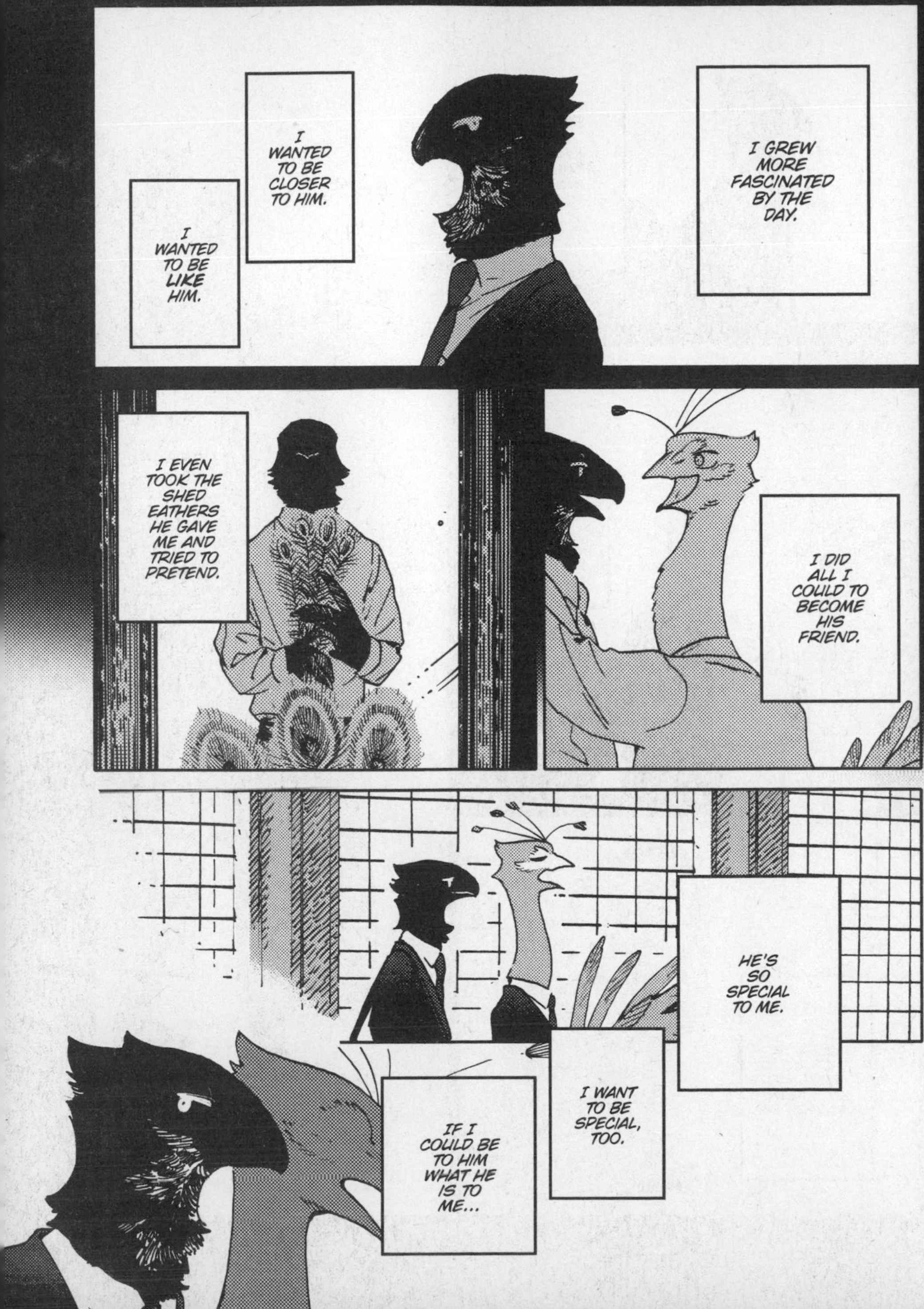
I GREW MORE FASCINATED BY THE DAY.
I WANTED TO BE CLOSER TO HIM.
I WANTED TO BE LIKE HIM.
I DID ALL I COULD TO BECOME HIS FRIEND.
I EVEN TOOK THE SHED EATHERS HE GAVE ME AND TRIED TO PRETEND.
HE'S SO SPECIAL TO ME.
I WANT TO BE SPECIAL, TOO.
IF I COULD BE TO HIM WHAT HE IS TO ME...

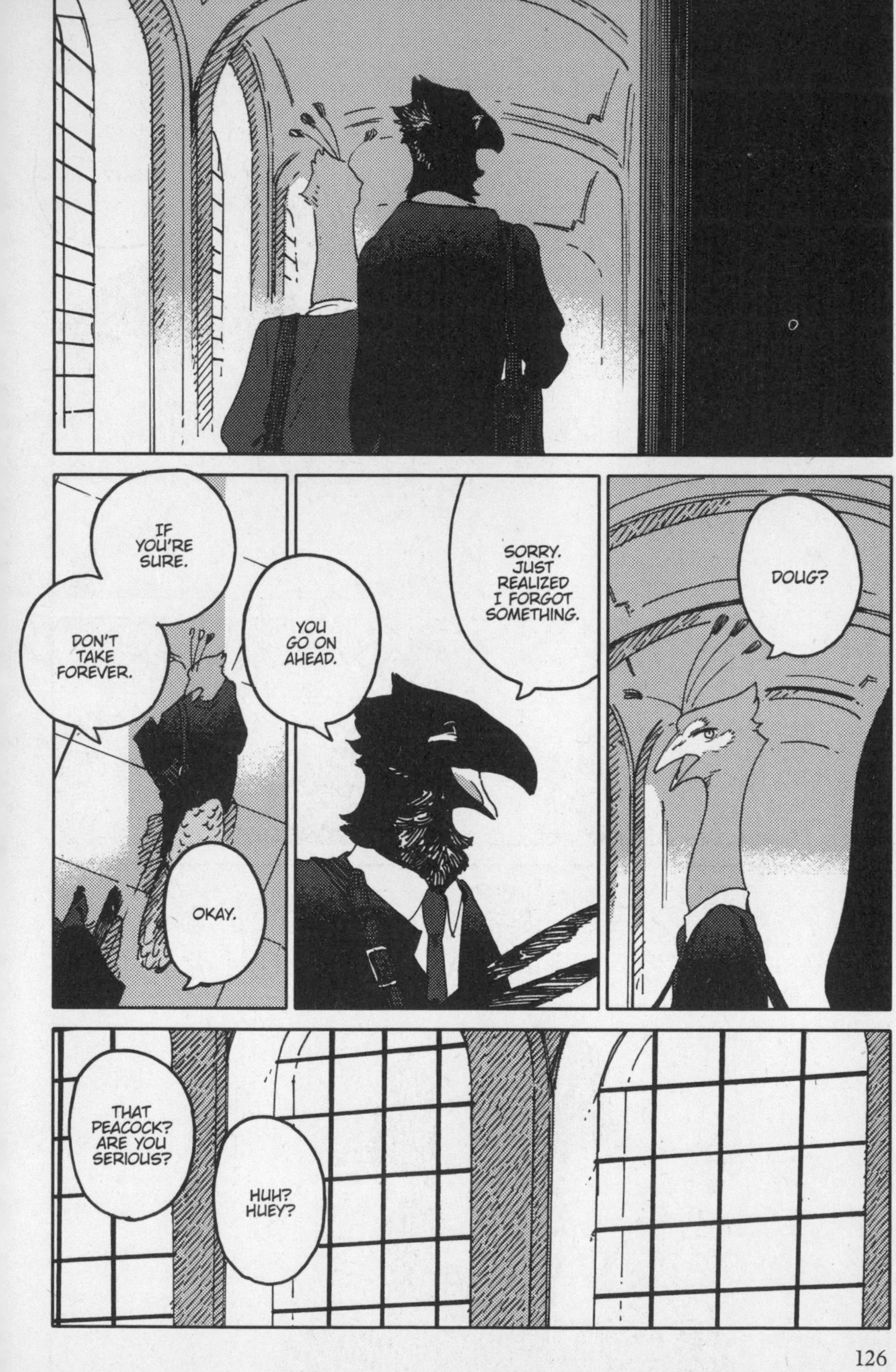
DOUG?
SORRY. JUST REALIZED I FORGOT SOMETHING.
YOU GO ON AHEAD.
IF YOU'RE SURE.
DON'T TAKE FOREVER.
OKAY.
HUH? HUEY?
THAT PEACOCK? ARE YOU SERIOUS?

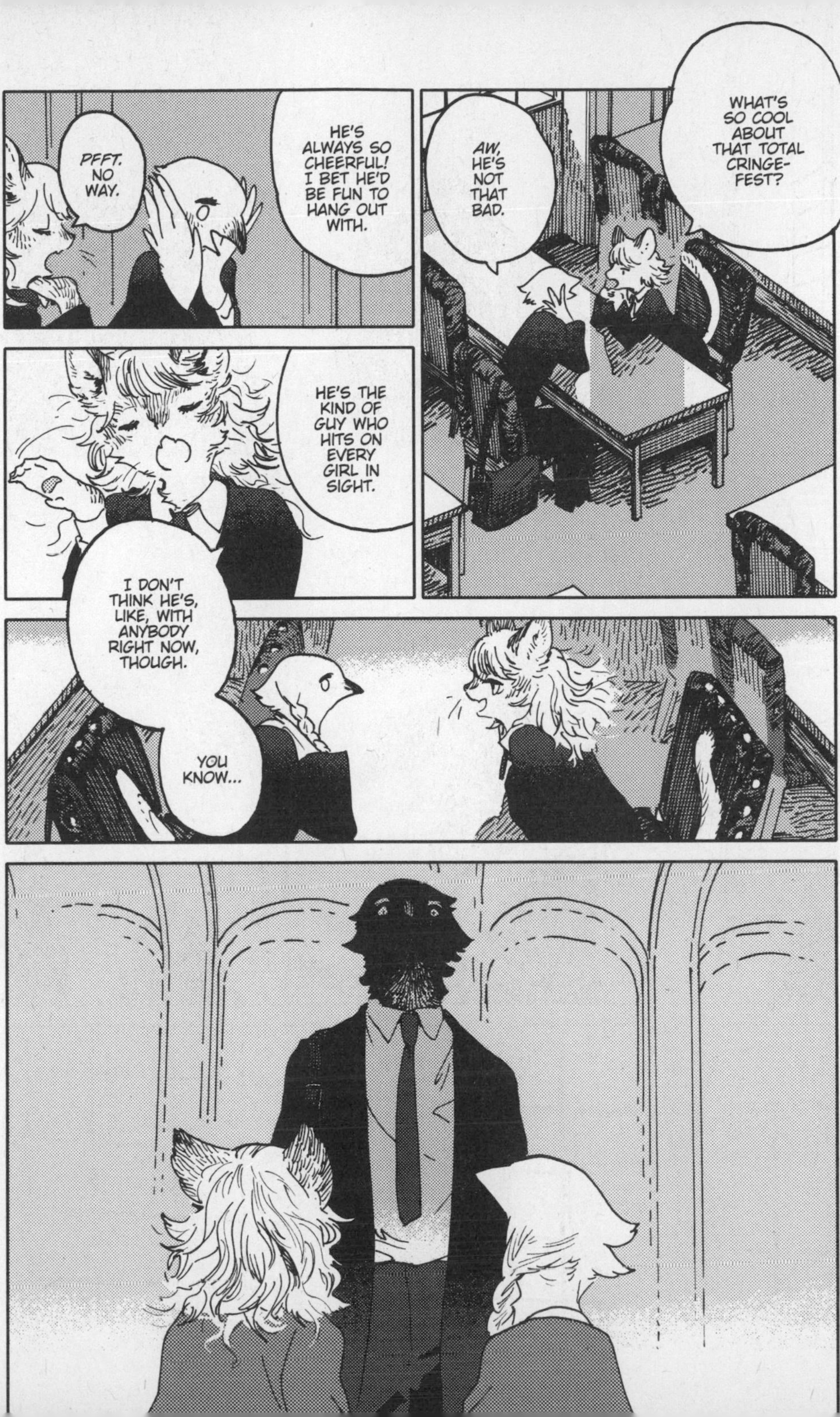
WHAT'S SO COOL ABOUT THAT TOTAL CRINGE-FEST?
AW, HE'S NOT THAT BAD.
HE'S ALWAYS SO CHEERFUL! I BET HE'D BE FUN TO HANG OUT WITH.
PFFT. NO WAY.
HE'S THE KIND OF GUY WHO HITS ON EVERY GIRL IN SIGHT.
I DON'T THINK HE'S, LIKE, WITH ANYBODY RIGHT NOW, THOUGH.
YOU KNOW...

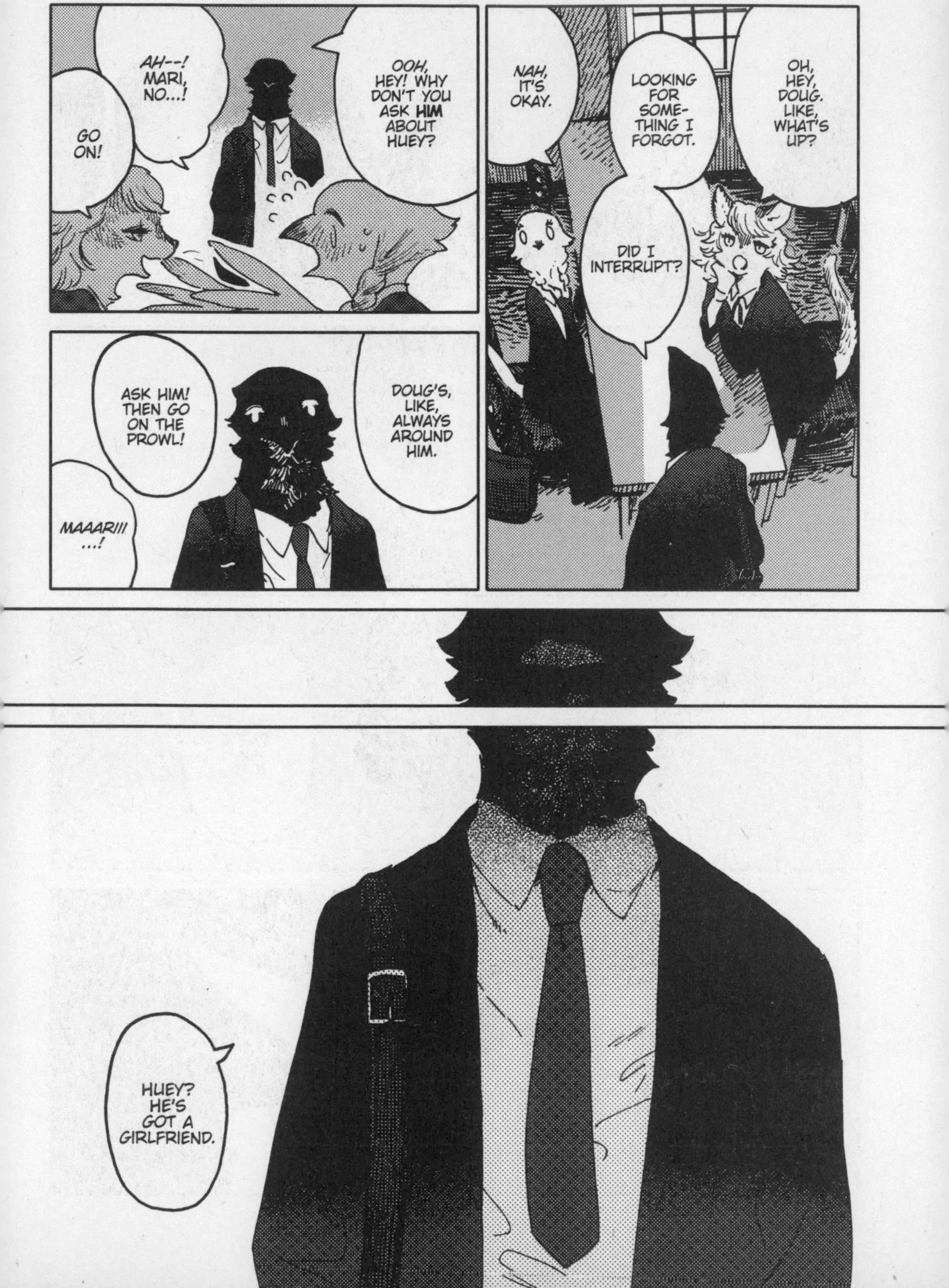
OH, HEY, DOUG. LIKE, WHAT'S UP?
LOOKING FOR SOMETHING I FORGOT.
DID I INTERRUPT?
NAH, IT'S OKAY.
OOH, HEY! WHY DON'T YOU ASK **HIM** ABOUT HUEY?
AH--! MARI, NO...!
GO ON!
DOUG'S, LIKE, ALWAYS AROUND HIM.
ASK HIM! THEN GO ON THE PROWL!
MAAARIII ...!
HUEY? HE'S GOT A GIRLFRIEND.

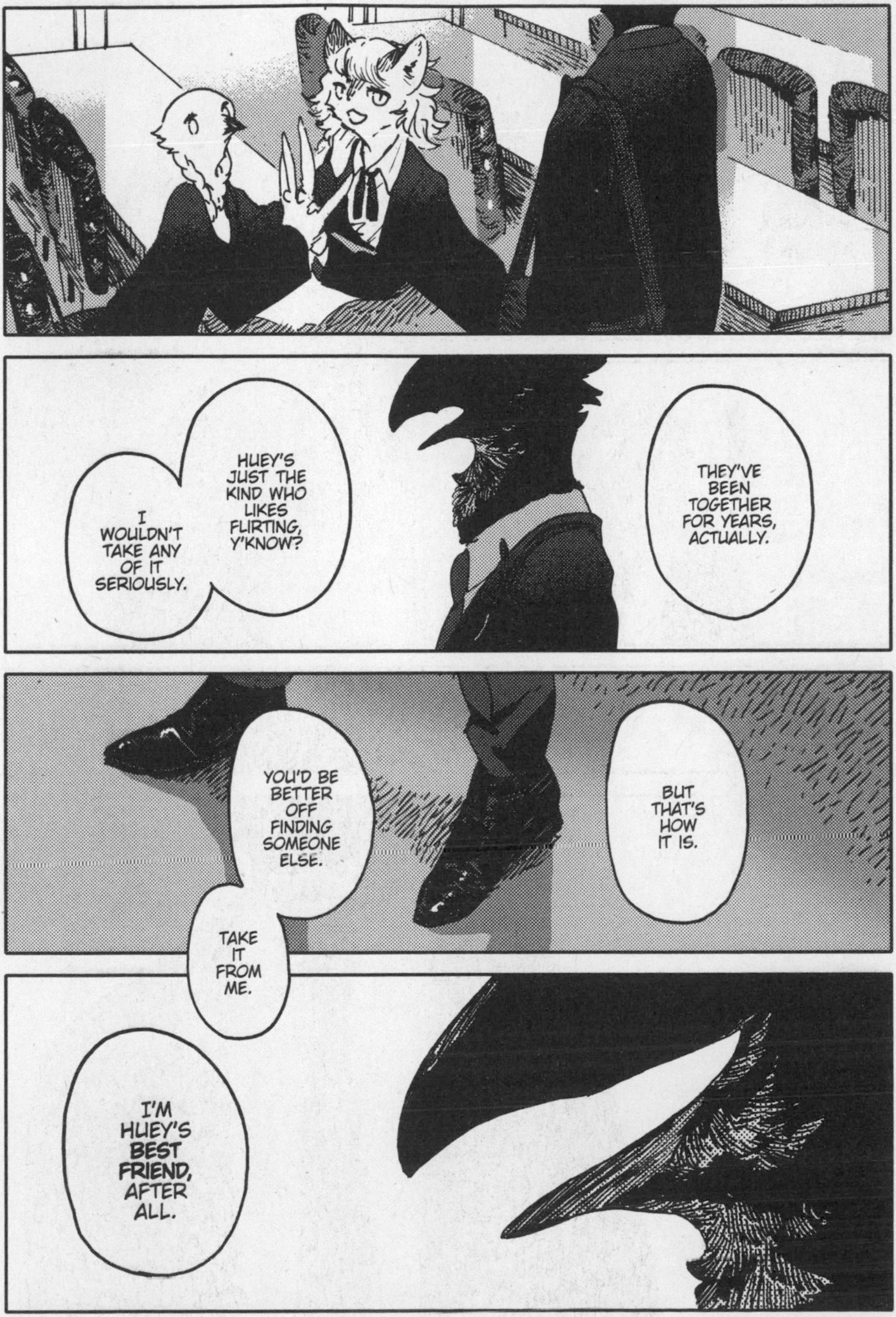
THEY'VE BEEN TOGETHER FOR YEARS, ACTUALLY.
HUEY'S JUST THE KIND WHO LIKES FLIRTING, Y'KNOW?
I WOULDN'T TAKE ANY OF IT SERIOUSLY.
BUT THAT'S HOW IT IS.
YOU'D BE BETTER OFF FINDING SOMEONE ELSE.
TAKE IT FROM ME.
I'M HUEY'S **BEST FRIEND,** AFTER ALL.

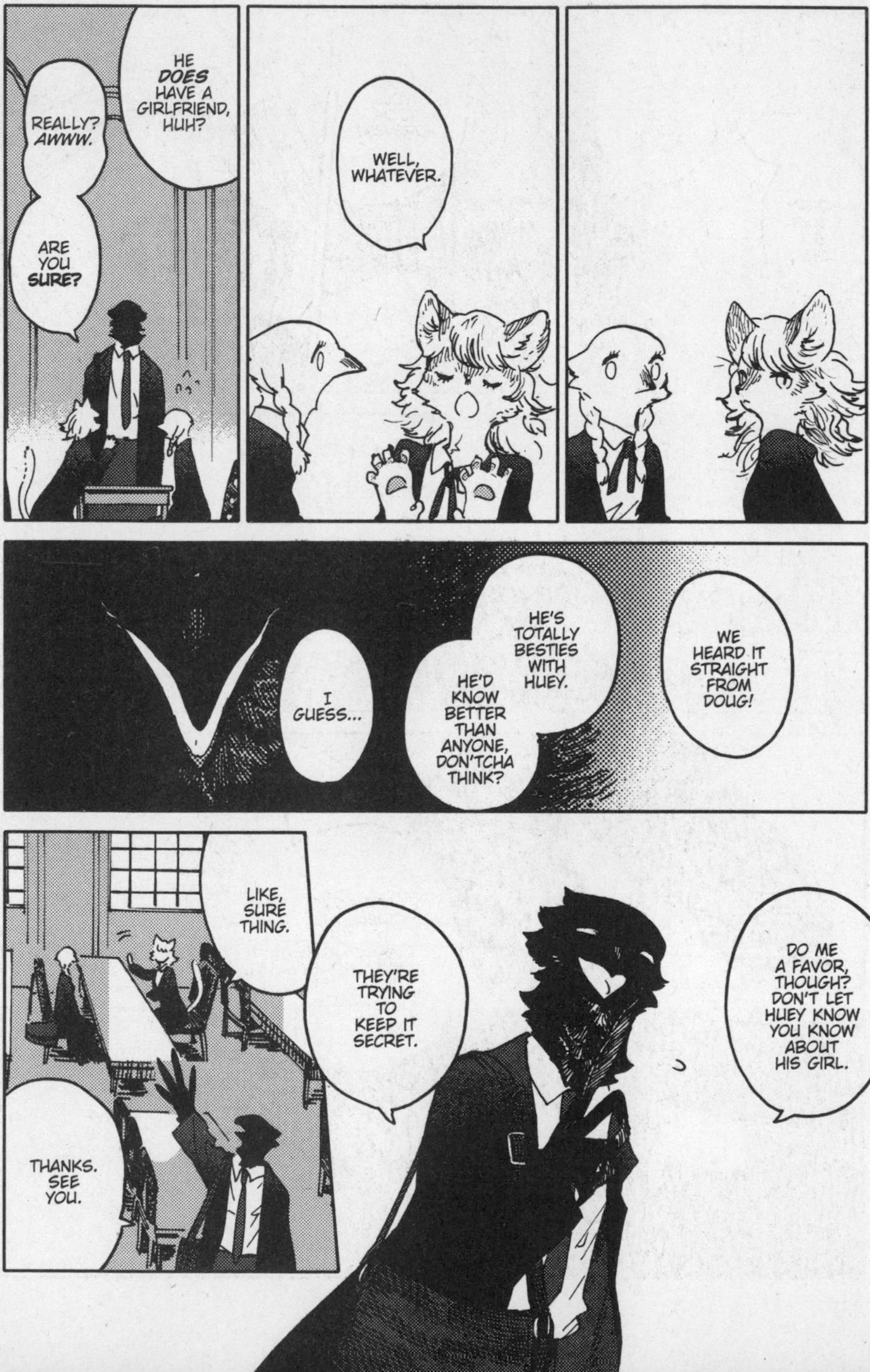
WELL, WHATEVER.
HE DOES HAVE A GIRLFRIEND, HUH?
REALLY? AWWW.
ARE YOU SURE?
WE HEARD IT STRAIGHT FROM DOUG!
HE'S TOTALLY BESTIES WITH HUEY.
HE'D KNOW BETTER THAN ANYONE, DON'TCHA THINK?
I GUESS...
DO ME A FAVOR, THOUGH? DON'T LET HUEY KNOW YOU KNOW ABOUT HIS GIRL.
THEY'RE TRYING TO KEEP IT SECRET.
LIKE, SURE THING.
THANKS. SEE YOU.

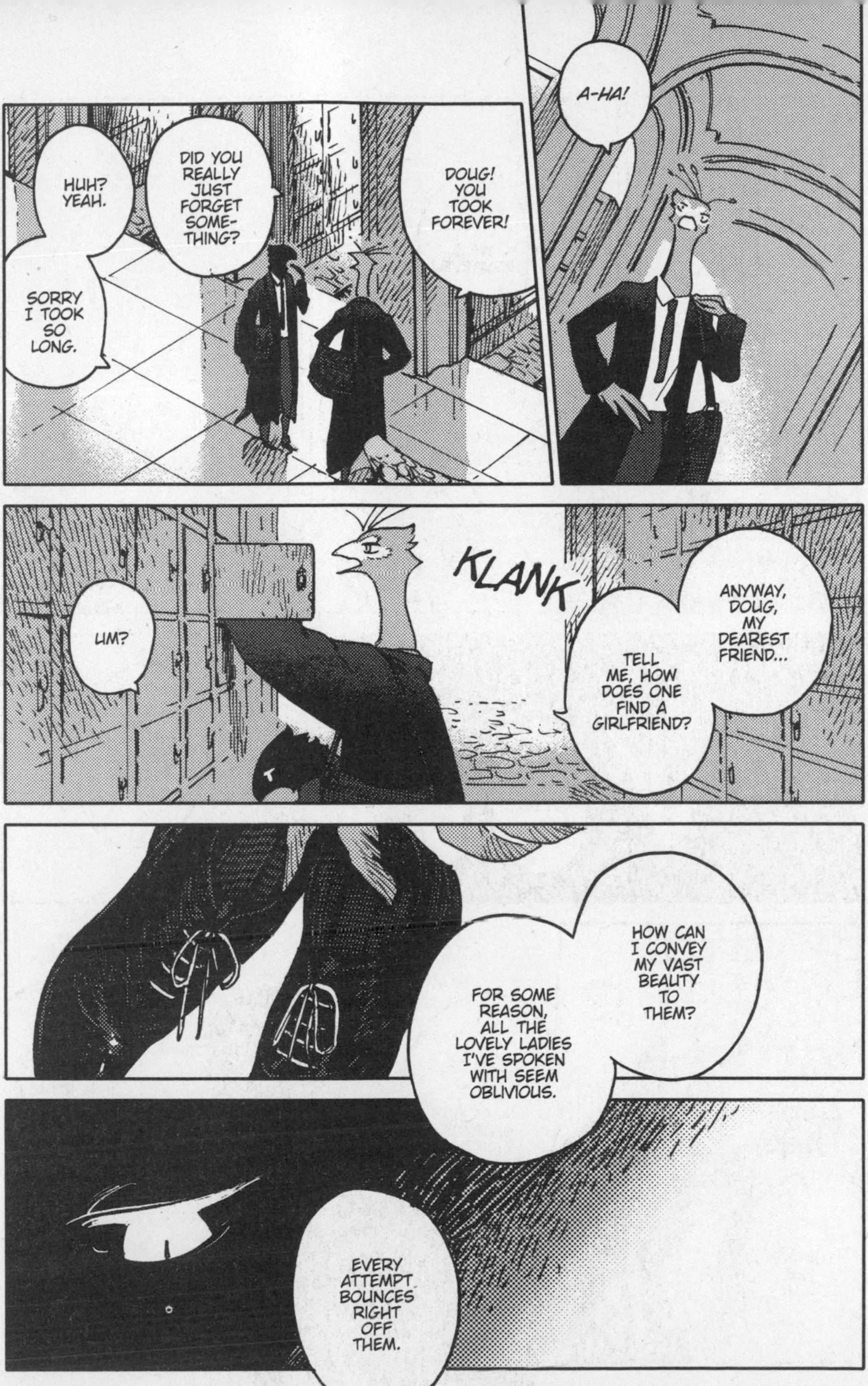
A-HA!
DOUG! YOU TOOK FOREVER!
DID YOU REALLY JUST FORGET SOME-THING?
HUH? YEAH.
SORRY I TOOK SO LONG.
KLANK
ANYWAY, DOUG, MY DEAREST FRIEND...
TELL ME, HOW DOES ONE FIND A GIRLFRIEND?
UM?
HOW CAN I CONVEY MY VAST BEAUTY TO THEM?
FOR SOME REASON, ALL THE LOVELY LADIES I'VE SPOKEN WITH SEEM OBLIVIOUS.
EVERY ATTEMPT BOUNCES RIGHT OFF THEM.

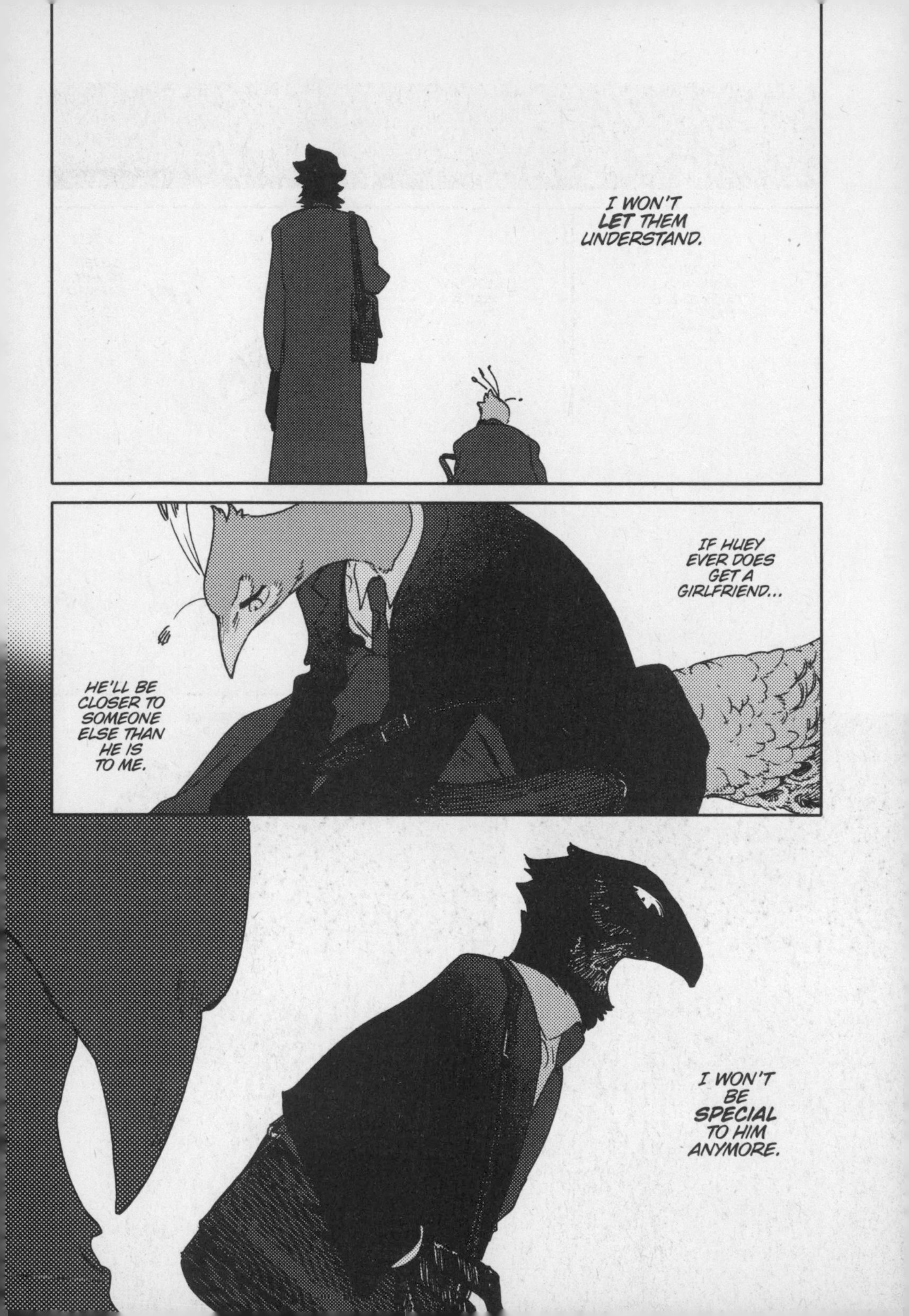
I WON'T LET THEM UNDERSTAND.
IF HUEY EVER DOES GET A GIRLFRIEND...
HE'LL BE CLOSER TO SOMEONE ELSE THAN HE IS TO ME.
I WON'T BE SPECIAL TO HIM ANYMORE.

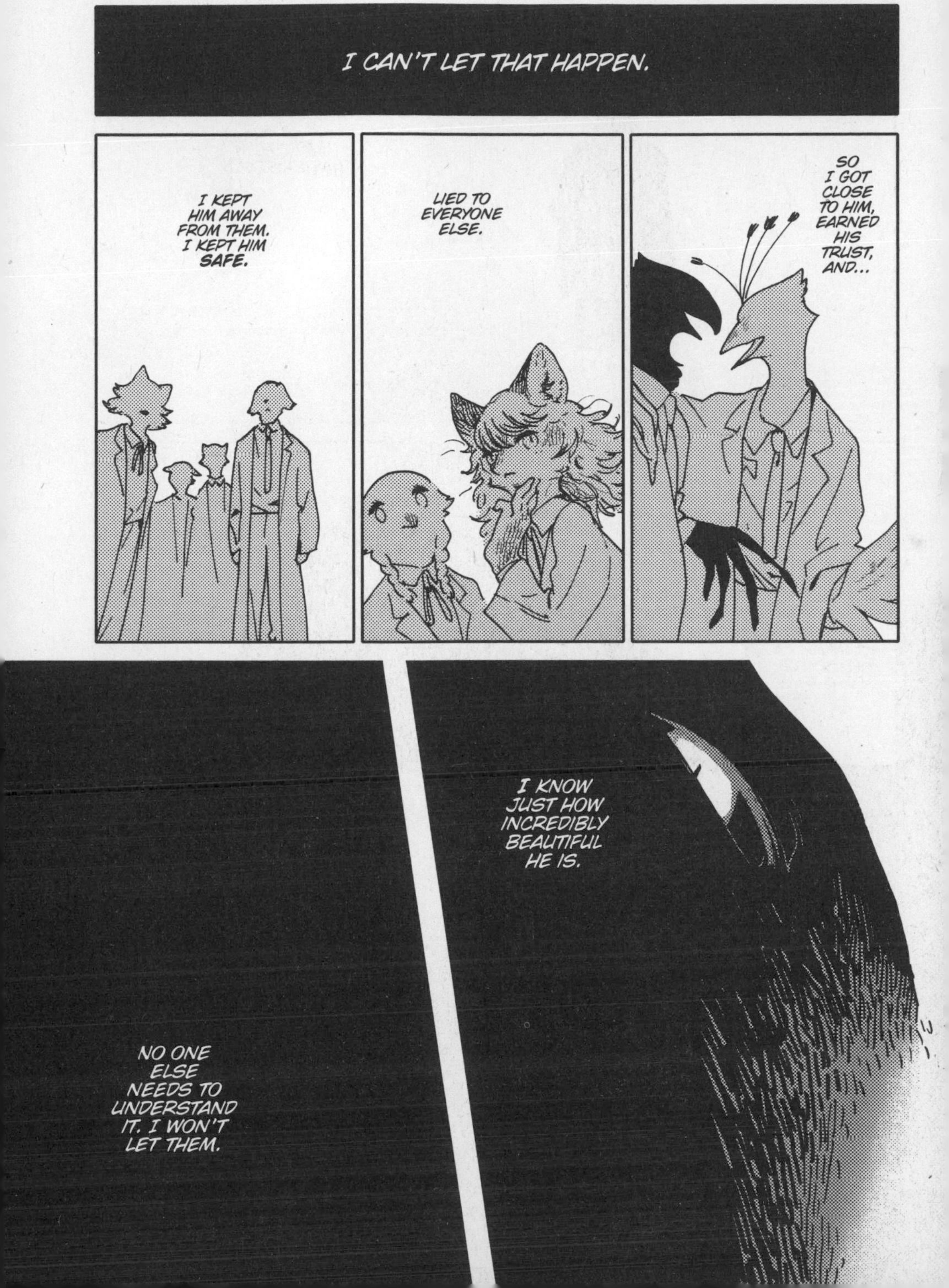
I CAN'T LET THAT HAPPEN.
SO I GOT CLOSE TO HIM, EARNED HIS TRUST, AND...
LIED TO EVERYONE ELSE.
I KEPT HIM AWAY FROM THEM. I KEPT HIM SAFE.
I KNOW JUST HOW INCREDIBLY BEAUTIFUL HE IS.
NO ONE ELSE NEEDS TO UNDERSTAND IT. I WON'T LET THEM.

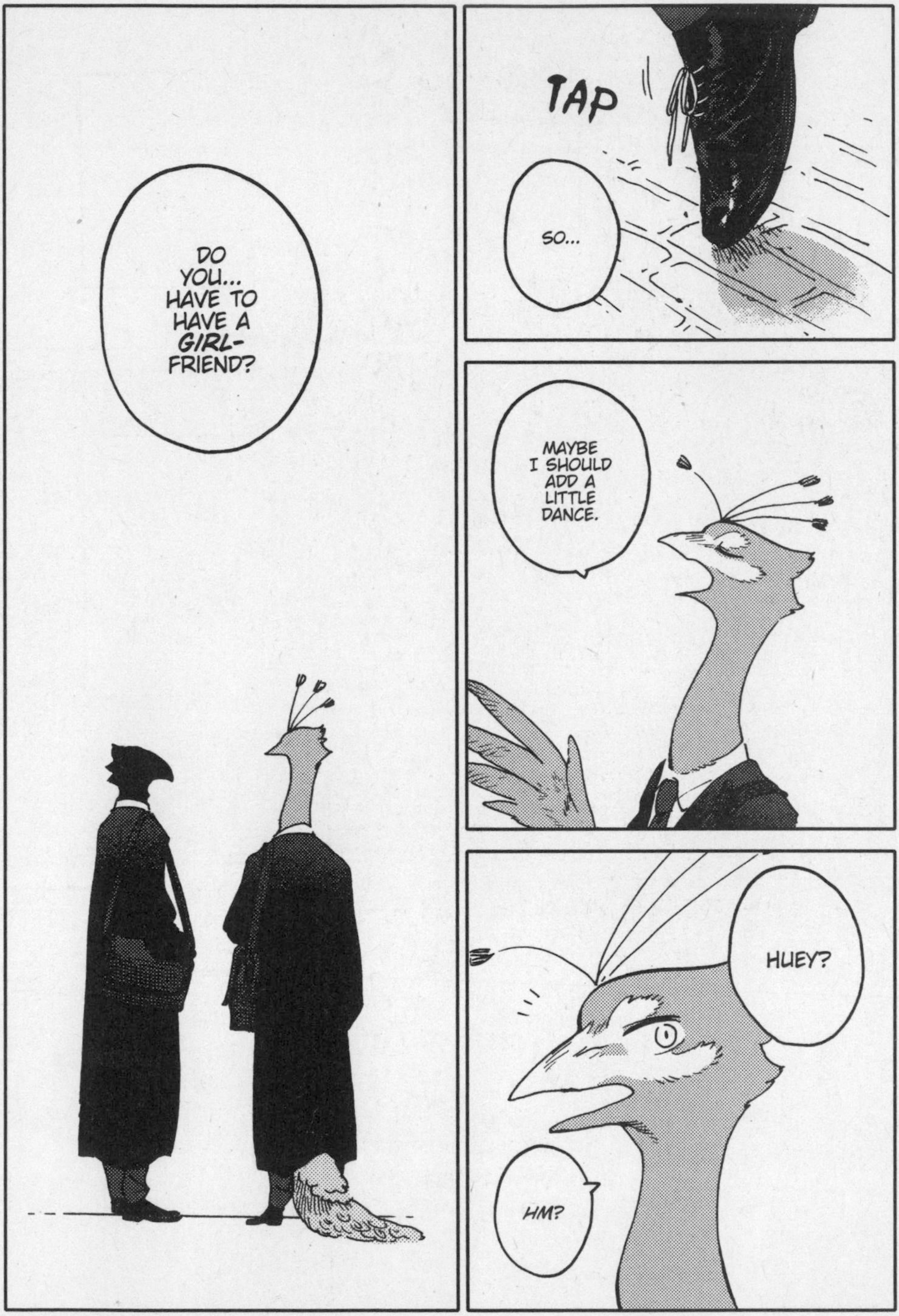
TAP
SO...
MAYBE I SHOULD ADD A LITTLE DANCE.
HUEY?
HM?
DO YOU... HAVE TO HAVE A *GIRL*-FRIEND?

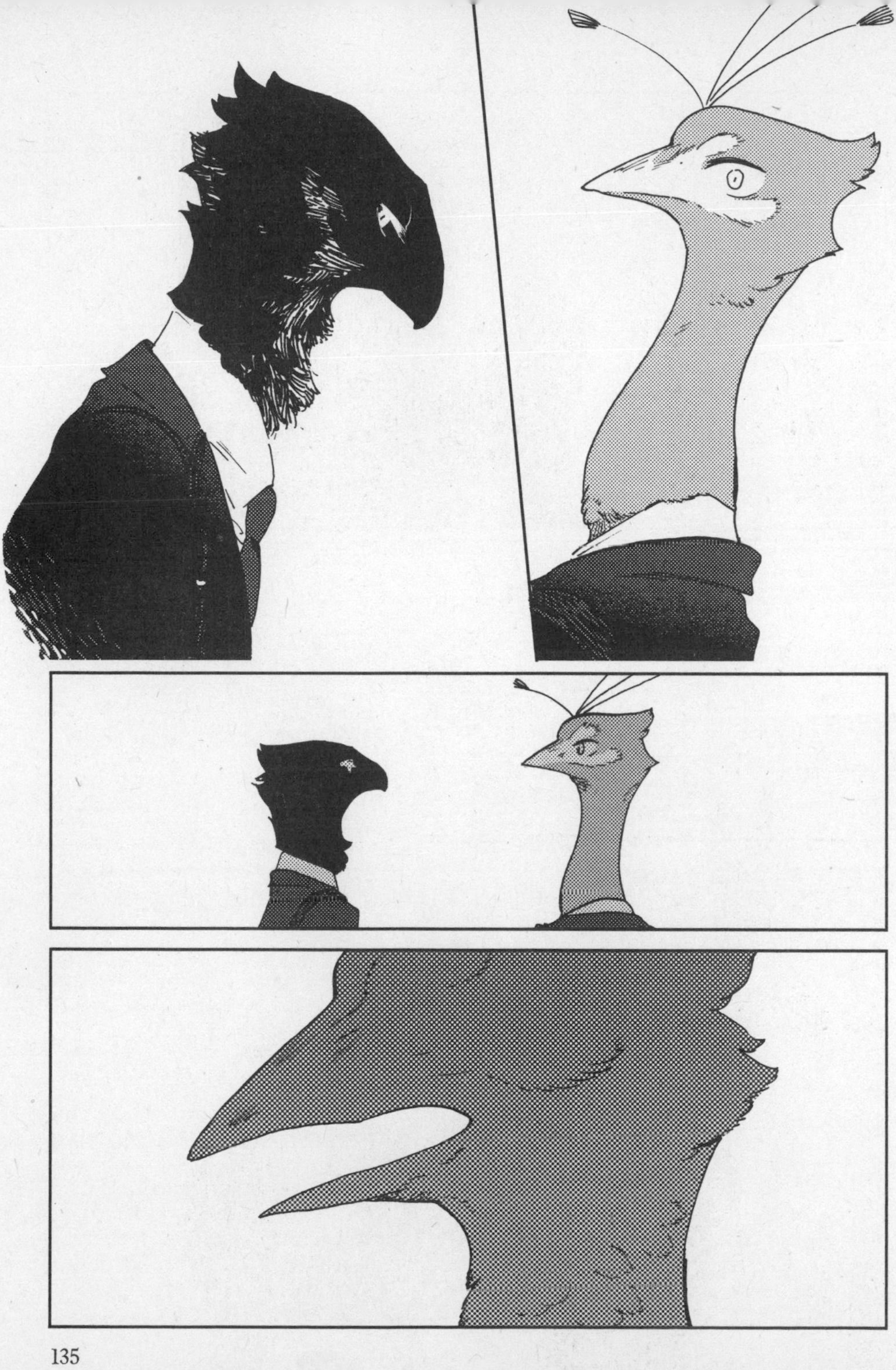

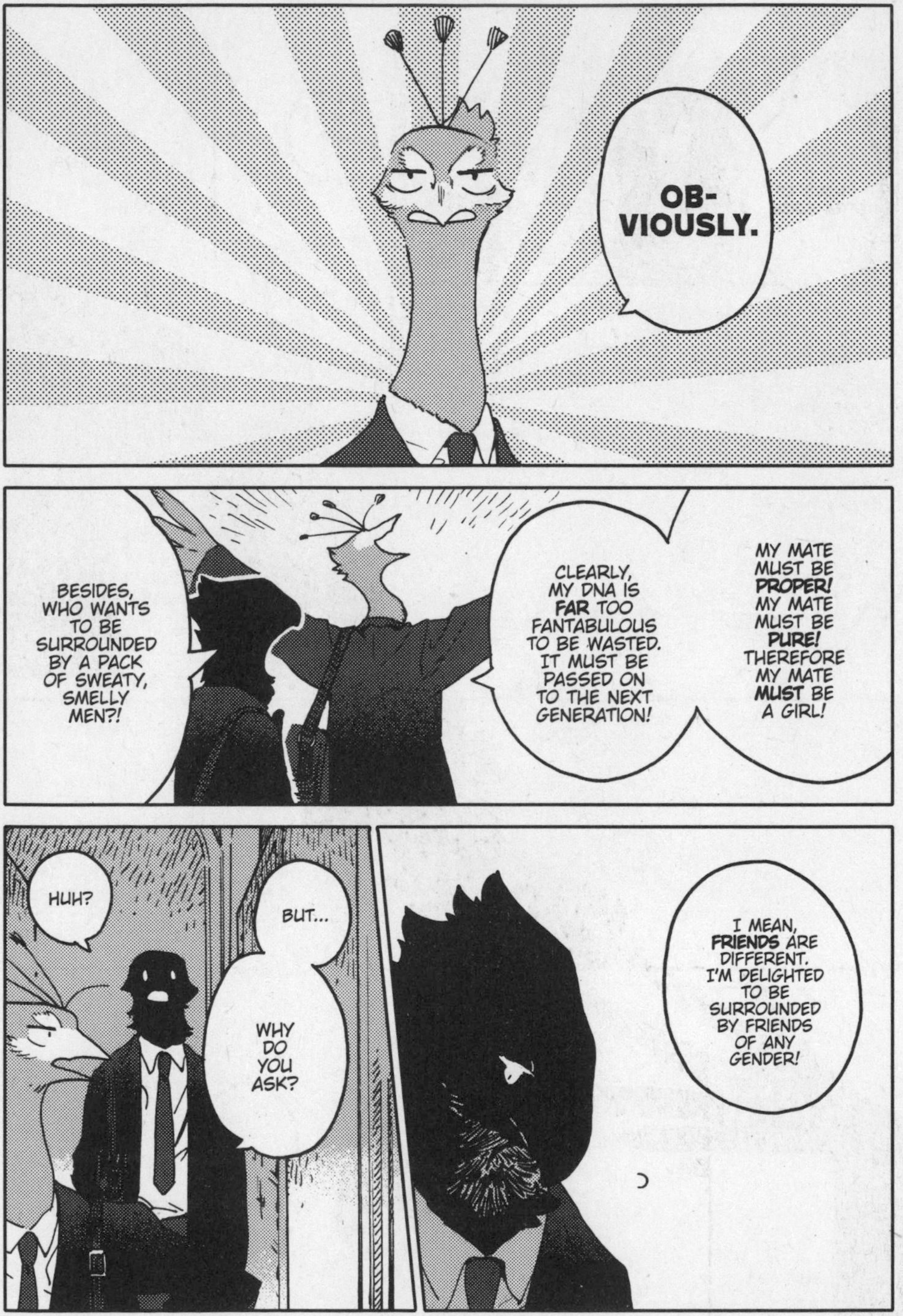
OB-VIOUSLY.
MY MATE MUST BE PROPER! MY MATE MUST BE PURE! THEREFORE MY MATE MUST BE A GIRL!
CLEARLY, MY DNA IS FAR TOO FANTABULOUS TO BE WASTED. IT MUST BE PASSED ON TO THE NEXT GENERATION!
BESIDES, WHO WANTS TO BE SURROUNDED BY A PACK OF SWEATY, SMELLY MEN?!
I MEAN, FRIENDS ARE DIFFERENT. I'M DELIGHTED TO BE SURROUNDED BY FRIENDS OF ANY GENDER!
BUT...
WHY DO YOU ASK?
HUH?

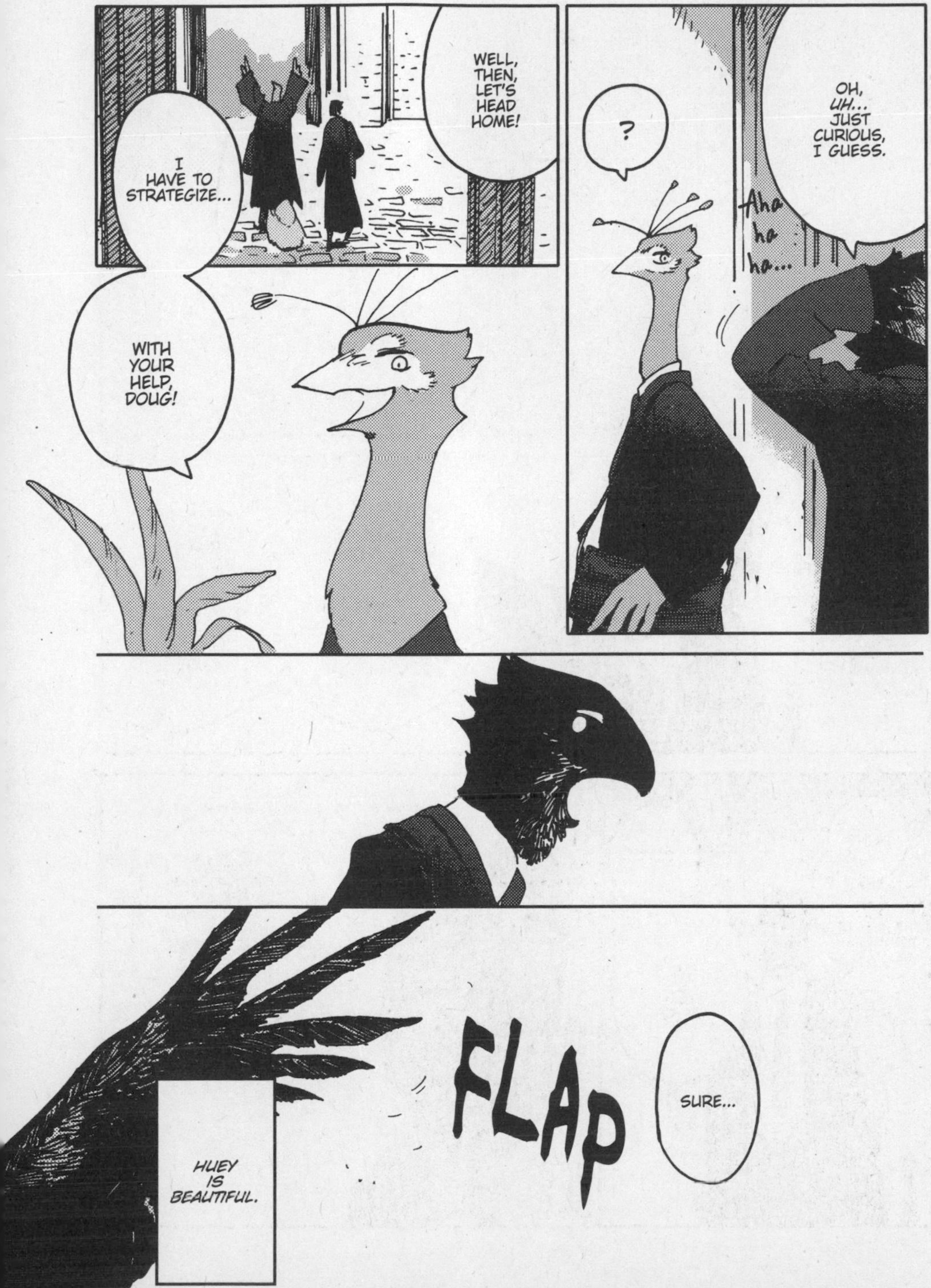
?
OH, UH... JUST CURIOUS, I GUESS.
Aha ha ha...
WELL, THEN, LET'S HEAD HOME!
I HAVE TO STRATEGIZE...
WITH YOUR HELP, DOUG!
SURE...
FLAP
HUEY IS BEAUTIFUL.

NO ONE ELSE UNDERSTANDS, BUT THEY DON'T HAVE TO.

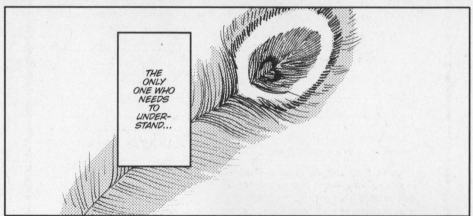

THE ONLY ONE WHO NEEDS TO UNDERSTAND...

IS ME.

◆ END ◆

INDIAN PEAFOWL

Pavo cristatus

Galliformes | Phasianidae *Pavo*

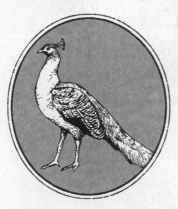

Peafowl are primarily ground-dwelling birds that prefer to live in open deciduous forests. As omnivores, they eat nuts, fruits, insects, and small mammals. The spectacular feathers of the male (called a peacock) are not actually tail feathers. They are 150 or so extremely long coverts that grow from the bird's back. A peacock's actual tail feathers are short and brown.

Peacocks spread those decorative feathers, called their train, during courtship displays and to intimidate possible predators by making themselves seem larger than they are.

CARRION CROW

Corvus corone

Passeriformes | Corvidae *Corvus*

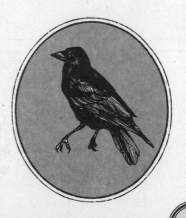

Crows have adapted to survive nearly anyplace, living everywhere from seaside cliffs to cities. They are also omnivores and will eat anything from meat and plants to carrion or even human garbage. They are usually solitary animals, although they will congregate during winter roosting.

Highly intelligent, they are capable of using tools, such as using rocks to crack open shellfish. They also use specific vocalizations to communicate with others by warning them of danger, informing them when food has been located, or even confirming their relative status in the pecking order.

The Wize Wize Beasts
of the Wizarding Wizdoms
by Nagabe

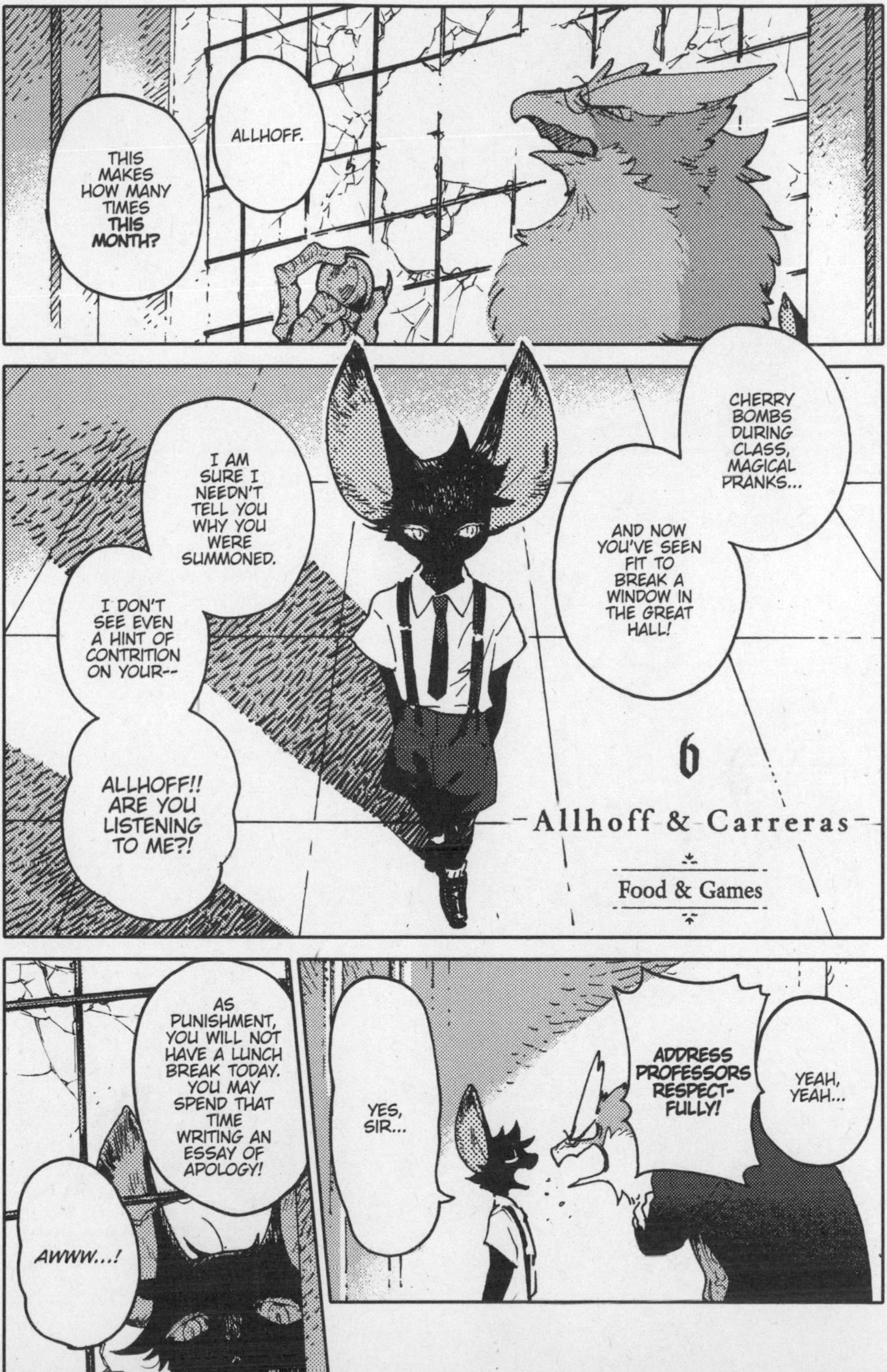
ALLHOFF.
THIS MAKES HOW MANY TIMES THIS MONTH?
CHERRY BOMBS DURING CLASS, MAGICAL PRANKS...
AND NOW YOU'VE SEEN FIT TO BREAK A WINDOW IN THE GREAT HALL!
I AM SURE I NEEDN'T TELL YOU WHY YOU WERE SUMMONED.
I DON'T SEE EVEN A HINT OF CONTRITION ON YOUR--
ALLHOFF!! ARE YOU LISTENING TO ME?!
6
Allhoff & Carreras
Food & Games
YEAH, YEAH...
ADDRESS PROFESSORS RESPECT-FULLY!
YES, SIR...
AS PUNISHMENT, YOU WILL NOT HAVE A LUNCH BREAK TODAY. YOU MAY SPEND THAT TIME WRITING AN ESSAY OF APOLOGY!
AWWW...!

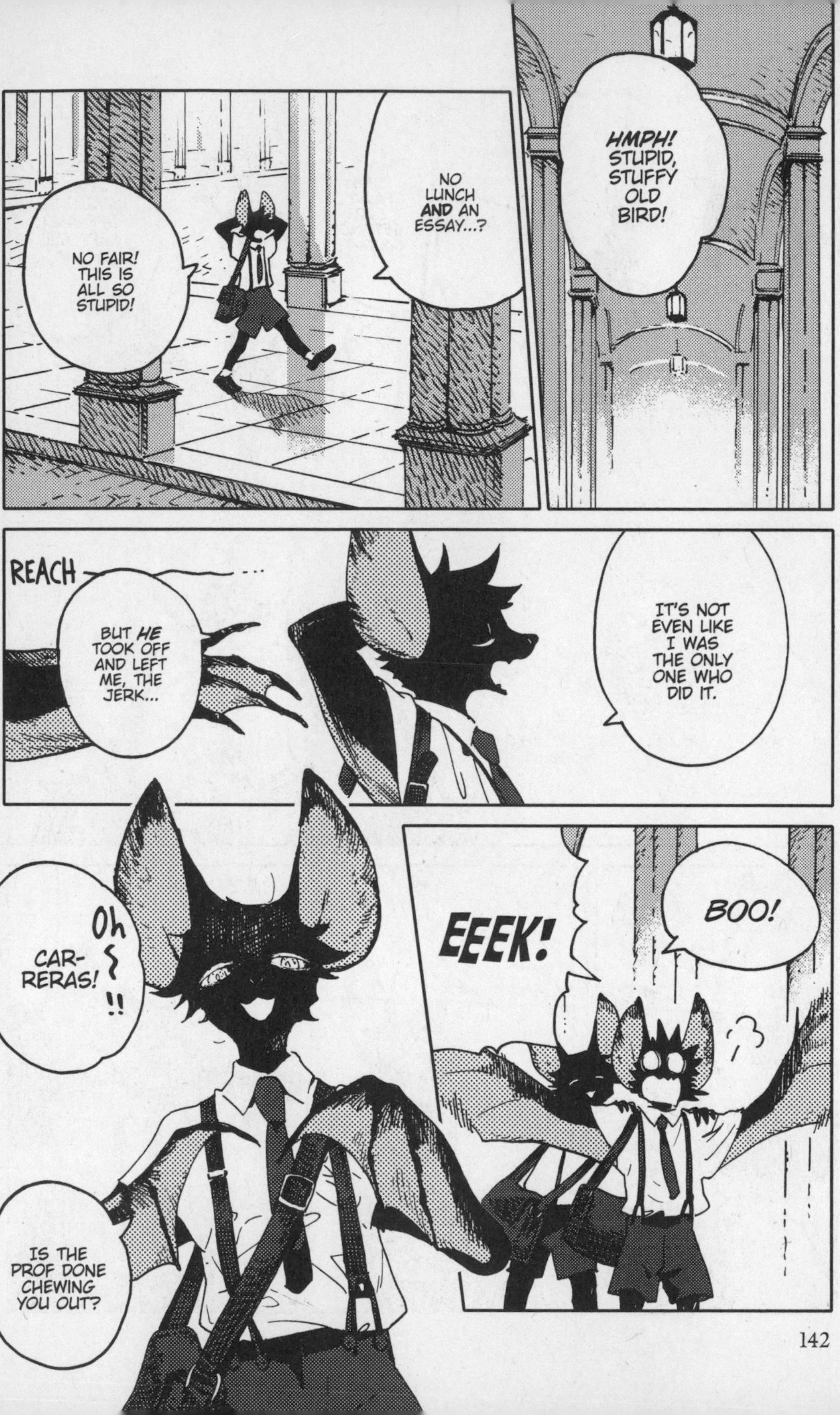
HMPH! STUPID, STUFFY OLD BIRD!
NO LUNCH AND AN ESSAY...?
NO FAIR! THIS IS ALL SO STUPID!
IT'S NOT EVEN LIKE I WAS THE ONLY ONE WHO DID IT.
REACH
BUT HE TOOK OFF AND LEFT ME, THE JERK...
BOO!
EEEK!
Oh~!!
CARRERAS!
IS THE PROF DONE CHEWING YOU OUT?

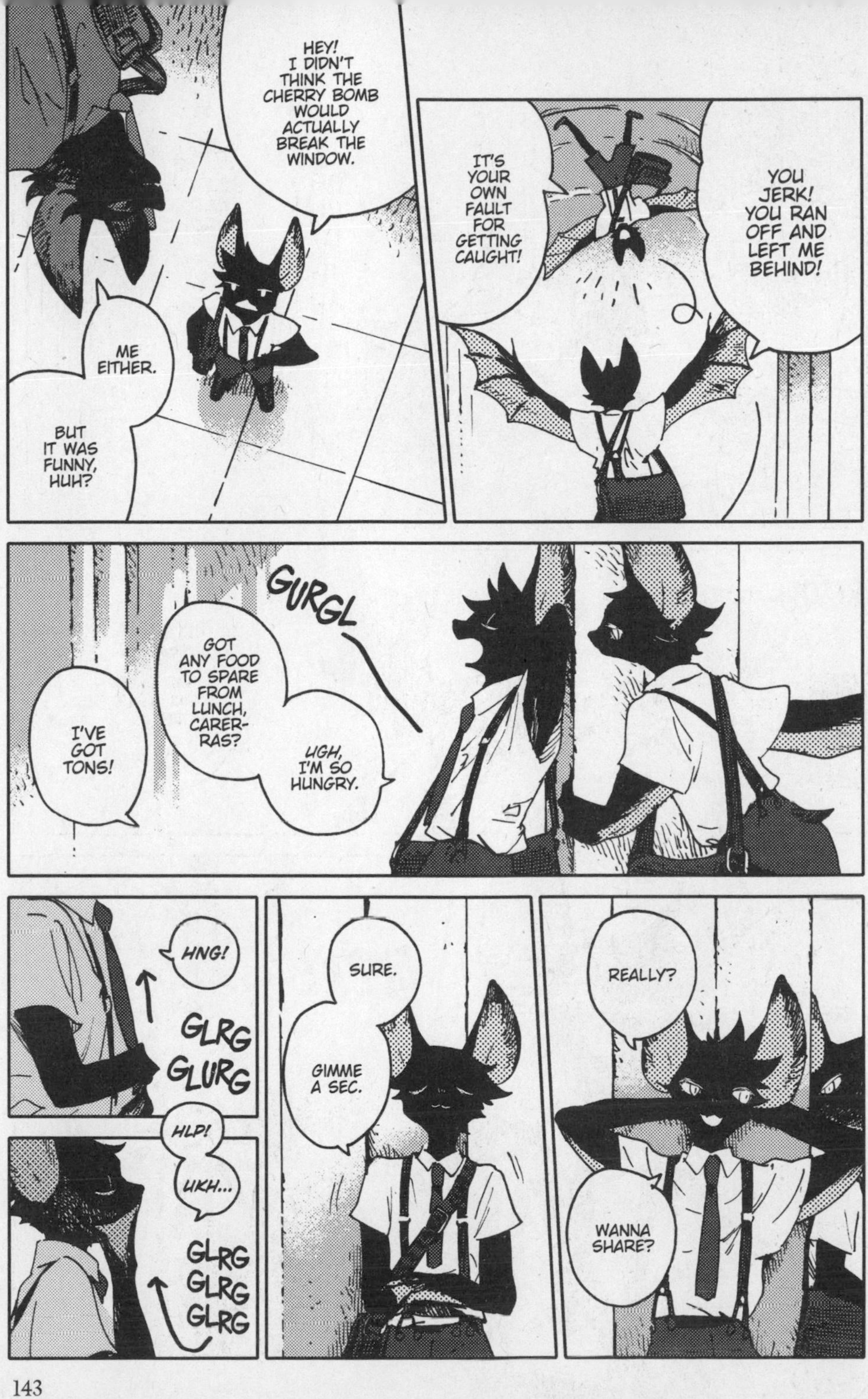
YOU JERK! YOU RAN OFF AND LEFT ME BEHIND!
IT'S YOUR OWN FAULT FOR GETTING CAUGHT!
HEY! I DIDN'T THINK THE CHERRY BOMB WOULD ACTUALLY BREAK THE WINDOW.
ME EITHER.
BUT IT WAS FUNNY, HUH?
GURGL
UGH, I'M SO HUNGRY.
GOT ANY FOOD TO SPARE FROM LUNCH, CARER-RAS?
I'VE GOT TONS!
REALLY?
WANNA SHARE?
SURE.
GIMME A SEC.
HNG!
GLRG GLURG
HLP!
UKH...
GLRG GLRG GLRG

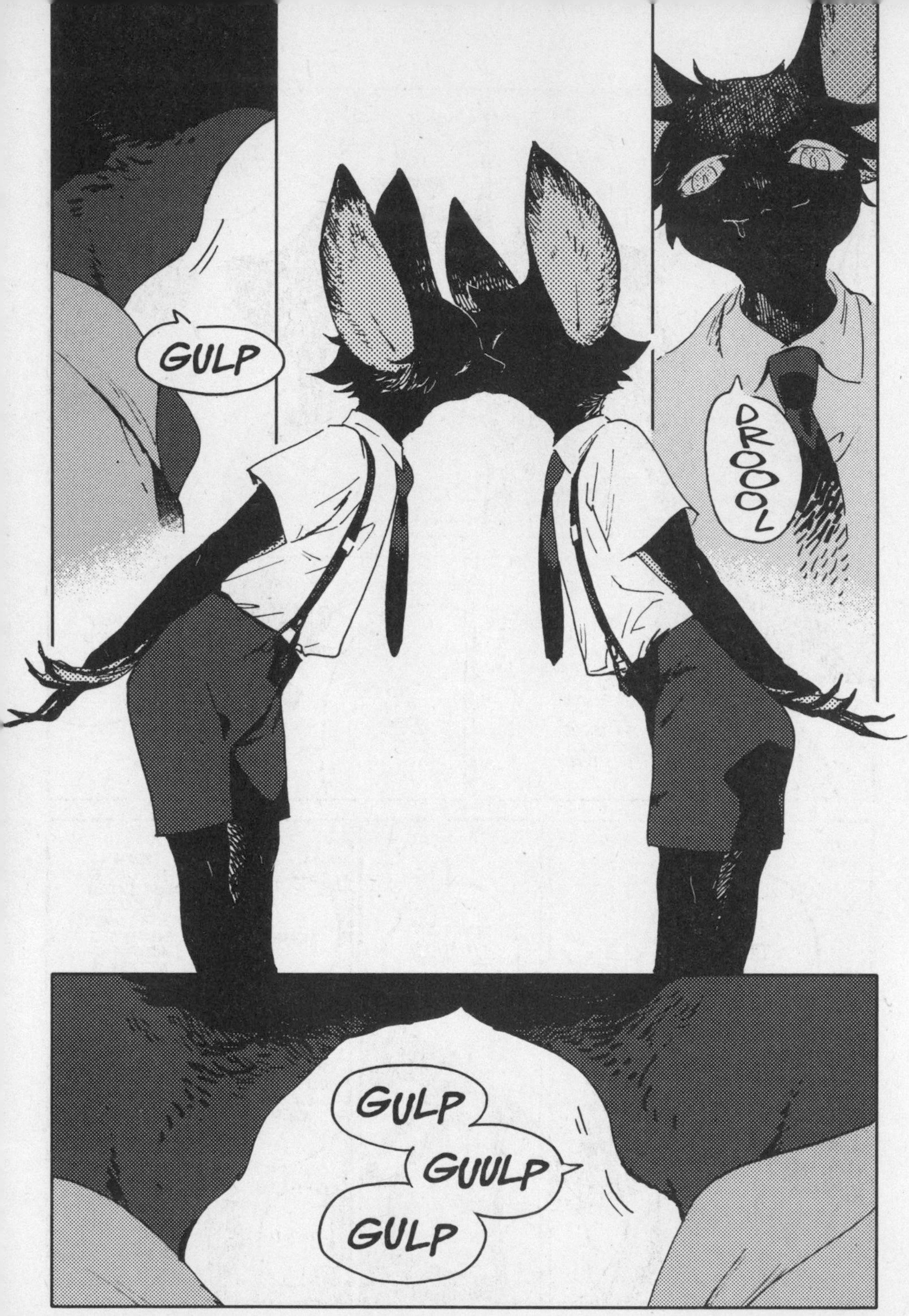
DROOOL
GULP
GULP
GUULP
GULP

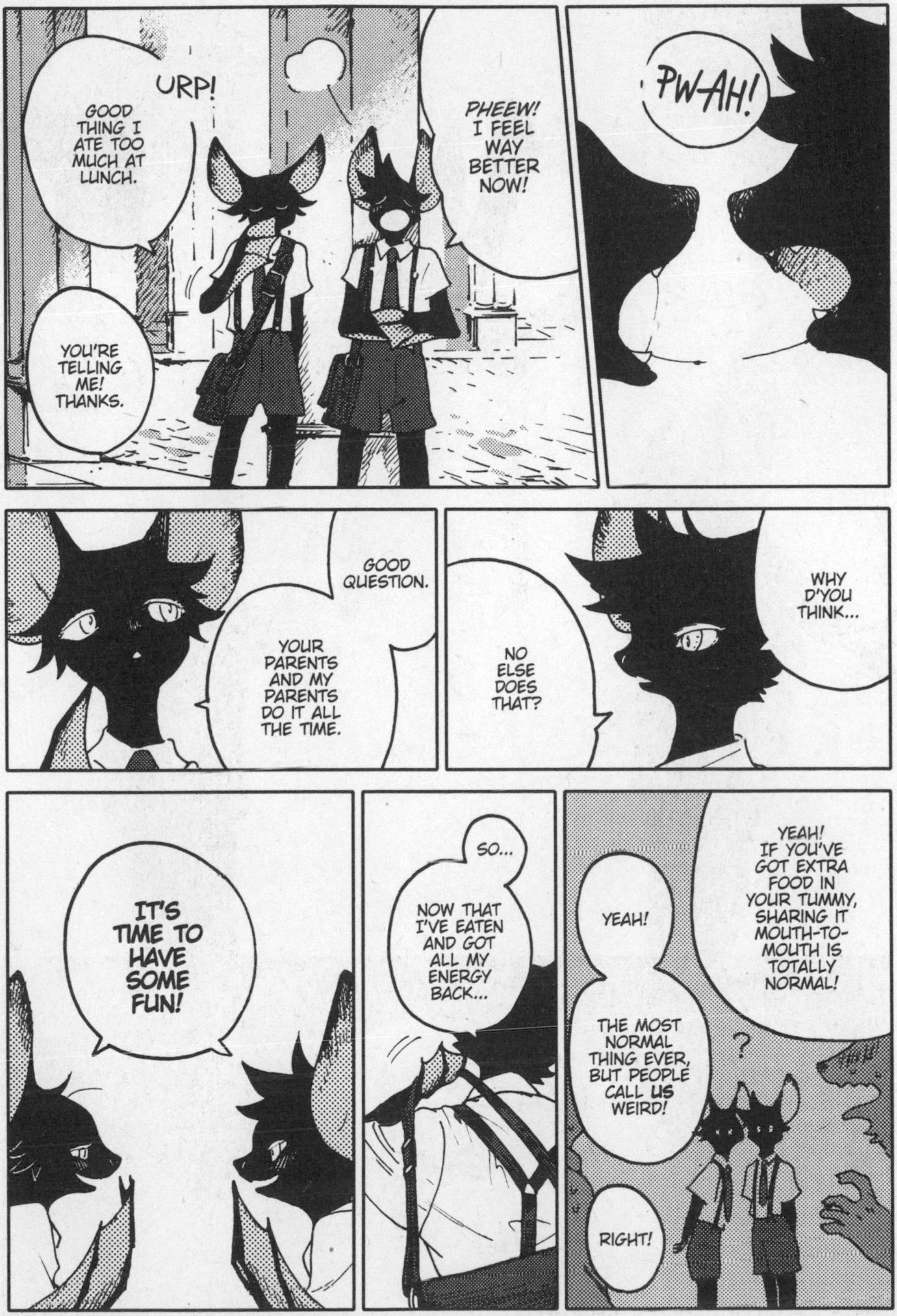
PW-AH!
PHEEW! I FEEL WAY BETTER NOW!
URP!
GOOD THING I ATE TOO MUCH AT LUNCH.
YOU'RE TELLING ME! THANKS.
WHY D'YOU THINK...
NO ELSE DOES THAT?
GOOD QUESTION.
YOUR PARENTS AND MY PARENTS DO IT ALL THE TIME.
YEAH! IF YOU'VE GOT EXTRA FOOD IN YOUR TUMMY, SHARING IT MOUTH-TO-MOUTH IS TOTALLY NORMAL!
YEAH!
THE MOST NORMAL THING EVER, BUT PEOPLE CALL **US** WEIRD!
RIGHT!
SO...
NOW THAT I'VE EATEN AND GOT ALL MY ENERGY BACK...
IT'S TIME TO HAVE SOME FUN!

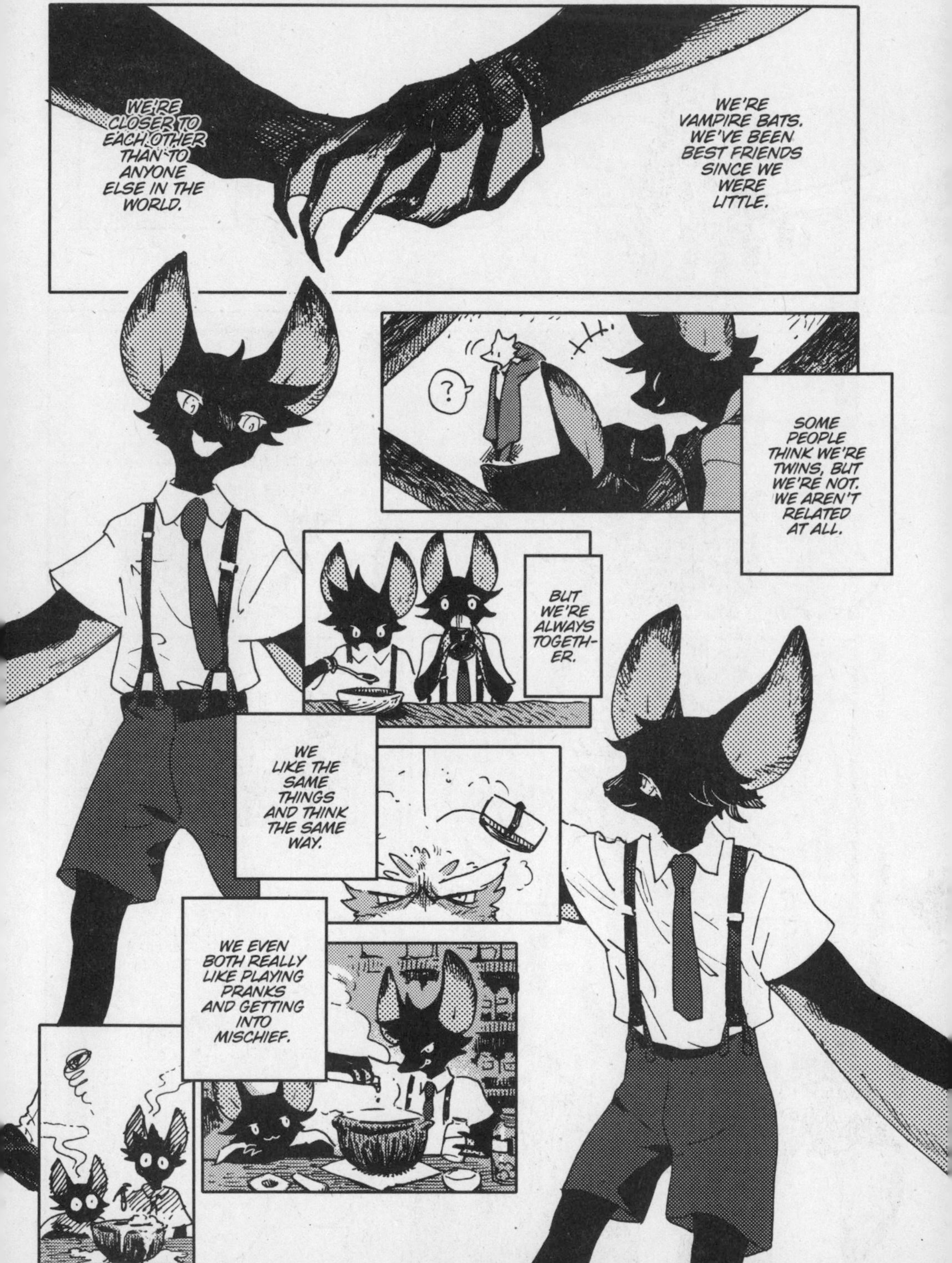
WE'RE VAMPIRE BATS. WE'VE BEEN BEST FRIENDS SINCE WE WERE LITTLE.
WE'RE CLOSER TO EACH OTHER THAN TO ANYONE ELSE IN THE WORLD.
?
SOME PEOPLE THINK WE'RE TWINS, BUT WE'RE NOT. WE AREN'T RELATED AT ALL.
BUT WE'RE ALWAYS TOGETHER.
WE LIKE THE SAME THINGS AND THINK THE SAME WAY.
WE EVEN BOTH REALLY LIKE PLAYING PRANKS AND GETTING INTO MISCHIEF.

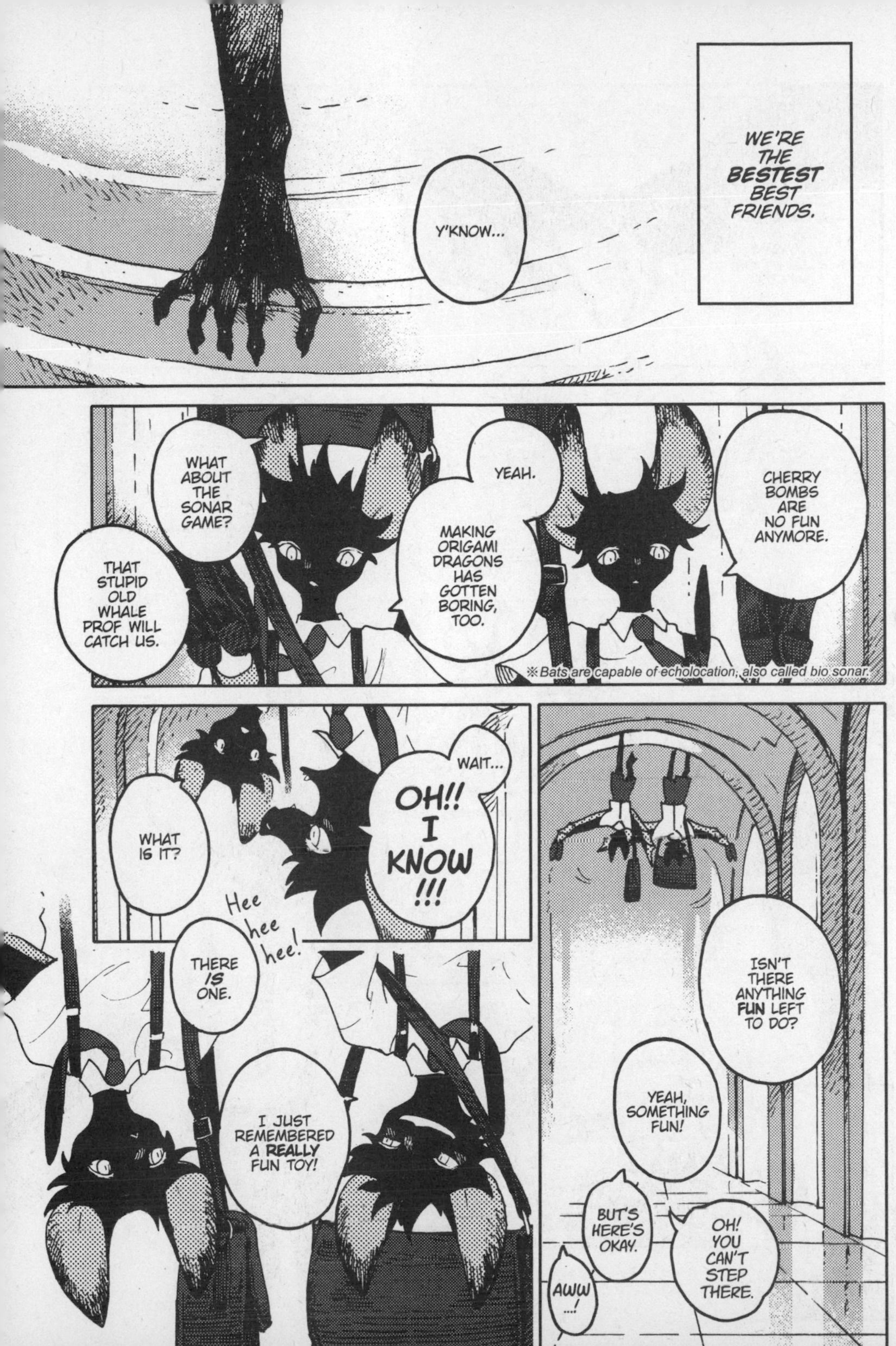
WE'RE THE BESTEST BEST FRIENDS.
Y'KNOW...
CHERRY BOMBS ARE NO FUN ANYMORE.
YEAH.
MAKING ORIGAMI DRAGONS HAS GOTTEN BORING, TOO.
WHAT ABOUT THE SONAR GAME?
THAT STUPID OLD WHALE PROF WILL CATCH US.
※Bats are capable of echolocation, also called bio sonar.
ISN'T THERE ANYTHING FUN LEFT TO DO?
YEAH, SOMETHING FUN!
OH! YOU CAN'T STEP THERE.
BUT'S HERE'S OKAY.
AWW...!
WAIT...
OH!! I KNOW!!!
WHAT IS IT?
Hee hee hee!
THERE IS ONE.
I JUST REMEMBERED A REALLY FUN TOY!

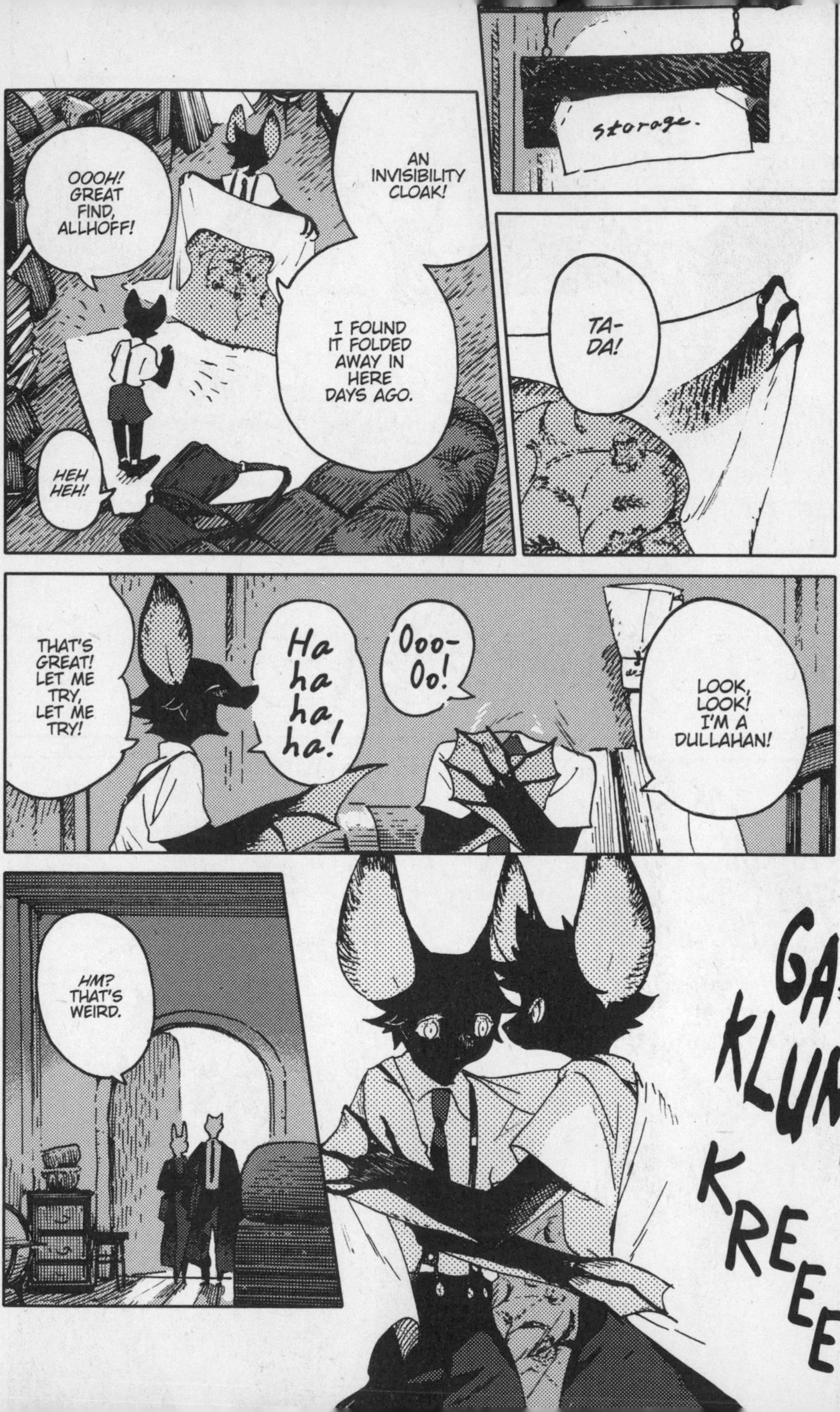
storage.
TA-DA!
AN INVISIBILITY CLOAK!
OOOH! GREAT FIND, ALLHOFF!
I FOUND IT FOLDED AWAY IN HERE DAYS AGO.
HEH HEH!
LOOK, LOOK! I'M A DULLAHAN!
Ooo-Oo!
Ha ha ha ha!
THAT'S GREAT! LET ME TRY, LET ME TRY!
GA-KLUNK
KREEE
HM? THAT'S WEIRD.

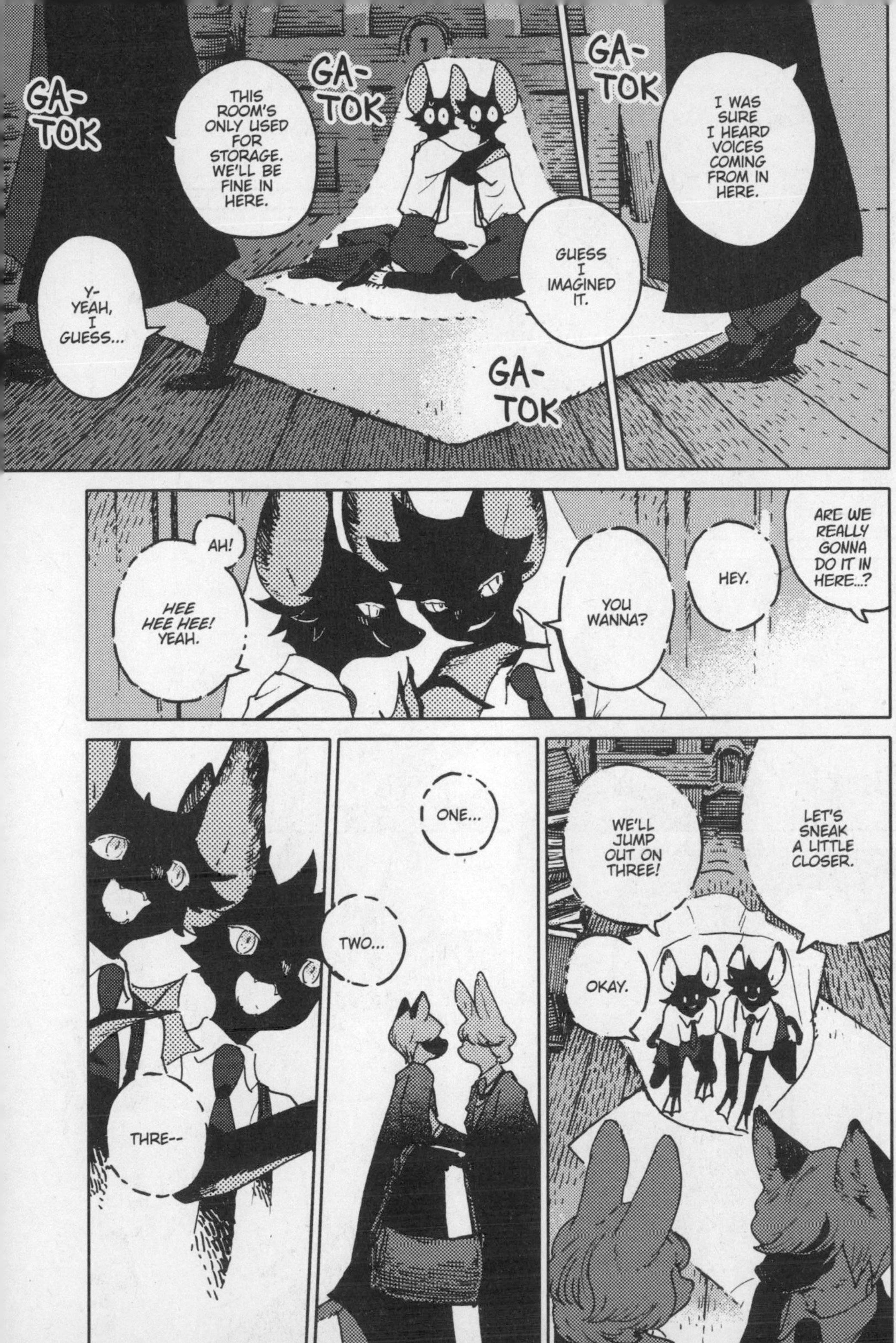
GA-TOK
I WAS SURE I HEARD VOICES COMING FROM IN HERE.
GA-TOK
THIS ROOM'S ONLY USED FOR STORAGE. WE'LL BE FINE IN HERE.
GA-TOK
GUESS I IMAGINED IT.
Y-YEAH, I GUESS...
GA-TOK
ARE WE REALLY GONNA DO IT IN HERE...?
HEY.
YOU WANNA?
AH!
HEE HEE HEE! YEAH.
LET'S SNEAK A LITTLE CLOSER.
WE'LL JUMP OUT ON THREE!
OKAY.
ONE...
TWO...
THRE--

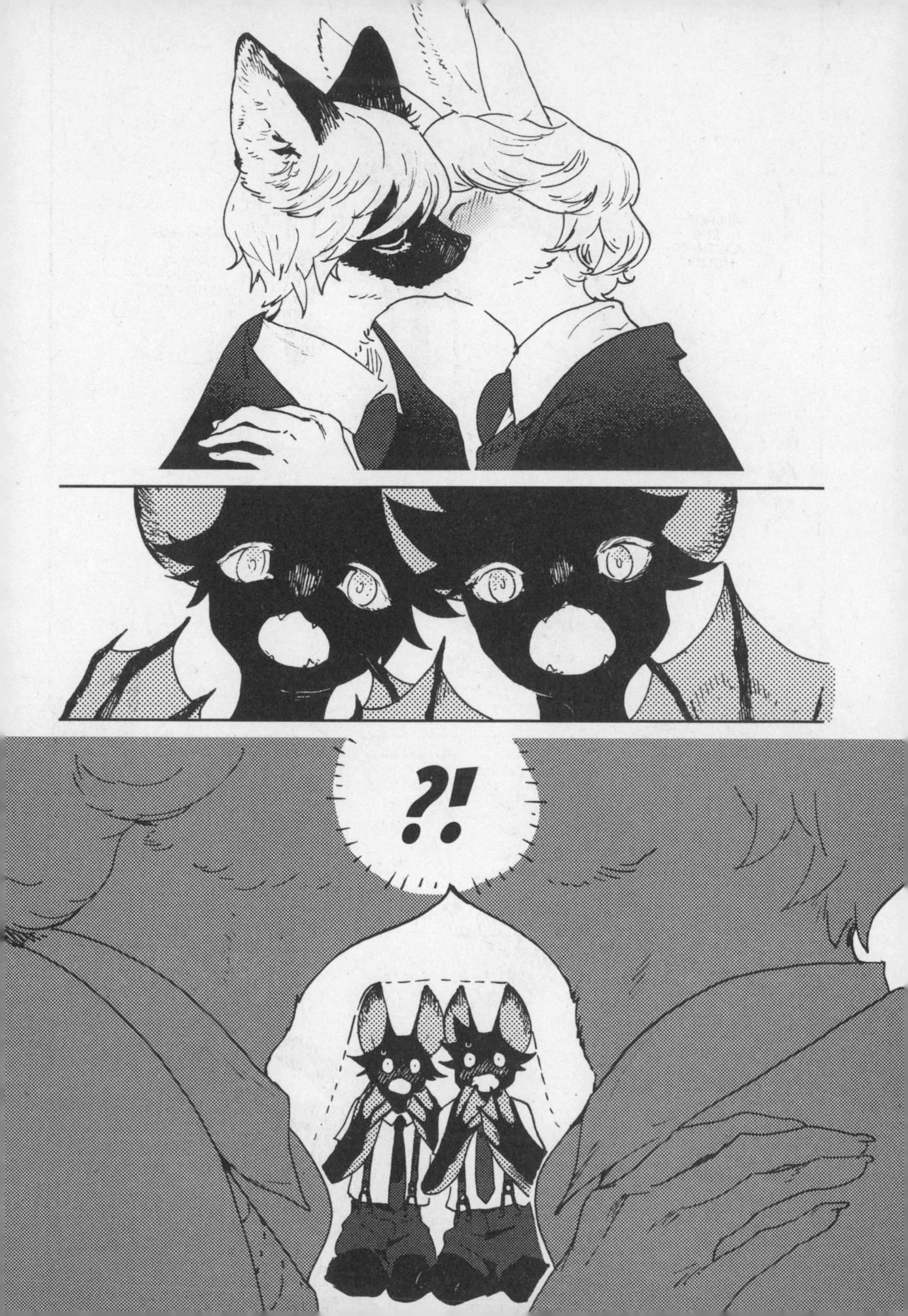
?!

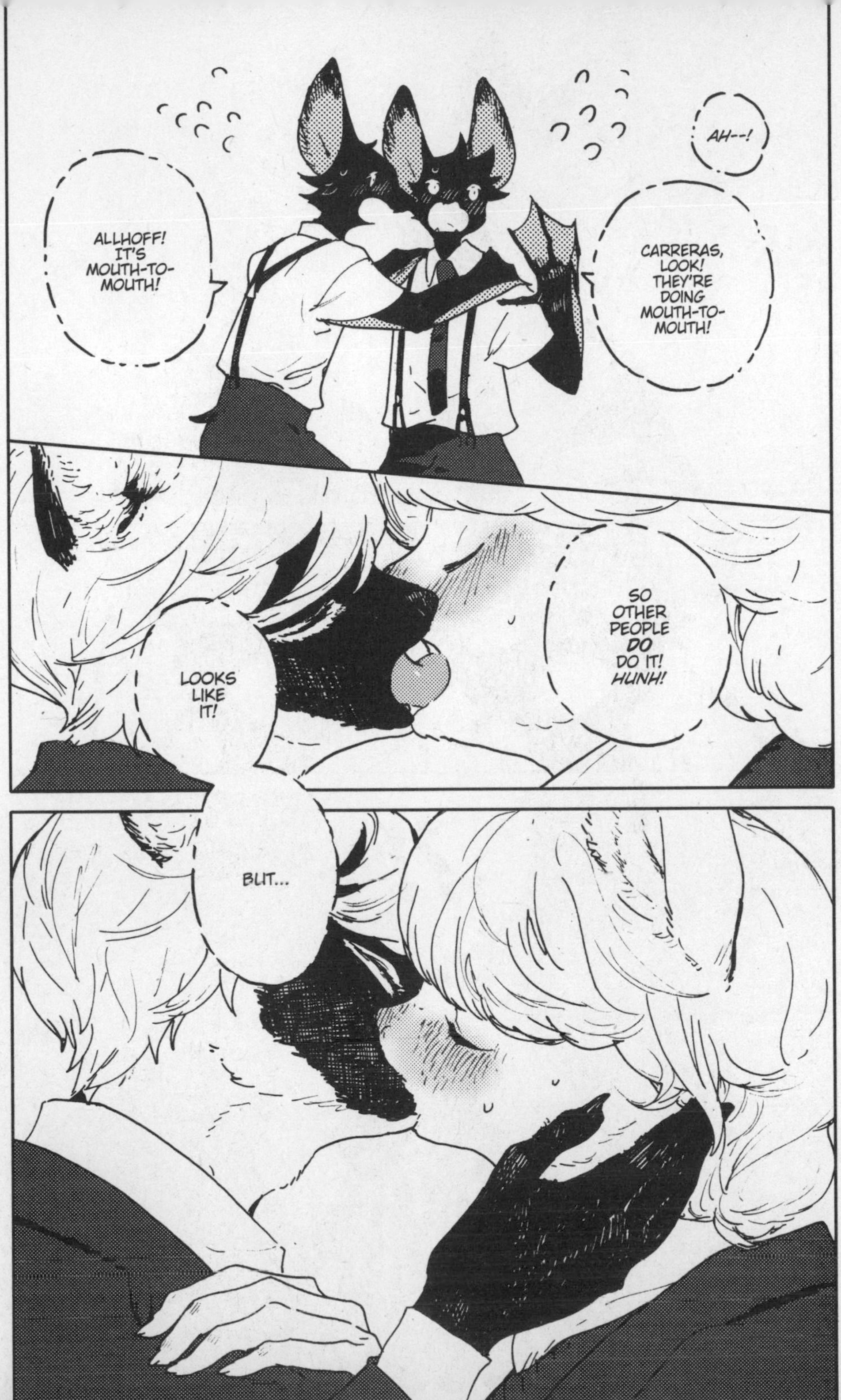
AH--!
CARRERAS, LOOK! THEY'RE DOING MOUTH-TO-MOUTH!
ALLHOFF! IT'S MOUTH-TO-MOUTH!
SO OTHER PEOPLE DO DO IT! HUNH!
LOOKS LIKE IT!
BUT...

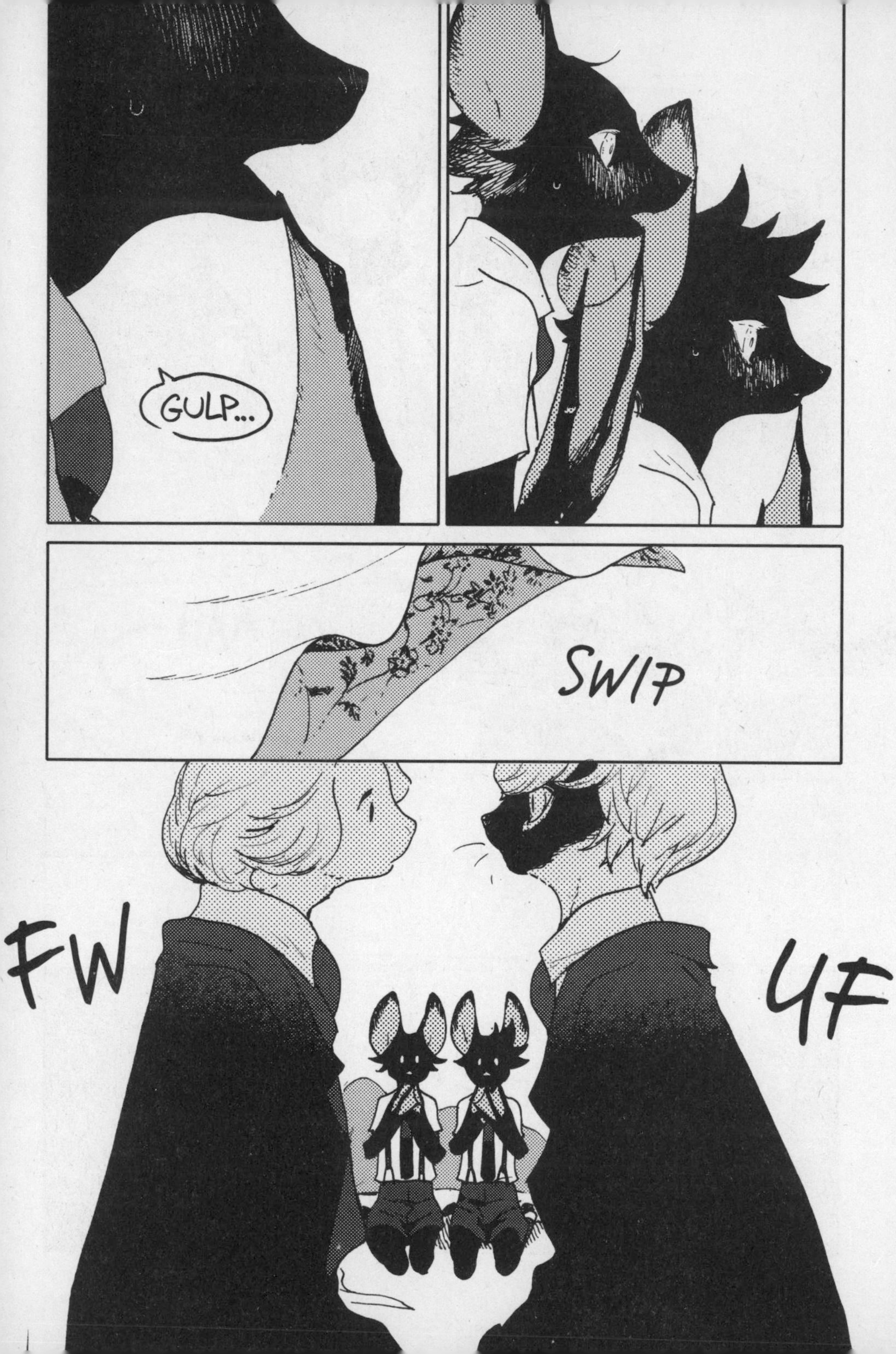
GULP...
SWIP
FW
UF

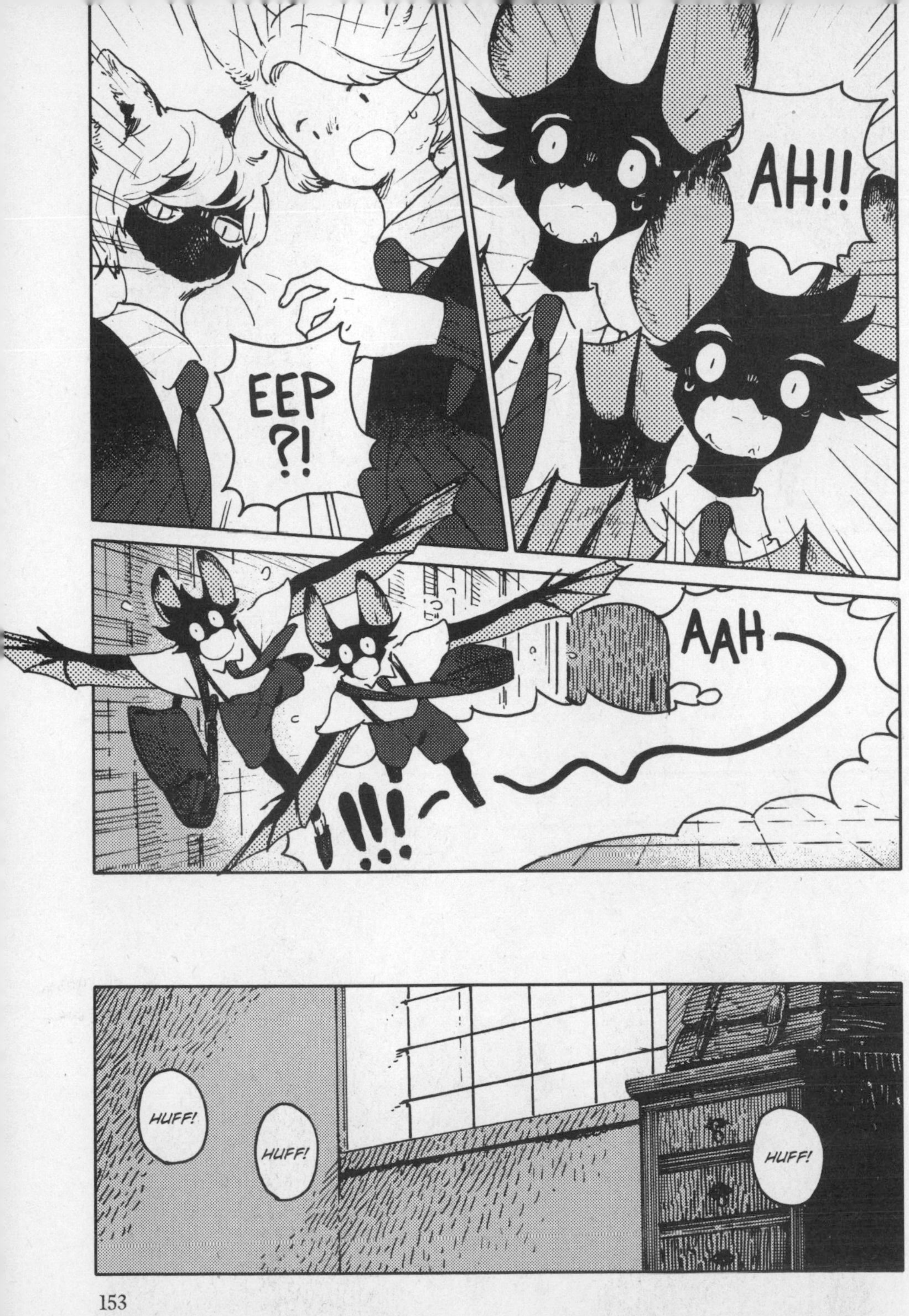
AH!!
EEP ?!
AAH
!!!
HUFF!
HUFF!
HUFF!

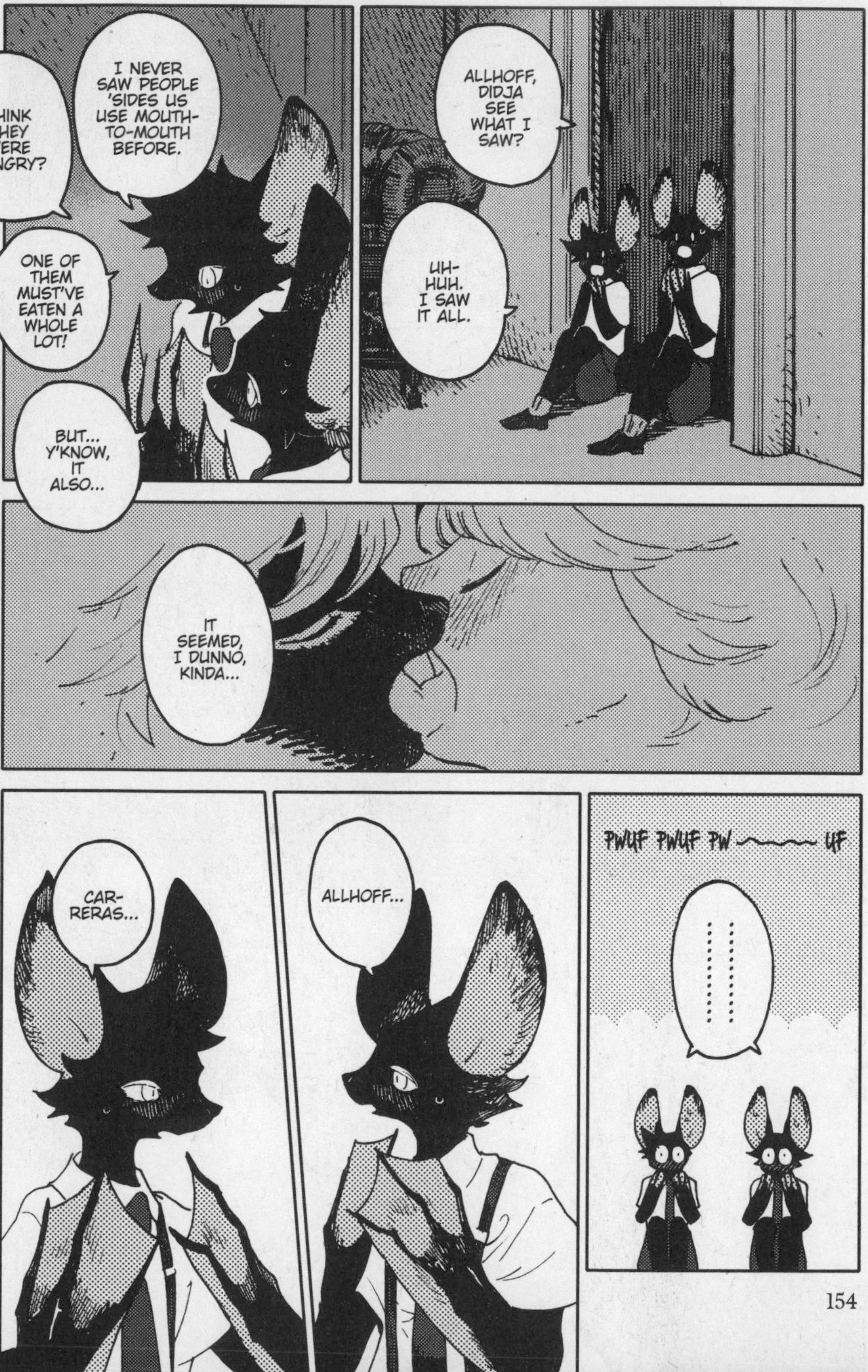
ALLHOFF, DIDJA SEE WHAT I SAW?
UH-HUH. I SAW IT ALL.
I NEVER SAW PEOPLE 'SIDES US USE MOUTH-TO-MOUTH BEFORE.
THINK THEY WERE HUNGRY?
ONE OF THEM MUST'VE EATEN A WHOLE LOT!
BUT... Y'KNOW, IT ALSO...
IT SEEMED, I DUNNO, KINDA...
PWUF PWUF PW~~~~UF
......
ALLHOFF...
CAR-RERAS...

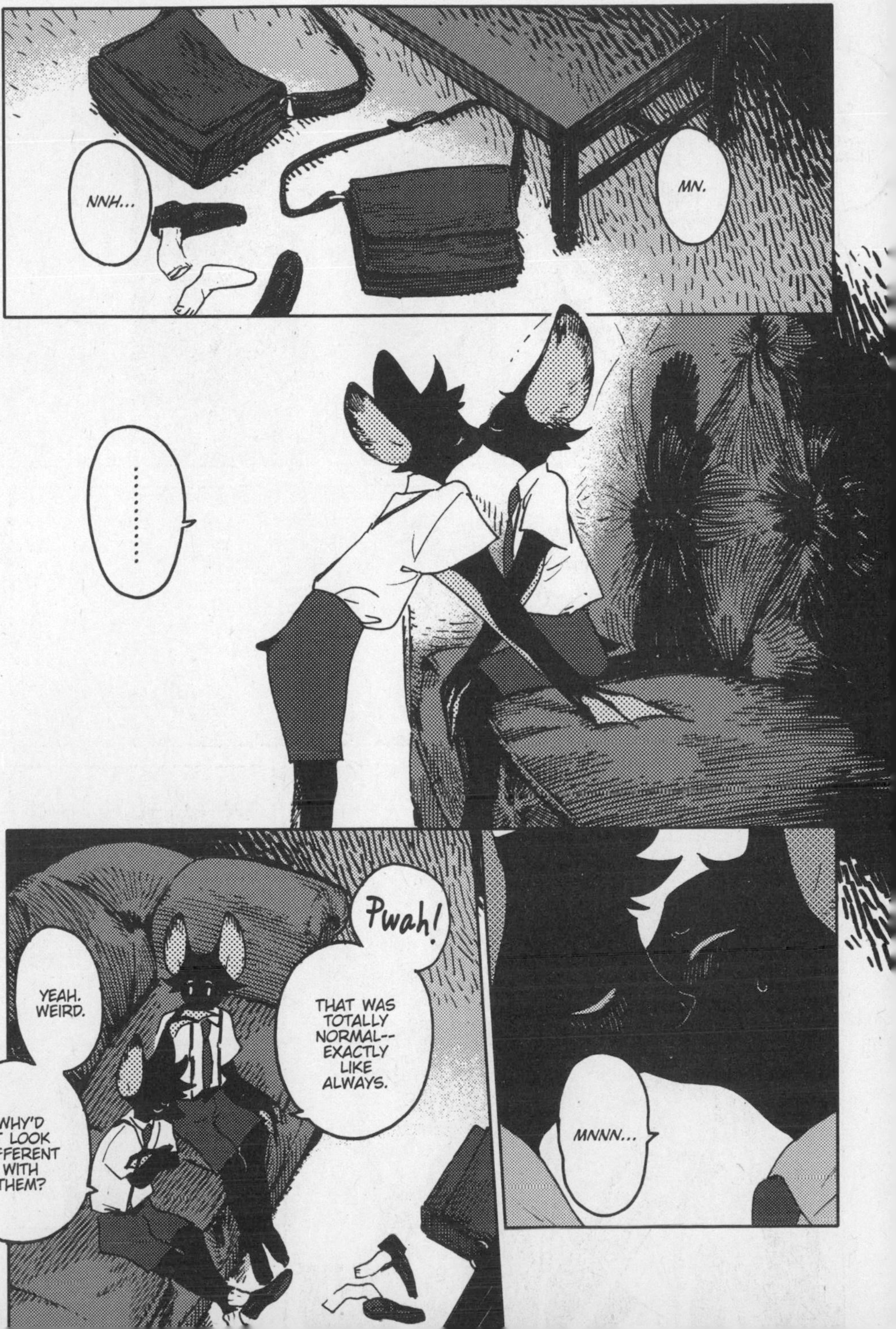
MN.
NNH...
......
MNNN...
Pwah!
THAT WAS TOTALLY NORMAL--EXACTLY LIKE ALWAYS.
YEAH. WEIRD.
WHY'D IT LOOK DIFFERENT WITH THEM?

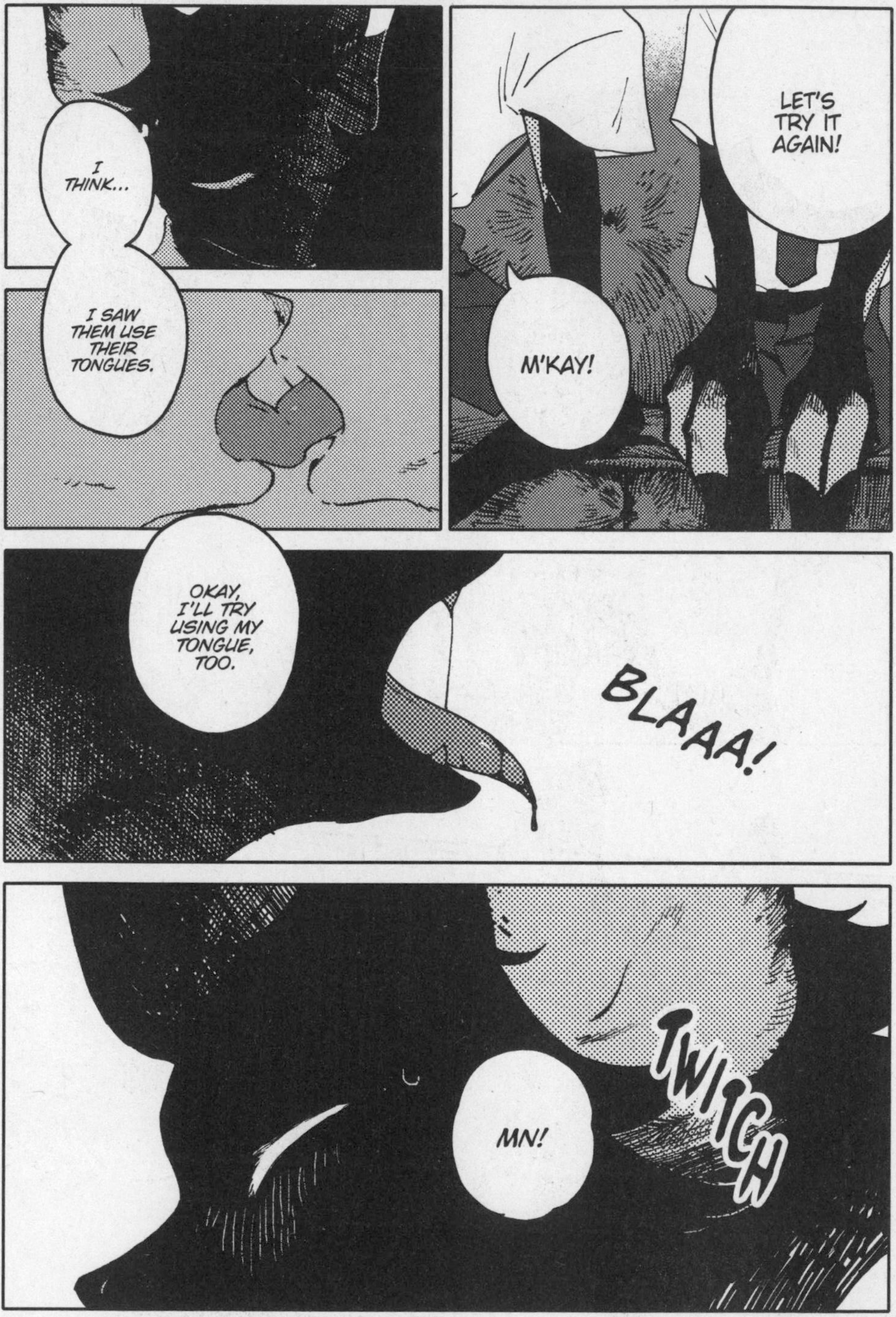
LET'S TRY IT AGAIN!
M'KAY!
I THINK...
I SAW THEM USE THEIR TONGUES.
OKAY, I'LL TRY USING MY TONGUE, TOO.
BLAAA!
TWITCH
MN!

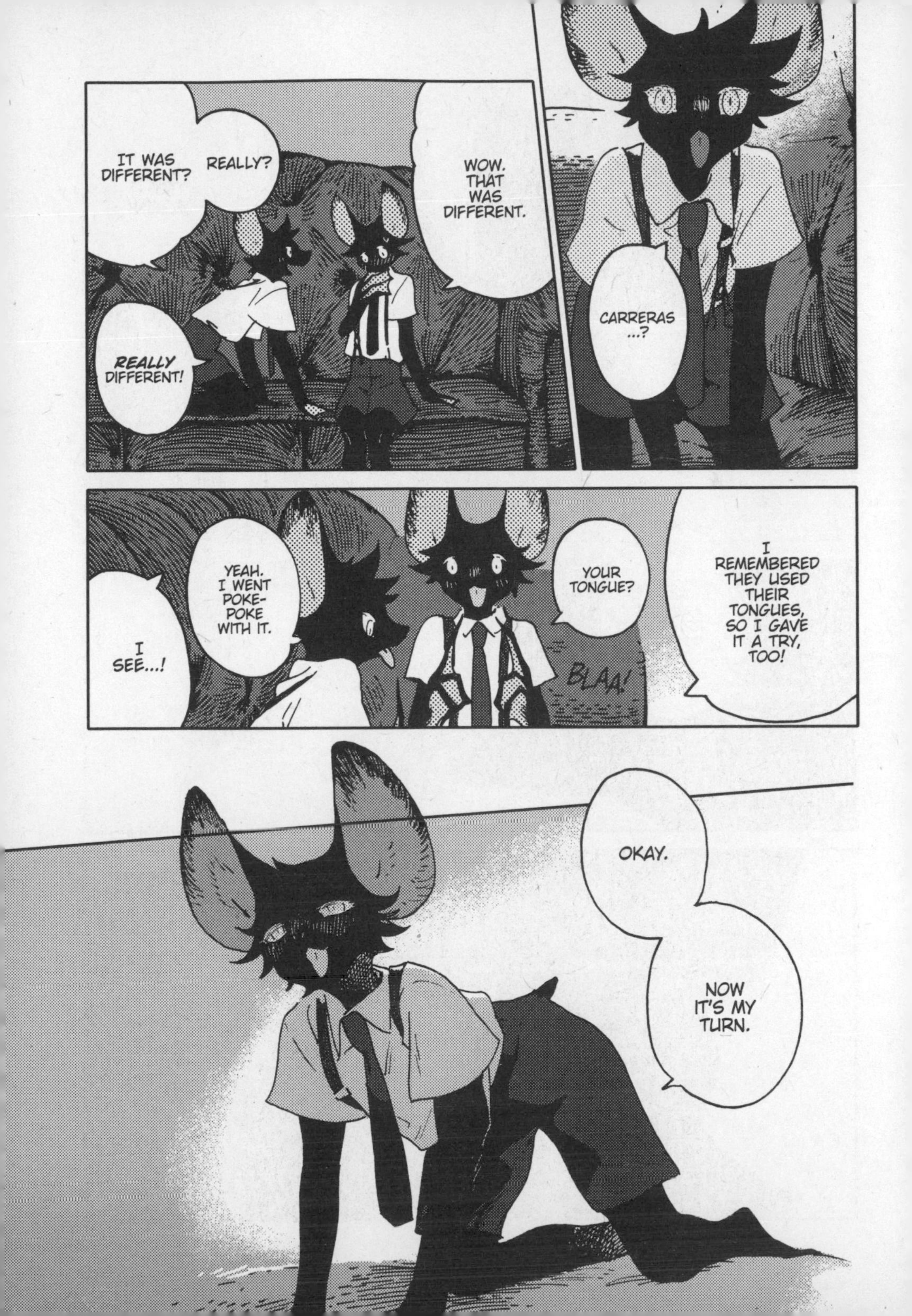
CARRERAS ...?
WOW. THAT WAS DIFFERENT.
REALLY?
IT WAS DIFFERENT?
REALLY DIFFERENT!
I REMEMBERED THEY USED THEIR TONGUES, SO I GAVE IT A TRY, TOO!
YOUR TONGUE?
BLAA!
YEAH. I WENT POKE-POKE WITH IT.
I SEE...!
OKAY.
NOW IT'S MY TURN.

MN...
MNN!
MFF!
NHH...
MNPH...
NN...
MNPH!
DRIBBLE

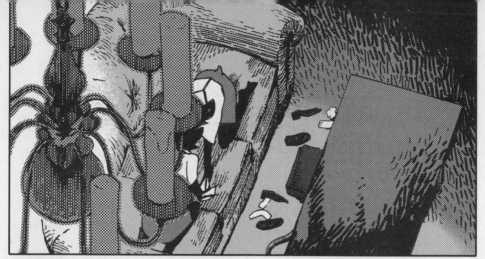

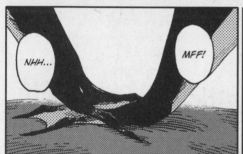

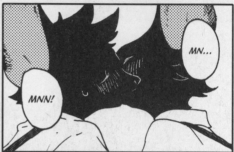

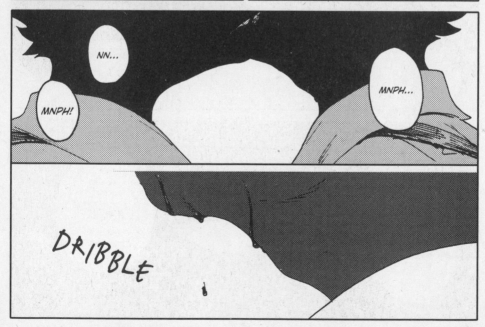

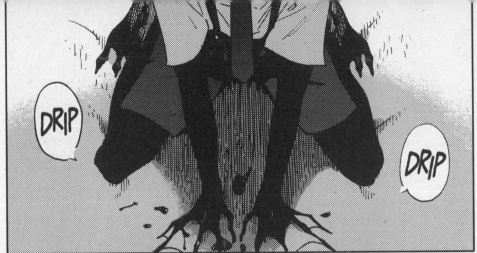

DRIP

DRIP

Pwah!

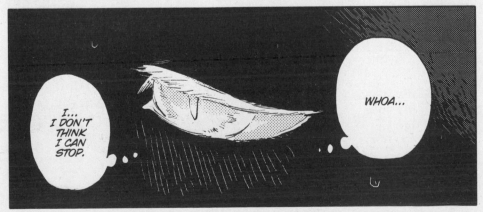

I... I DON'T THINK I CAN STOP.

WHOA...

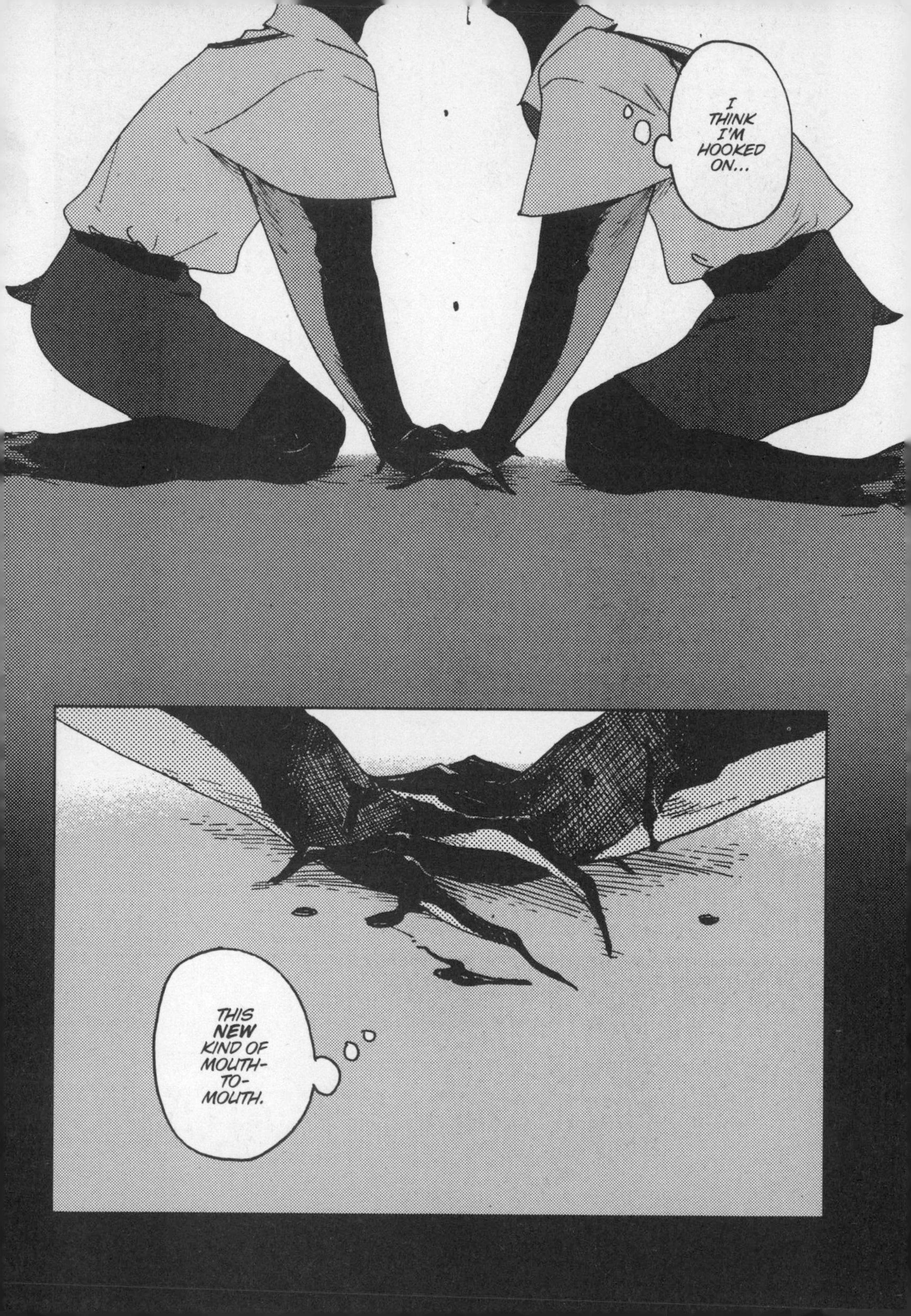
I THINK I'M HOOKED ON...
THIS NEW KIND OF MOUTH-TO-MOUTH.

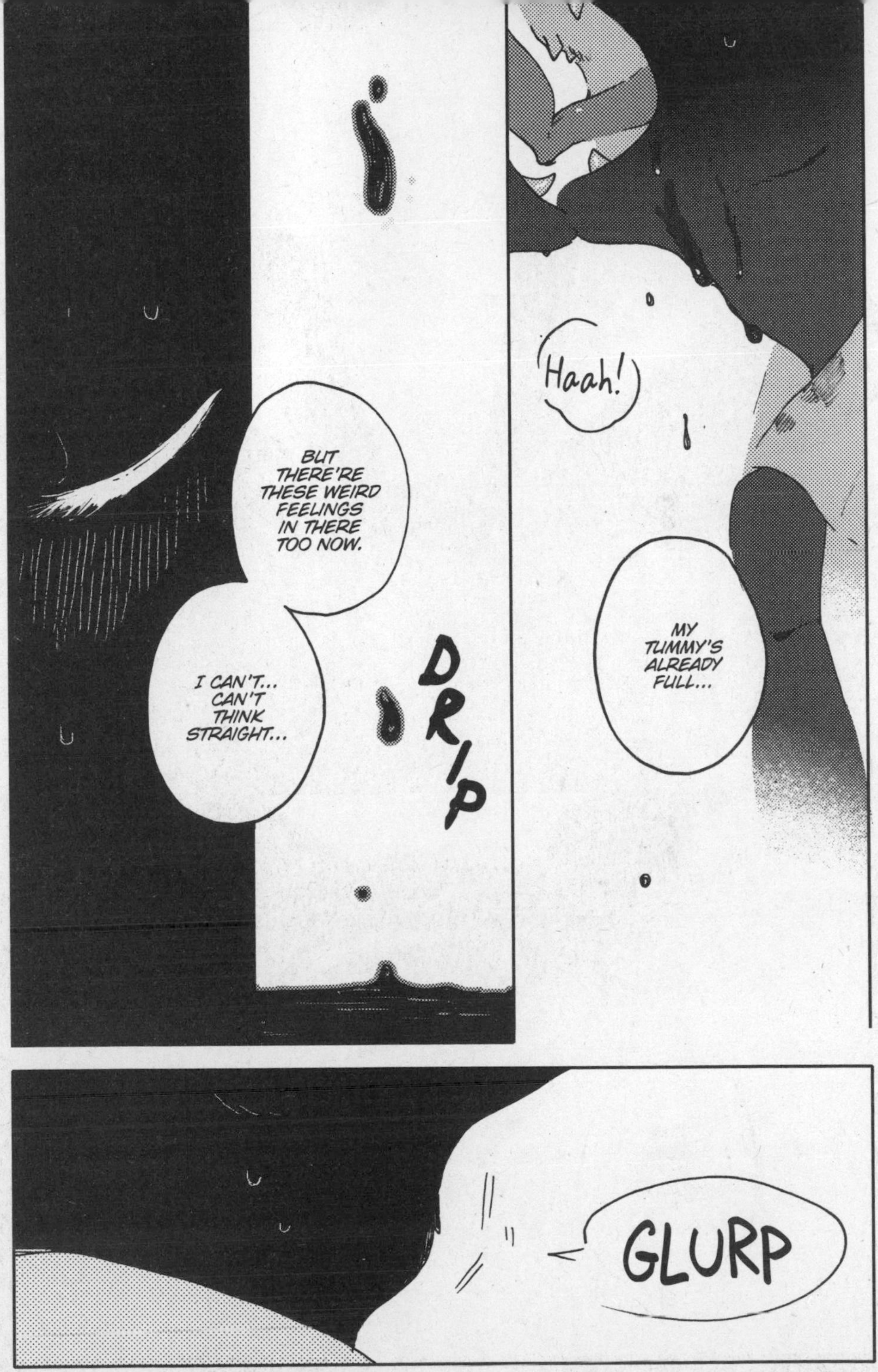
Haah!
MY TUMMY'S ALREADY FULL...
BUT THERE'RE THESE WEIRD FEELINGS IN THERE TOO NOW.
I CAN'T... CAN'T THINK STRAIGHT...
DRIP
GLURP

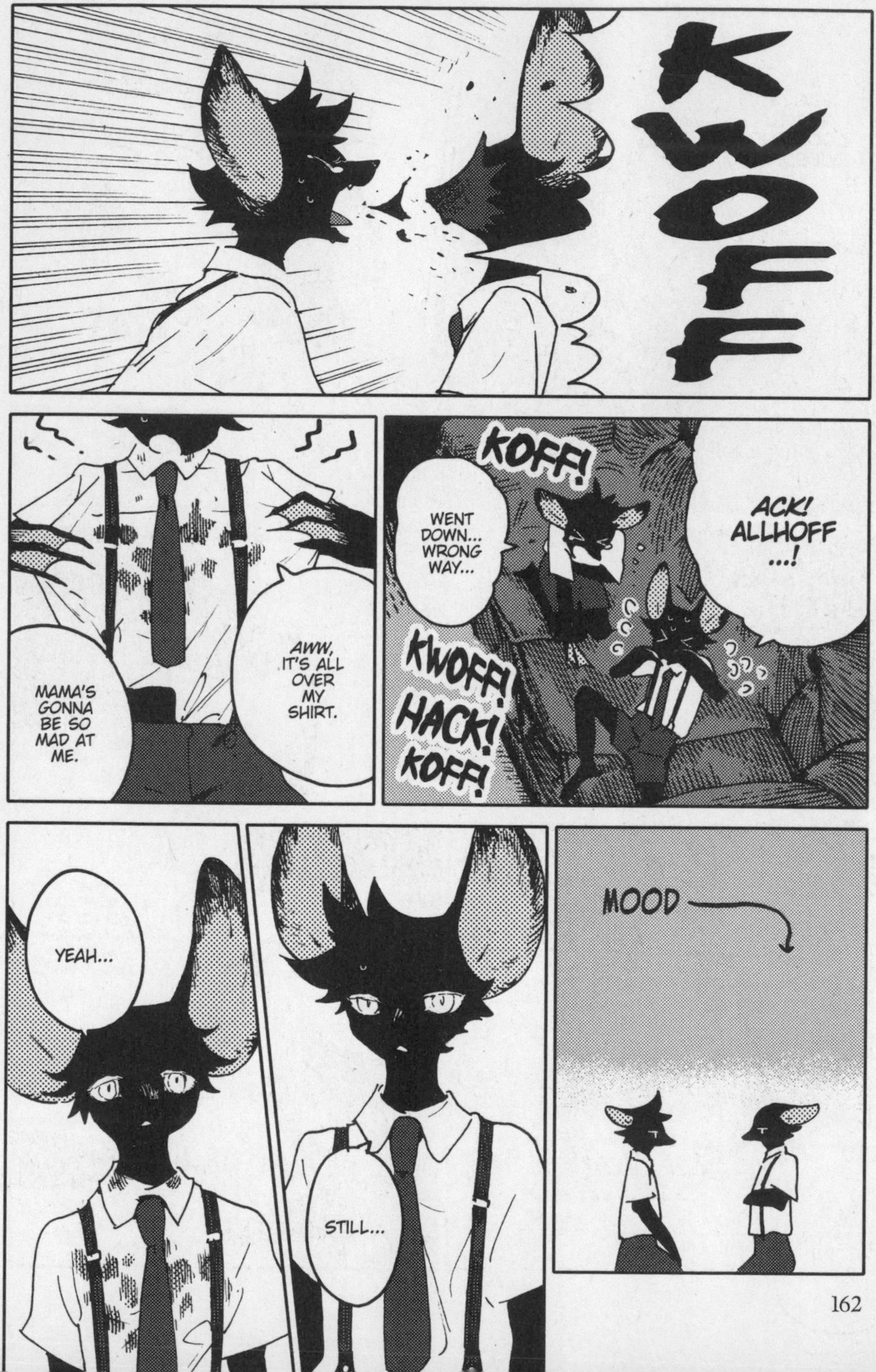
KWOFF
ACK! ALLHOFF ...!
KOFF!
WENT DOWN... WRONG WAY...
KWOFF! HACK! KOFF!
AWW, IT'S ALL OVER MY SHIRT.
MAMA'S GONNA BE SO MAD AT ME.
MOOD
STILL...
YEAH...

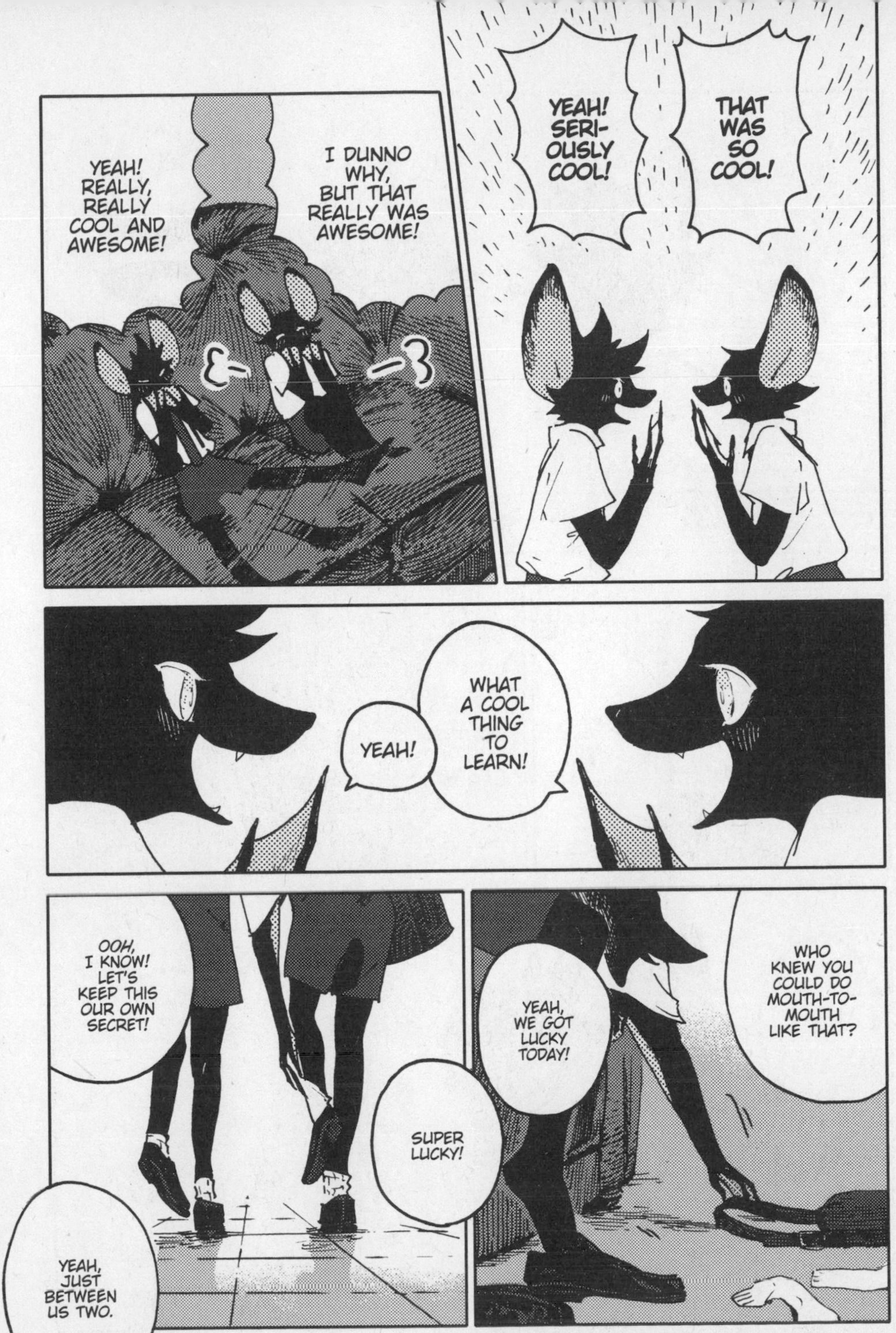
THAT WAS SO COOL!
YEAH! SERI-OUSLY COOL!
I DUNNO WHY, BUT THAT REALLY WAS AWESOME!
YEAH! REALLY, REALLY COOL AND AWESOME!
WHAT A COOL THING TO LEARN!
YEAH!
WHO KNEW YOU COULD DO MOUTH-TO-MOUTH LIKE THAT?
YEAH, WE GOT LUCKY TODAY!
SUPER LUCKY!
OOH, I KNOW! LET'S KEEP THIS OUR OWN SECRET!
YEAH, JUST BETWEEN US TWO.

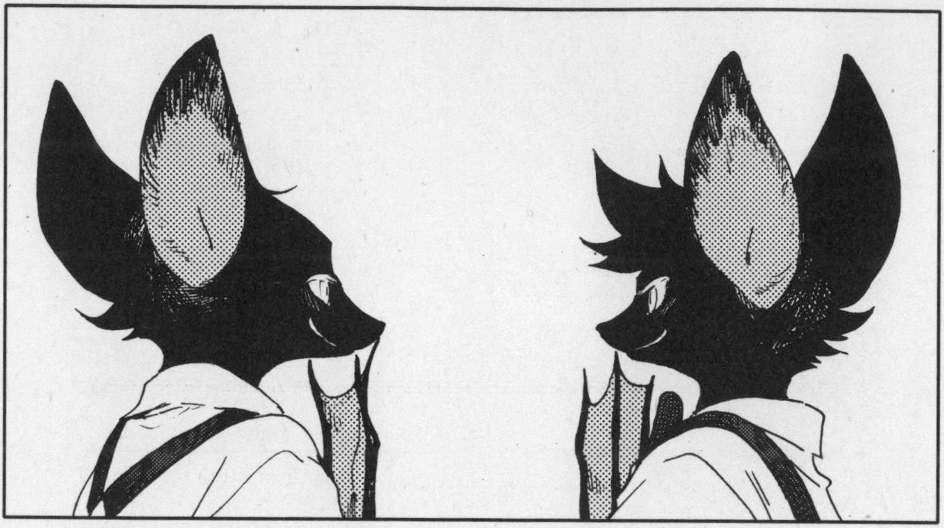

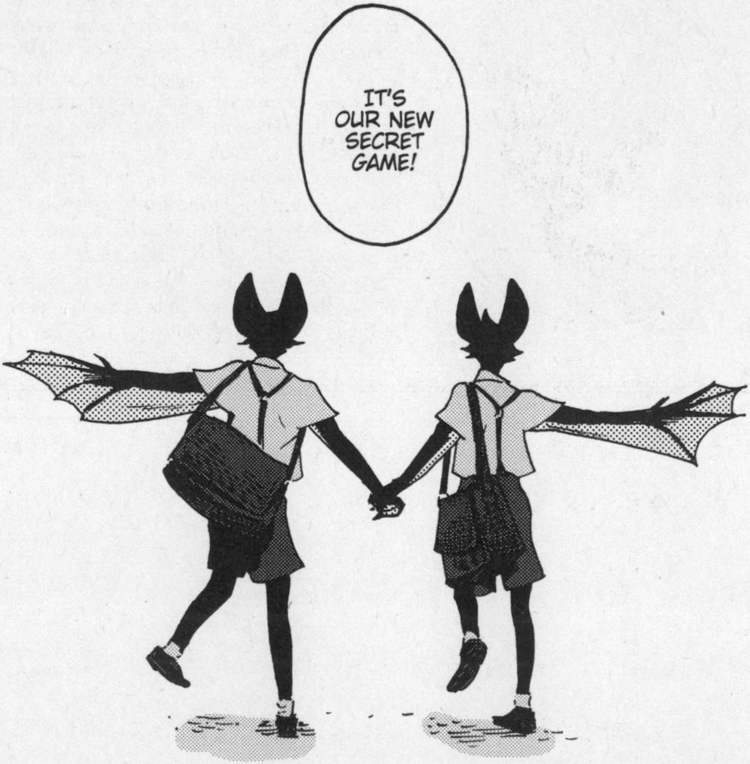
IT'S OUR NEW SECRET GAME!

◆ END ◆

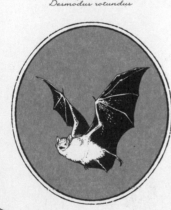

Chiroptera | Phyllostomidae *Desmodus*

COMMON VAMPIRE BAT

Desmodus rotundus

Bats are the only living winged mammals capable of flight. Their wing membranes are an extension of their back and flank skin, connected to their arms. They have large wingspans for their size.

As nocturnal animals, they use echolocation to maneuver in the dark and detect their prey. They feed exclusively on blood, a practice called hematophagy, preying on other mammals (and the occasional human) like livestock. Once a likely target is located, they will land and approach their prey quietly from the ground, then bite them and lap blood from the wound. It takes them upwards of half an hour to drink only 25ml or so. Their teeth are so sharp their prey barely notices the 5mm incision in their skin, and their saliva contains anticoagulants, which prolongs bleeding.

The Wize Wize Beasts
of the Wizarding Wizdoms
by Nagabe

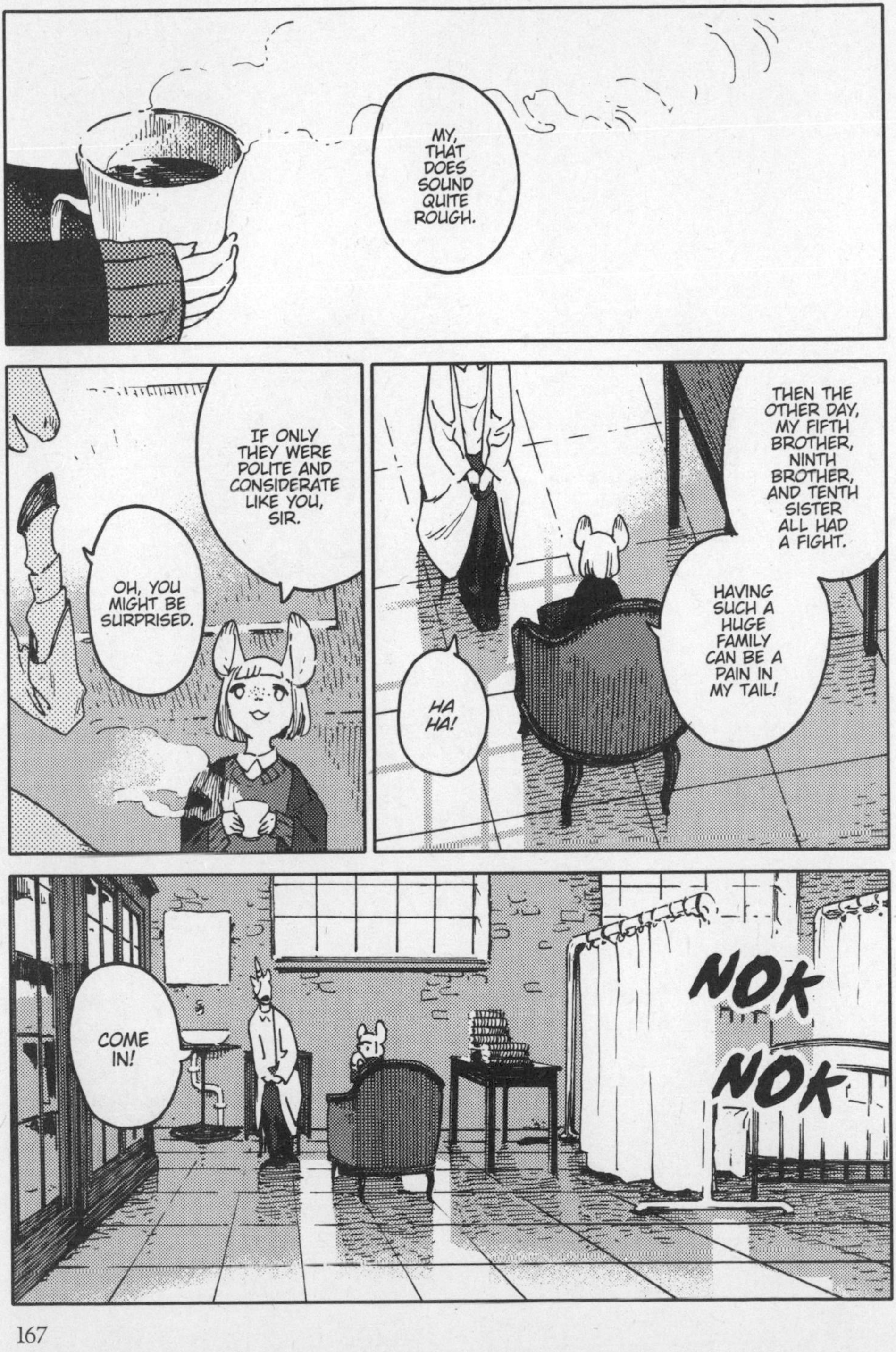
MY, THAT DOES SOUND QUITE ROUGH.
THEN THE OTHER DAY, MY FIFTH BROTHER, NINTH BROTHER, AND TENTH SISTER ALL HAD A FIGHT.
HAVING SUCH A HUGE FAMILY CAN BE A PAIN IN MY TAIL!
HA HA!
IF ONLY THEY WERE POLITE AND CONSIDERATE LIKE YOU, SIR.
OH, YOU MIGHT BE SURPRISED.
NOK NOK
COME IN!

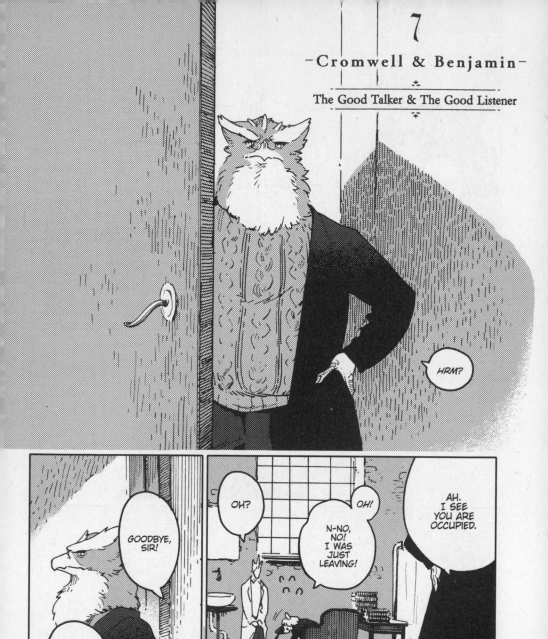

7

-Cromwell & Benjamin-

The Good Talker & The Good Listener

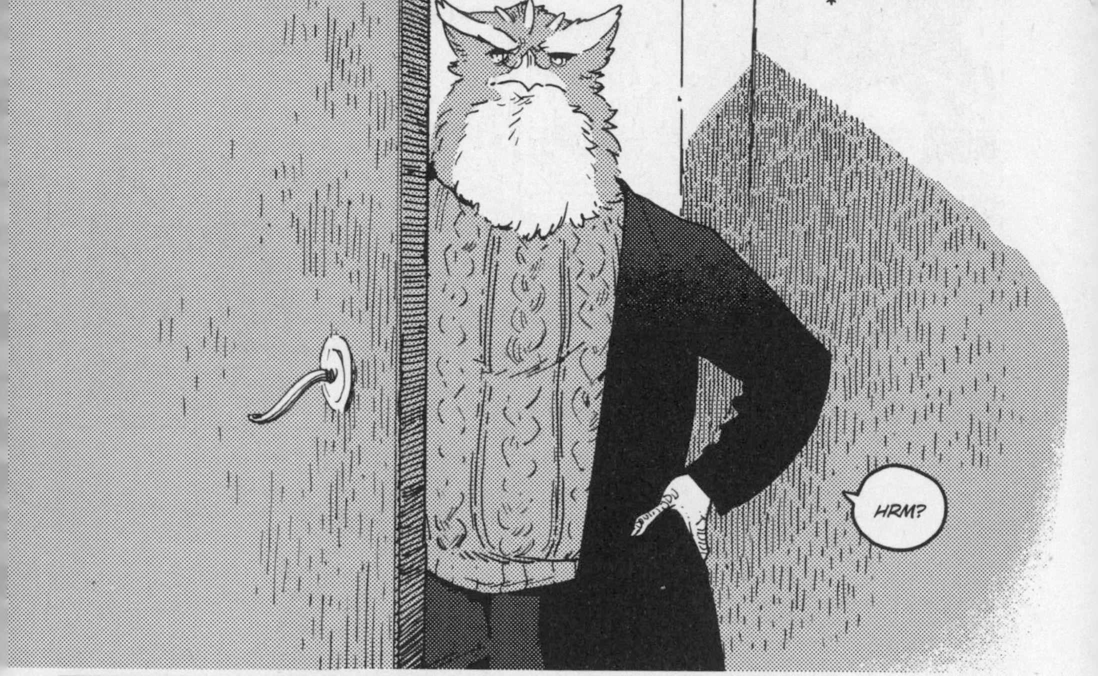
HRM?

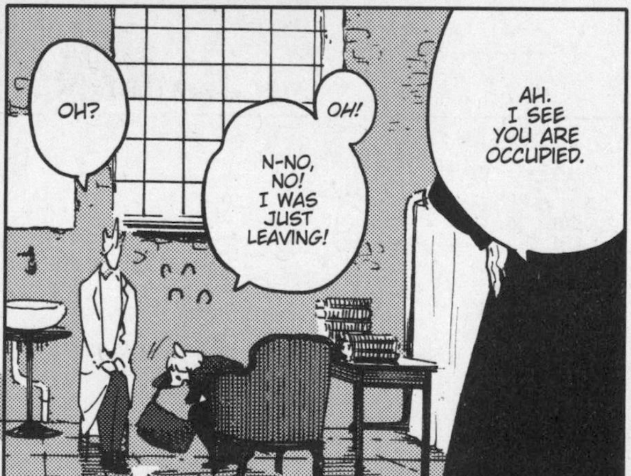
AH. I SEE YOU ARE OCCUPIED.
OH!
N-NO, NO! I WAS JUST LEAVING!
OH?

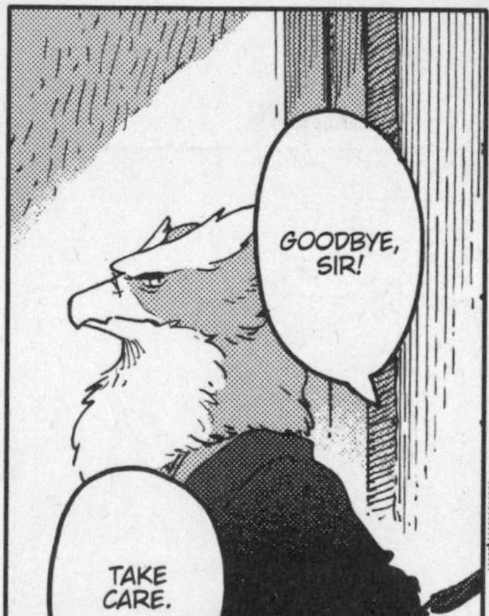
GOODBYE, SIR!
TAKE CARE.

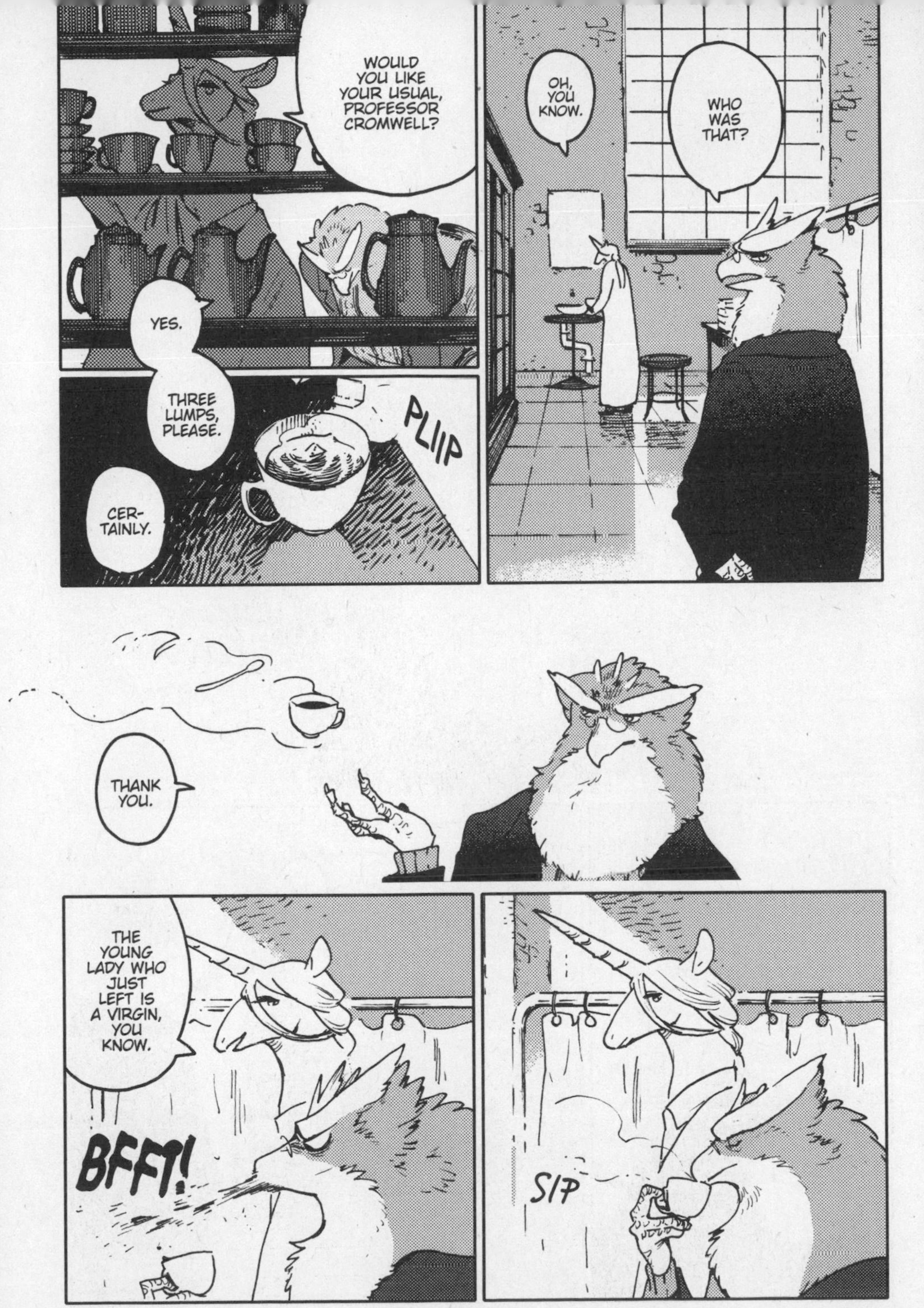
WHO WAS THAT?
OH, YOU KNOW.
WOULD YOU LIKE YOUR USUAL, PROFESSOR CROMWELL?
YES.
THREE LUMPS, PLEASE.
PLIIP
CER-TAINLY.
THANK YOU.
SIP
THE YOUNG LADY WHO JUST LEFT IS A VIRGIN, YOU KNOW.
BFFT!

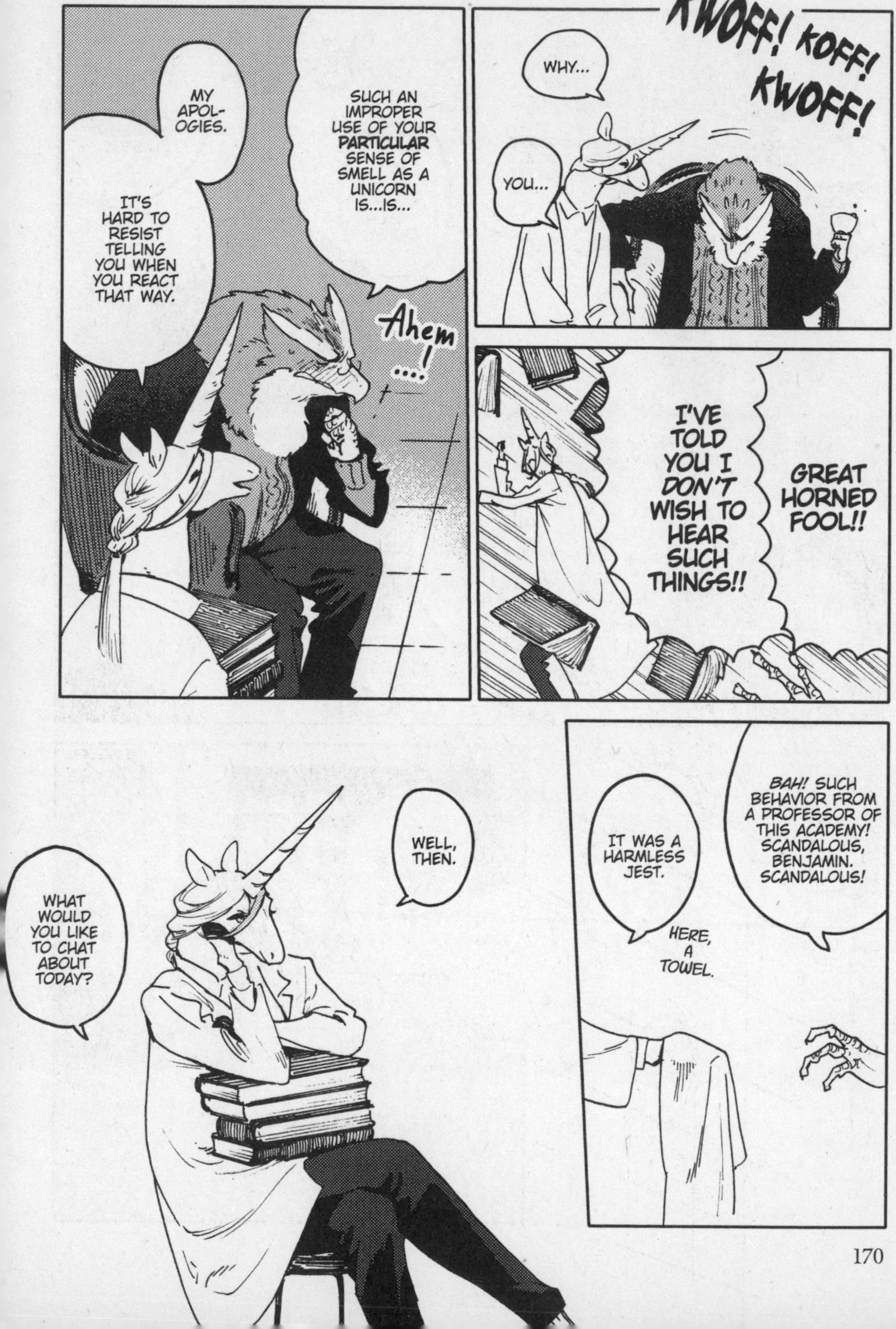
SUCH AN IMPROPER USE OF YOUR PARTICULAR SENSE OF SMELL AS A UNICORN IS...IS...
MY APOL-OGIES.
IT'S HARD TO RESIST TELLING YOU WHEN YOU REACT THAT WAY.
Ahem ...!
KWOFF! KOFF! KWOFF!
WHY...
YOU...
I'VE TOLD YOU I DON'T WISH TO HEAR SUCH THINGS!!
GREAT HORNED FOOL!!
BAH! SUCH BEHAVIOR FROM A PROFESSOR OF THIS ACADEMY! SCANDALOUS, BENJAMIN. SCANDALOUS!
IT WAS A HARMLESS JEST.
HERE, A TOWEL.
WELL, THEN.
WHAT WOULD YOU LIKE TO CHAT ABOUT TODAY?

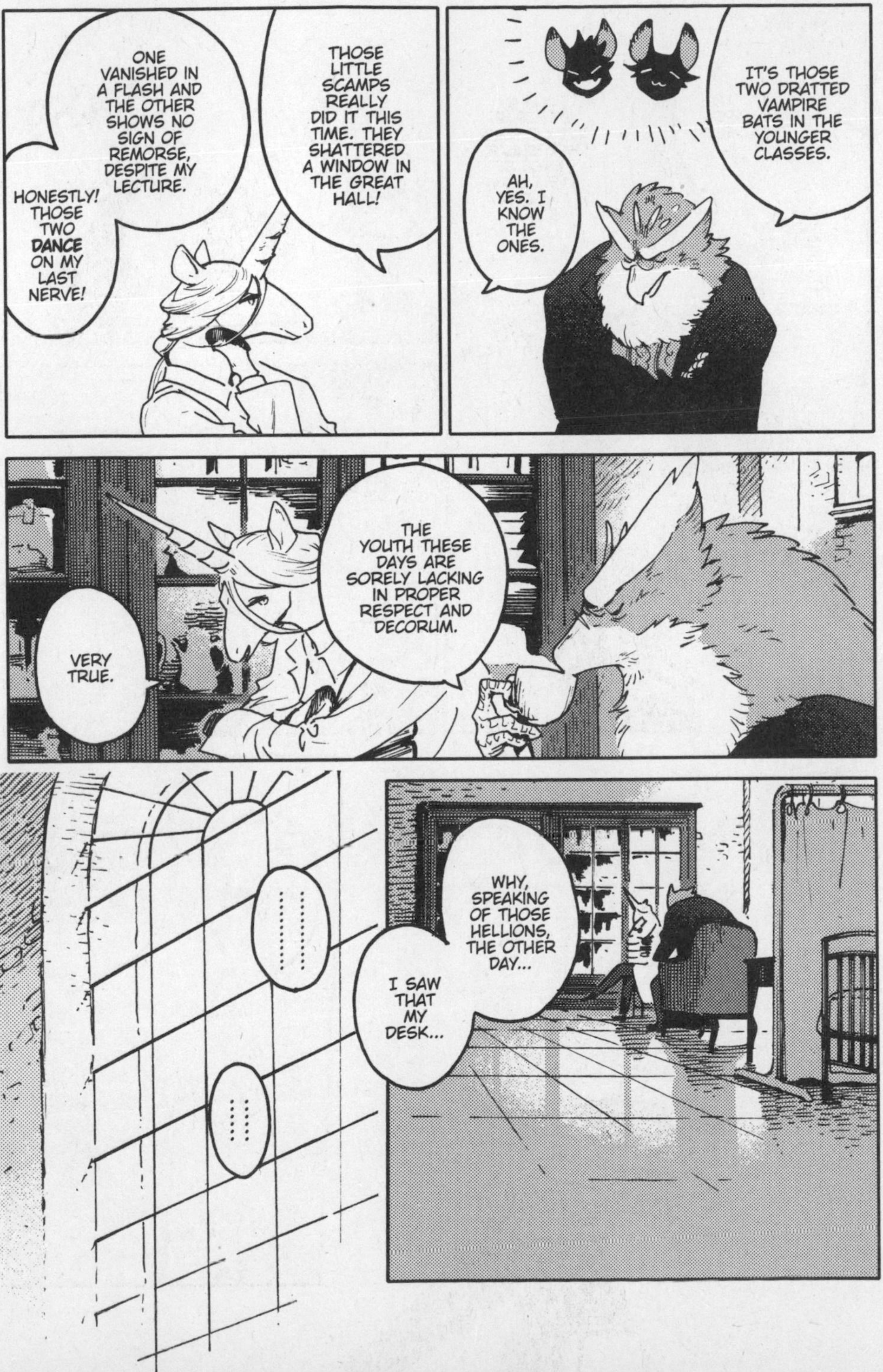
IT'S THOSE TWO DRATTED VAMPIRE BATS IN THE YOUNGER CLASSES.
AH, YES. I KNOW THE ONES.
THOSE LITTLE SCAMPS REALLY DID IT THIS TIME. THEY SHATTERED A WINDOW IN THE GREAT HALL!
ONE VANISHED IN A FLASH AND THE OTHER SHOWS NO SIGN OF REMORSE, DESPITE MY LECTURE.
HONESTLY! THOSE TWO DANCE ON MY LAST NERVE!
THE YOUTH THESE DAYS ARE SORELY LACKING IN PROPER RESPECT AND DECORUM.
VERY TRUE.
WHY, SPEAKING OF THOSE HELLIONS, THE OTHER DAY...
I SAW THAT MY DESK...

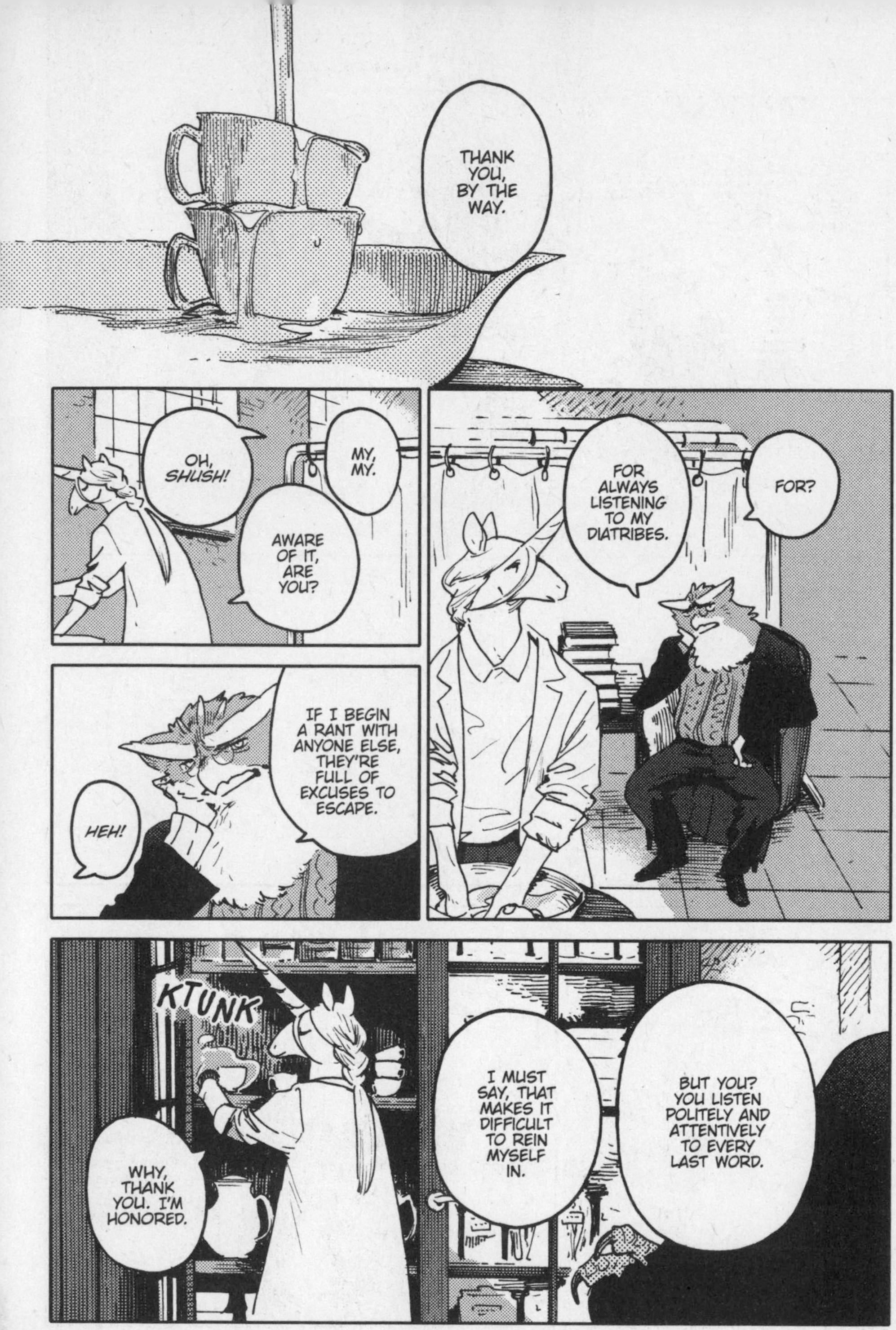
THANK YOU, BY THE WAY.
FOR?
FOR ALWAYS LISTENING TO MY DIATRIBES.
MY, MY.
OH, SHUSH!
AWARE OF IT, ARE YOU?
IF I BEGIN A RANT WITH ANYONE ELSE, THEY'RE FULL OF EXCUSES TO ESCAPE.
HEH!
BUT YOU? YOU LISTEN POLITELY AND ATTENTIVELY TO EVERY LAST WORD.
I MUST SAY, THAT MAKES IT DIFFICULT TO REIN MYSELF IN.
KTUNK
WHY, THANK YOU. I'M HONORED.

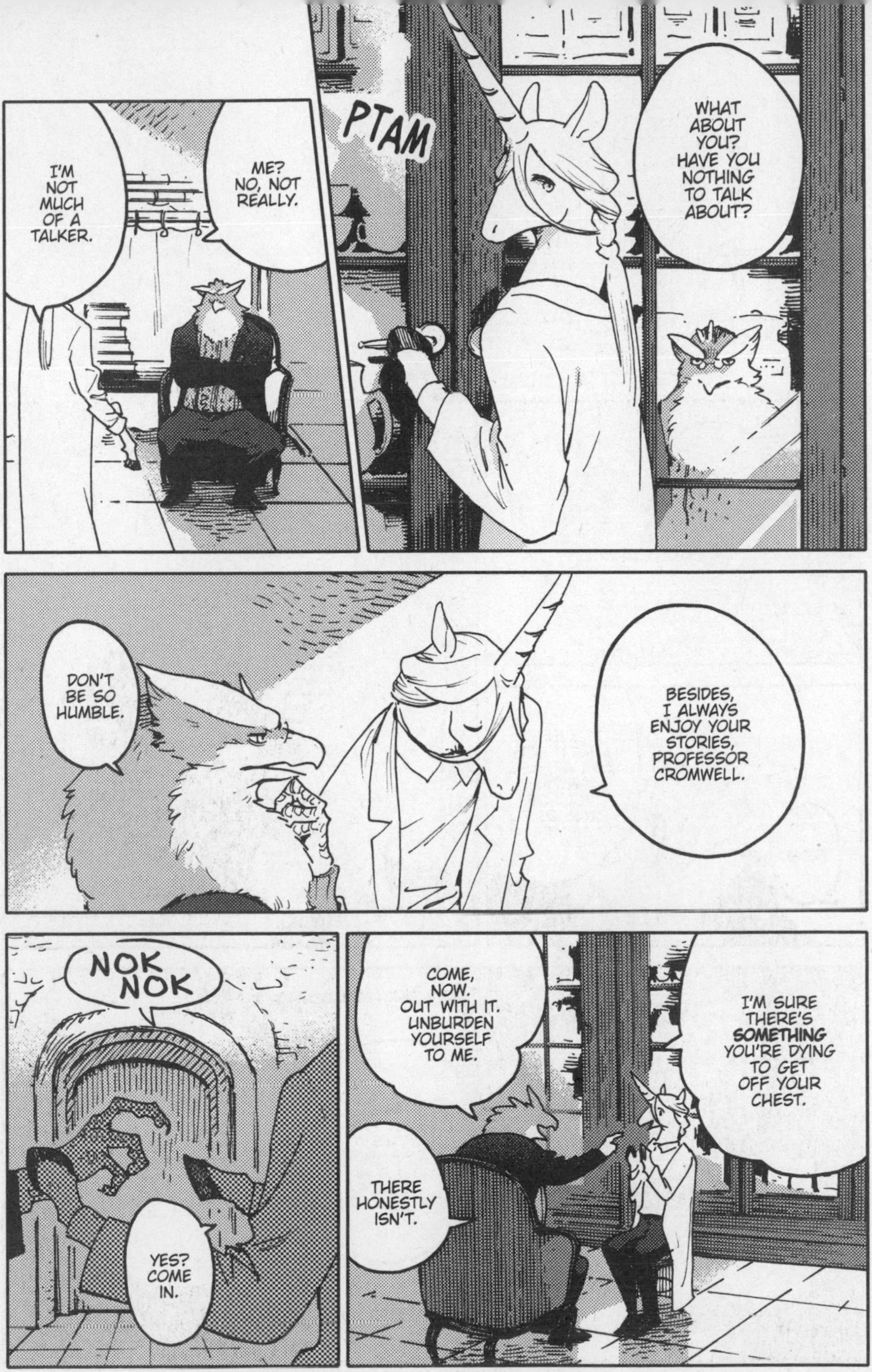
WHAT ABOUT YOU? HAVE YOU NOTHING TO TALK ABOUT?
PTAM
ME? NO, NOT REALLY.
I'M NOT MUCH OF A TALKER.
BESIDES, I ALWAYS ENJOY YOUR STORIES, PROFESSOR CROMWELL.
DON'T BE SO HUMBLE.
I'M SURE THERE'S SOMETHING YOU'RE DYING TO GET OFF YOUR CHEST.
COME, NOW. OUT WITH IT. UNBURDEN YOURSELF TO ME.
THERE HONESTLY ISN'T.
NOK NOK
YES? COME IN.

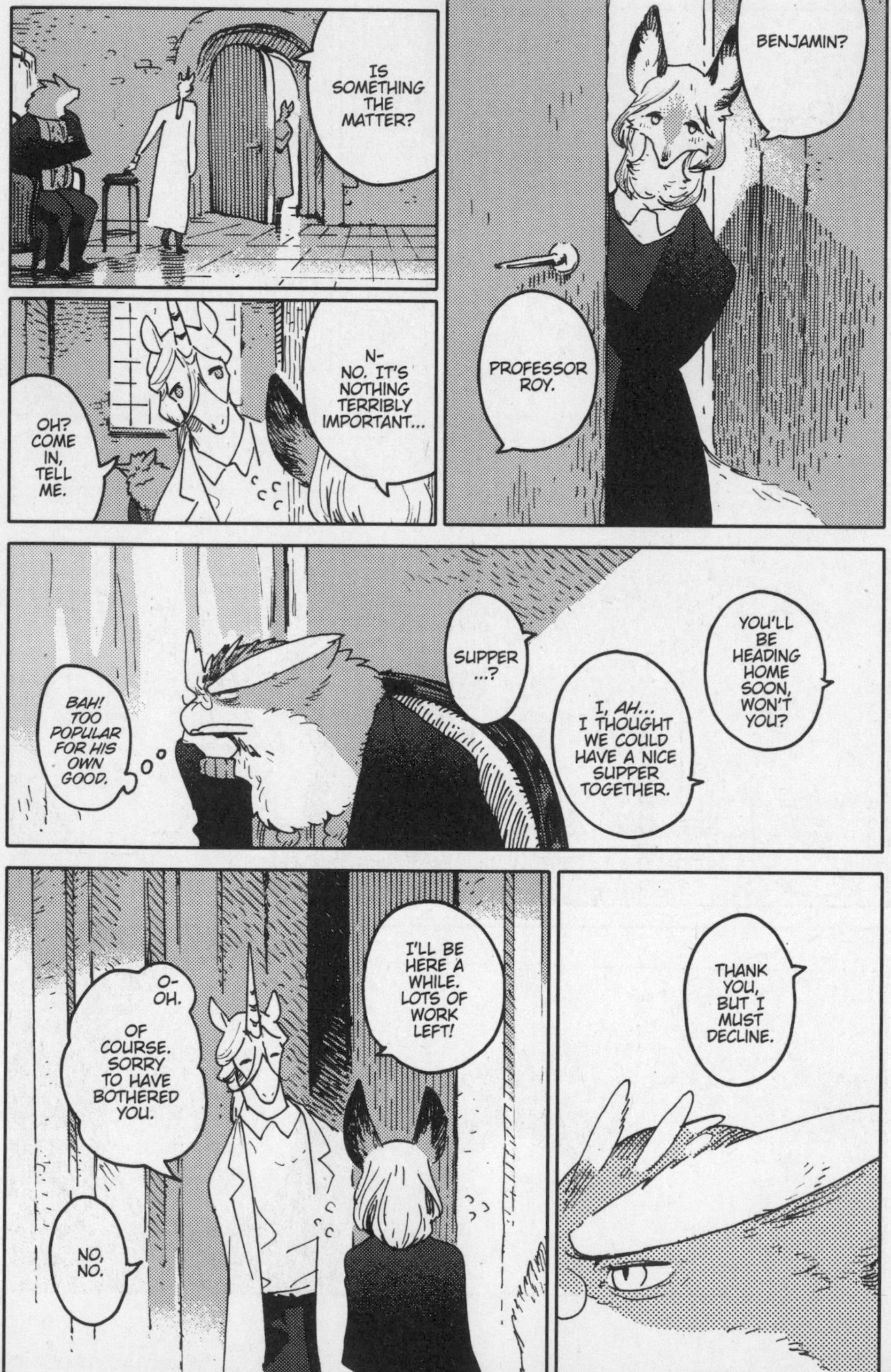
BENJAMIN?
PROFESSOR ROY.
IS SOMETHING THE MATTER?
N-NO. IT'S NOTHING TERRIBLY IMPORTANT...
OH? COME IN, TELL ME.
YOU'LL BE HEADING HOME SOON, WON'T YOU?
I, AH... I THOUGHT WE COULD HAVE A NICE SUPPER TOGETHER.
SUPPER...?
BAH! TOO POPULAR FOR HIS OWN GOOD.
THANK YOU, BUT I MUST DECLINE.
I'LL BE HERE A WHILE. LOTS OF WORK LEFT!
O-OH. OF COURSE. SORRY TO HAVE BOTHERED YOU.
NO, NO.

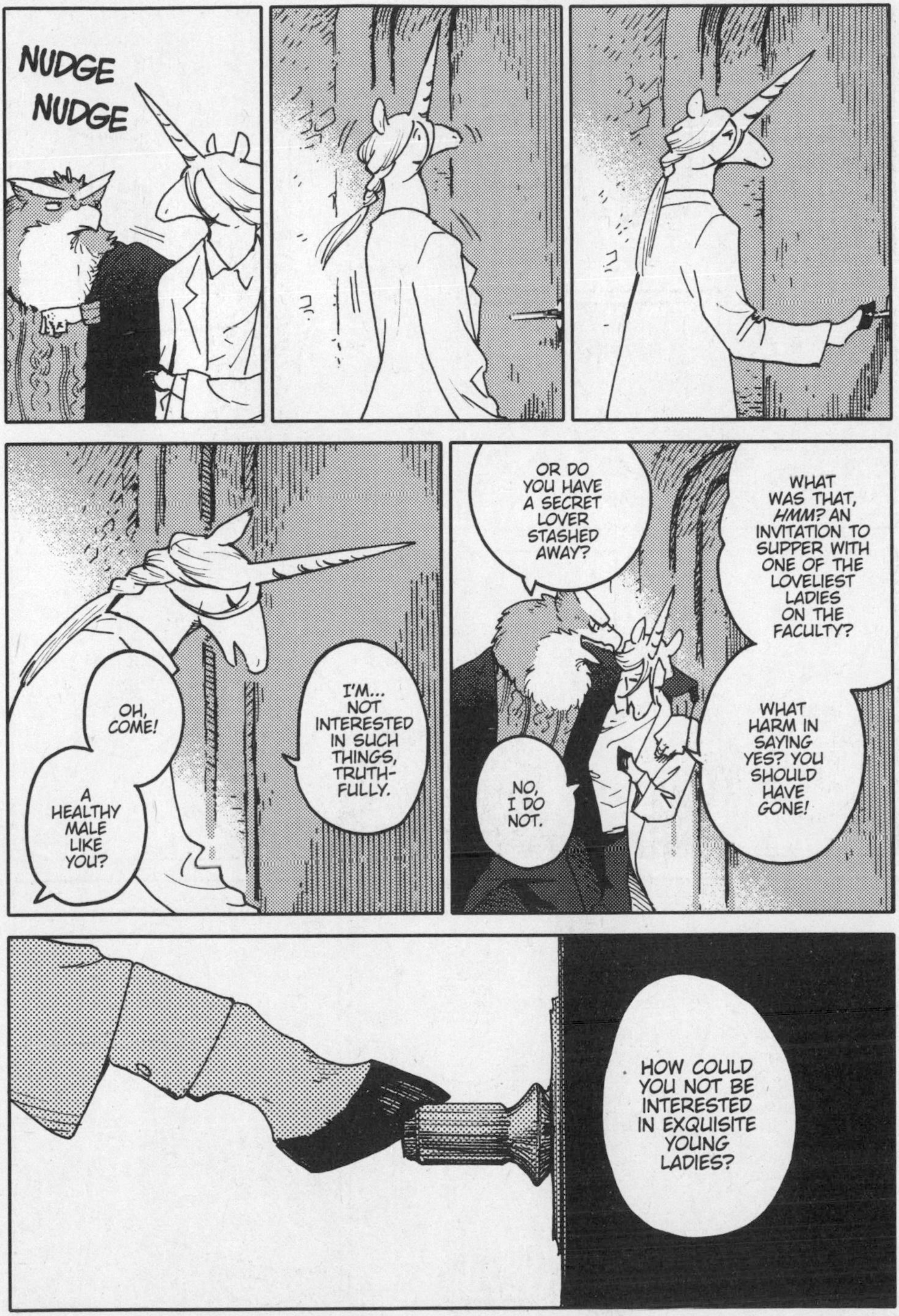
NUDGE NUDGE
WHAT WAS THAT, *HMM?* AN INVITATION TO SUPPER WITH ONE OF THE LOVELIEST LADIES ON THE FACULTY?
OR DO YOU HAVE A SECRET LOVER STASHED AWAY?
WHAT HARM IN SAYING YES? YOU SHOULD HAVE GONE!
NO, I DO NOT.
I'M... NOT INTERESTED IN SUCH THINGS, TRUTHFULLY.
OH, COME!
A HEALTHY MALE LIKE YOU?
HOW COULD YOU NOT BE INTERESTED IN EXQUISITE YOUNG LADIES?

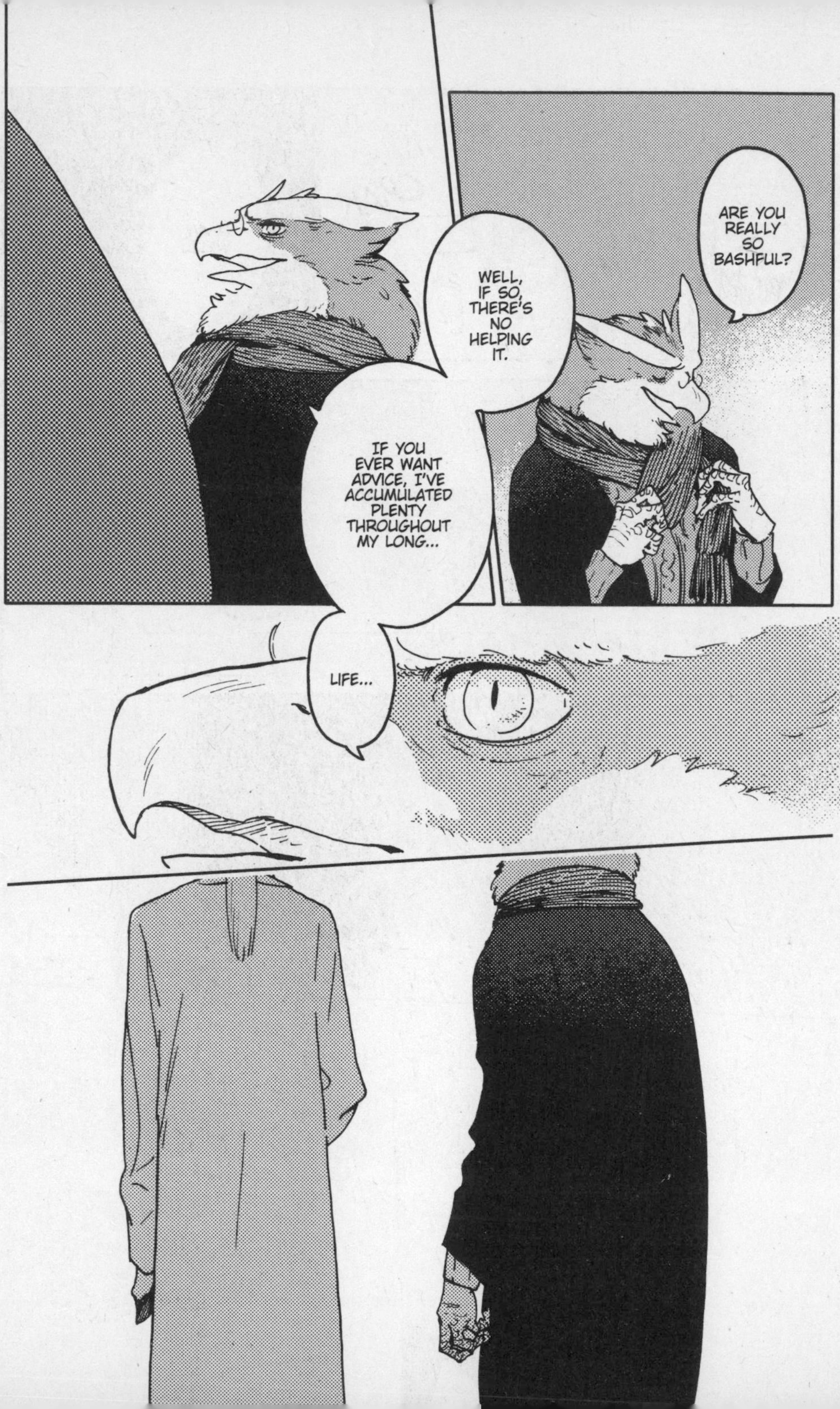
ARE YOU REALLY SO BASHFUL?
WELL, IF SO, THERE'S NO HELPING IT.
IF YOU EVER WANT ADVICE, I'VE ACCUMULATED PLENTY THROUGHOUT MY LONG...
LIFE...

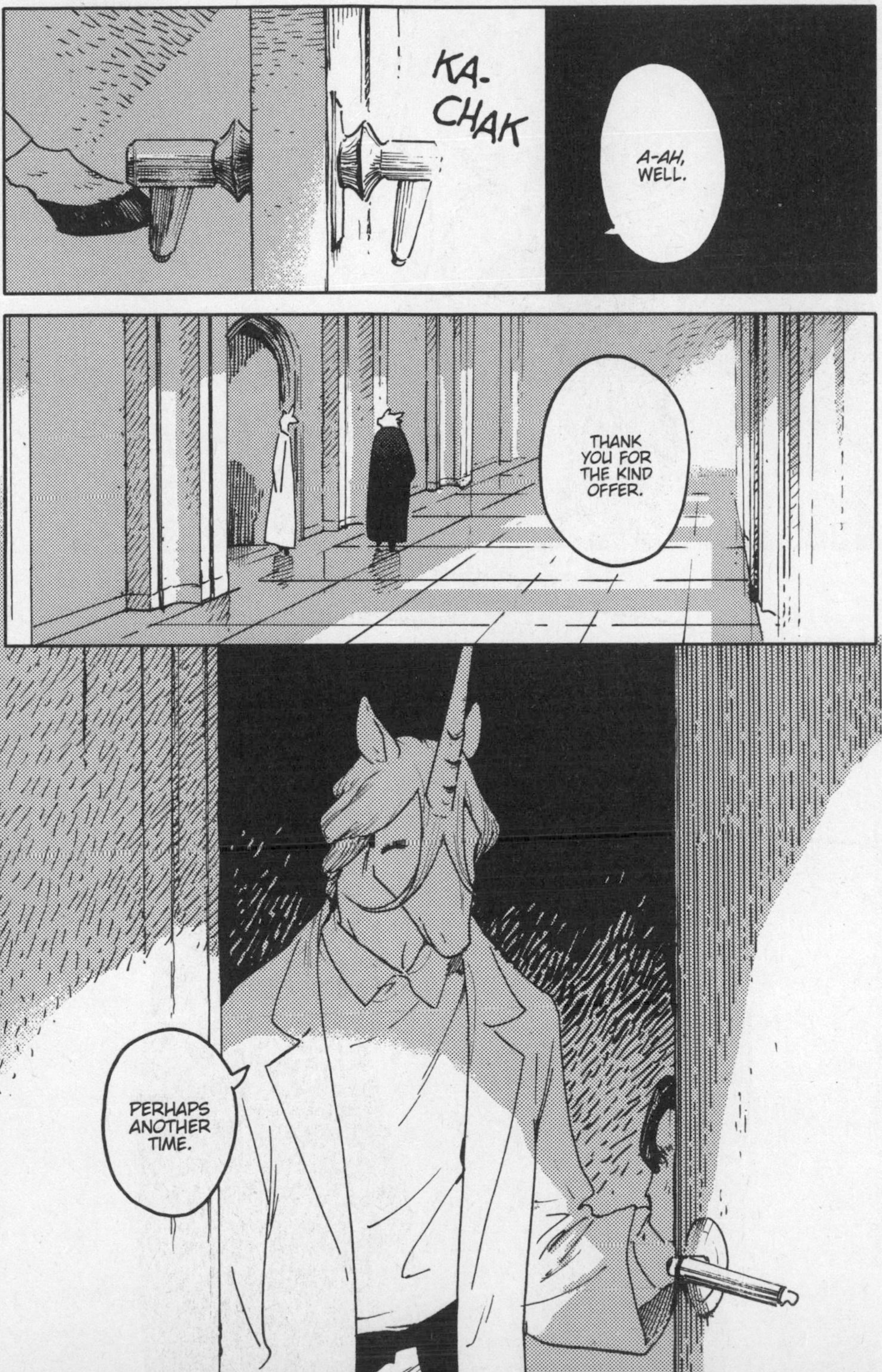
A-AH, WELL.
KA-CHAK
THANK YOU FOR THE KIND OFFER.
PERHAPS ANOTHER TIME.

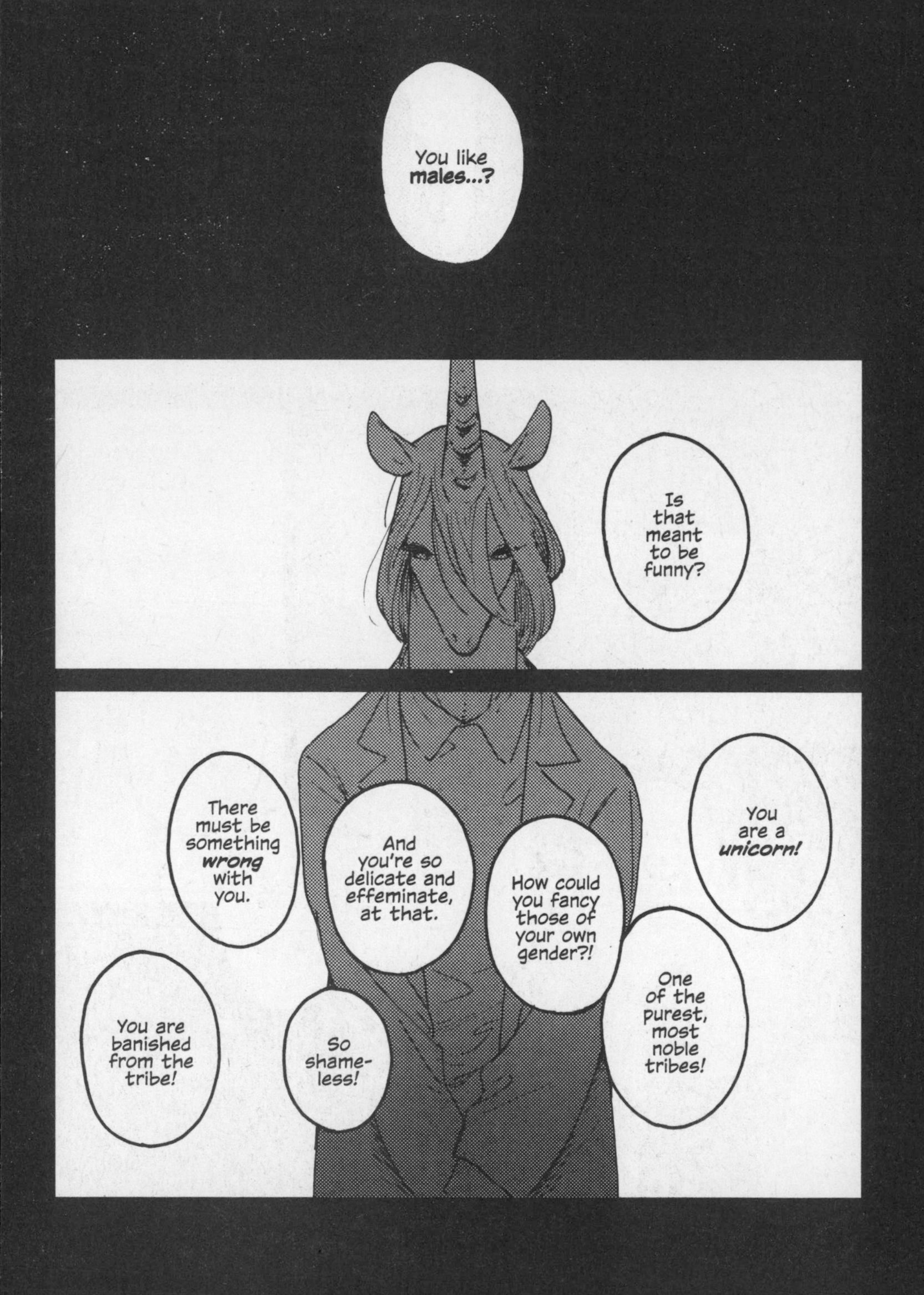
You like males...?
Is that meant to be funny?
You are a unicorn!
One of the purest, most noble tribes!
How could you fancy those of your own gender?!
And you're so delicate and effeminate, at that.
There must be something wrong with you.
So shameless!
You are banished from the tribe!

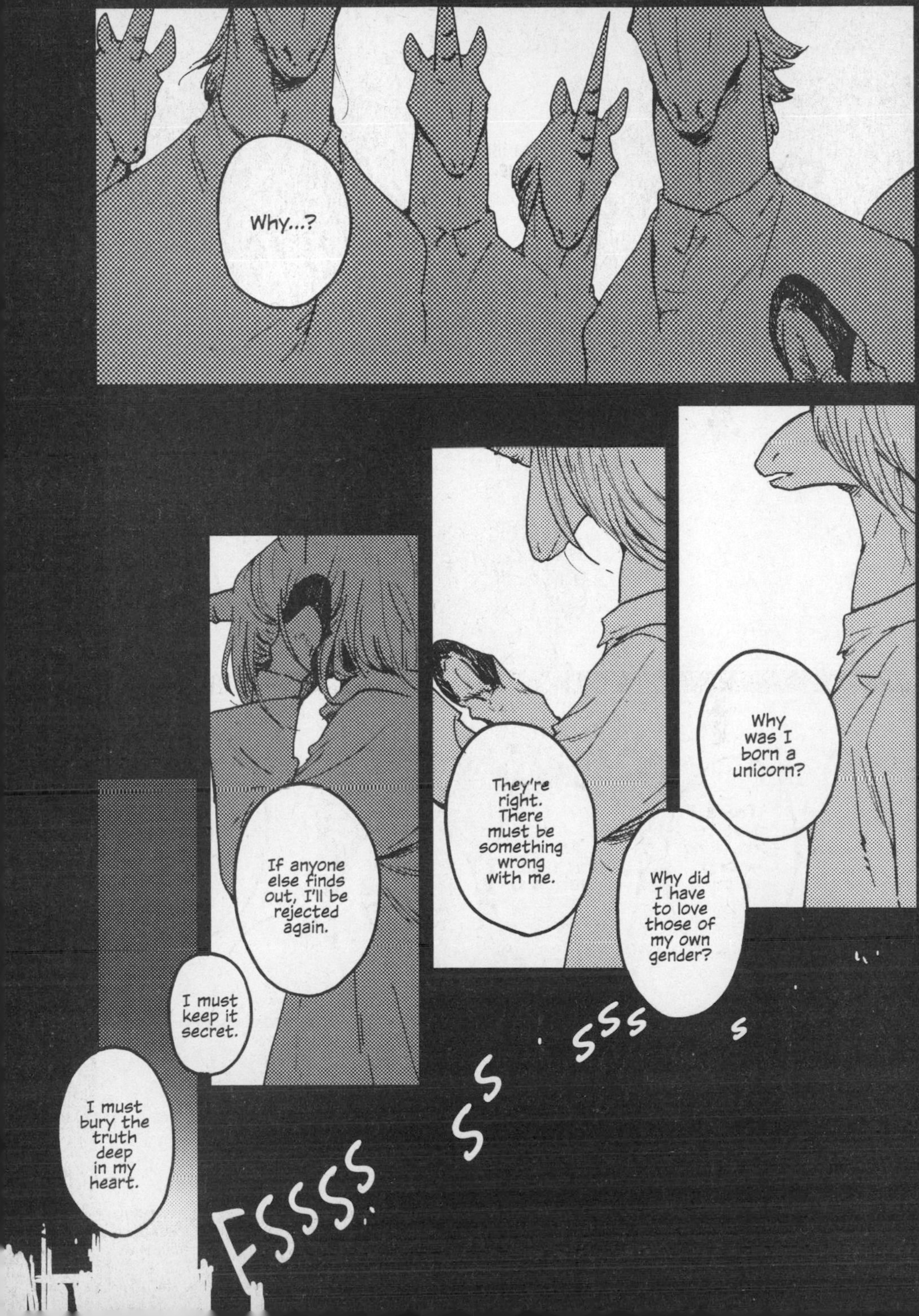
Why...?
Why was I born a unicorn?
Why did I have to love those of my own gender?
They're right. There must be something wrong with me.
If anyone else finds out, I'll be rejected again.
I must keep it secret.
I must bury the truth deep in my heart.
FSSSS

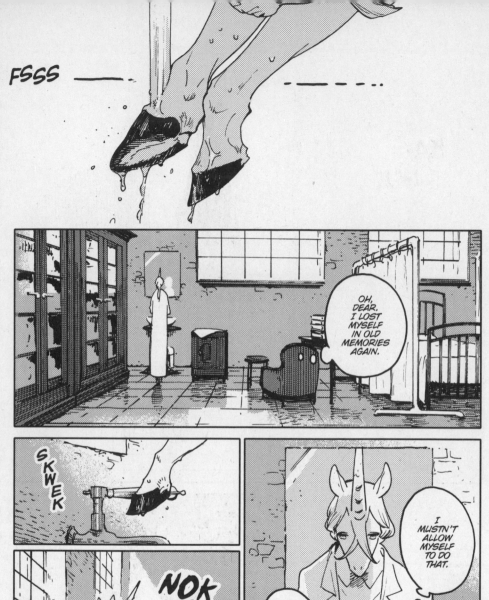

FSSS ————. ————————...

OH, DEAR. I LOST MYSELF IN OLD MEMORIES AGAIN.

SKWEK

I MUSTN'T ALLOW MYSELF TO DO THAT.

I MUST STAY COMPOSED.

NOK NOK

YES? COME IN!

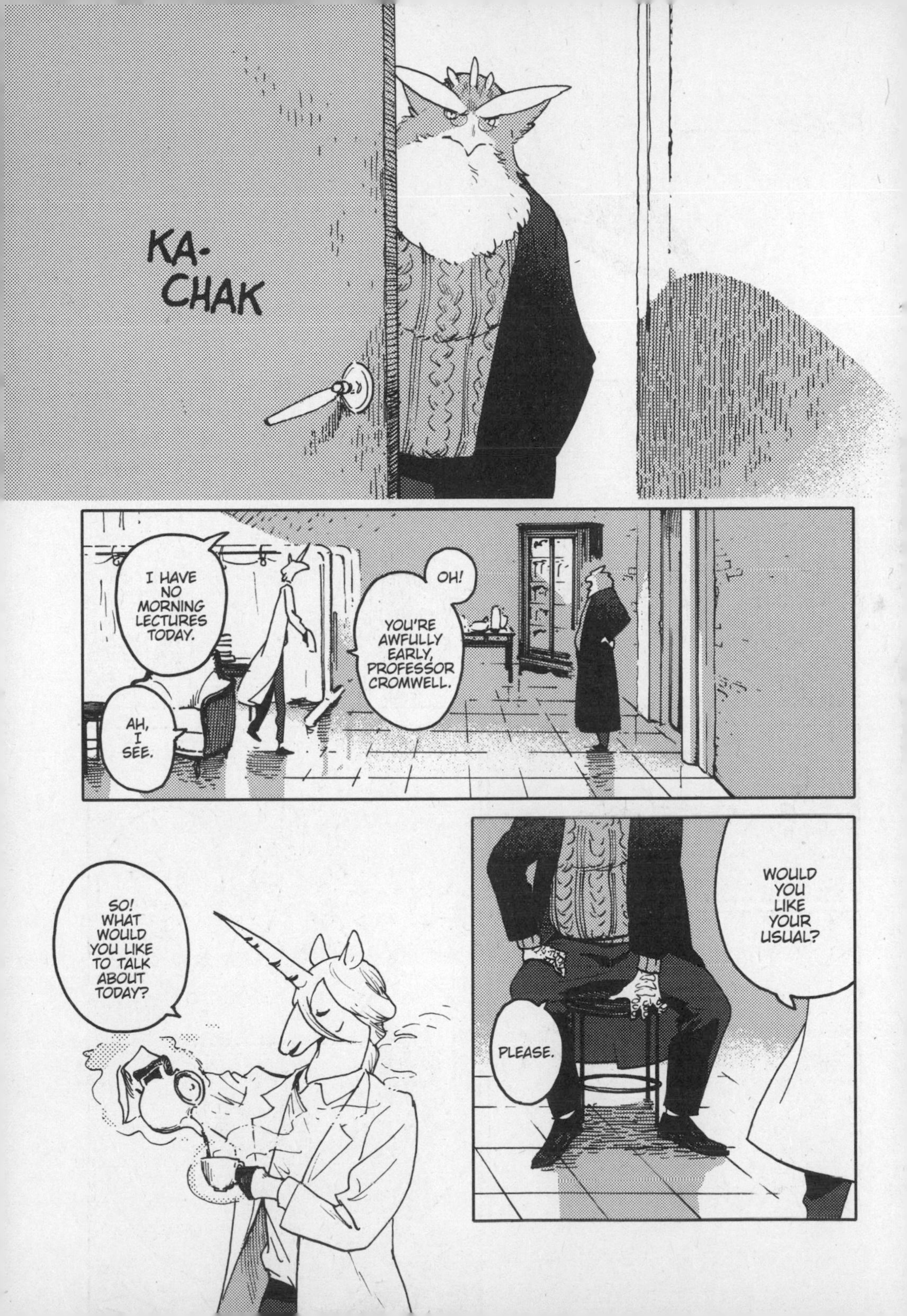
KA-CHAK
OH!
YOU'RE AWFULLY EARLY, PROFESSOR CROMWELL.
I HAVE NO MORNING LECTURES TODAY.
AH, I SEE.
WOULD YOU LIKE YOUR USUAL?
PLEASE.
SO! WHAT WOULD YOU LIKE TO TALK ABOUT TODAY?

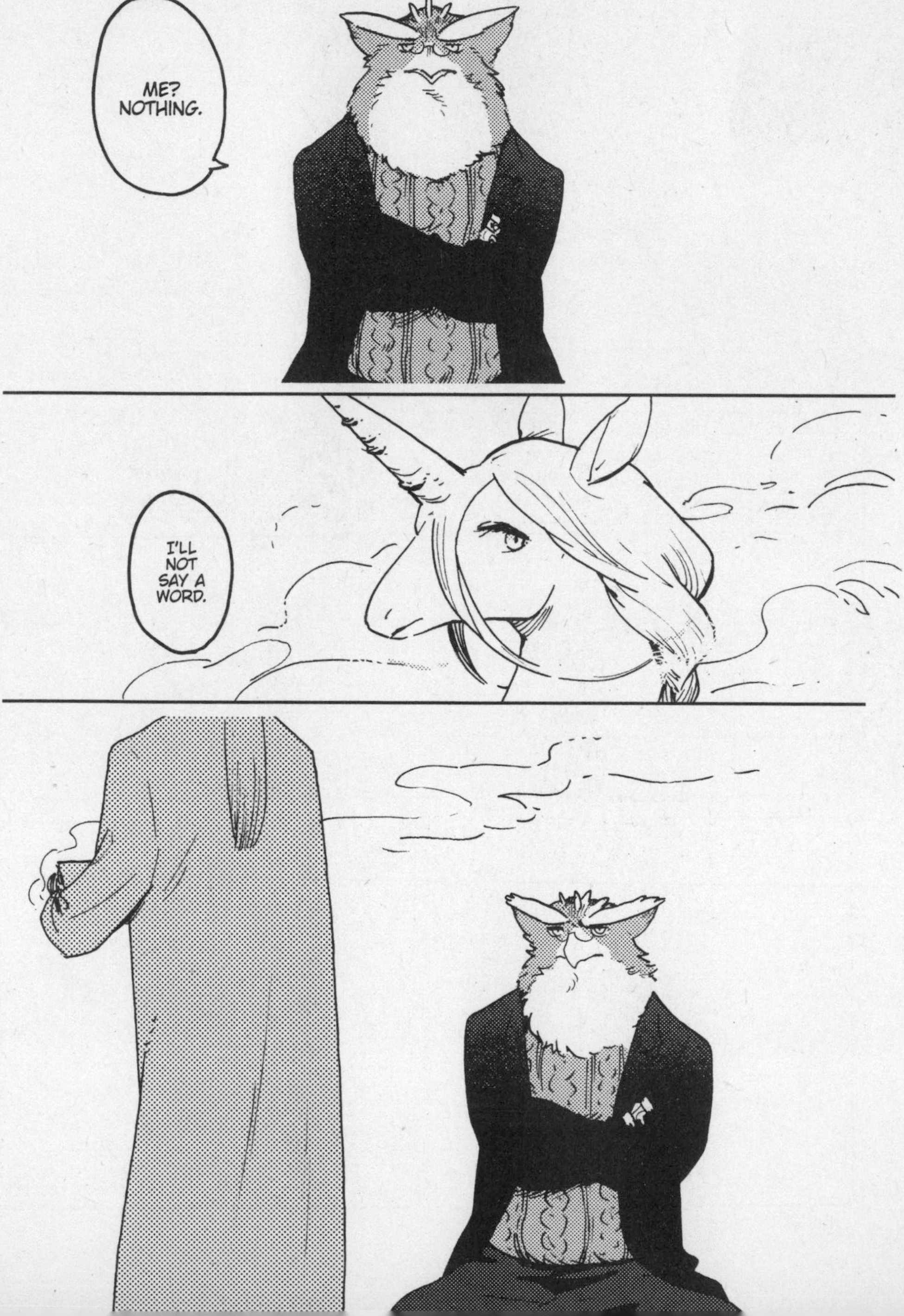
ME? NOTHING.
I'LL NOT SAY A WORD.

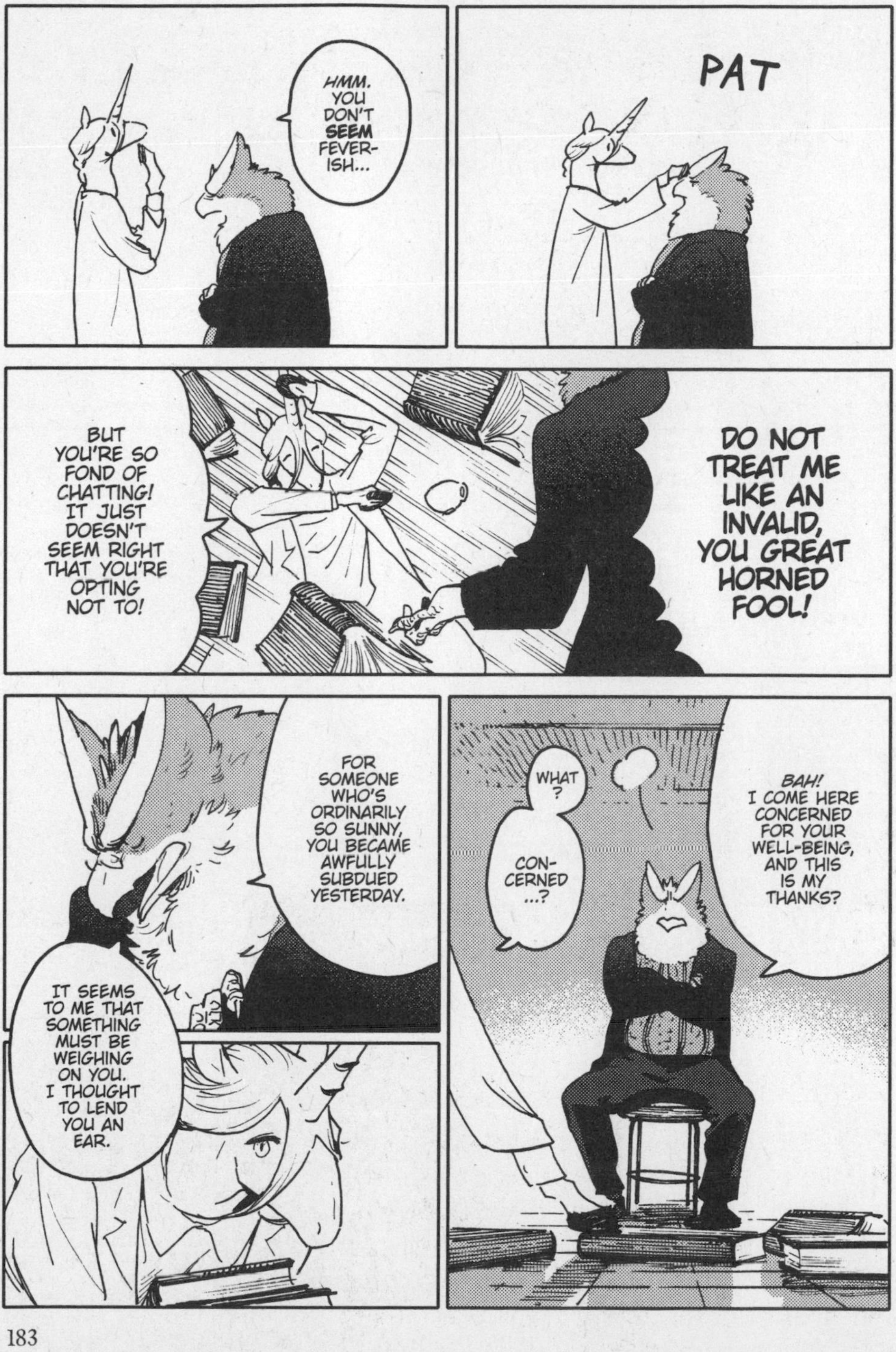
PAT
HMM. YOU DON'T SEEM FEVERISH...
DO NOT TREAT ME LIKE AN INVALID, YOU GREAT HORNED FOOL!
BUT YOU'RE SO FOND OF CHATTING! IT JUST DOESN'T SEEM RIGHT THAT YOU'RE OPTING NOT TO!
BAH! I COME HERE CONCERNED FOR YOUR WELL-BEING, AND THIS IS MY THANKS?
WHAT?
CONCERNED...?
FOR SOMEONE WHO'S ORDINARILY SO SUNNY, YOU BECAME AWFULLY SUBDUED YESTERDAY.
IT SEEMS TO ME THAT SOMETHING MUST BE WEIGHING ON YOU. I THOUGHT TO LEND YOU AN EAR.

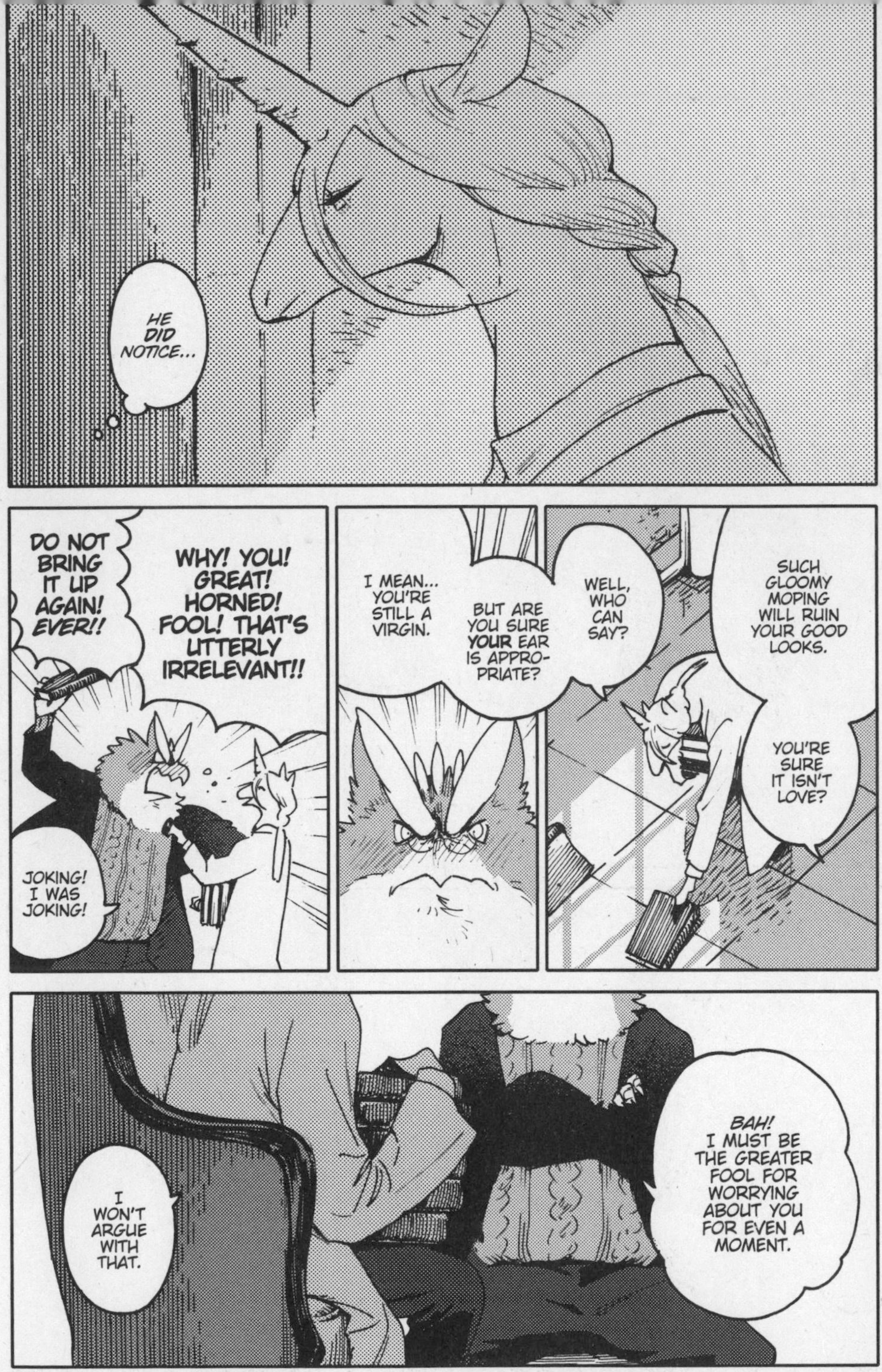
HE DID NOTICE...
SUCH GLOOMY MOPING WILL RUIN YOUR GOOD LOOKS.
YOU'RE SURE IT ISN'T LOVE?
WELL, WHO CAN SAY?
BUT ARE YOU SURE YOUR EAR IS APPROPRIATE?
I MEAN... YOU'RE STILL A VIRGIN.
WHY! YOU! GREAT! HORNED! FOOL! THAT'S UTTERLY IRRELEVANT!!
DO NOT BRING IT UP AGAIN! EVER!!
JOKING! I WAS JOKING!
BAH! I MUST BE THE GREATER FOOL FOR WORRYING ABOUT YOU FOR EVEN A MOMENT.
I WON'T ARGUE WITH THAT.

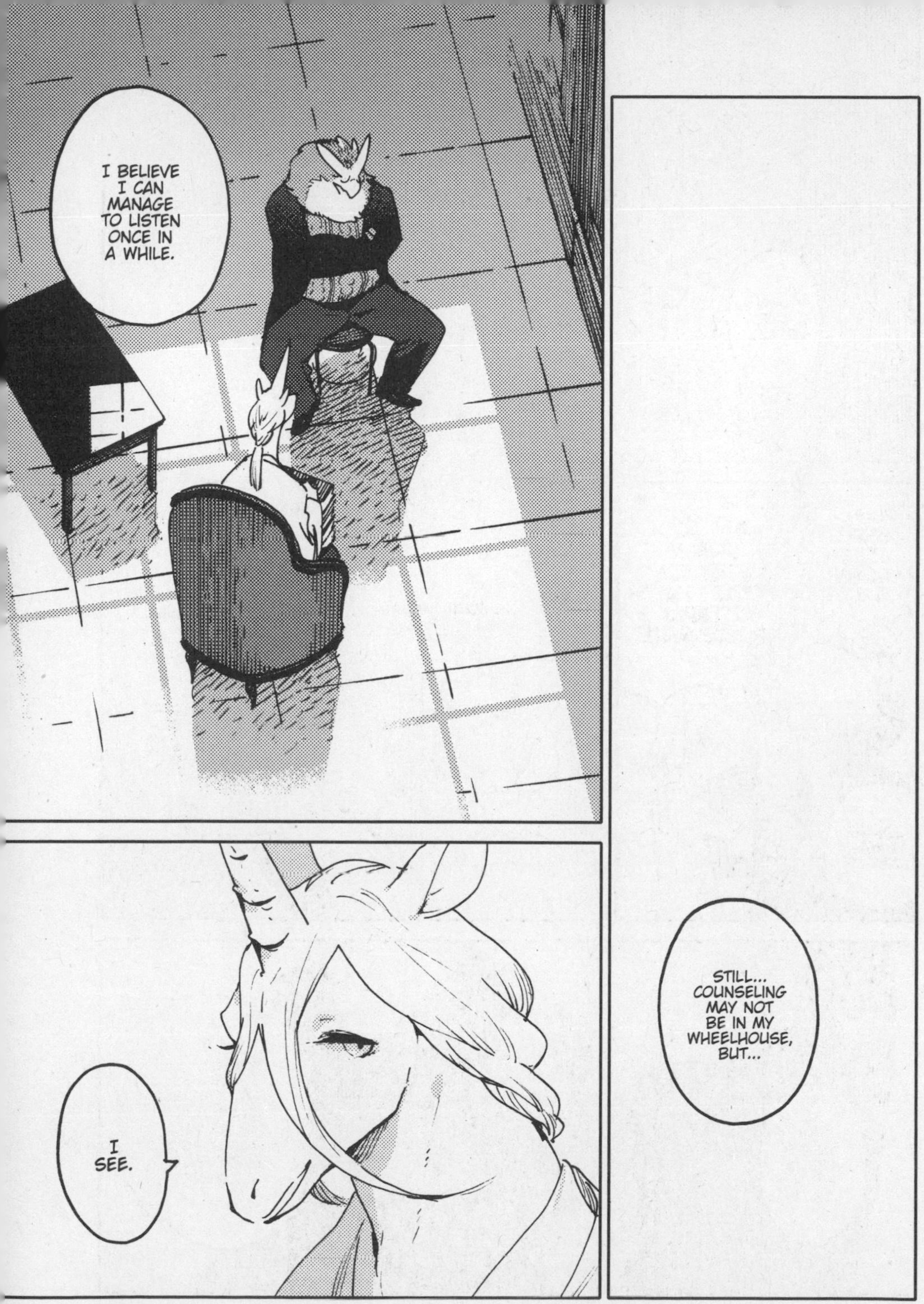
STILL... COUNSELING MAY NOT BE IN MY WHEELHOUSE, BUT...
I BELIEVE I CAN MANAGE TO LISTEN ONCE IN A WHILE.
I SEE.

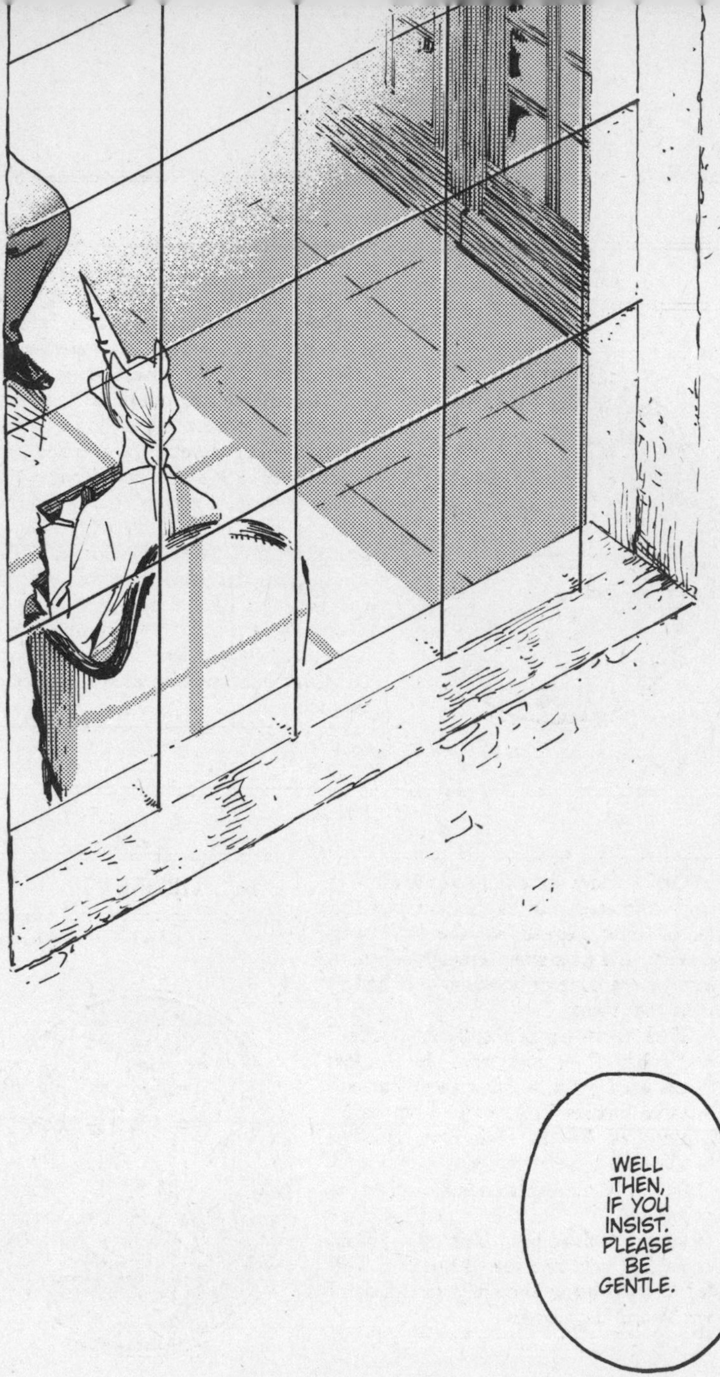
WELL THEN, IF YOU INSIST. PLEASE BE GENTLE.

◆ END ◆

UNICORN

Unicorn

A unicorn is a mystical creature combining traits of horses and deer. Its signature characteristic is the single spiraling horn in the center of its forehead. They are fiercely proud, powerful, and brave, and are nimble and swift enough to outrun a horse and outmaneuver a deer. Their horns, which are supposedly capable of piercing any material, are long, sharp, and strong.

Several mystical powers are attributed to unicorns, from the ability to purify water or neutralize toxins with a touch of their horn to discerning virginity by scent. It's also said that they have a particular fondness for virgins, preferring their company and being calmer and quieter in their presence. Unicorns are often considered a symbol of the moon.

Griffons have the torso and wings of an eagle combined with the hindquarters and tail of a lion. Legends say they are strong enough, and have sharp enough talons, to seize several cows or horses at once and fly away with them.

Their name—spelled "griffon," "griffin," or "gryphon"—comes from the Ancient Greek word *gryps,* which means "curved." As their bodies blend traits from eagles (masters of the sky) and lions (masters of the earth), some regard the griffon as a symbol of the earth and sky united, or of the sun.

Early mythologies claimed griffons could find gold and would hoard it. That led to them being known as guardians of wealth and knowledge.

GRIFFON

Griffon

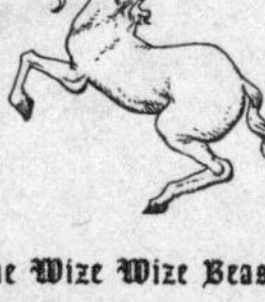

The Wize Wize Beasts
of the Wizarding Wizdoms
by Nagabe

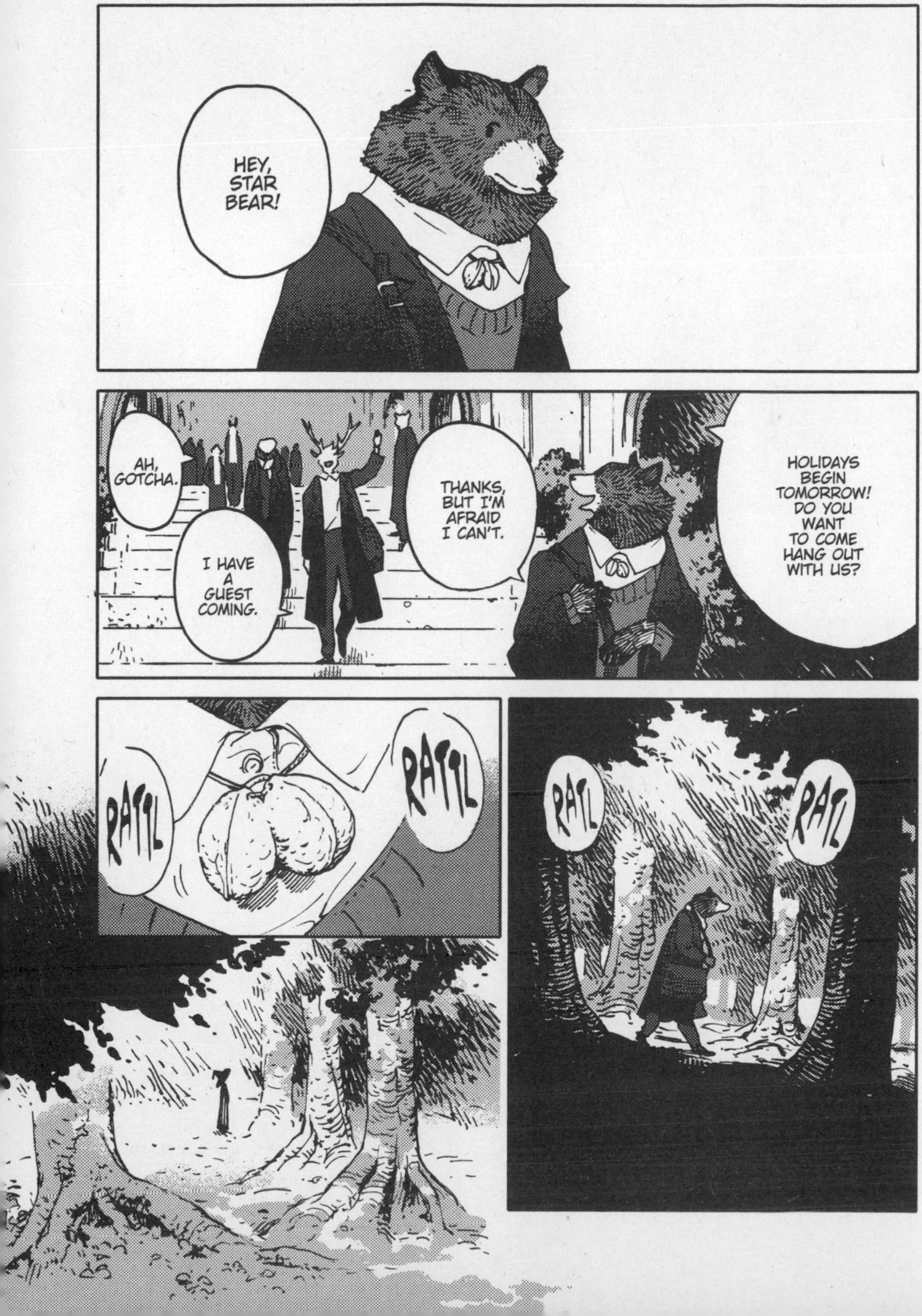
HEY, STAR BEAR!
HOLIDAYS BEGIN TOMORROW! DO YOU WANT TO COME HANG OUT WITH US?
THANKS, BUT I'M AFRAID I CAN'T.
I HAVE A GUEST COMING.
AH, GOTCHA.
RATL
RATL
RATTL
RATTL

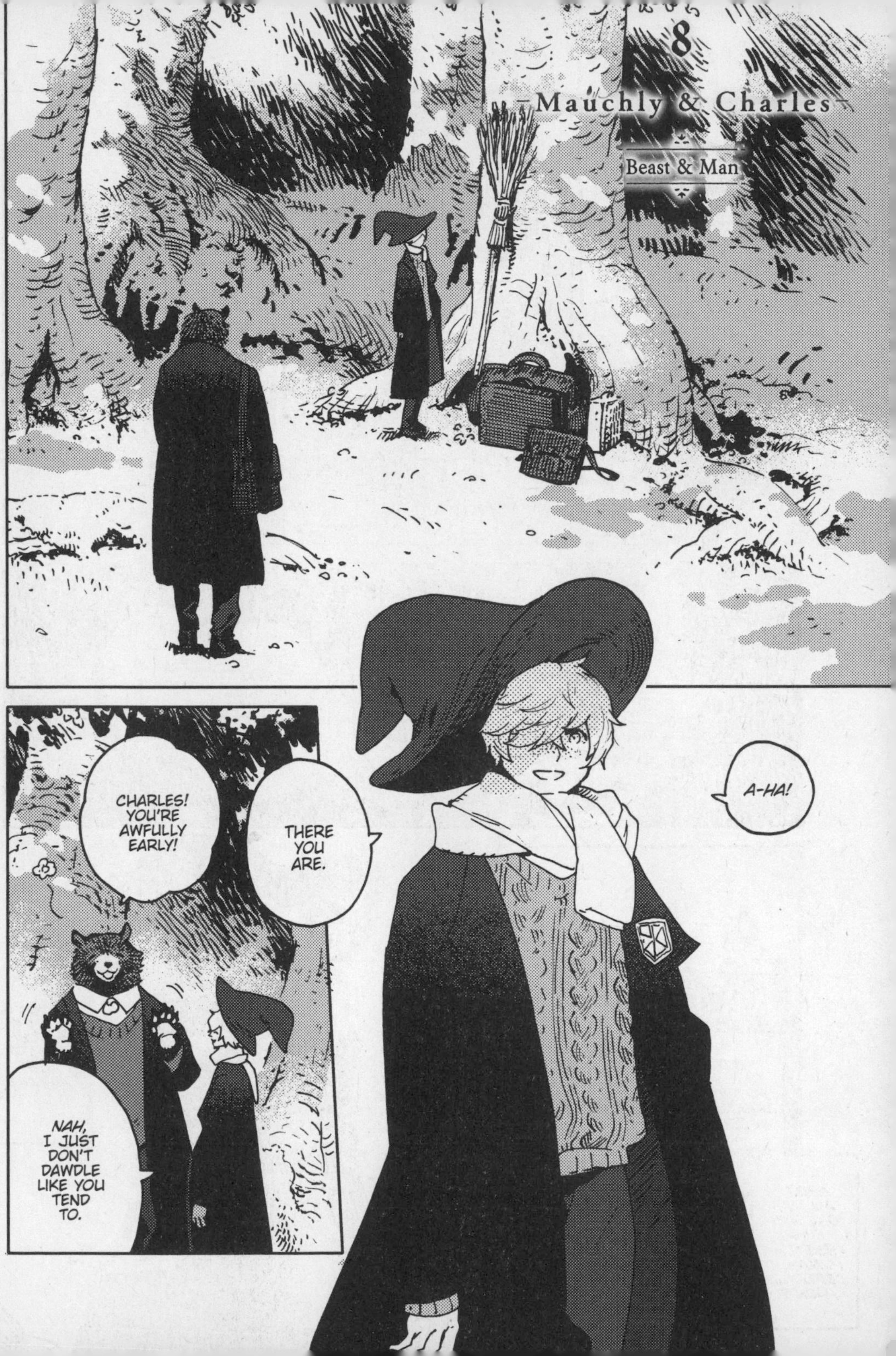
8
Mauchly & Charles
Beast & Man
A-HA!
THERE YOU ARE.
CHARLES! YOU'RE AWFULLY EARLY!
NAH, I JUST DON'T DAWDLE LIKE YOU TEND TO.

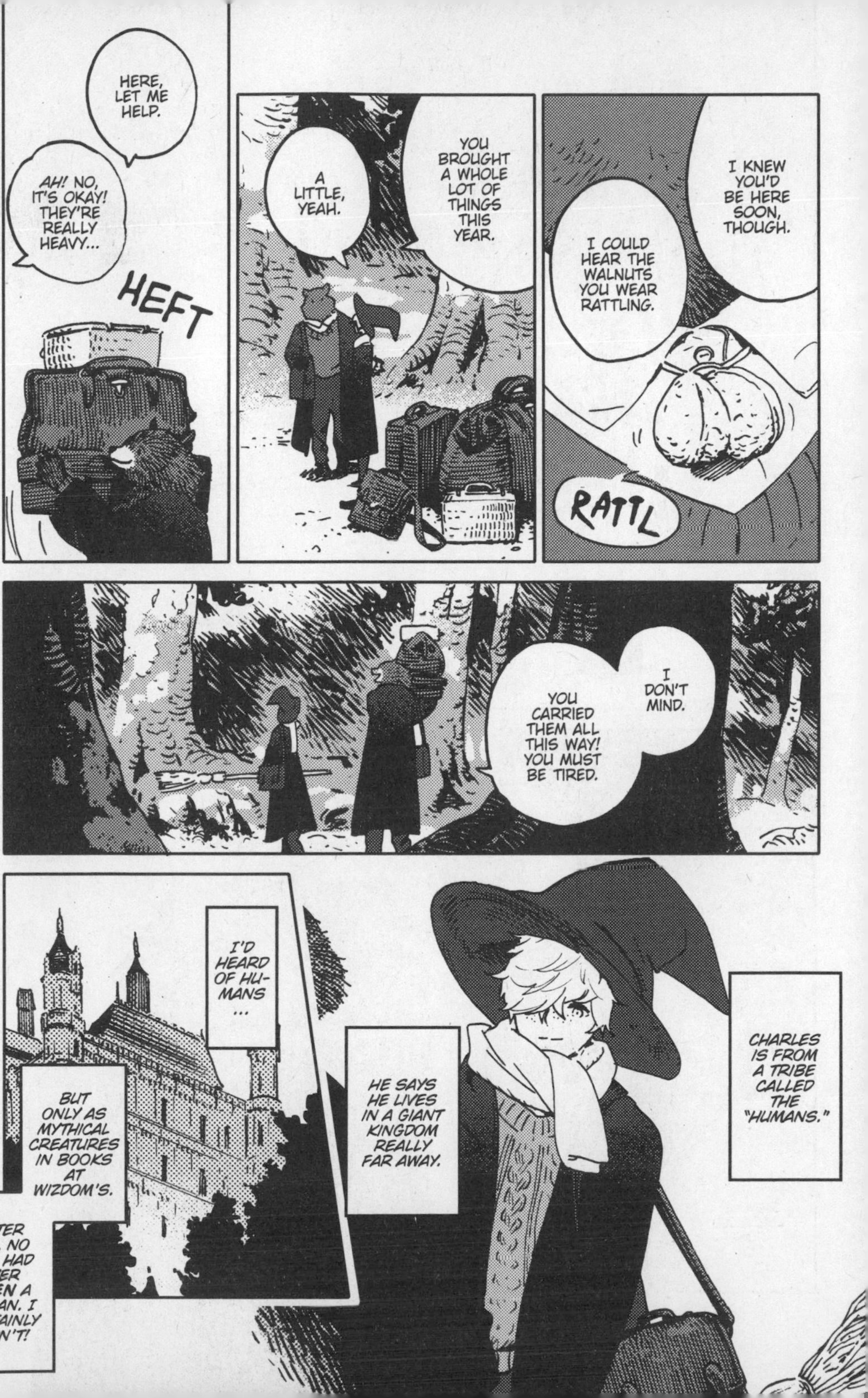

I KNEW YOU'D BE HERE SOON, THOUGH.
I COULD HEAR THE WALNUTS YOU WEAR RATTLING.
RATTL
YOU BROUGHT A WHOLE LOT OF THINGS THIS YEAR.
A LITTLE, YEAH.
HERE, LET ME HELP.
AH! NO, IT'S OKAY! THEY'RE REALLY HEAVY...
HEFT
I DON'T MIND.
YOU CARRIED THEM ALL THIS WAY! YOU MUST BE TIRED.
CHARLES IS FROM A TRIBE CALLED THE "HUMANS."
HE SAYS HE LIVES IN A GIANT KINGDOM REALLY FAR AWAY.
I'D HEARD OF HU-MANS...
BUT ONLY AS MYTHICAL CREATURES IN BOOKS AT WIZDOM'S.
AFTER ALL, NO ONE HAD EVER SEEN A HUMAN. I CERTAINLY HADN'T!

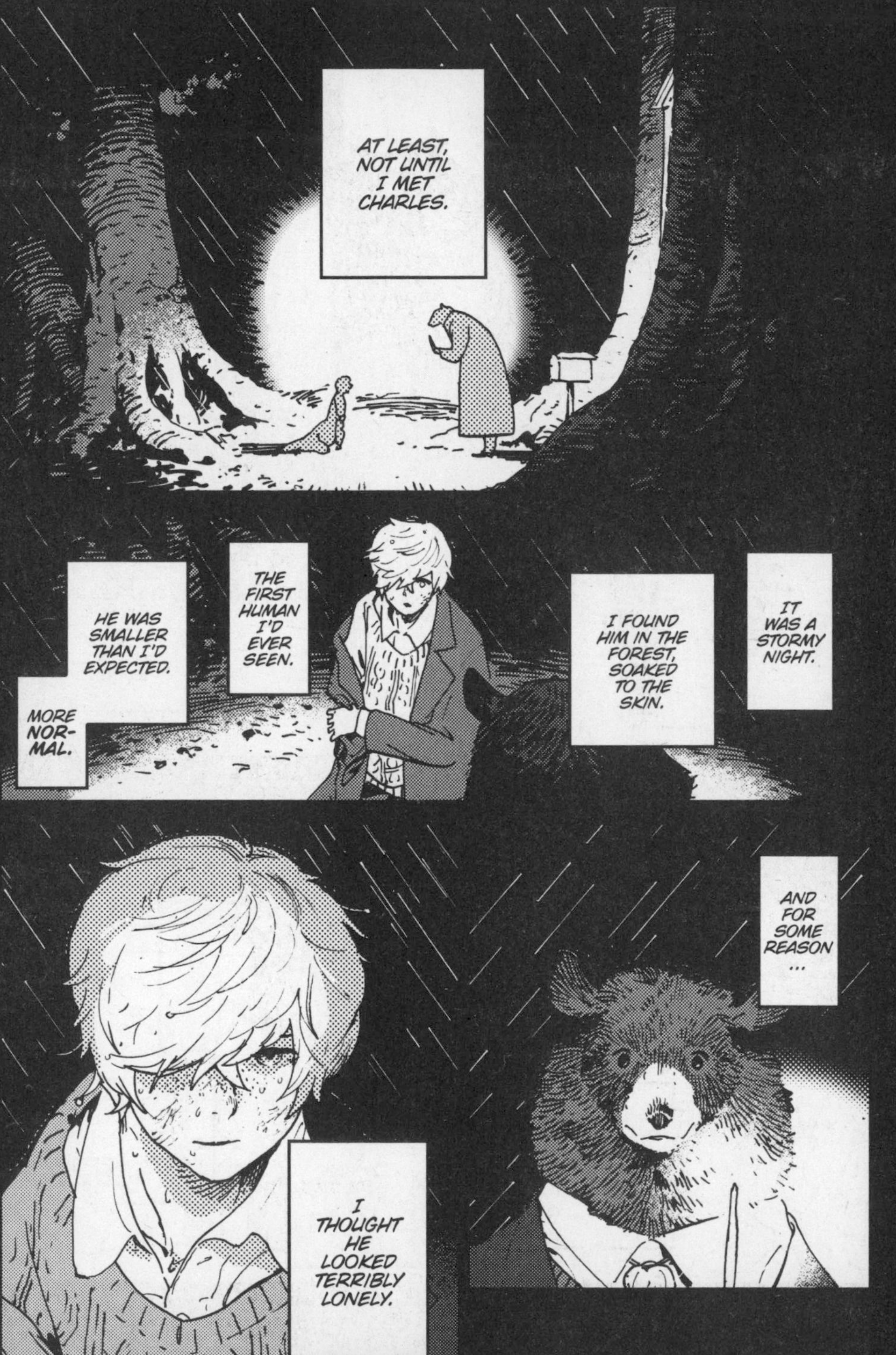
AT LEAST, NOT UNTIL I MET CHARLES.
IT WAS A STORMY NIGHT.
I FOUND HIM IN THE FOREST, SOAKED TO THE SKIN.
THE FIRST HUMAN I'D EVER SEEN.
HE WAS SMALLER THAN I'D EXPECTED.
MORE NOR-MAL.
AND FOR SOME REASON ...
I THOUGHT HE LOOKED TERRIBLY LONELY.

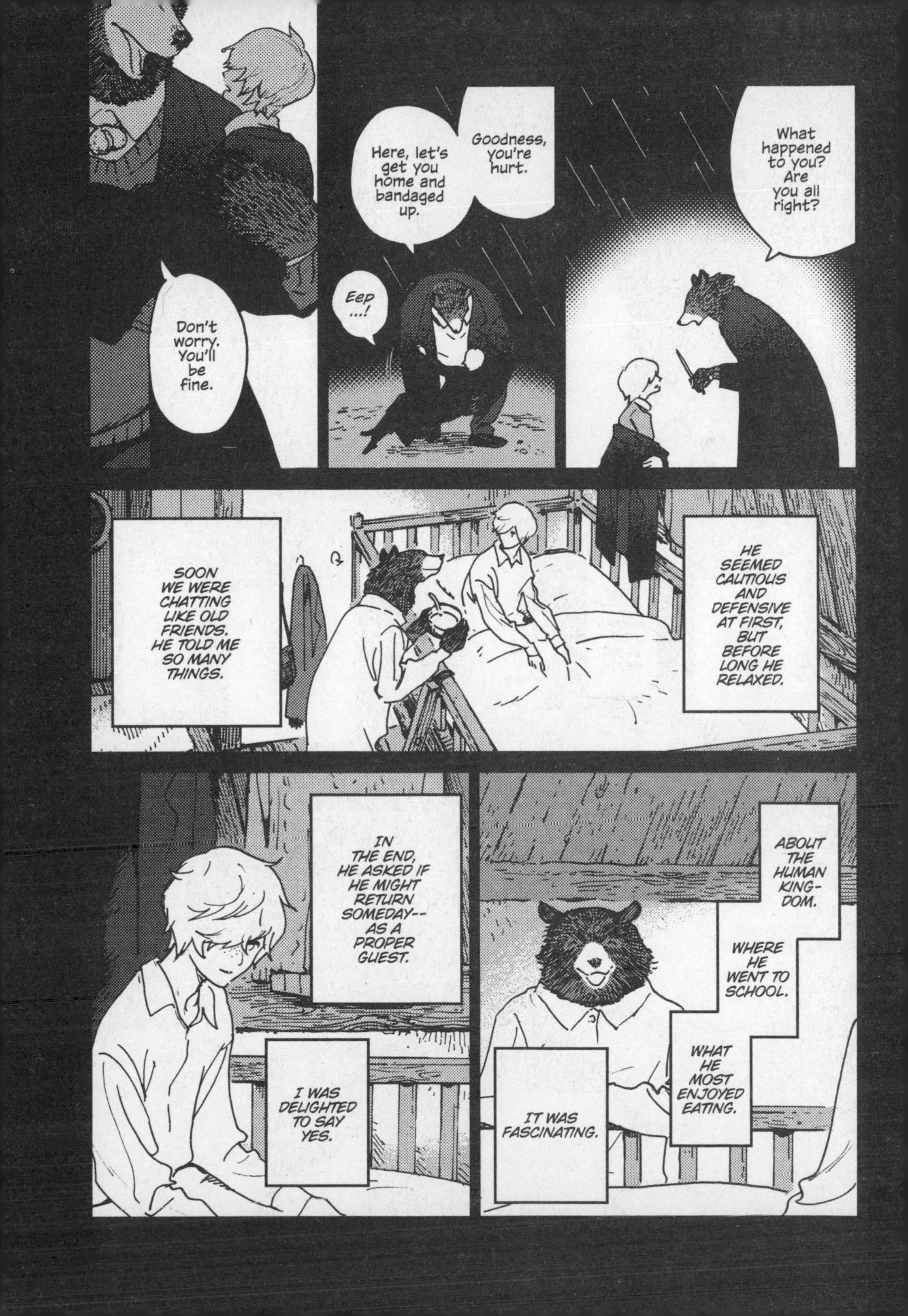
What happened to you? Are you all right?
Goodness, you're hurt.
Here, let's get you home and bandaged up.
Eep ...!
Don't worry. You'll be fine.
HE SEEMED CAUTIOUS AND DEFENSIVE AT FIRST, BUT BEFORE LONG HE RELAXED.
SOON WE WERE CHATTING LIKE OLD FRIENDS. HE TOLD ME SO MANY THINGS.
ABOUT THE HUMAN KING-DOM.
WHERE HE WENT TO SCHOOL.
WHAT HE MOST ENJOYED EATING.
IT WAS FASCINATING.
IN THE END, HE ASKED IF HE MIGHT RETURN SOMEDAY-- AS A PROPER GUEST.
I WAS DELIGHTED TO SAY YES.

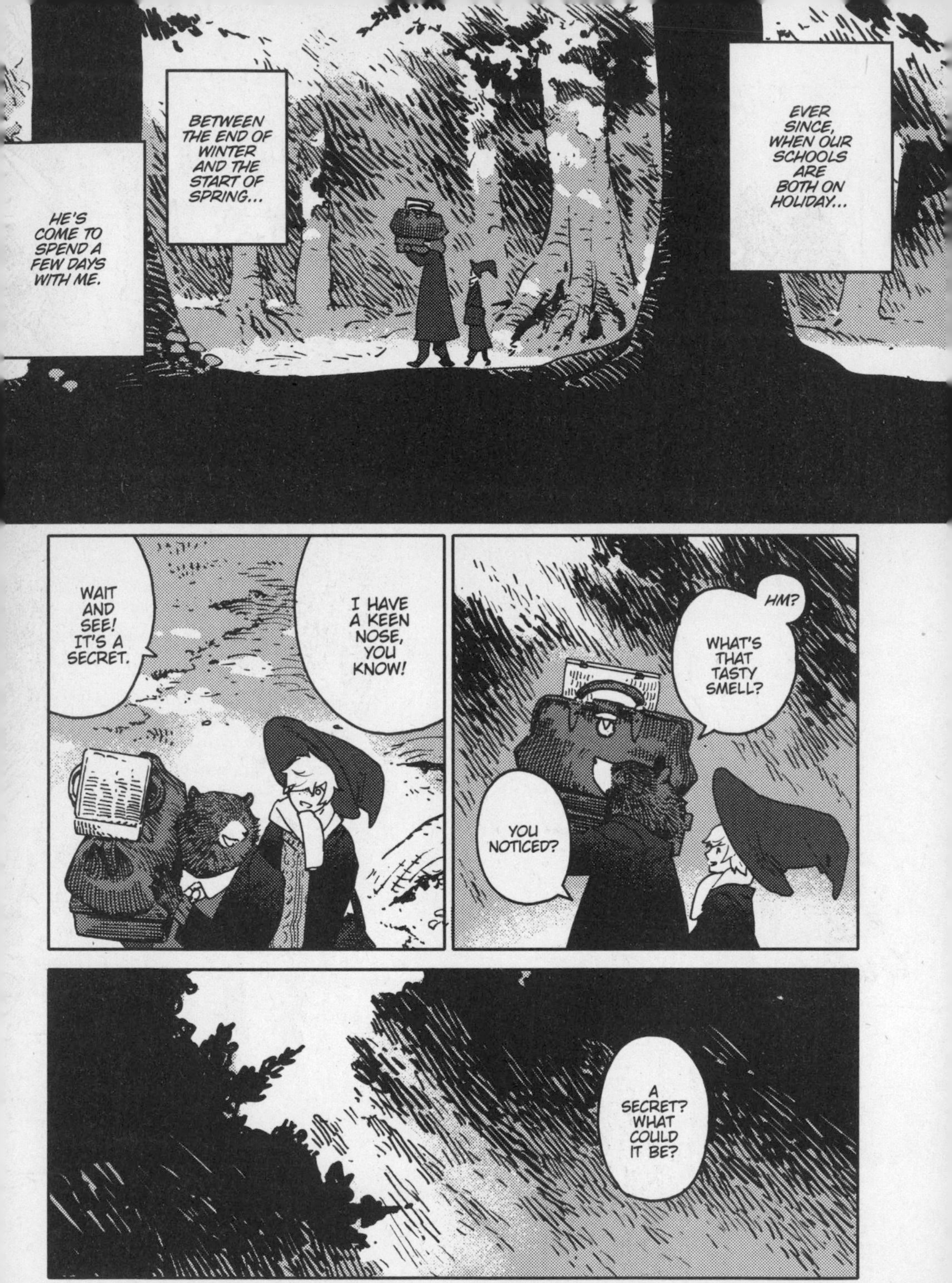
EVER SINCE, WHEN OUR SCHOOLS ARE BOTH ON HOLIDAY...
BETWEEN THE END OF WINTER AND THE START OF SPRING...
HE'S COME TO SPEND A FEW DAYS WITH ME.
HM?
WHAT'S THAT TASTY SMELL?
YOU NOTICED?
I HAVE A KEEN NOSE, YOU KNOW!
WAIT AND SEE! IT'S A SECRET.
A SECRET? WHAT COULD IT BE?

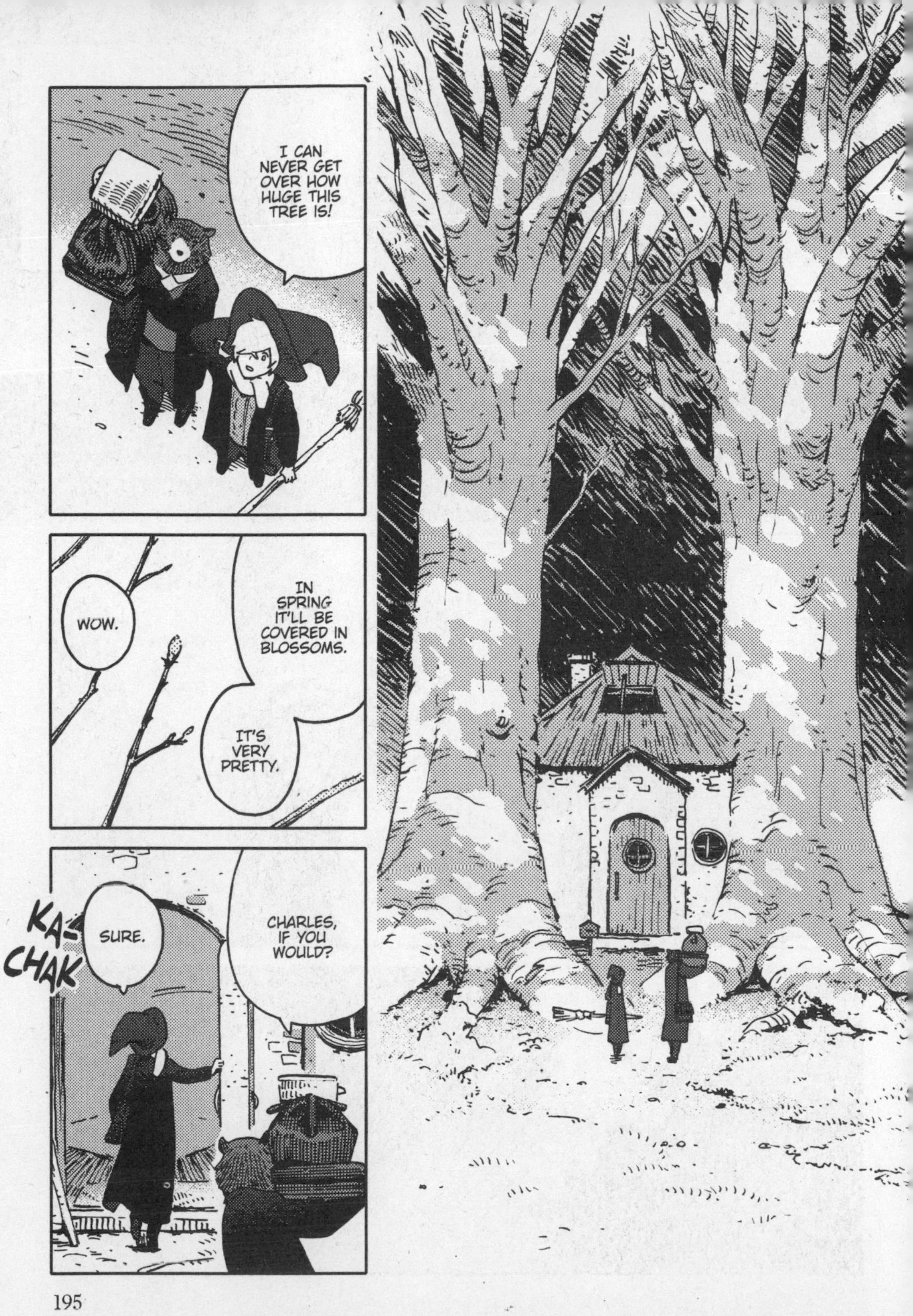
I CAN NEVER GET OVER HOW HUGE THIS TREE IS!
IN SPRING IT'LL BE COVERED IN BLOSSOMS.
WOW.
IT'S VERY PRETTY.
CHARLES, IF YOU WOULD?
SURE.
KA-CHAK

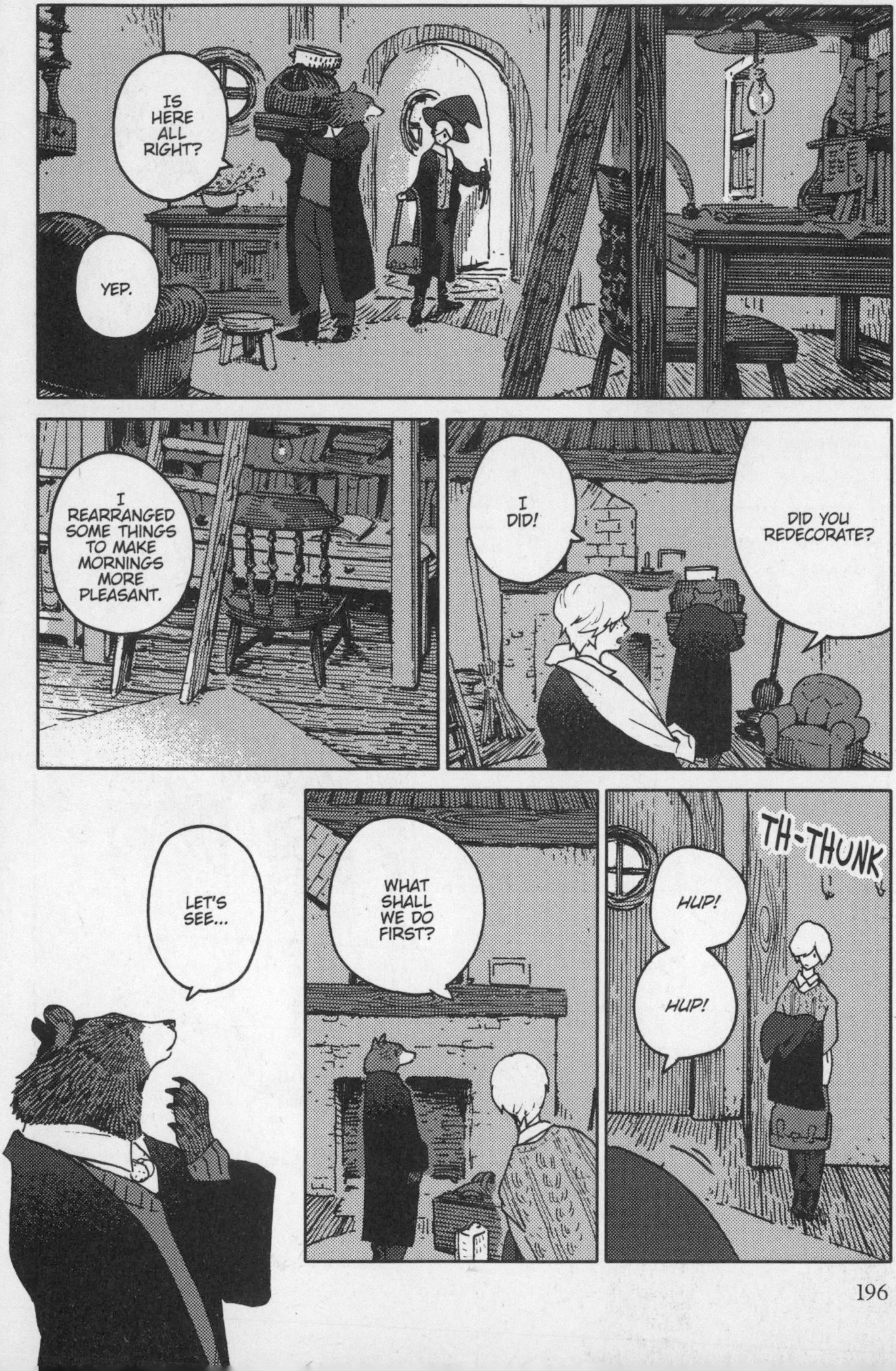
IS HERE ALL RIGHT?
YEP.
DID YOU REDECORATE?
I DID!
I REARRANGED SOME THINGS TO MAKE MORNINGS MORE PLEASANT.
TH-THUNK
HUP!
HUP!
WHAT SHALL WE DO FIRST?
LET'S SEE...

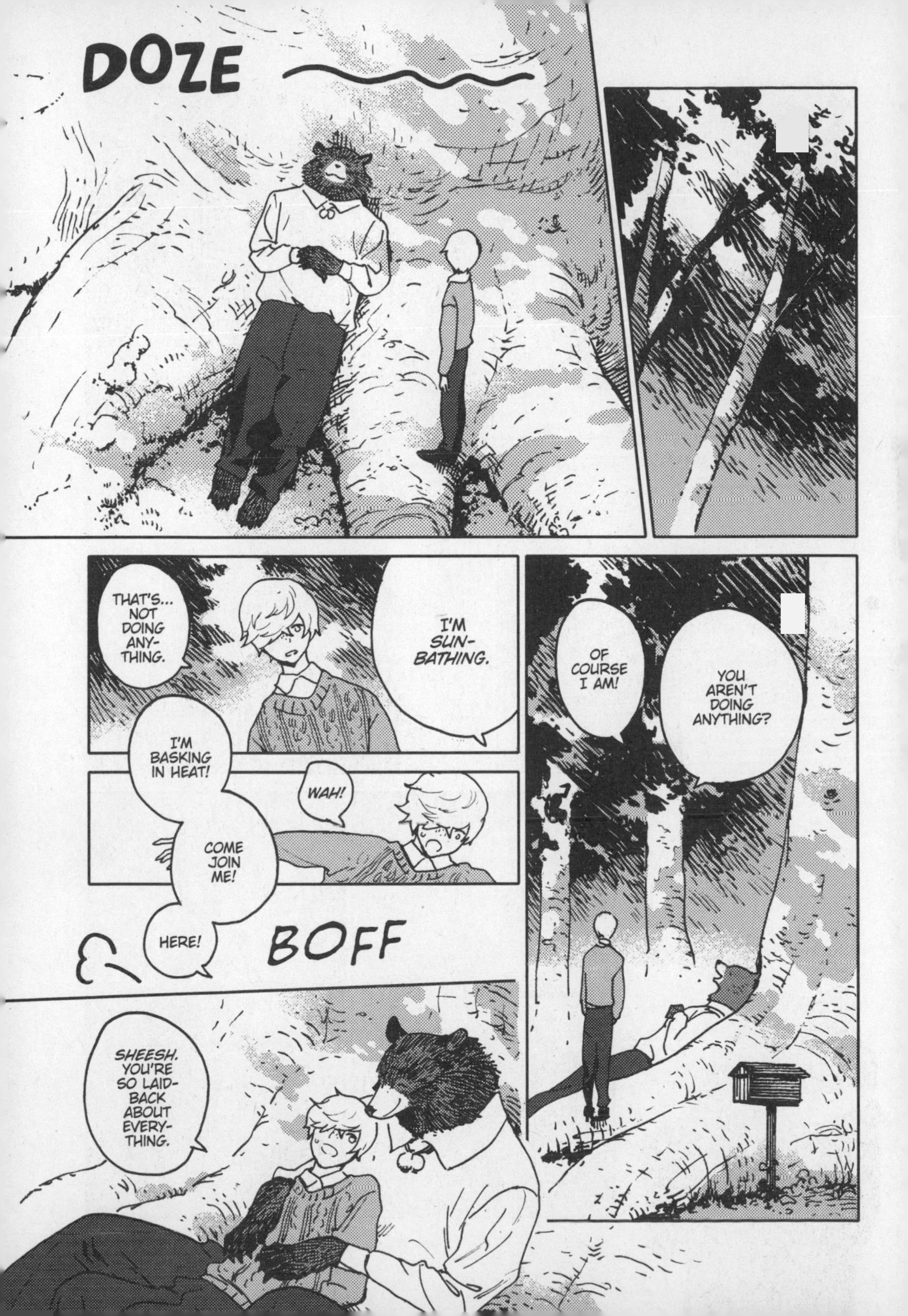
DOZE
YOU AREN'T DOING ANYTHING?
OF COURSE I AM!
I'M SUN-BATHING.
THAT'S... NOT DOING ANY-THING.
I'M BASKING IN HEAT!
WAH!
COME JOIN ME!
HERE!
BOFF
SHEESH. YOU'RE SO LAID-BACK ABOUT EVERY-THING.

AH,
WELL.

RUFL...

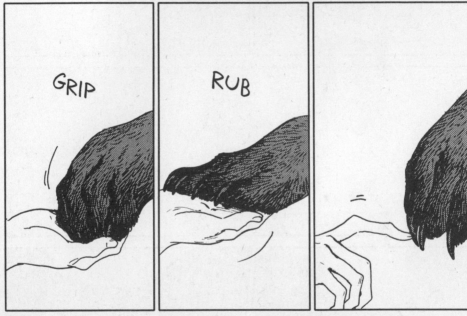

GRIP

RUB

IS SOMETHING ON MY PAW?

199

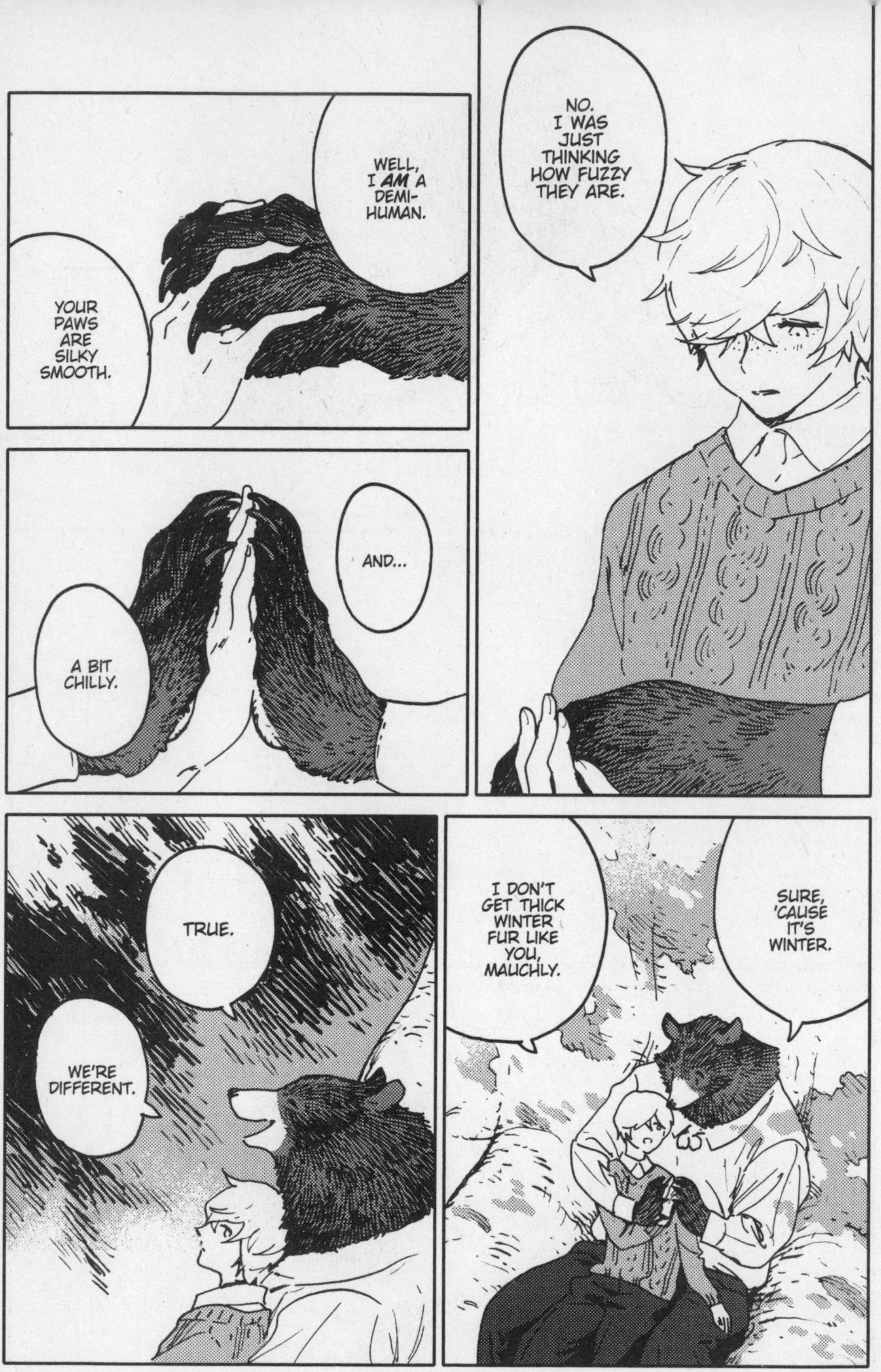
NO. I WAS JUST THINKING HOW FUZZY THEY ARE.
WELL, I AM A DEMI-HUMAN.
YOUR PAWS ARE SILKY SMOOTH.
AND...
A BIT CHILLY.
SURE, 'CAUSE IT'S WINTER.
I DON'T GET THICK WINTER FUR LIKE YOU, MAUCHLY.
TRUE.
WE'RE DIFFERENT.

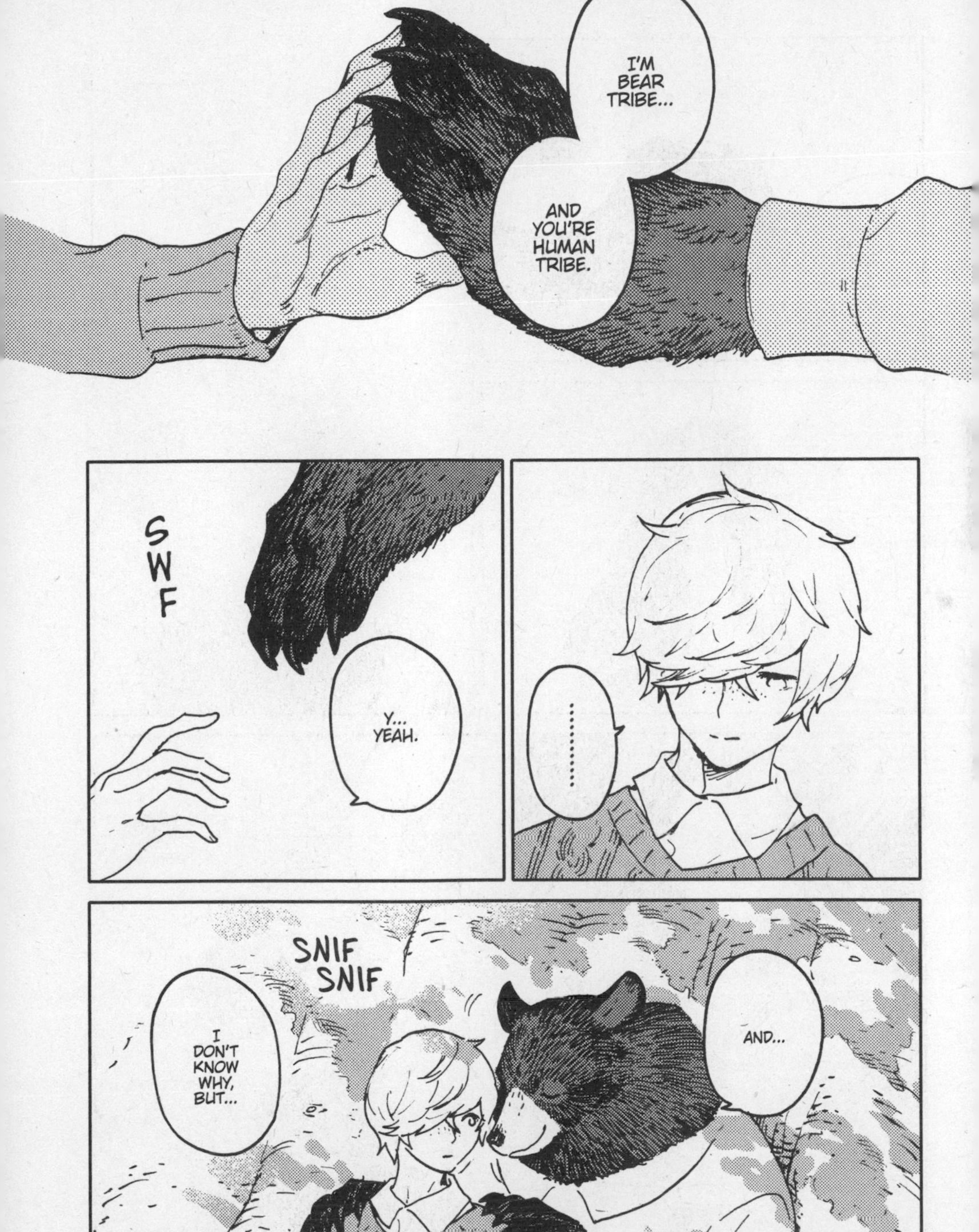
I'M BEAR TRIBE...
AND YOU'RE HUMAN TRIBE.
......
SWF
Y... YEAH.
AND...
SNIF SNIF
I DON'T KNOW WHY, BUT...

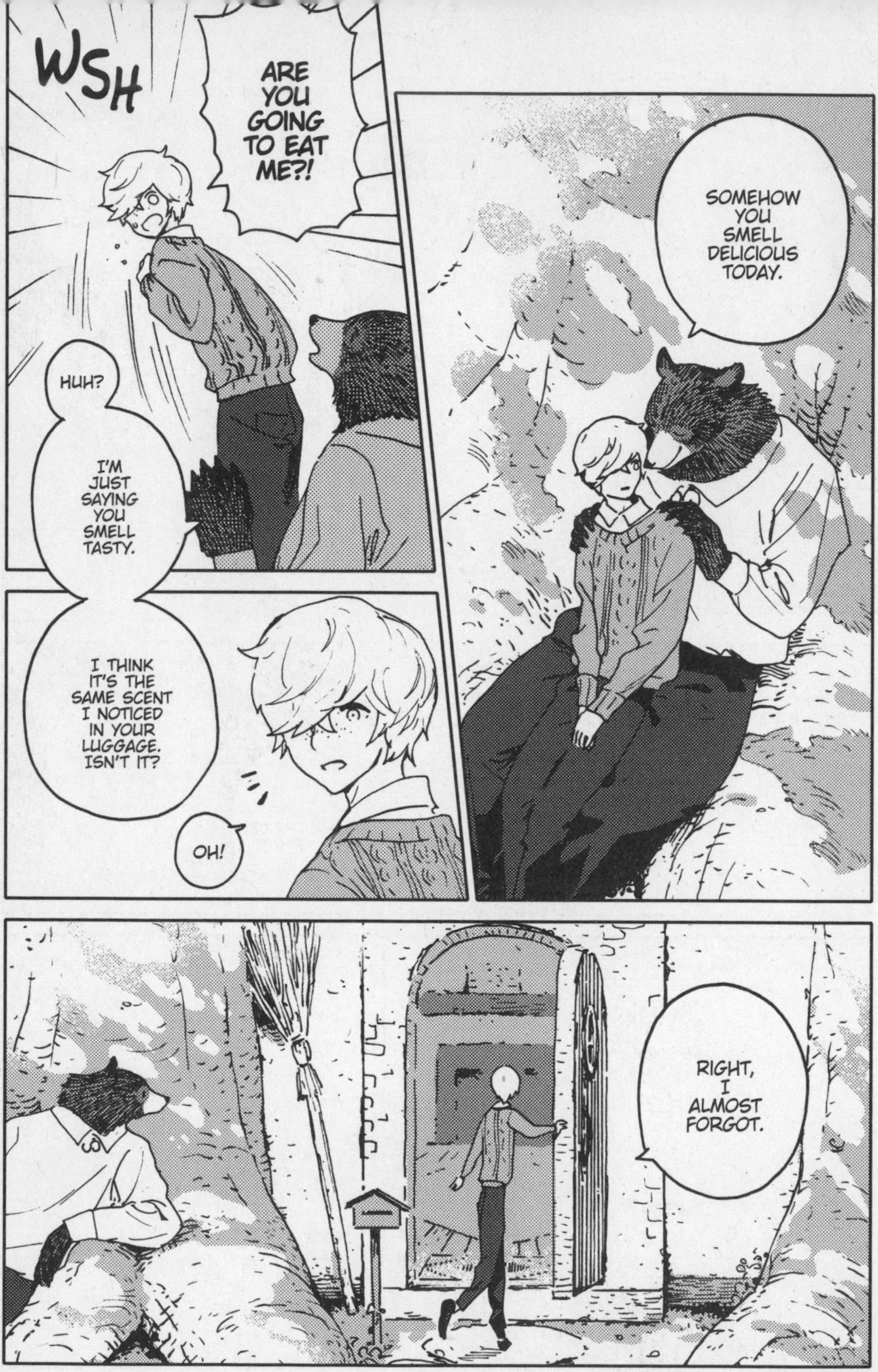
SOMEHOW YOU SMELL DELICIOUS TODAY.
WSH
ARE YOU GOING TO EAT ME?!
HUH?
I'M JUST SAYING YOU SMELL TASTY.
I THINK IT'S THE SAME SCENT I NOTICED IN YOUR LUGGAGE. ISN'T IT?
OH!
RIGHT, I ALMOST FORGOT.

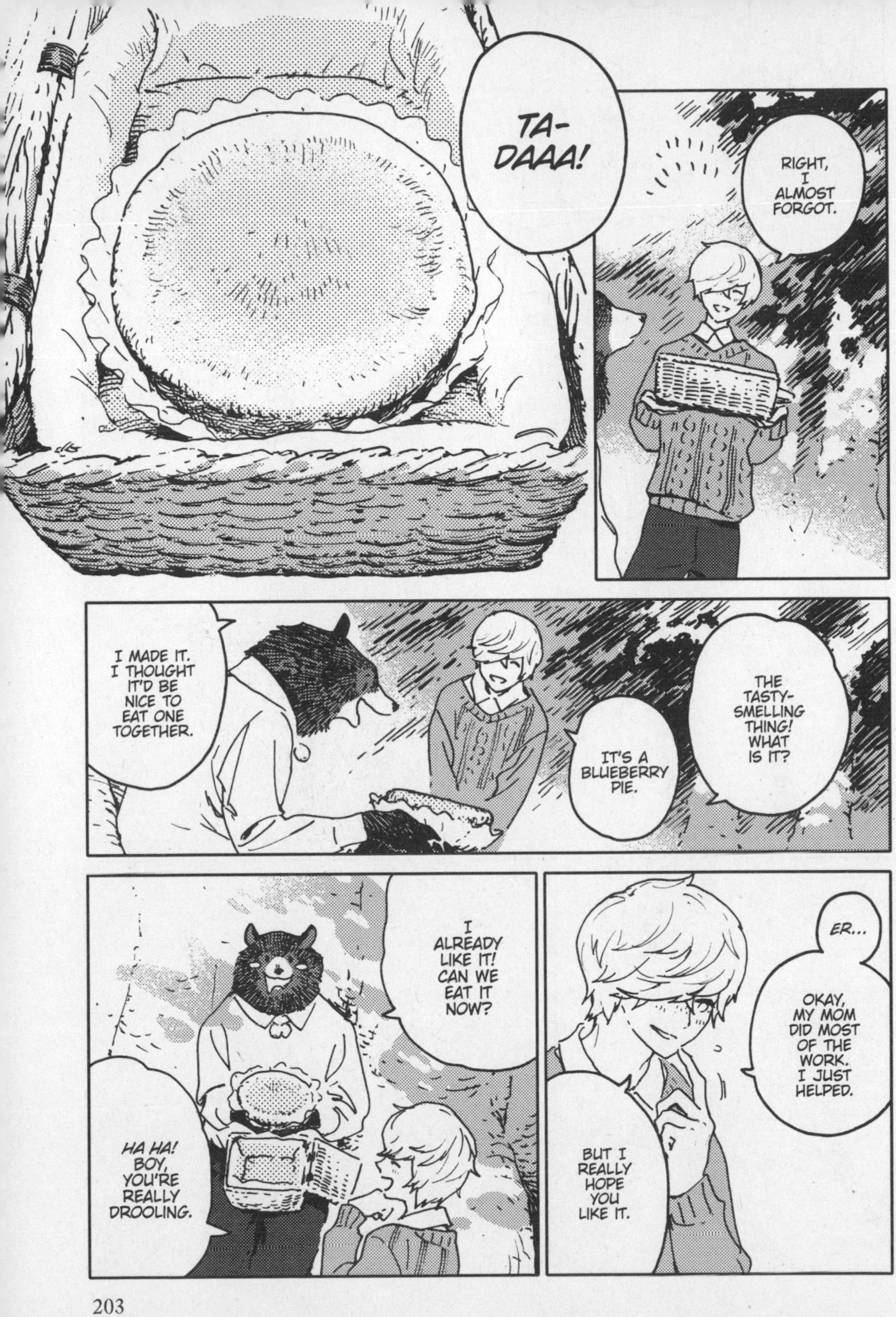
RIGHT, I ALMOST FORGOT.
TA-DAAA!
THE TASTY-SMELLING THING! WHAT IS IT?
IT'S A BLUEBERRY PIE.
I MADE IT. I THOUGHT IT'D BE NICE TO EAT ONE TOGETHER.
ER...
OKAY, MY MOM DID MOST OF THE WORK. I JUST HELPED.
BUT I REALLY HOPE YOU LIKE IT.
I ALREADY LIKE IT! CAN WE EAT IT NOW?
HA HA! BOY, YOU'RE REALLY DROOLING.

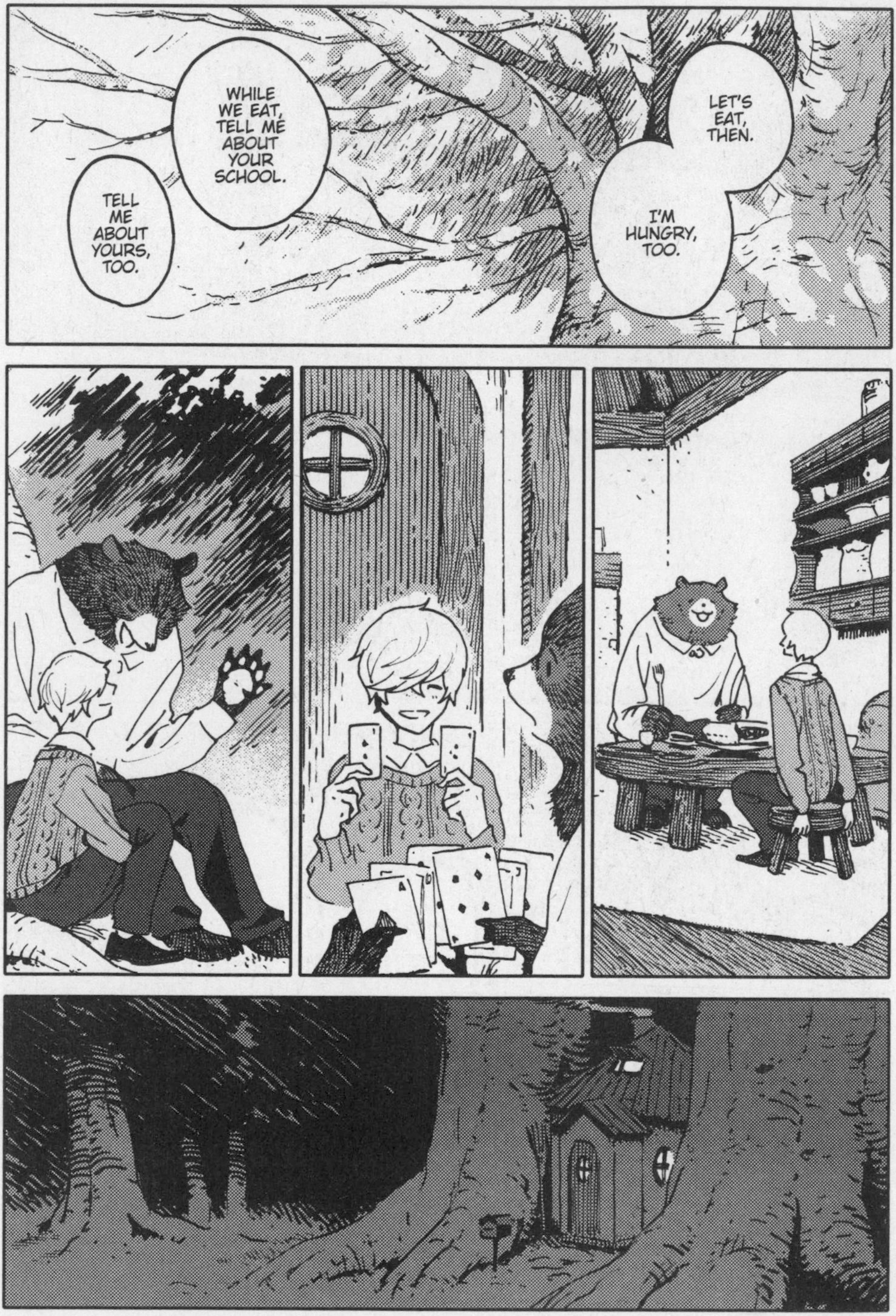
LET'S EAT, THEN.
I'M HUNGRY, TOO.
WHILE WE EAT, TELL ME ABOUT YOUR SCHOOL.
TELL ME ABOUT YOURS, TOO.

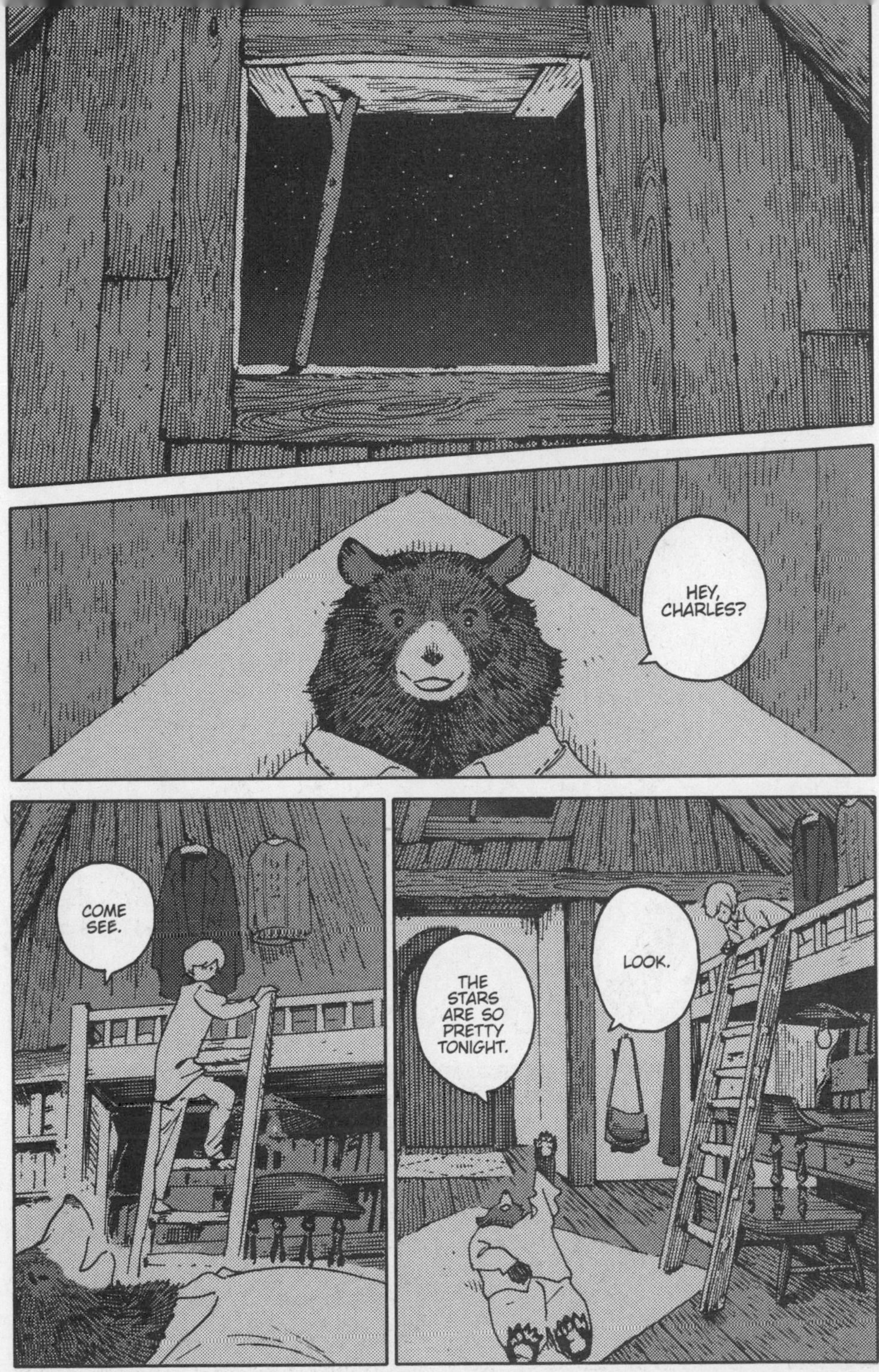
HEY, CHARLES?
LOOK.
THE STARS ARE SO PRETTY TONIGHT.
COME SEE.

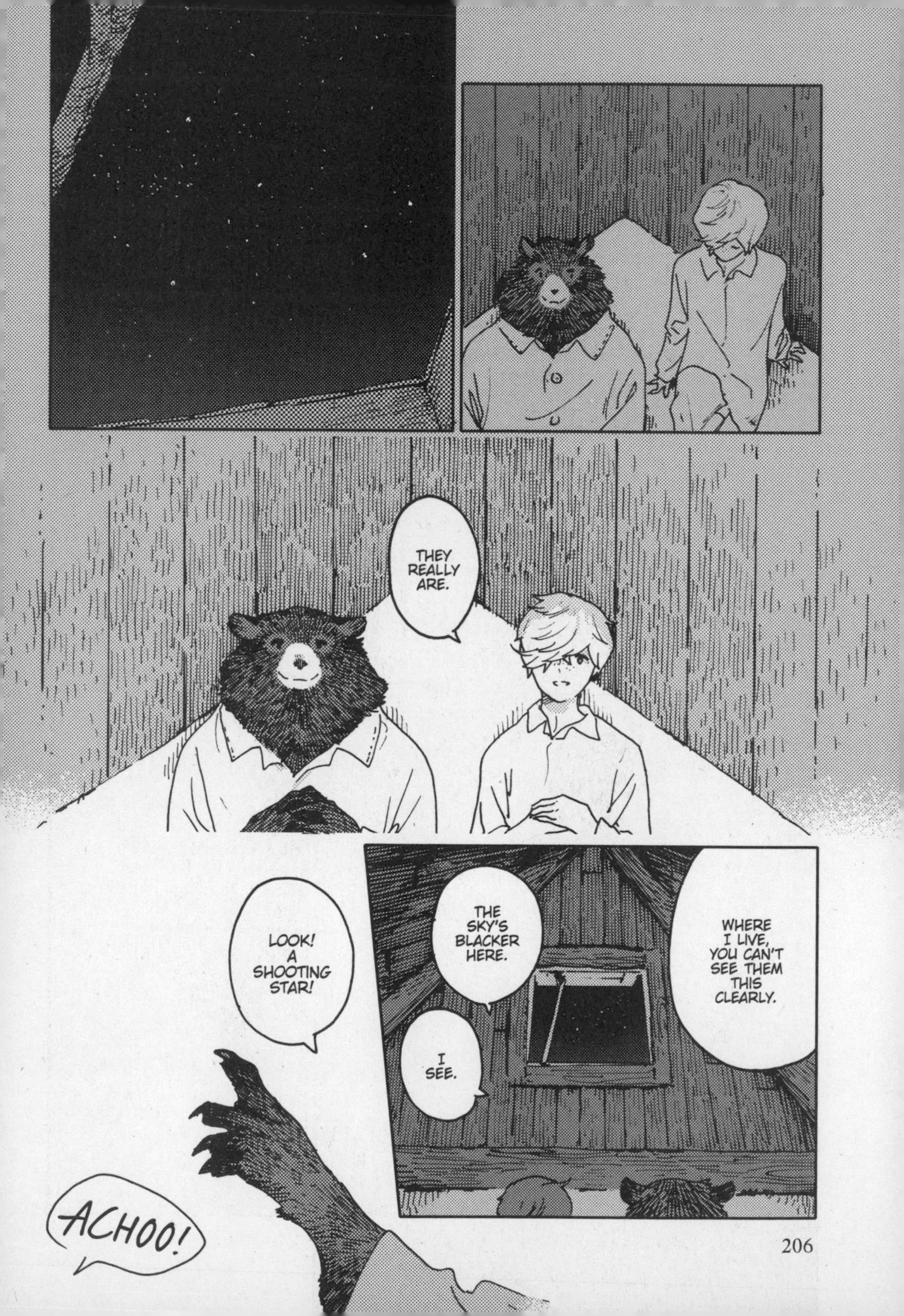
THEY REALLY ARE.
WHERE I LIVE, YOU CAN'T SEE THEM THIS CLEARLY.
THE SKY'S BLACKER HERE.
I SEE.
LOOK! A SHOOTING STAR!
ACHOO!

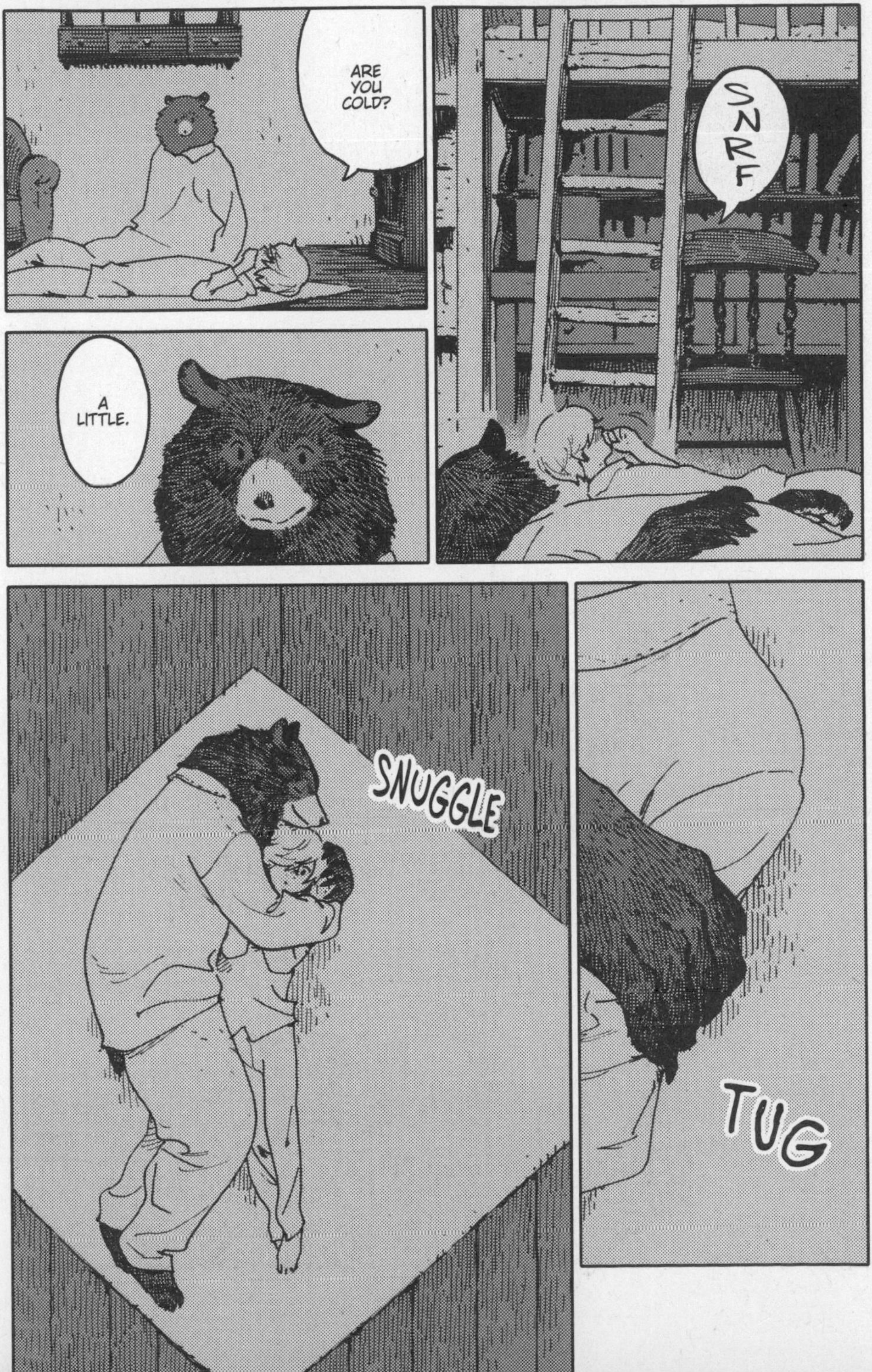
SNRF
ARE YOU COLD?
A LITTLE.
TUG
SNUGGLE

THERE.
DO YOU
FEEL
WARMER
NOW?

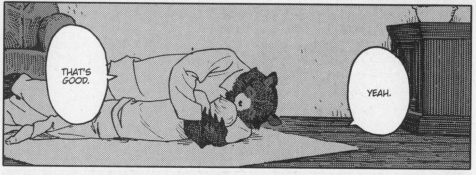

THAT'S
GOOD.

YEAH.

HEY,
MAUCHLY?

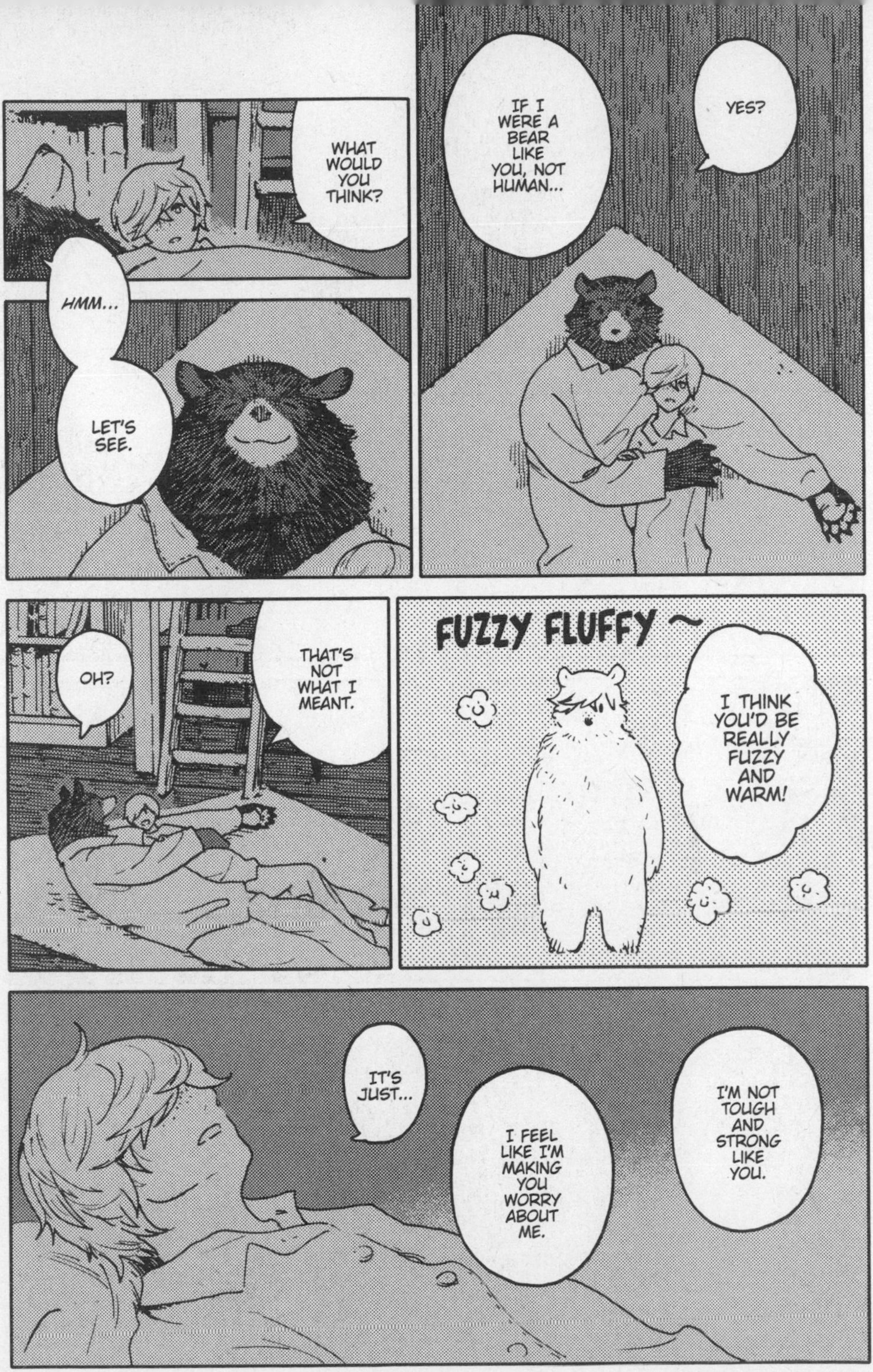
YES?
IF I WERE A BEAR LIKE YOU, NOT HUMAN...
WHAT WOULD YOU THINK?
HMM...
LET'S SEE.
FUZZY FLUFFY ~
I THINK YOU'D BE REALLY FUZZY AND WARM!
THAT'S NOT WHAT I MEANT.
OH?
I'M NOT TOUGH AND STRONG LIKE YOU.
I FEEL LIKE I'M MAKING YOU WORRY ABOUT ME.
IT'S JUST...

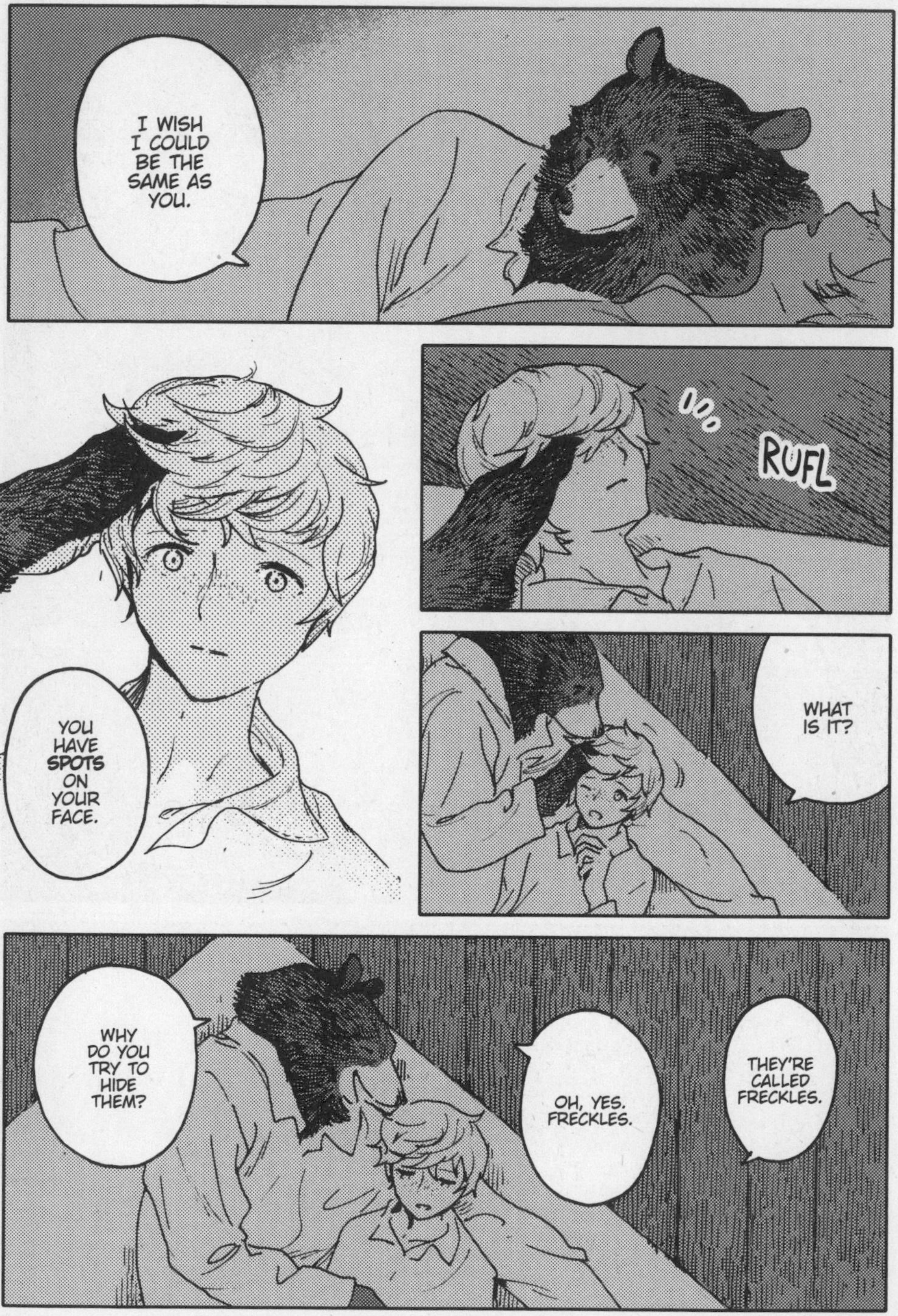
I WISH I COULD BE THE SAME AS YOU.
RUFL
WHAT IS IT?
YOU HAVE **SPOTS** ON YOUR FACE.
THEY'RE CALLED FRECKLES.
OH, YES. FRECKLES.
WHY DO YOU TRY TO HIDE THEM?

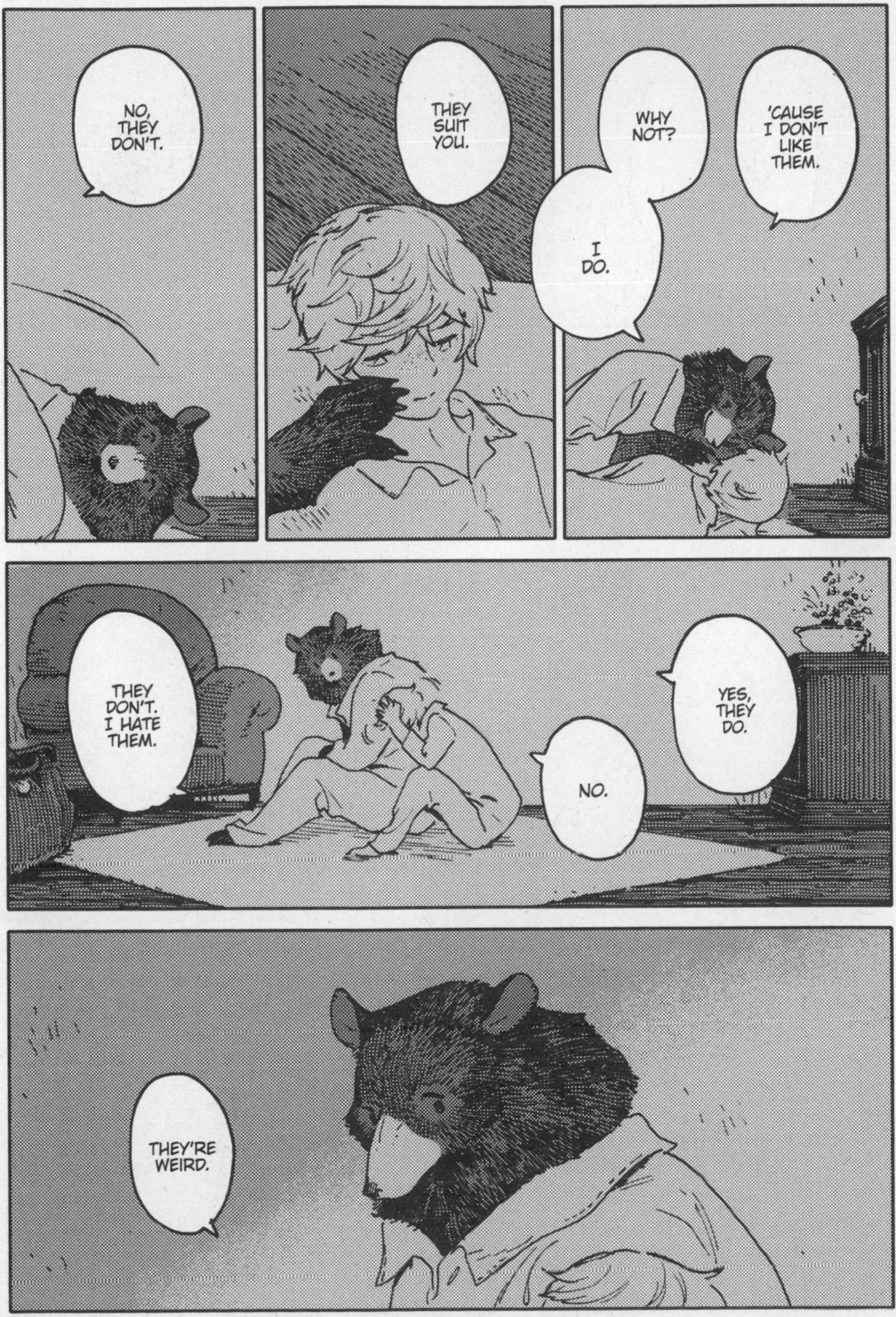
'CAUSE I DON'T LIKE THEM.
WHY NOT?
I DO.
THEY SUIT YOU.
NO, THEY DON'T.
YES, THEY DO.
NO.
THEY DON'T. I HATE THEM.
THEY'RE WEIRD.

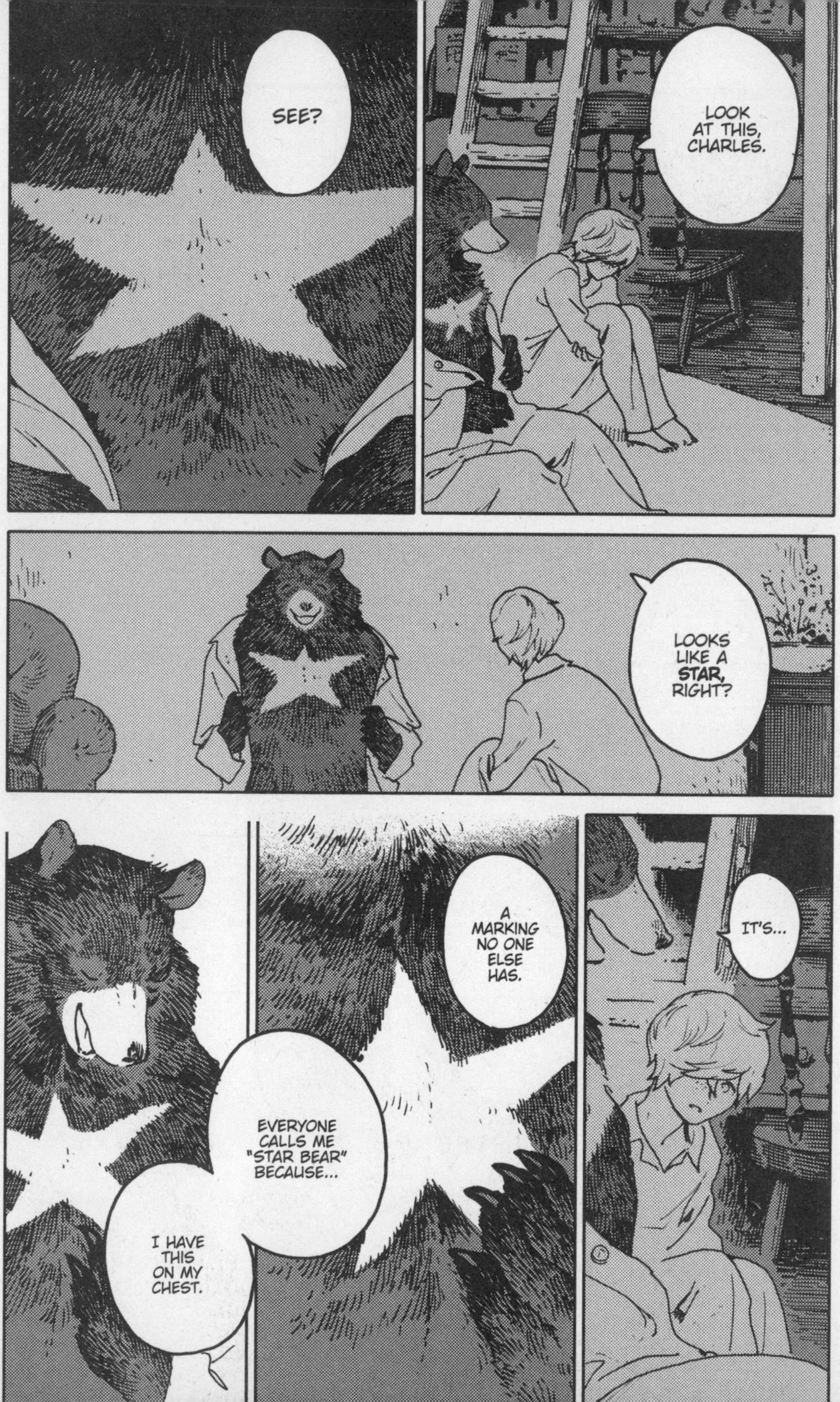
LOOK AT THIS, CHARLES.
SEE?
LOOKS LIKE A STAR, RIGHT?
IT'S...
A MARKING NO ONE ELSE HAS.
EVERYONE CALLS ME "STAR BEAR" BECAUSE...
I HAVE THIS ON MY CHEST.

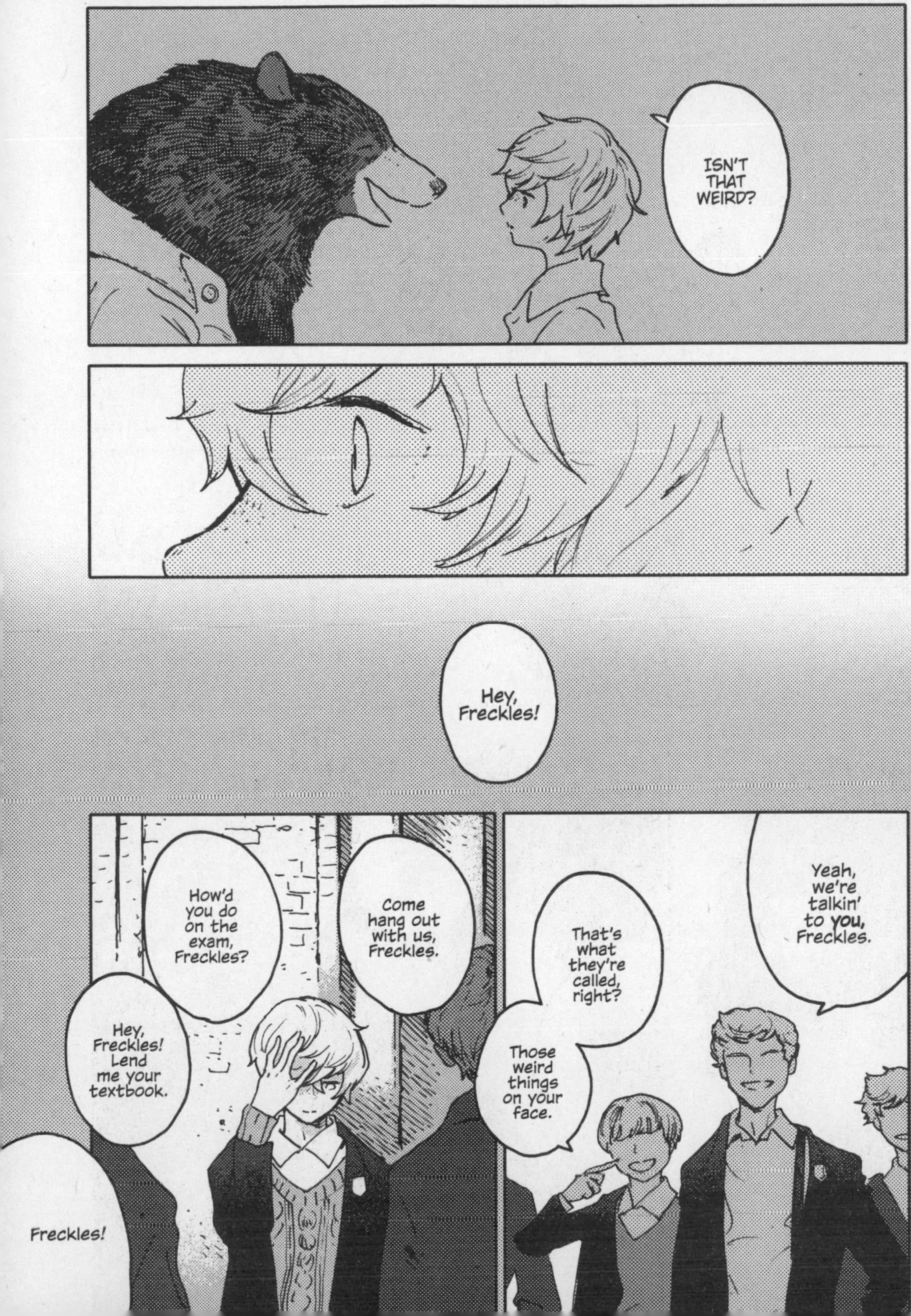
ISN'T THAT WEIRD?
Hey, Freckles!
Yeah, we're talkin' to you, Freckles.
That's what they're called, right?
Those weird things on your face.
Come hang out with us, Freckles.
How'd you do on the exam, Freckles?
Hey, Freckles! Lend me your textbook.
Freckles!

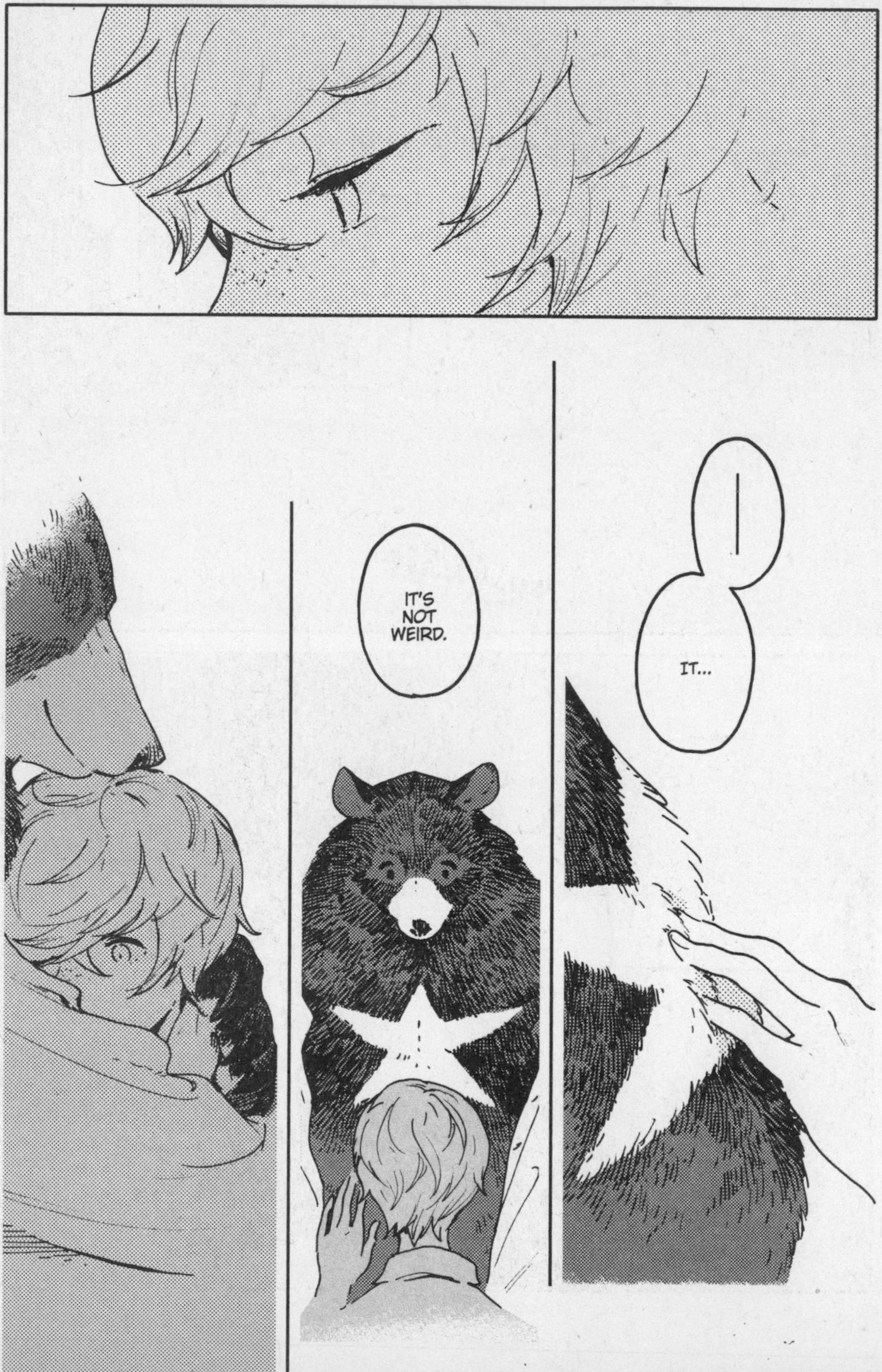
IT...
IT'S NOT WEIRD.

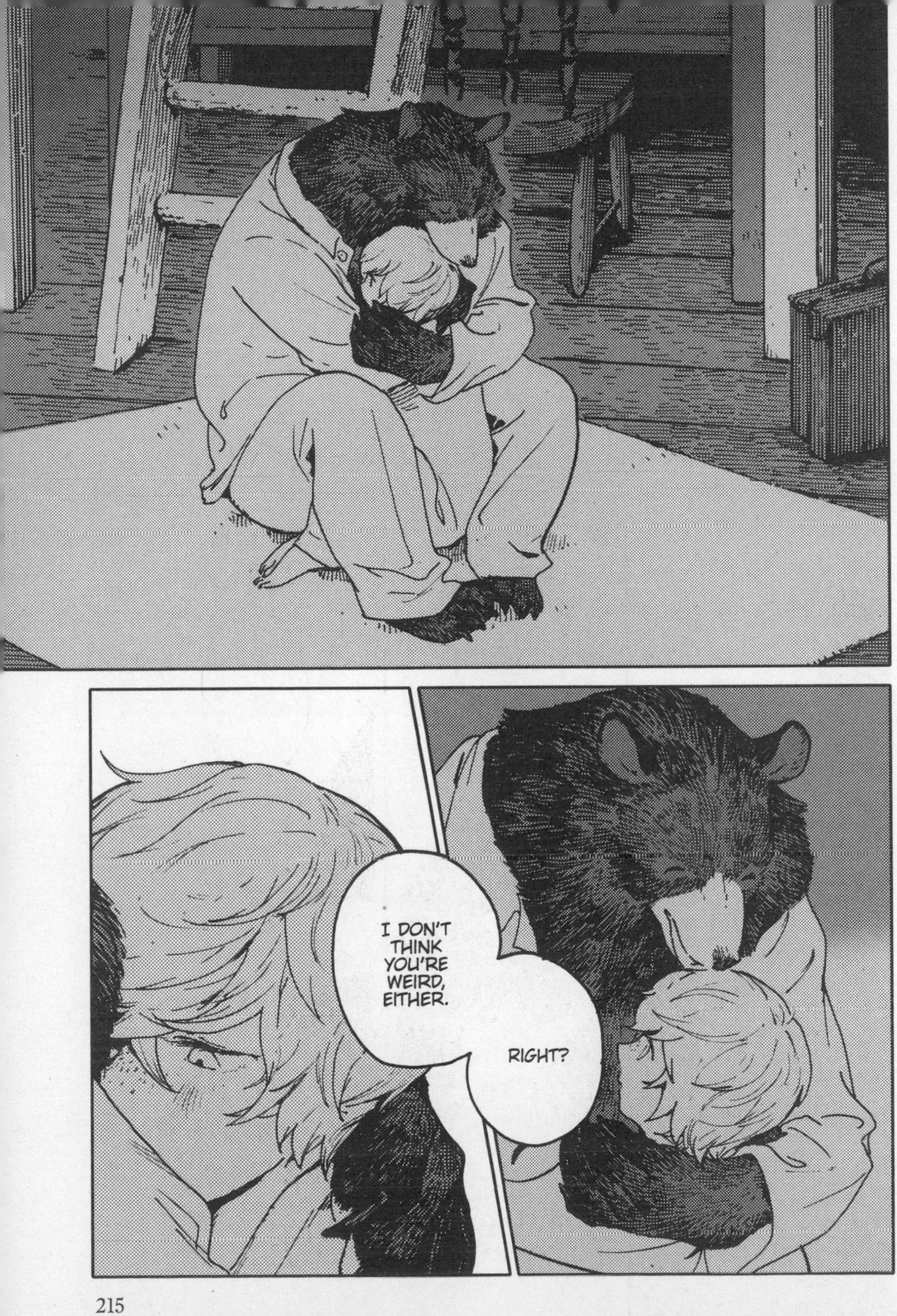
I DON'T THINK YOU'RE WEIRD, EITHER.
RIGHT?

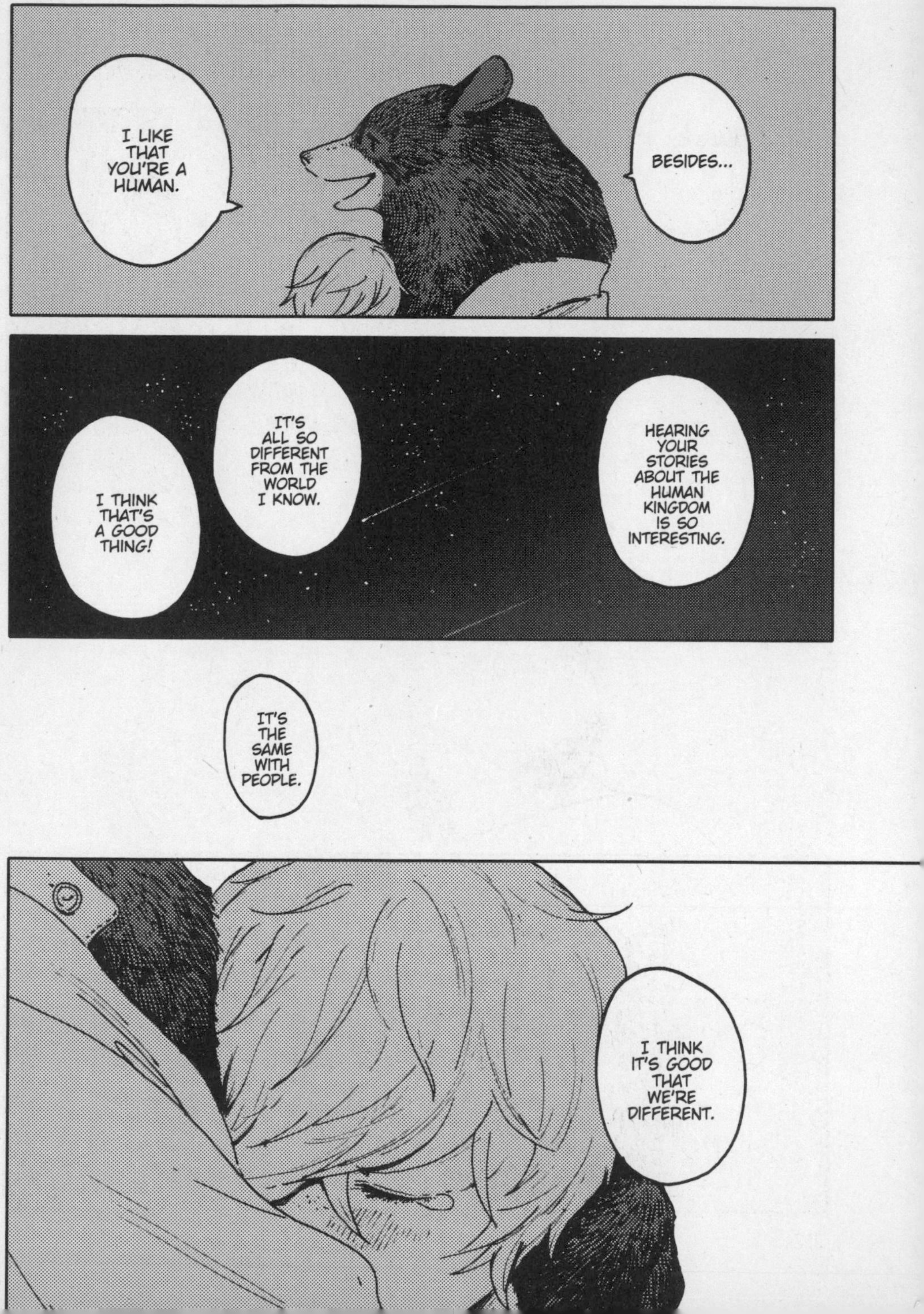
BESIDES...
I LIKE THAT YOU'RE A HUMAN.
HEARING YOUR STORIES ABOUT THE HUMAN KINGDOM IS SO INTERESTING.
IT'S ALL SO DIFFERENT FROM THE WORLD I KNOW.
I THINK THAT'S A GOOD THING!
IT'S THE SAME WITH PEOPLE.
I THINK IT'S GOOD THAT WE'RE DIFFERENT.

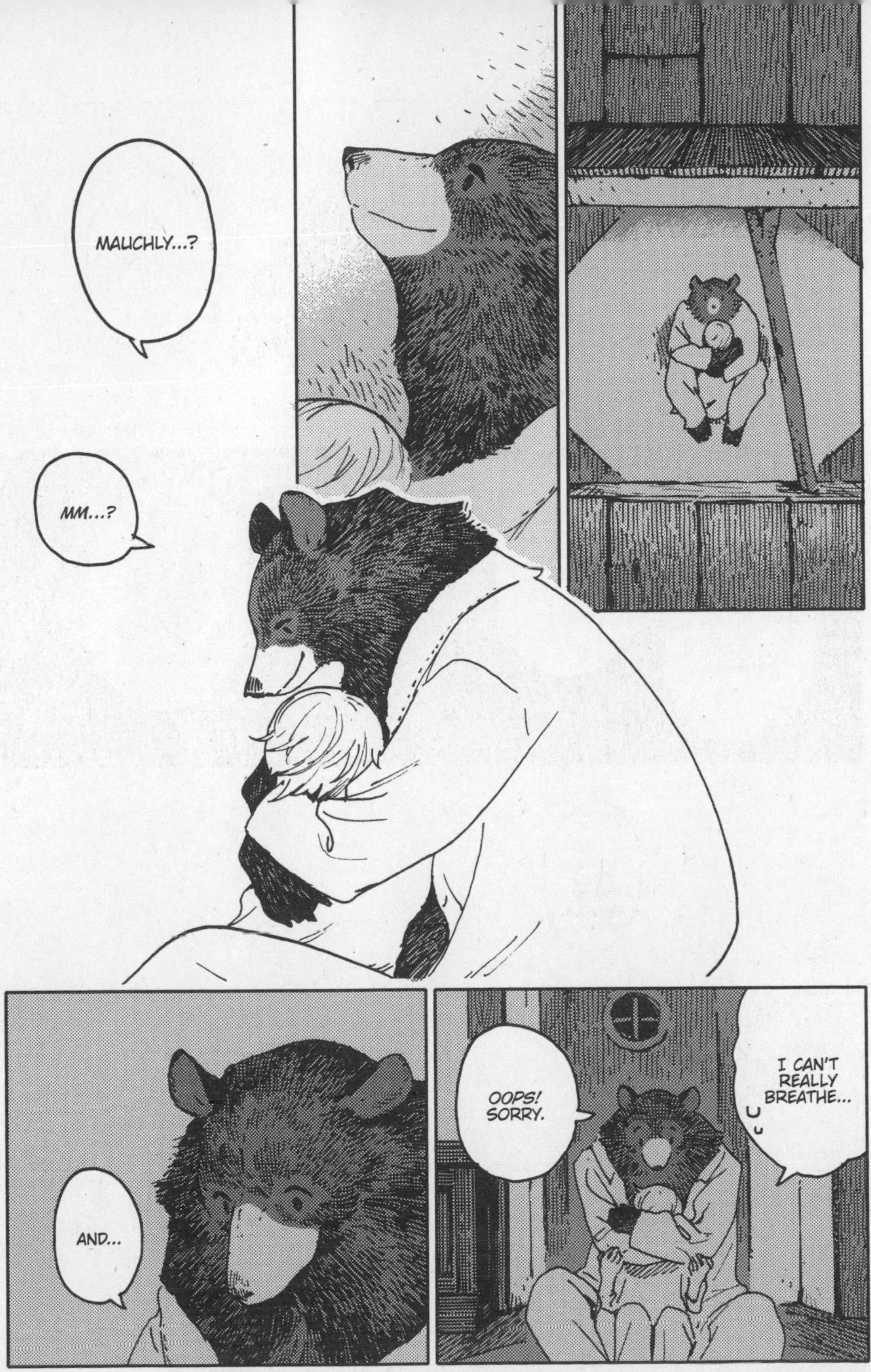
MAUCHLY...?
MM...?
I CAN'T REALLY BREATHE...
OOPS! SORRY.
AND...

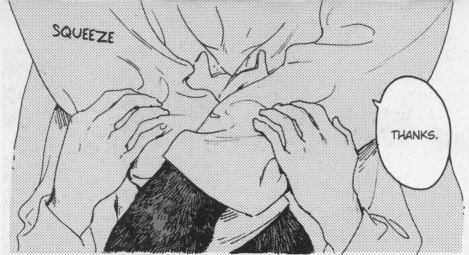

SQUEEZE

THANKS.

YOU'RE WELCOME.

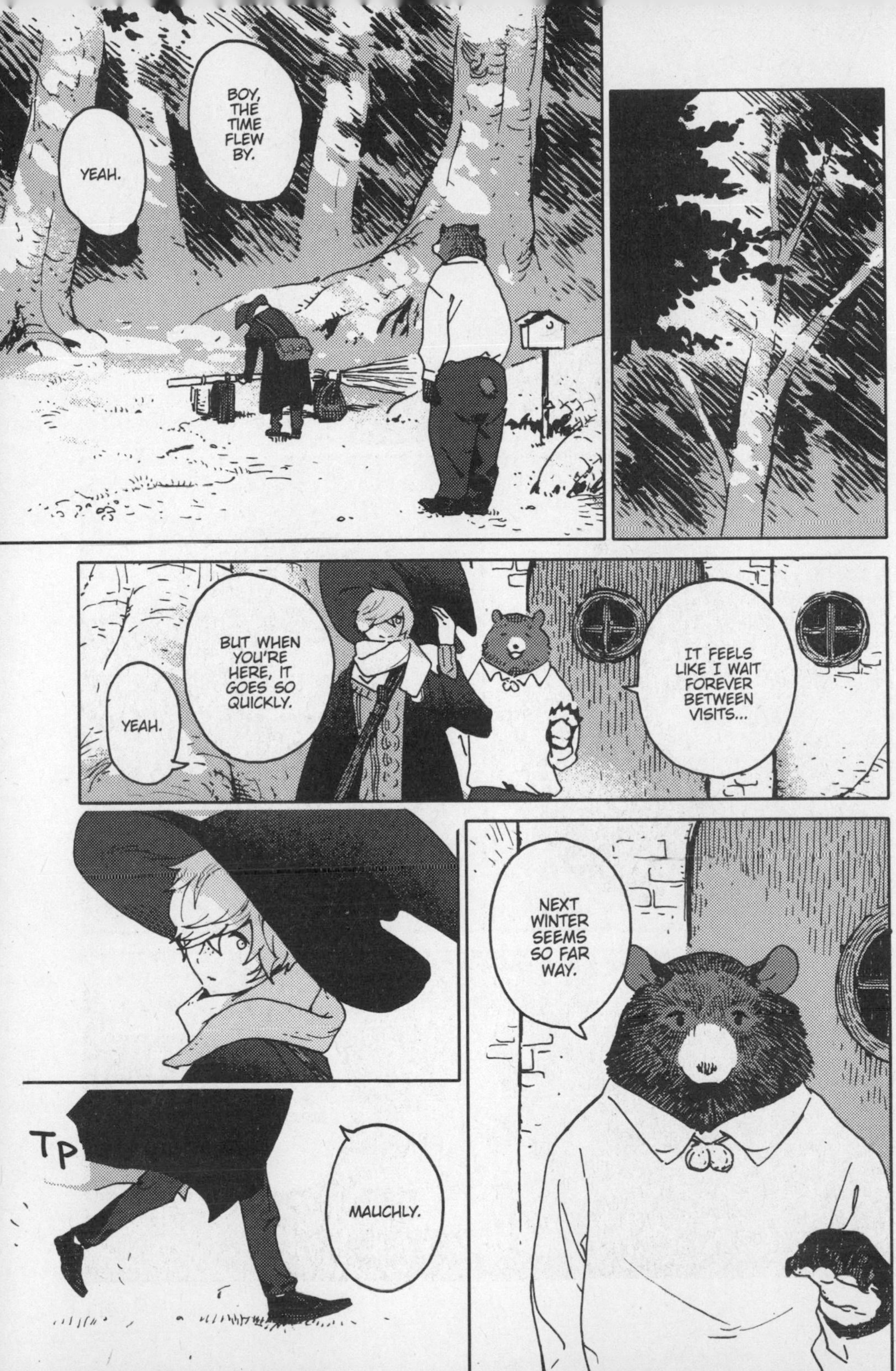
BOY, THE TIME FLEW BY.
YEAH.
IT FEELS LIKE I WAIT FOREVER BETWEEN VISITS...
BUT WHEN YOU'RE HERE, IT GOES SO QUICKLY.
YEAH.
NEXT WINTER SEEMS SO FAR WAY.
MAUCHLY.
TP

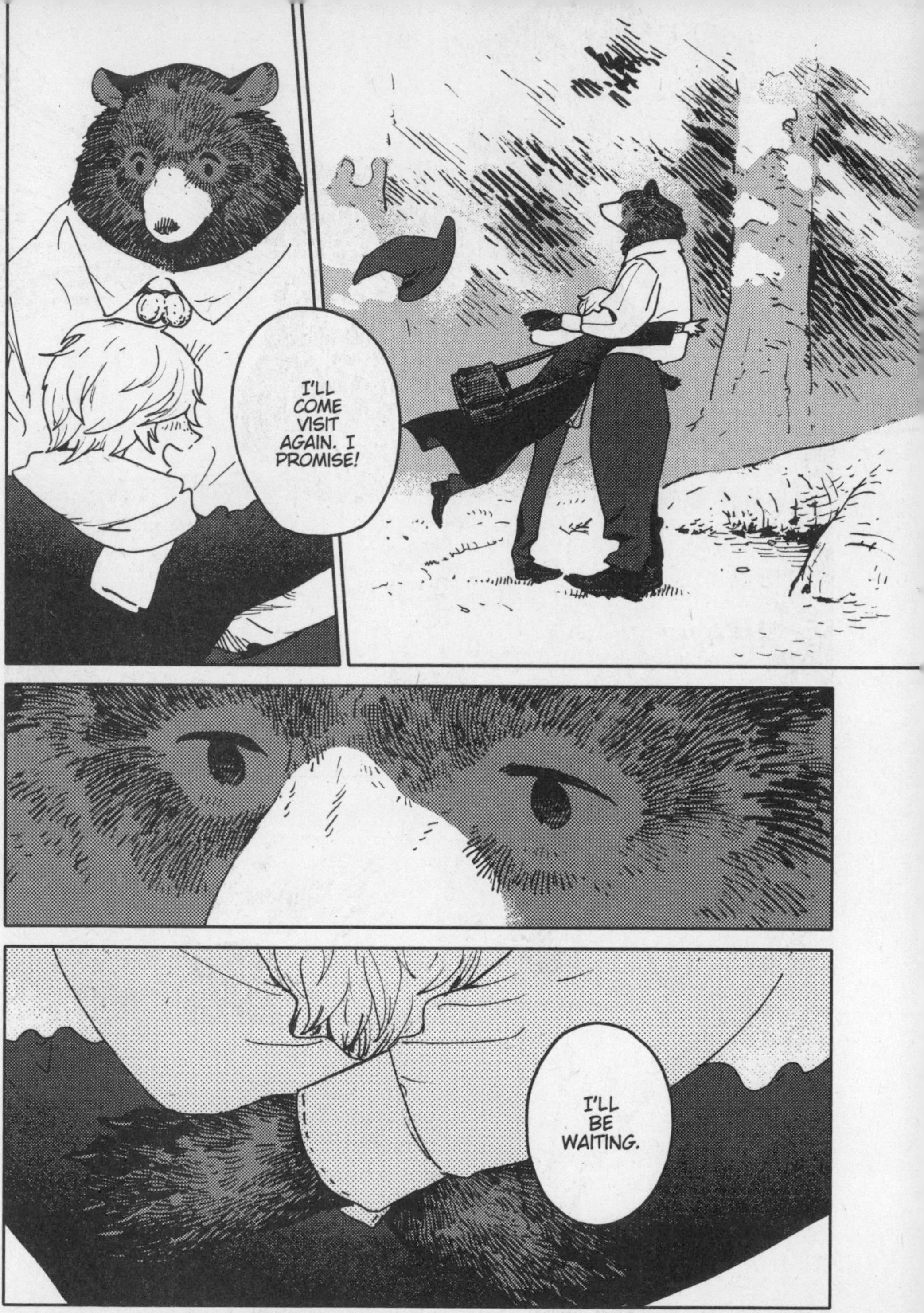
I'LL COME VISIT AGAIN. I PROMISE!
I'LL BE WAITING.

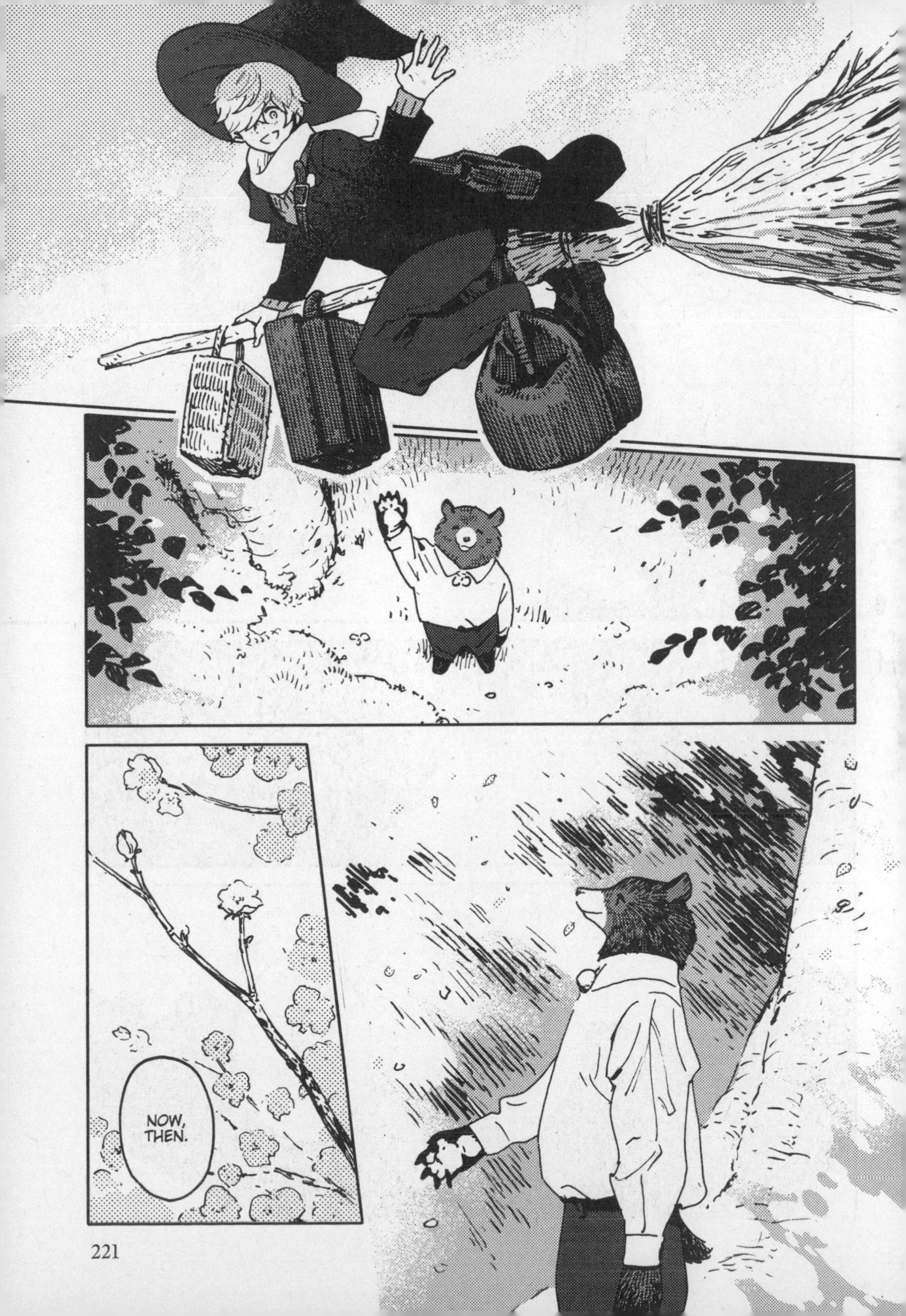
NOW, THEN.

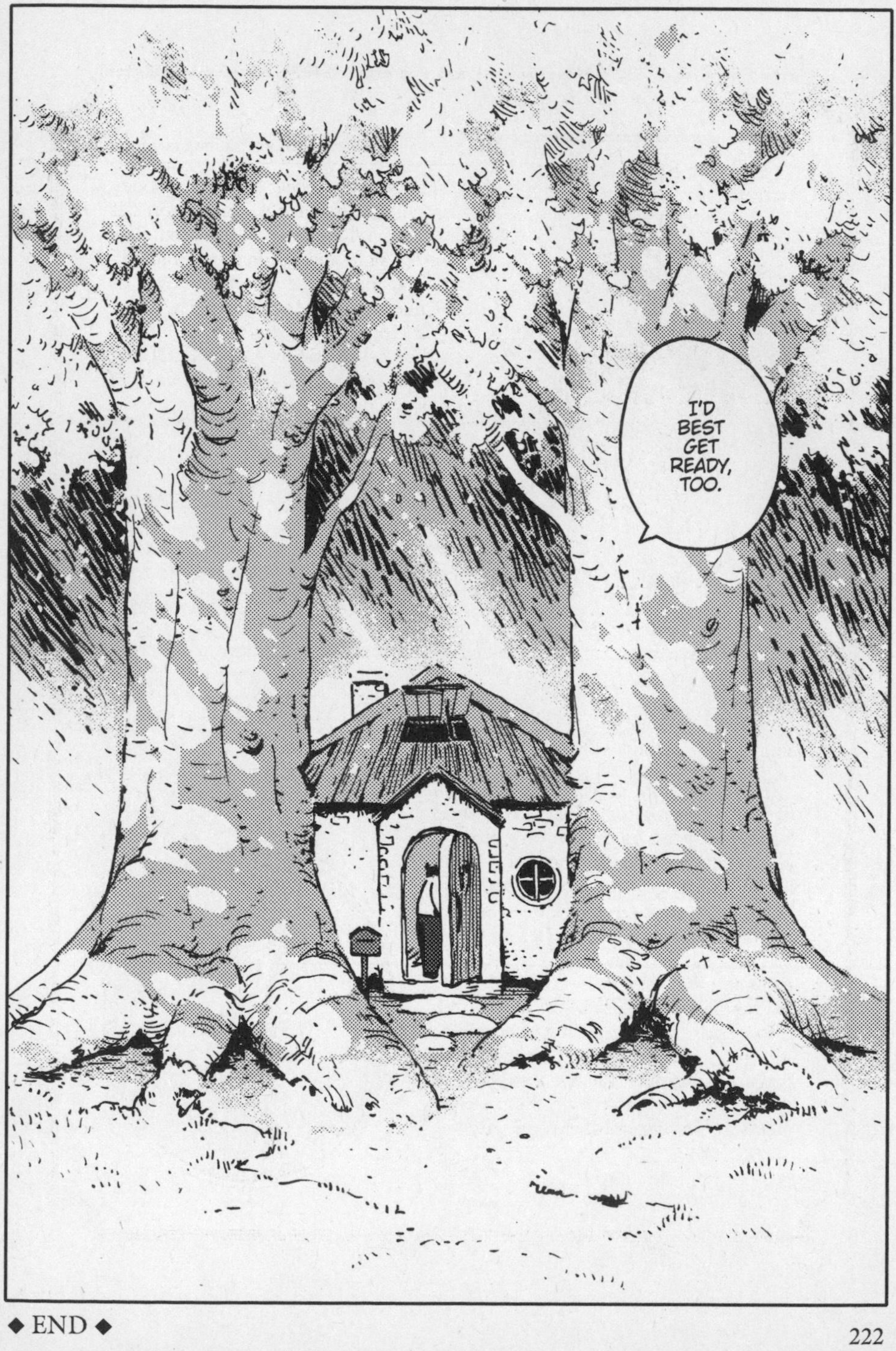
I'D BEST GET READY, TOO.

◆ END ◆

ASIAN BLACK BEAR

Ursus thibetanus

Carnivora | Ursidae *Ursus*

The Asian black bear has a stocky body, a large head, thick limbs, and a short tail. They have a sharp sense of smell, but their senses of sight and hearing are more limited. The thick layer of subcutaneous fat dulls their sense of touch, too. They have large sharp claws that don't retract.

Since they're largely herbivorous, they have flat, rounded molars that are ideal for grinding and crushing plant matter. They're known to feed on a wide variety of things, such as acorns, beech nuts, pinecones, cherries, honey, grasses, herbs, insects, and occasionally meat. They hibernate during the winter. The white patch of fur across their chest looks like a crescent, so they're sometimes nicknamed "moon bears."

Primates | Hominidae *Homo*

Homo sapiens means "wise human" in Latin. Humans have highly developed brains and vocal cords, allowing them to create intricate communication systems using speech, gestures, and written symbols. Language acquisition is thought to be an ability inherent to the species.

They are the only fully erect bipedal mammal, and they have no tails, only a few vestigial tail bones at the base of their spine. Their hind legs are longer than their forelimbs, and they have fully developed heels. Another rare trait for a mammal is that their bodies are nearly hairless, leaving their skin almost completely exposed.

HUMAN

Homo sapiens

|| A Cat's Specialty ||

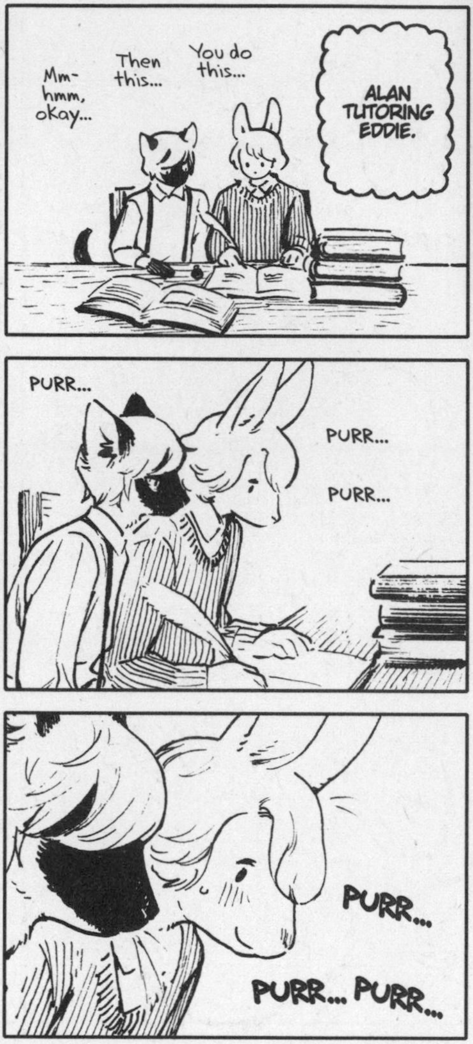
ALAN TUTORING EDDIE.
You do this...
Then this...
Mm-hmm, okay...
PURR...
PURR...
PURR...
PURR...
PURR... PURR...
HE'S PURRING SO LOUDLY!
WHAT'S WRONG?
?
NOTHING...!

|| Hug Pillow ||

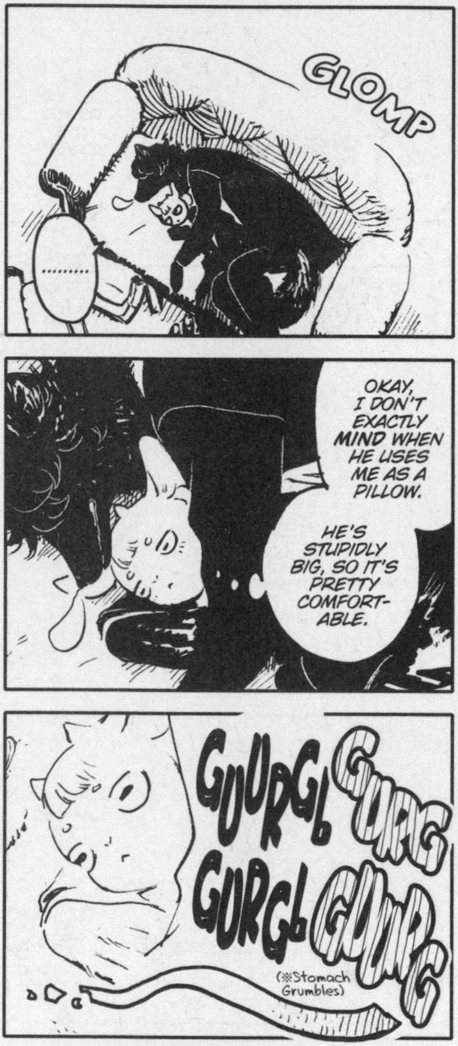
GLOMP
....
OKAY, I DON'T EXACTLY MIND WHEN HE USES ME AS A PILLOW.
HE'S STUPIDLY BIG, SO IT'S PRETTY COMFORTABLE.
GURG GURG
GURGL GURGL
(※Stomach Grumbles)
GURRGL... GURGL...
IT'S THIS PART THAT TERRIFIES ME!

|| Formula for a *Dere* ||

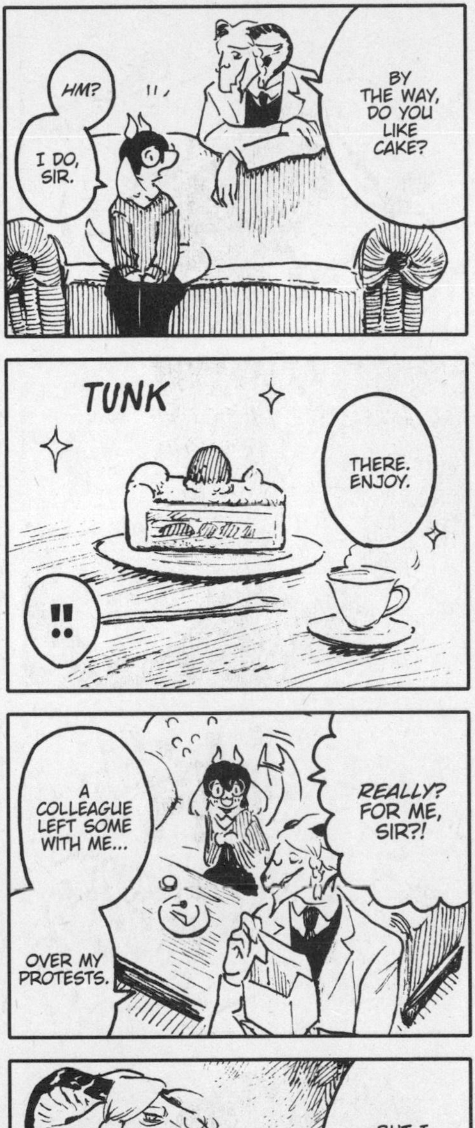
BY THE WAY, DO YOU LIKE CAKE?
HM?
I DO, SIR.
TUNK
THERE. ENJOY.
!!
REALLY? FOR ME, SIR?!
A COLLEAGUE LEFT SOME WITH ME...
OVER MY PROTESTS.
BUT I THOUGHT YOU MIGHT ENJOY IT, SO I KEPT IT.
BE MINDFUL OF THAT AS YOU EAT.
??
AH... YES, SIR.

|| Shedding Season ||

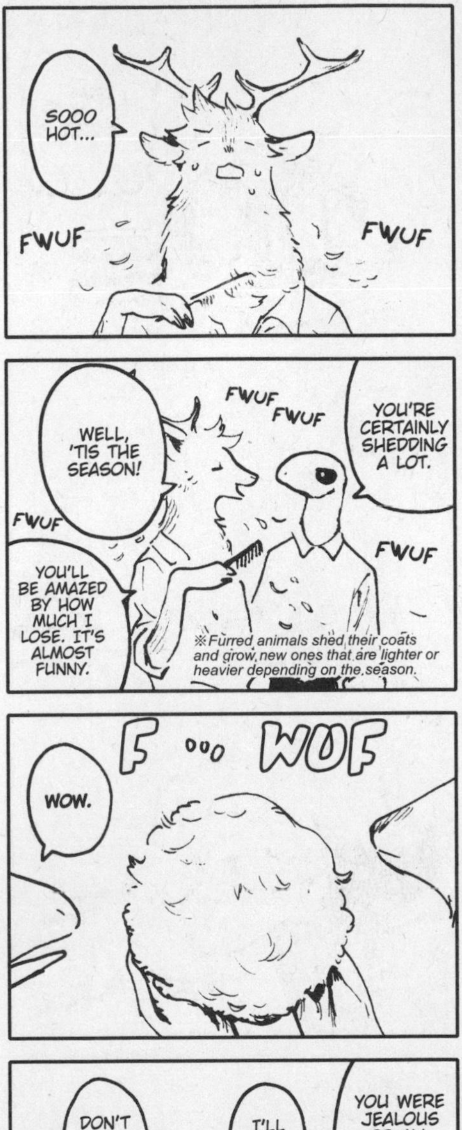
FWUF
SOOO HOT...
FWUF
YOU'RE CERTAINLY SHEDDING A LOT.
FWUF FWUF
WELL, 'TIS THE SEASON!
FWUF
FWUF
YOU'LL BE AMAZED BY HOW MUCH I LOSE. IT'S ALMOST FUNNY.
※Furred animals shed their coats and grow new ones that are lighter or heavier depending on the season.
F...WUF
WOW.
YOU WERE JEALOUS OF ALL MY FUR, RIGHT? HERE!
I'LL PASS.
DON'T BE SHY.
NO. REALLY.

|| Cool Dude ||

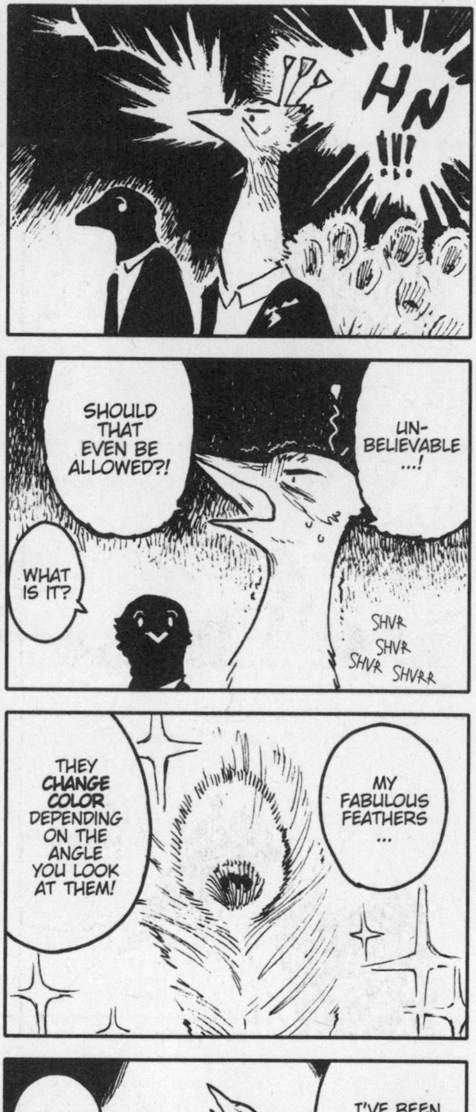
HN!!!
UN-BELIEVABLE ...!
SHOULD THAT EVEN BE ALLOWED?!
WHAT IS IT?
SHVR SHVR SHVR SHVRR
MY FABULOUS FEATHERS ...
THEY **CHANGE COLOR** DEPENDING ON THE ANGLE YOU LOOK AT THEM!
I'VE BEEN SPREADING EVEN **MORE** BEAUTY THAN I REALIZED!
AM I THE GREATEST, OR WHAT?!
YOU ARE.

|| Which Twin is Which? ||

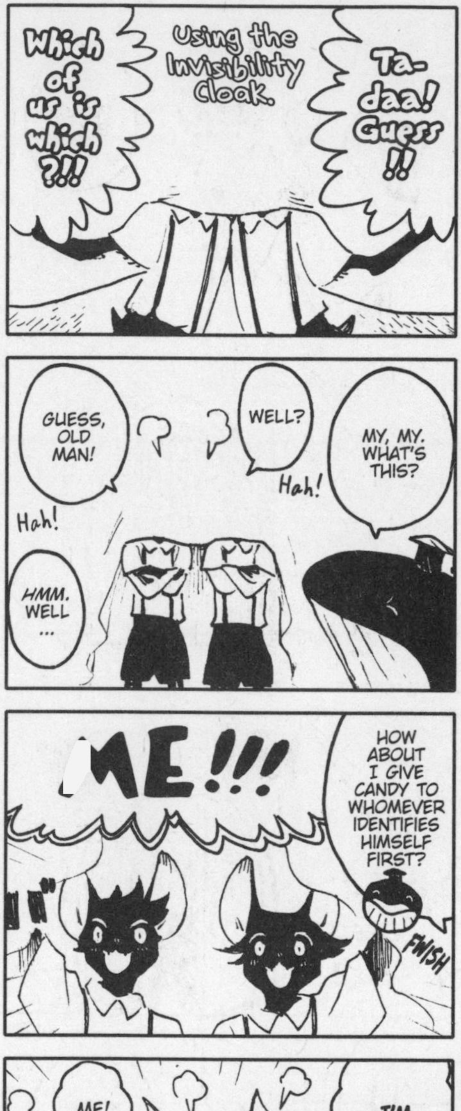
Ta-daa! Guess!!
Using the Invisibility Cloak.
Which of us is which?!!
MY, MY. WHAT'S THIS?
Hah!
WELL?
GUESS, OLD MAN!
Hah!
HMM. WELL ...
HOW ABOUT I GIVE CANDY TO WHOMEVER IDENTIFIES HIMSELF FIRST?
FWISH
ME!!!
I'M FIRST!
NO, ME!
Ho ho!
ME!
ME!

|| Real-Time Attack ||

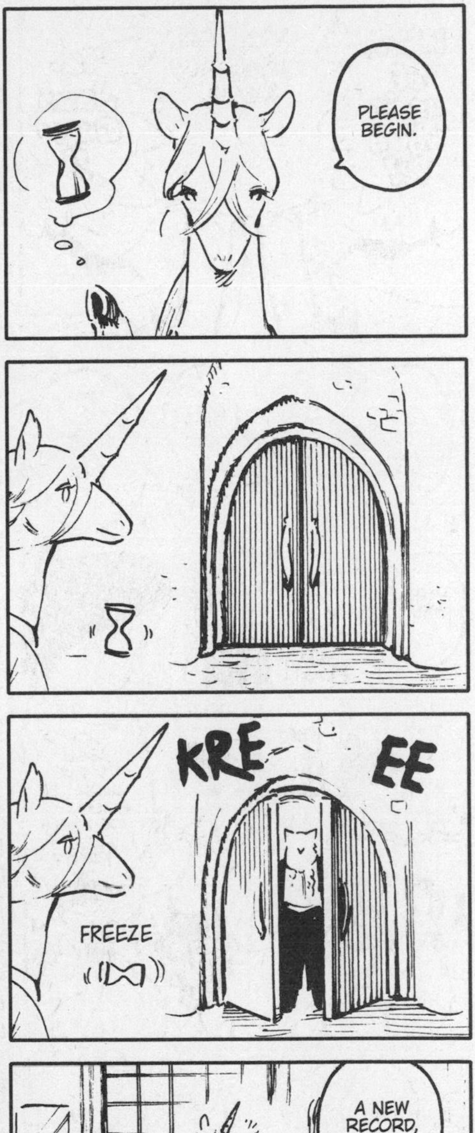
PLEASE BEGIN.
KRE EE
FREEZE
A NEW RECORD, PRO- FESSOR.
WHAT NOW?

|| Pooh Bear ||

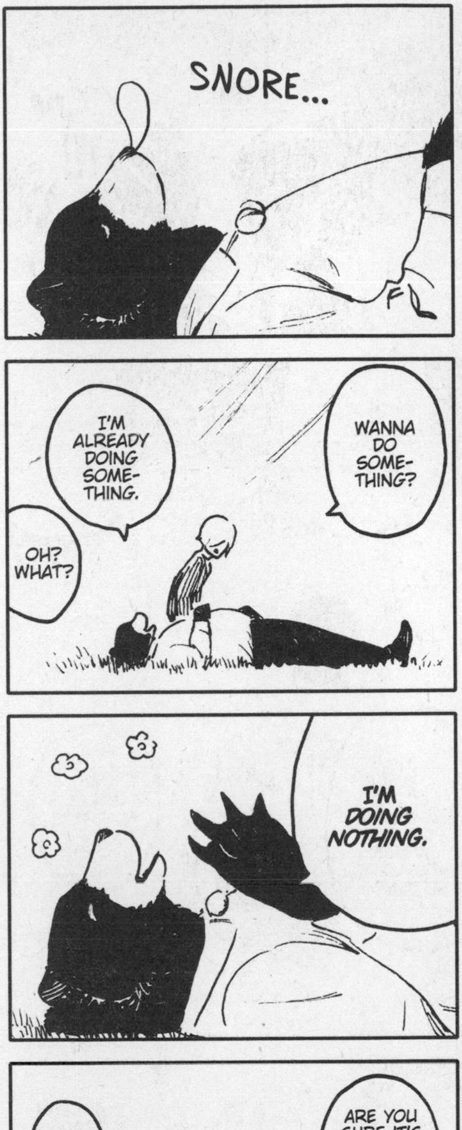
SNORE...
WANNA DO SOME- THING?
I'M ALREADY DOING SOME- THING.
OH? WHAT?
I'M *DOING NOTHING.*
ARE YOU SURE IT'S OKAY FOR YOU TO SAY THAT?
HM?

◆ END ◆

Afterword

HELLO TO FURRIES AND NON-FURRIES ALIKE!
NAGABE THE FURRY HERE!
ON AN EARLIER TITLE OF MINE...
BUCHOU WA ONEE (THE BOSS IS A SISTER), SOMEONE COMMENTED AND SAID, "THE ONLY NON-HUMAN THING ABOUT THE CHARACTERS IS THEIR LOOKS!"
SO THIS TIME, I ADDED MORE NON-HUMAN ELEMENTS.
I USED CHARACTERS' ANIMAL TYPES TO DECIDE WHAT THEIR ABILITIES, ENVIRONMENTS, AND RELATIONSHIPS WOULD BE LIKE.
Bears have keen noses.
IF THEY HAD ANY UNIQUE QUIRKS, I TRIED TO IMPLEMENT THOSE INTO THE STORY AS MUCH AS POSSIBLE.
Vampire bats share blood with each other.
Et cetera...
I'M A LITTLE SAD THAT I COULDN'T GO REALLY IN DEPTH AND OUT THERE WITH ANY OF THIS...
BUT I'M DEEPLY GRATEFUL TO MY PUBLISHER FOR GIVING ME THIS MUCH FREEDOM!
I GIVE MY HUMBLEST THANKS TO MY EDITOR, E-SAN!
YEAH, NON-HUMANS ARE GREAT.

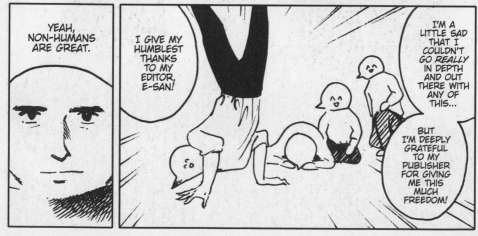

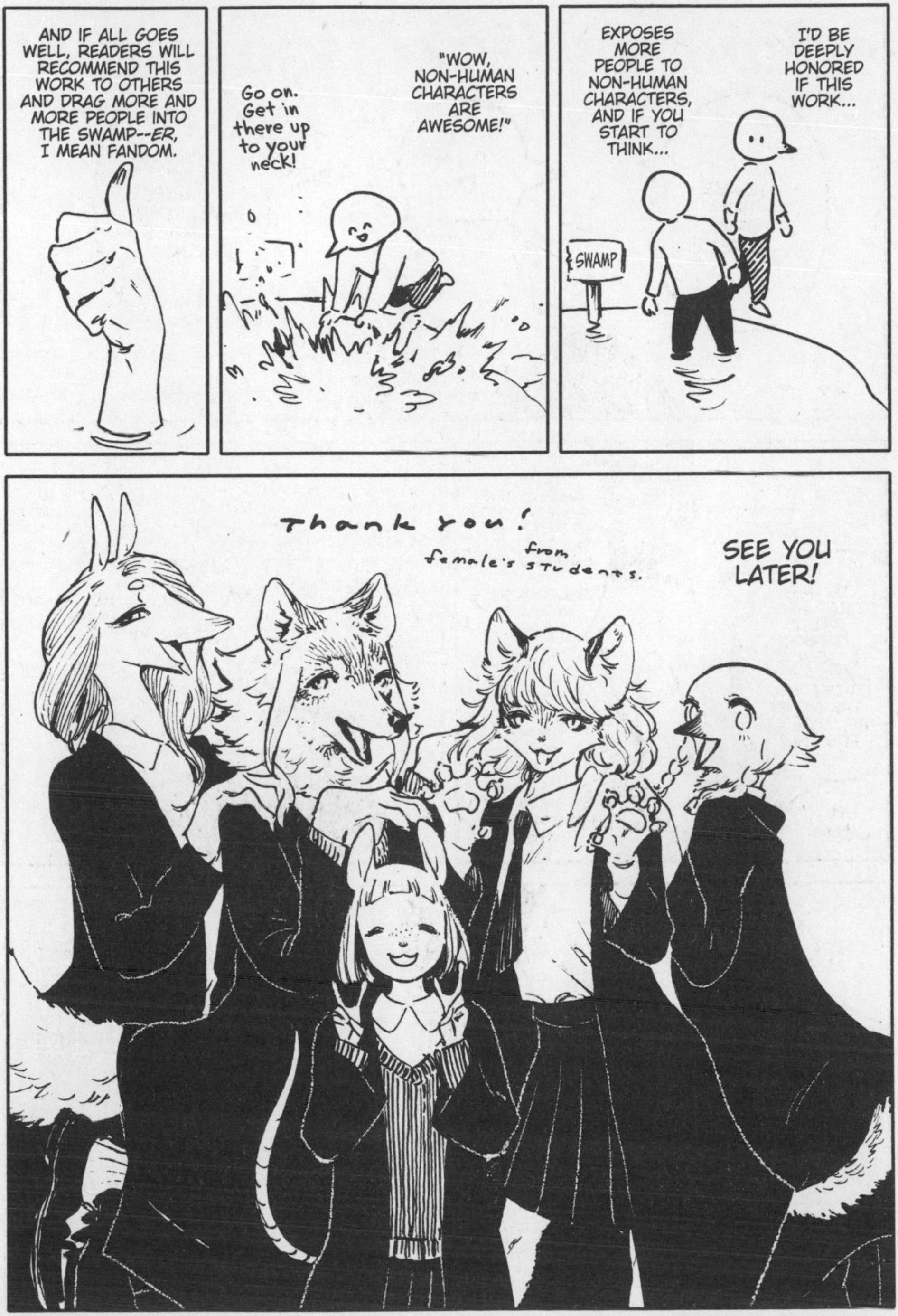
I'D BE DEEPLY HONORED IF THIS WORK...
EXPOSES MORE PEOPLE TO NON-HUMAN CHARACTERS, AND IF YOU START TO THINK...
SWAMP
"WOW, NON-HUMAN CHARACTERS ARE AWESOME!"
Go on. Get in there up to your neck!
AND IF ALL GOES WELL, READERS WILL RECOMMEND THIS WORK TO OTHERS AND DRAG MORE AND MORE PEOPLE INTO THE SWAMP--ER, I MEAN FANDOM.
SEE YOU LATER!
Thank you!
from female's students.

◆ END ◆

SEVEN SEAS ENTERTAINMENT PRESENTS

The Wize Wize Beasts of the Wizarding Wizdoms
story and art by NAGABE

TRANSLATION
Adrienne Beck

ADAPTATION
Ysabet MacFarlane

LETTERING AND LAYOUT
Karis Page

COVER DESIGN
KC Fabellon

PROOFREADER
Stephanie Cohen
Kurestin Armada

ASSISTANT EDITOR
Jenn Grunigen

PRODUCTION MANAGER
Lissa Pattillo

MANAGING EDITOR
Julie Davis

EDITOR-IN-CHIEF
Adam Arnold

PUBLISHER
Jason DeAngelis

THE WIZE WIZE BEASTS OF THE WIZARDING WIZDOMS
©nagabe 2018
Originally published in Japan in 2018 by AKANESHINSHA, Tokyo.
English translation rights arranged with COMIC HOUSE, Tokyo,
through TOHAN CORPORATION, Tokyo.

Seven Seas press and purchase enquiries can be sent to Marketing Manager
Lianne Sentar at press@gomanga.com. Information regarding the distribution
and purchase of digital editions is available from Digital Manager CK Russell
at digital@gomanga.com.

Seven Seas and the Seven Seas logo are trademarks of
Seven Seas Entertainment. All rights reserved.

ISBN: 978-1-64275-709-5

Printed in Canada

First Printing: October 2019

10 9 8 7 6 5 4 3 2 1

FOLLOW US ONLINE: *www.sevenseasentertainment.com*

READING DIRECTIONS

This book reads from *right to left*, Japanese style.
If this is your first time reading manga, you start
reading from the top right panel on each page and
take it from there. If you get lost, just follow the
numbered diagram here. It may seem backwards at
first, but you'll get the hang of it! Have fun!!

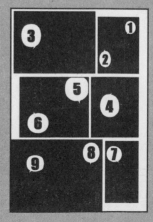